Newnes
PC Troubleshooting
Pocket Book

Newnes PC Troubleshooting Pocket Book

Michael Tooley

Second edition

OXFORD BOSTON JOHANNESBURG
MELBOURNE NEW DELHI SINGAPORE

Newnes
An imprint of Butterworth-Heinemann
Linacre House, Jordan Hill, Oxford OX2 8DP
225 Wildwood Avenue, Woburn, MA 01801–2041
A division of Reed Educational and Professional Publishing Ltd

A member of the Reed Elsevier plc group

First published 1994
Reprinted 1997 (twice)

Second edition 1998

British Library Cataloguing in Publication Data
A catalogue record for this book is available from the British Library

ISBN 0 7506 39016

Typeset by The Midland Book Typesetting Company, Loughborough
Printed and bound in Great Britain.

Contents

Preface

Sooner or later, most PC users find themselves confronted with hardware or software failure or the need to upgrade or optimise a system for some new application. The *PC Troubleshooting Pocket Book* provides a concise and compact reference which describes in a clear and straightforward manner the principles and practice of fault finding and upgrading IBM PCs and compatible systems.

This book is aimed at anyone who is involved with the installation, configuration, maintenance, upgrading, repair or support of PC systems. It also provides non-technical users with sufficient background information to diagnose basic faults and carry out simple modifications and repairs.

In computer troubleshooting, as with any field of endeavour, there are a number of short-cuts which can be instrumental in helping to avoid hours of frustration and costly effort. I have thus included a number of 'tips' which will help you avoid many of these pitfalls. These snippets of information are the culmination of 20 years of practical computing experience, the past twelve of which has been with IBM and compatible systems.

The book also includes the commented source code for five diagnostic utilities. These programs have been written in Microsoft's immensely popular QuickBASIC and will help you to check and modify the configuration of your system as well as carry out routine tests and adjustments of such items as disk drives, printers and monitors. Microsoft QuickBASIC was previously supplied as part of the MS-DOS package and it is eminently suitable for the complete beginner to programming. If you don't have access to Microsoft QuickBASIC, or if you would prefer not to type in the programs, they can be downloaded from the author's Web site. Finally, the programs may be freely adapted, copied and modified and you are encouraged to use them as the basis for your own personalised diagnostic routines.

To take into account the relentless advance in PC technology, this second edition has been considerably updated and extended and a completely new section has been included on troubleshooting in the Windows environment.

Happy troubleshooting!

Michael Tooley

Preface

1
Introduction

PC troubleshooting covers a very wide variety of activities including diagnosing and correcting hardware faults and ensuring that systems are correctly configured for the applications which run on them. This chapter sets the scene for the rest of the book and explains the underlying principles of troubleshooting and fault finding.

A word about you

This book makes very few assumptions about your previous experience and the level of underpinning knowledge which you might (or might not) have. You should at least be familiar with the basic constituents of a PC system: system unit, display, keyboard and mouse. In addition, you have probably had some experience of using DOS and/or Windows. That's all!

Don't panic if you are a complete beginner to fault finding and repair. You can begin by tackling simple faults and slowly gain experience by moving on to progressively more difficult (and more challenging) faults. With very little experience you should be able to diagnose and rectify simple hardware problems, install a wide variety of upgrades and otpimise your system by making changes to the CONFIG.SYS and AUTOEXEC.BAT files.

With more experience you will be able to tackle fault finding to 'replaceable unit' level. Examples of this could be diagnosing and replacing a faulty I/O card, a power supply or a disk drive.

Fault finding to component level requires the greatest skill. It also requires an investment in specialised diagnostic equipment and tools. Nowadays, however, component level fault finding is often either impractical or uneconomic; you may require equipment available only to the specialist and it may be cheaper to replace a card or disk drive rather than spend several hours attempting to repair it.

Approach to troubleshooting

Whatever your background it is important to develop a systematic approach to troubleshooting right from the start. This will help you to cope with obscure as well as routine faults.

The following stages are typical:

(a) Perform functional tests and observations. If the fault has been reported by someone else, it is important to obtain all relevant information and not make any assumptions which may lead you along a blind alley.

(b) Eliminate functional parts of the system from your investigation.

(c) Isolate the problem to a particular area of the system. This will often involve associating the fault with one or more of the following:
   (i) power supply (including mains cable and fuse)
   (ii) system motherboard (includes CPU, ROM and RAM)

(iii) graphics adapter (includes video RAM)
(iv) disk adapter (includes disk controller)
(v) other I/O adapter cards (e.g. serial communications cards, modem cards etc.)
(vi) floppy disk drive (including disk drive cables and connectors)
(vii) hard disk drive (including disk drive cables and connectors)
(viii) keyboard and mouse
(ix) display
(x) software (including configuration programs such as CONFIG.SYS and AUTOEXEC.BAT)
(xi) external hardware (such as a printer sharer or external drive)
(xii) communications or network problems.

(d) Disassemble (as necessary) and investigate individual components and sub-systems (e.g. carry out RAM diagnostics, gain access to system board, remove suspect SIMM).

(e) Identify and replace faulty components (e.g. check SIMM and replace with functional component).

(f) Perform appropriate functional tests (e.g. re-run RAM diagnostics, check memory is fully operational).

(g) Re-assemble system and, if appropriate, 'soak-test' or 'burn-in' for an appropriate period.

TIP

If you have more than one system available, items such as the system unit, display, keyboard, and external cables can all be checked (and eliminated from further investigation) without having to remove or dismantle anything. Simply disconnect the suspect part and substitute the equivalent part from an identical or compatible system which is known to be functional.

Where to start

It is 'perhaps' worth saying that a system which appears to be totally dead can be a much easier prospect than one which displays an intermittent fault.

Start at the beginning and move progressively towards the end. This sounds obvious but many would-be troubleshooters ignore this advice and jump in at a later stage. By so doing, they often make erroneous assumptions and all too often ignore some crucial piece of information.

What to ask

If you are troublehooting someone else's system you may be presented with a box and no information other than that 'it doesn't work'. It has to be said that the average user is remarkably inadequate when it comes to describing faults on items of technical equipment. Furthermore he/she rarely connects the circumstances which lead up to equipment failure with the actual appearance of the fault. For example, a PC which has been relocated to a shelf over a radiator is bound to be a candidate for a very early death.

If you do have to deal with non-technical users it is well worth producing your own checklist of questions. To help you, the questions that I regularly use are as follows:

1. Has the fault just appeared or has it got progressively worse?
2. Is the fault present all the time?
3. If the fault is intermittent, under what circumstances does the fault appear?
4. Did the system work satisfactorily before? If not, in what way were you disatisfied with its performance?
5. Has the configuration of the system changed in any way? If so, how has it changed?
6. What action (if any) have you taken to rectify the fault?
7. How did you first become aware of the fault?
8. Did you hear, see, or smell anything when the system failed?
9. What was actually happening when the system crashed?

In addition, you may wish to ask supplementary questions or make a few simple suggestions such as:

10. Have you checked the power to the system?
11. Is the printer on-line and is it loaded with paper?
12. Is the network 'up and running'?

In judging what reliance to place on the user's responses, it usually helps to make some assessment of the level of the user's technical expertise. You can do this by asking a few simple (but non-technical) questions and noting what comes back. Try something along the following lines:

13. How long have you been using the system?
14. Is this the first PC that you have used/owned?
15. How confident do you feel when you use the system?

In any event, it is important to have some empathy with the user and ensure that they do not feel insulted by your questions. A user who feels ignorant or threatened may often consciously or subconsciously withold information. After all, the secretary who spills a cup of coffee over a keyboard is unlikely to admit to it within the boss's hearing.

Categorising faults

It helps to divide faults into the following categories: hardware faults, software faults and configuration problems. This book is organised on this basis.

Hardware faults

Hardware faults are generally attributable to component malfunction or component failure. Electronic components do not generally wear out with age but they become less reliable at the end of their normal service life. It is very important to realise that component reliability is greatly reduced when components are operated at, or near, their maximum ratings. As an example, a capacitor rated at 25V and operated at 10V at a temperature of 20°C will exhibit a mean-time-to-failure (MTTF) of around 200,000 hours. When operated at 40°C with 20V applied, however, its MTTF will be reduced by a factor of 10 to about 20,000 hours.

TIP

The mean-time-to-failure (MTTF) of a system can be greatly extended by simply keeping it cool. Always ensure that your PC is kept out of direct sunlight and away from other heat producing sources (such as radiators). Ventilation slots should be kept clear of obstructions and there must be adequate air flow all around the system enclosure. For this reason it is important to avoid placing tower systems under desks, in corners or sandwiched between shelves.

Software faults

Software faults can arise from a number of causes including defective coding, corrupted data, viruses, 'software bombs' and 'trojan horses'. Software faults attributable to defective coding can be minimised by comprehensive software testing before a product is released. Unfortunately, this does not always happen. Furthermore, modern software can be extremely complex and 'bugs' can often appear in 'finished' products due to quite unforeseen circumstances (such as changes in operating system code). Most reputable software houses respond favourably to reports from users and offer software upgrades, 'bug fixes' and 'work arounds' which can often be instrumental in overcoming most problems. The moral to this is that if you do not get satisfactory service from your software distributor/supplier you should tell all your friends and take your business elsewhere.

In recent years, computer viruses have become an increasing nuisance. A persistent virus can be extremely problematic and, in severe cases, can result in total loss of your precious data. You can avoid this trauma by adhering to a strict code of practice and by investing in a proprietary anti-virus package.

Configuration problems

Configuration problems exist when both hardware and software are operating correctly but neither has been optimised for use *with the other*. Incorrectly configured systems may operate slower or provide significantly reduced functionality when compared with their fully optimised counterparts. Unfortunately, there is a 'grey' area in which it is hard to decide upon whether a system has been correctly optimised as different software packages may require quite different configurations.

A brief history of the PC

The original IBM PC was announced in 1981 and made its first appearance in 1982. The PC had an 8088 central processing unit and a mere 64Kbytes of system board RAM. The basic RAM was, however, expandable to an almost unheard of total of 640Kbytes. The original PC supported two 360Kbyte floppy disk drives, an 80 column × 25 line text display and up to 16 colours using a Colour Graphics Adapter (CGA).

The XT (eXtended Technology) version of the PC appeared in 1983. This machine provided users with a single 360Kbyte floppy drive and a 10Mbyte hard disk. This was later followed by AT (Advanced Technology) specification machines which were based on an 80286 microprocessor (rather than the 8088 used in its predecessors) together with 256Kbytes of RAM fitted to the system board. The standard AT provided 1.2Mbytes of floppy disk storage together with a 20Mbyte hard disk.

Not surprisingly, the standards set by IBM attracted much interest from other manufacturers, notable amongst whom were Compaq and Olivetti. These companies were not merely content to produce machines with an identical specification but went on to make their own significant improvements to IBM's basic specifications. Other manufacturers were happy to 'clone' the PC; indeed, one could be forgiven for thinking that the highest accolade that could be offered by the computer press was that a machine was 'IBM compatible'.

Since those early days, the IBM PC has become the 'de facto' standard for personal computing. Other manufacturers (such as Apple, Commodore and Atari) have produced systems with quite different specifications but none has been as phenomenally successful as IBM.

'386, '486 and Pentium-based systems now provide performance specifications which would have been quite unheard of a decade ago and which have allowed software developers to produce an increasingly powerful and sophisticated range of products which will support multi-users on networked systems as well as single-users running multiple tasks on stand-alone machines.

IBM compatible systems are now produced by a very large number of well-known manufacturers (including Viglen, Dell, Elonex, Dan Technology, Amstrad and Research Machines). Machines are invariably produced to exacting specifications and you can be reasonably certain that the company will provide a good standard of after-sales service. Indeed, most reputable manufacturers will support their equipment for a number of years after it ceases to be part of a 'current product range'.

Finally, many small companies have begun assembling PC-compatible systems in recent years using individual components and boards imported from Far-East manufacturers. In many cases, these systems offer performance specifications which rival those of well-known brands, however, the constituent parts may be of uncertain pedigree.

Burn-in

Any reputable manufacturer or distributor will check and 'burn-in' (or 'soak test') a system prior to despatching it to the end-user. This means running the system for several hours in an environment which simulates the range of operational conditions which the system in question is likely to encounter.

'Burn-in' can be instrumental in detecting components that may quickly fail either due to defective manufacture or to incorrect specification. In the case of a PC, 'burn-in' should continuously exercise *all* parts of the system, including floppy and hard disk drives.

TIP

It is always wise to 'soak test' a system following any troubleshooting activity (particularly if it involves the replacement of an item of hardware). Chapter 18 includes a program which you can use.

Conventions used in this book

The following conventions are used in this book:

1. Special keys and combinations of special keys are enclosed within angled brackets and the simultaneous depression of two

(or more keys) is indicated using a hyphen. Hence <SHIFT-F1> means 'press the shift key down and, whilst keeping it held down, press the F1 key'.

2. In addition, many of the special function keys (such as Control, Alternate etc) have been abbreviated. Thus <CTRL> refers to the Control key, <ALT> refers to the Alternate key and <DEL> refers to the Delete key. <CTRL-ALT-DEL> refers to the *simultaneous* depression of all three keys.
3. DOS commands and optional switches and parameters (where appropriate) have all been shown in upper case. In practice, DOS will invariably accept entries made in either upper or lower case. Thus, as far as DOS is concerned, **dir a**: is the same as **DIR A**:. For consistency, we have used upper case but you may make entries in either upper or lower case, as desired.
4. Where several complete lines of text are to be entered (such as those required to create a batch file) each line should be terminated with the <ENTER> key.
5. Unless otherwise stated, addresses and data values are given in hexadecimal (base 16).
6. Finally, where several DOS commands are likely to be used together (e.g. within a batch file) or where we provide examples of output to a printer or a screen display, we have made use of a monospaced Courier font.

2
PC fundamentals

An understanding of the basic operation of a microcomputer system is an essential first step to getting the best out of your PC. This chapter provides the basic under-pinning knowledge required to carry out successful upgrading and troubleshooting.

The chapter begins by describing the basic components of a microcomputer and how data are represented within it. The chapter includes a quick tour of a system with particular reference to the central processing unit (CPU), memory (ROM and RAM) and the means of input and output. The chapter concludes with a brief introduction to some of the facilities provided by an operating system.

Microcomputer basics

The basic components of a microcomputer system are:

(a) a central processing unit (CPU)

(b) a memory, comprising both 'read/write' and 'read only' devices (commonly called RAM and ROM respectively)

(c) a mass storage device for programs and/or data (e.g. a floppy and/or hard disk drive)

(d) a means of providing user input and output (via a keyboard and display interface)

(e) interface circuits for external input and output (I/O). These circuits (commonly called 'ports') simplify the connection of peripheral devices such as printers, modems, mice and joysticks.

In a microcomputer (as distinct from a mini or mainframe machine), the functions of the CPU are provided by a single VLSI microprocessor chip (e.g. an Intel 8086, 8088, 80286, 80386, 80486 or Pentium). The microprocessor is crucial to the overall performance of the system. Indeed, successive generations of PC are normally categorised by reference to the type of chip used. The 'original' PC used an 8088, AT systems are based on an 80286, '386 machines use an 80386, and so on.

Semiconductor devices are also used for the fast read/write and read-only memory. Strictly speaking, both types of memory permit 'random access' since any item of data can be retrieved with equal ease regardless of its actual location within the memory. Despite this, the term 'RAM' has become synonymous with semiconductor read/write memory.

The semiconductor ROM provides non-volatile storage for part of the operating system code (this 'BIOS' code remains intact when the power supply is disconnected). The semiconductor RAM provides storage for the remainder of the operating system code (the 'DOS'), applications programs and transient data (including that which corresponds to the screen display).

It is important to note that any program or data stored in RAM will be lost when the power supply is switched off or disconnected. The only exception to this is a small amount of 'CMOS memory' kept alive by means of a battery. This 'battery-backed' memory (used on AT and later machines) is used to retain important configuration data such as the type of hard and floppy disk fitted to the system and the amount of RAM present.

> **TIP**
>
> It is well worth noting down the contents of the CMOS memory to avoid the frustration of having to puzzle out the settings for your own particular system when the backup battery eventually fails and has to be replaced. To view the current CMOS configuration settings press the 'Del' key during the boot-up sequence and enter the 'Setup' routine.

Catching the bus

The basic components of the system (CPU, RAM, ROM and I/O) are linked together using a multiple-wire connecting system know as a 'bus' (see Figure 2.1). Three different buses are present (together with any specialised 'local' buses used for high-speed data transfer). The three main buses are:

(a) an 'address bus', used to specify memory locations

(b) a 'data bus', on which data is transferred between devices

(c) a 'control bus', which provides timing and control signals throughout the system.

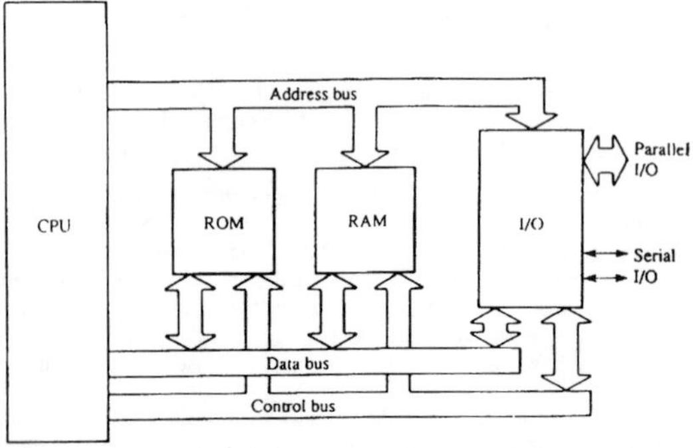

Figure 2.1 Basic components of a microcomputer system

Expanding the system

In the generalised system shown in Figure 2.1, we have included the keyboard, display and disk interface within the block marked 'I/O'. The IBM PC provides the user with somewhat greater flexibility by making the bus and power connections available at a number of 'expansion connectors'. The connectors permit the use of 'adapter cards' (see Figure 2.2). These adapters allow the system to be configured for different types of display, mass storage device etc. Commonly available expansion cards include: floppy and hard disk adapters, expansion memory cards, games (joystick) adapters, sound and video cards, internal modems, CD-ROM cards and additional serial/parallel ports.

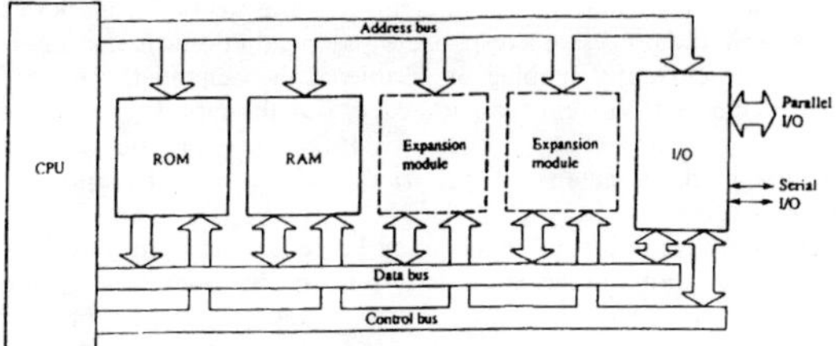

Figure 2.2 System expansion using adapter cards

Clocks and timing

To distinguish valid data from the transient and indeterminate states that occur when data is changing, all bus data transfers must occur at known times within a regular cycle of 'reading' and 'writing'. Therefore the movement of data around a microcomputer system is synchronised using a master 'system clock'. This signal is the basic heartbeat of the system; the faster the clock frequency the smaller the time taken to execute a single machine instruction.

Some microprocessors have internal clock circuitry but the Intel processor family requires the services of an external clock generator. The PC's clock signal is thus generated using external logic, the basic timing element of which is a quartz crystal. This device ensures that the clock signal is both highly accurate and extremely stable. On the original PC, the 'system clock' signal was obtained by dividing this fundamental output frequency by a factor of 4.

Interrupting the system

Another control signal of particular note is the 'interrupt'. Interrupts provide an efficient means of responding to the needs of external

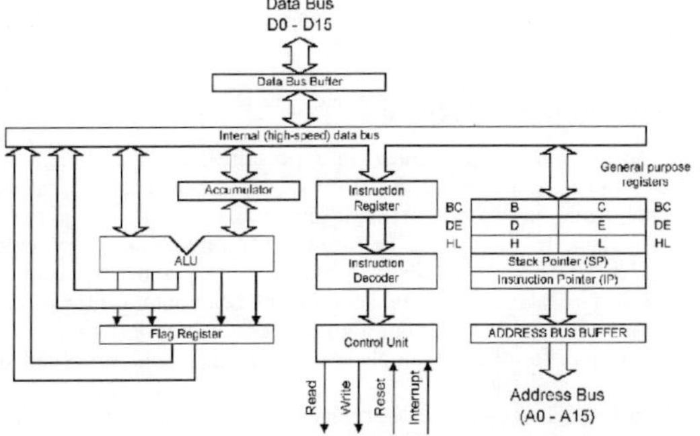

Figure 2.3 Simplified internal architecture of a CPU

hardware, such as a keyboard or a modem connected to the serial port. The Intel family of processors provides interrupts which are both 'maskable' and 'non-maskable'.

When a non-maskable interrupt input is asserted, the processor must suspend execution of the current instruction and respond immediately to the interrupt. In the case of a maskable interrupt, the processor's response will depend upon whether interrupts are currently enabled or disabled (when enabled, the CPU will suspend its current task and carry out the requisite interrupt service routine). The response to interrupts can be enabled or disabled by means of program instructions (EI and DI, respectively).

In practice, interrupt signals may be generated from a number of sources and since each will require its own customised response, a mechanism must be provided for identifying the source of the interrupt and vectoring to the appropriate interrupt service routine. In order to assist in this task, the PC uses a programmable interrupt controller chip (based on an 8239A, or its equivalent).

A further type of interrupt is generated by software. These 'software interrupts' provide an efficient means of accessing the BIOS and DOS services (see page 233 for an example of this).

Data representation

The number of individual lines present within the address bus and data bus depends upon the particular microprocessor employed (see Table 2.1). Some processors (notably the 80386SX, 80486SX etc.) only have a 16-bit external data bus to permit the use of a lower-cost motherboard whilst still retaining software compatibility with their full bus width processors (such as the 80386DX, 80486DX etc.).

Signals on all lines, no matter whether they are used for address, data or control, can exist in only two basic states: logic 0 ('low') or logic 1 ('high'). Data and addresses are represented by binary numbers (a sequence of 1s and 0s) that appear on the data and address bus, respectively.

The largest binary number that can appear on a 16-bit data bus corresponds to the condition when all 16 of the lines are at logic 1. Therefore, the largest value of data that can be present on the bus at any instant of time is equivalent to the binary number 1111111111111111 (or 65535). Similarly, the highest address that can appear on a 20-bit address bus is 11111111111111111111 (or 1,048,575).

Binary and hexadecimal

For convenience, the binary data present within a system is often converted to hexadecimal (base 16). This format is easier for mere humans to comprehend and offers the advantage over denary (base 10) that it can be converted to and from binary with ease. The first sixteen numbers in binary, denary and hexadecimal are shown in Table 2.2. A single hexadecimal character (in the range zero to F) is used to represent a group of four binary digits (bits). This group of four bits (or single hex. character) is sometimes called a 'nibble'.

A 'byte' of data comprises a group of eight bits. Thus a byte can be represented by just two hex. characters. A group of sixteen bits (a 'word') can be represented by four hex. characters, thirty-two bits (a 'double word') by eight hex. characters, and so on.

Table 2.1 Intel CPU specifications

Processor type	Register size (bits)	Data bus size (bits)	Address bus size (bits)	Addressing range (bytes)	Clock speed (typical, MHz)	Year of introduction (approx.)
8086	16	16	20	1M	4.7	1978
80286	16	16	24	16M	12, 16, 20	1982
80386DX	32	32	32	4G	16, 20, 25, 33, 40	1985
80386SX	32	16	24	16M	16, 20, 25	1987
80486DX	32	32	32	4G	33, 50, 66, 100	1990
80486SX	32	32	32	4G	25, 50	1991
Pentium	64	32	32	4G	75, 90, 100, 120, 133	1993
Pentium II	64	32	32	4G	233, 266	1997

Table 2.2 Binary, denary and dexadecimal numbers

Binary (base 2)	Denary (base 10)	Hexadecimal (base 16)
0000	0	0
0001	1	1
0010	2	2
0011	3	3
0100	4	4
0101	5	5
0110	6	6
0111	7	7
1000	8	8
1001	9	9
1010	10	A
1011	11	B
1100	12	C
1101	13	D
1110	14	E
1111	15	F

TIP

The value of a byte expressed in binary can be easily converted to hexadecimal by arranging the bits in groups of four and converting each nibble into hexadecimal using Table 2.2. Taking 10100011 as an example; 1010 = A and 0011 = 3, thus 0100011 can be represented by hex. A3.

Data in memory

A byte of data can be stored at each address within the total memory space of a computer. Hence, one byte can be stored at each of the 1,048,576 memory locations within a machine offering 1Mbyte of RAM. In the case of words and double words, the least significant data byte is stored at the lowest memory address (a word will require two bytes of memory storage whilst a long word will require four bytes). To illustrate this, a byte of 3F, a word of 2C3E, and a double word of F0A29E41 are shown as they would appear stored in memory in Figure 2.4.

Individual bits within a word are numbered from 0 (least significant bit) to 15 (most significant bit). In the case of double words, the bits are numbered from 0 (least significant bit) to 31 (most significant bit). Negative (or 'signed') numbers can be represented using 'two's complement' notation where the leading (most significant) bit indicates the sign of the number (1 = negative, 0 = positive).

The range of integer data values that can be represented as bytes, words and long words are shown in the Table 2.3.

Byte data		Word data		Double word data	
				Address + 3	F0
				Address + 2	A2
		Address + 1	2C	Address + 1	9E
Address	3F	Address	3E	Address	41

Figure 2.4 Comparison of byte, word and double word data

Table 2.3 Data types

Unsigned byte	8	0 to 255
Signed byte	8	–128 to +127
Unsigned word	16	0 to 65,535
Signed word	16	–32,768 to +32,767
Unsigned double word	32	0 to 4,294,836,225
Signed double word	32	–1,073,741,824 to 1,073,676,289

A quick tour of the system

To explain the operation of the microcomputer system shown in the Figure 2.1 in greater detail, we shall examine each major system component individually, starting with the single most important component of the system, the CPU.

The CPU

The CPU forms the heart of any microcomputer and, consequently, its operation is crucial to the entire system. The primary function of the microprocessor is that of fetching, decoding and executing instructions resident in memory. As such, it must be able to transfer data from external memory into its own internal registers and vice versa. Furthermore, it must operate predictably, distinguishing, for example, between an operation contained within an instruction and any accompanying addresses of read/write memory locations. In addition, various system housekeeping tasks need to be performed, including responding to interrupts from external devices.

The main parts of a microprocessor are:

(a) registers for temporary storage of addresses and data

(b) an 'arithmetic logic unit' (ALU) that performs arithmetic and logic operations

(c) a means of controlling and timing operations within the system.

The majority of operations performed by a microprocessor involve the movement of data. Indeed, the program code (a set of instructions stored in ROM or RAM) must itself be fetched from memory prior to execution. The microprocessor thus performs a continuous sequence of instruction fetch and execute cycles. The act of fetching an instruction code (or operand or data value) from memory involves a read operation whilst the act of moving data from the microprocessor to a memory location involves a write operation.

Microprocessors determine the source of data (when it is being read) and the destination of data (when it is being written) by placing a unique address on the address bus. The address at which the data is to be placed (during a write operation) or from which it is to be fetched (during a read operation) can either constitute part of the memory of the system (in which case it may be within ROM or RAM) or it can be considered to be associated with input/output (I/O).

Since the data bus is connected to a number of VLSI devices, an essential requirement of such chips (e.g. ROM or RAM) is that their data outputs should be capable of being isolated from the bus whenever necessary. These VLSI devices are fitted with select or enable inputs which are driven by address decoding logic (not shown in Figures 2.1 and 2.3). This logic ensures that ROM, RAM and I/O devices never simultaneously attempt to place data on the bus!

The inputs of the address decoding logic are derived from one, or more, of the address bus lines. The address decoder effectively divides the available memory into blocks corresponding to a particular function (ROM, RAM, I/O etc.). Hence, where the processor is reading and writing to RAM, for example, the address decoding logic will ensure that only the RAM is selected whilst the ROM and I/O remain isolated from the data bus.

Within the CPU, data is stored in several 'registers'. Registers themselves can be thought of as a simple pigeon-hole arrangement that can store as many bits as there are holes available. Generally, these devices can store groups of 16 or 32-bits. Additionally, some registers may be configured as either one register of 16 bits or two registers of 32-bits.

Some microprocessor registers are accessible to the programmer whereas others are used by the microprocessor itself. Registers may be classified as either 'general purpose' or 'dedicated'. In the latter case, a particular function is associated with the register, such as holding the result of an operation or signalling the result of a comparison.

The ALU can perform arithmetic operations (addition and subtraction) and logic (complementation, logical AND, logical OR etc.). The ALU operates on two inputs (16 or 32-bits in length depending upon the CPU type) and it provides one output (again of 16 or 32-bits). In addition, the ALU status is preserved in the 'flag register' so that, for example, an overflow, zero or negative result can be detected.

The control unit is reponsible for the movement of data within the CPU and the management of control signals, both internal and external. The control unit asserts the requisite signals to read or write data as appropriate to the current instruction.

Parallel input and output

The transfer of data within a microprocessor system involves moving groups of 8, 16 or 32-bits using the bus architecture described earlier. Consequently, it is a relatively simple matter to transfer data into and out of the system in parallel form. This process is further simplified by using a Programmable Parallel I/O device (8255, or equivalent). This device provides registers for the temporary storage of data that not only 'buffer' the data but also provide a degree of electrical isolation from the system data bus.

Serial input and output

Parallel data transfer is primarily suited to high-speed operation over relatively short distances, a typical example being the linking of a microcomputer to an adjacent dot matrix printer. There are, however, some applications in which parallel data transfer is inappropriate, the most common example being data communication by means of telephone lines. In such cases, data must be sent serially (one bit after another) rather than in parallel form.

To transmit data in serial form, the parallel data from the microprocessor must be reorganised into a stream of bits. This task is greatly simplified by using an LSI interface device that contains a shift register which is loaded with parallel data from the data bus. These data are then read out as a serial bit stream by successive shifting. The reverse process, serial-to-parallel conversion, also uses a shift register. Here, data is loaded in serial form, each bit shifting further into the register until it becomes full. Data is then placed simultaneously on the parallel output lines. The basic principles of parallel-to-serial and serial-to-parallel data conversion are illustrated in Figures 2.5(a) and (b), respectively.

(a)

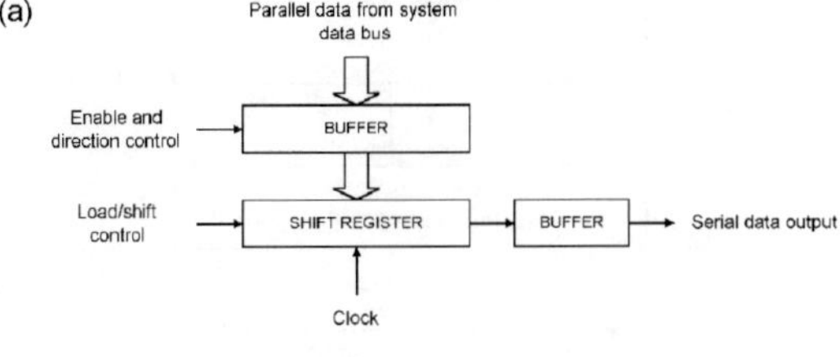

(b)

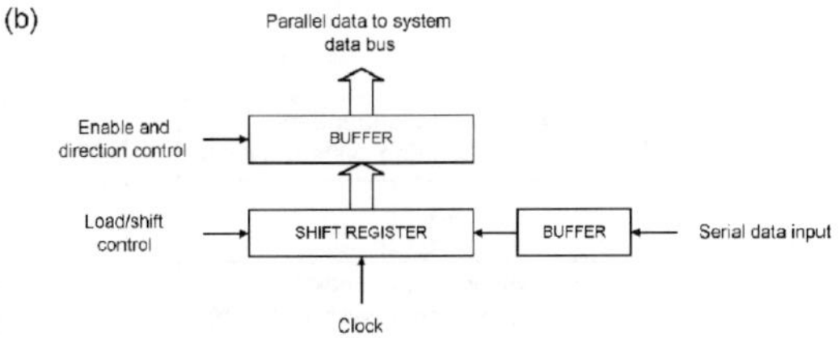

Figure 2.5 Basic principles of parallel-to-serial and serial-to-parallel data conversion

Operating systems

Many of the functions of an operating system (like those associated with disk filing) are obvious. Others, however, are so closely related to the machine's hardware that the average user remains blissfully unaware of them. This, of course, is as it should be. As far as most end-users of computer systems are concerned, the operating system provides an environment from which it is possible to launch and run applications programs and to carry out elementary maintenance of disk files. Here, the operating system is perhaps better described as a 'computer resource manager'.

The operating system provides an essential bridge between the user's applications programs and the system hardware. In order to provide a standardised environment (which will cater for a variety of different hardware configurations) and ensure a high degree of software portability, part of the operating system (the 'DOS') is hardware independent. The hardware-dependent remainder (the 'BIOS') provides the individual low-level routines required by the machine in question.

A well-behaved applications program will interact with the hardware independent (DOS) routines. These, in turn, will interact with the lower-level hardware dependent (BIOS) routines. Figure 2.6 illustrates this important point.

The operating system also provides the user with a number of utility programs which can be used for housekeeping tasks such as disk formatting, disk copying etc.

In order to provide a means of interaction with the user (via keyboard entered commands and on-screen prompts and messages), the operating system incorporates a shell program (e.g. the COMMAND.COM program provided within MS-DOS).

In order to optimise the use of the available memory, most modern operating systems employ memory management techniques which allocate memory to transient programs and then release the memory

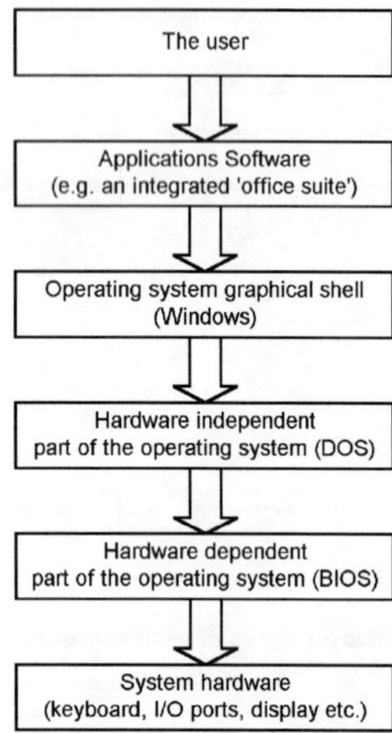

Figure 2.6 Relationship between COMMAND.COM, DOS and BIOS

when the program is terminated. A special type of 'terminate and stay resident' (TSR) program can remain resident in memory for execution whilst an application program is running.

TIP

TSRs can consume valuable memory which can, in some instances prevent applications programs from functioning correctly. Use the **MEM /C** or **MEM /D** command to determine which TSRs are present and how much of your valuable memory is being consumed!

3
System architecture and construction

This chapter sets out to introduce the PC and provide an insight into the architecture, operation and construction of a 'generic PC'. This chapter also deals with the safety and static hazards associated with PC equipment.

PC architecture

The term 'PC' now applies to such a wide range of equipment that it is difficult to pin down the essential ingredients of such a machine. However, at the risk of over-simplifying matters, a PC need only satisfy two essential criteria:

(a) be based upon an Intel 16, 32, or 64-bit processor (such as an 80486, Pentium, or an equivalent device such as a 5x86 from AMD or a 6x86 from IBM)

(b) be able to support the MS-DOS or compatible operating system (e.g. PC-DOS, DR-DOS, Novell DOS or Caldera's Open-DOS).

Other factors, such as available memory size, display technology, and disk storage, remain secondary.

The generic PC, whether a 'desktop' or 'tower' system, comprises three units: System Unit, Keyboard and Display.

The System Unit contains a number of items including:

- the system board or 'motherboard' to which is attached a number of memory modules and adapter cards
- the power supply
- one or more floppy drive(s)
- one or more hard drives(s).

In addition, the following may be contained within the system unit:

- a CD-ROM drive
- a backup tape or disk drive.

Fortunately, all of these units are fairly easy to spot and easy to recognise.

The original PC system board

The original IBM PC System Board employed approximately 100 integrated circuit devices including an 8088 CPU, an 8259A Interrupt Controller, an optional 8087 Maths Coprocessor, an 8288 Bus Controller, an 8284A Clock Generator, an 8253 Timer/Counter, an 8237A DMA Controller, and an 8255A Parallel Interface together with a host of discrete logic (including bus buffers, latches and transceivers). Figure 3.1 shows the simplified bus architecture of the system.

Much of this architecture was carried forward to the PC-XT and the PC-AT. This latter machine employed an 80286 CPU, 80287 Maths Coprocessor, two 8237A DMA Controllers, 8254–2 Programmable Timer, 8284A Clock Generator, two 8259A Interrupt Controllers and a 74LS612N Memory Mapper.

In order to significantly reduce manufacturing costs as well as to save on space and increase reliability, more recent XT and AT-compatible microcomputers are based on a significantly smaller number of devices (many of which may be surface mounted types). This trend has been continued with today's powerful '386- and '486-based systems. However, the functions provided by the highly integrated chipsets are merely a superset of those provided by the much large number of devices found in their predecessors.

PC specifications

PC's tend to conform to one of the basic specifications shown in Table 3.1.

TIP

With PC specifications things may not always be what they seem. The original Pentium processor with its 64-bit data bus promised to offer PC-users the advantages of 64-bit processing. In fact, Pentium architecture is based on two interconnected 32-bit '486-type processors. When the Pentium was first launched, it was sobering to find that the first generation of these much heralded chips could only just match the speed of the 'clock doubled' '486 chips that they were designed to replace (real benefits didn't materialise until the much faster Pentiums appeared). As far as memory is concerned and because of its 32-bit address bus, the Pentium is able to address exactly the same range as its predecessor. Not surprisingly, many people who rushed out to purchase the first Pentium-based systems were very disappointed with their performance – there must be a moral here somewhere!

Architecture of the original PC

Figure 3.1 shows the architecture of a generic 8088-based PC. There is more to this diagram than mere historical interest might indicate as all modern PCs can trace their origins to this particular arrangement. It is, therefore, worth spending a few moments developing an understanding of the configuration.

The 'CPU bus' (comprising lines A8 to A19 and AD0 to AD7 on the left side of Figure 3.1) is separated from the 'system bus' which links the support devices and expansion cards.

The eight least significant address and all eight of the data bus lines share a common set of eight CPU pins. These lines are labelled AD0 to AD7. The term used to describe this form of bus (where data and address information take turns to be present on a shared set of bus lines) is known as 'multiplexing'. This saves pins on the CPU package and it allowed Intel to make use of standard 40-pin packages for the 8088 and 8086 processors.

The system address bus (available on each of the expansion connectors) comprises 20 address lines, A0 to A19. The system data bus comprises eight lines, D0 to D7. Address and data information is alternately latched onto the appropriate set of bus lines by means of the four 74LS373 8-bit data latches. The control signals, ALE (address latch enable) and DIR (direction) derived from the 8288 bus controller are used to activate the two pairs of data latches.

Table 3.1 Typical PC specifications

Standard	Processor	RAM	Cache	Floppy disk	Hard disk	Graphics	Parallel port(s)	Serial port(s)	Clock speed	Bus
PC	8088	256K DRAM	Nil	1 or 2 5¼" 360K	None	Text or CGA	1 or 2	1 or 2	8 MHz	ISA (8-bit)
XT	8088 or 80286	640K DRAM	Nil	1 or 2 5¼" 360K	10M	Text and CGA	1 or 2	1 or 2	8 or 10MHz	ISA (8-bit)
AT	80286	1M DRAM	Nil	1 or 2 5¼" 1.2M	20M	Text, CGA or EGA	1 or 2	1 or 2	12 or 16MHz	ISA (16 bit)
PS/2	80286 or 80386	1M to 16M DRAM	Nil	1 3½" 720K or 1.44M	44M, 70M or 117M	Text, EGA or VGA	1 or 2	1 or 2	8, 10, 16 or 20MHz	MCA
PS/1	80286 or 80386	1M to 16M DRAM	Nil	1 3.5" 1.44M	85M or 130M	Text, VGA or SVGA	1 or 2	1 or 2	8, 10, 16 or 20MHz	MCA
386SX-based	80386SX	1M to 8M DRAM	64K	1 or 2 3½" 1.44M or 5¼" 1.2M	80M IDE	Text, VGA or SVGA	1 or 2	1 or 2	16 or 20MHz	ISA (16-bit)

Table 3.1 Continued

Standard	Processor	RAM	Cache	Floppy disk	Hard disk	Graphics	Parallel port(s)	Serial port(s)	Clock speed	Bus
386DX-based	80386DX	1M to 16M DRAM	128K	1 or 2 3½" 1.44M or 5¼" 1.2M	120M IDE	Text, VGA or SVGA	1 or 2	1 or 2	25 or 35MHz	ISA (16-bit)
486SX-based	80486SX	4M to 16M DRAM	256K	1 or 2 3½" 1.44M or 5¼" 1.2M	230M EIDE	Text, VGA or SVGA	1 or 2	1 or 2	25 or 33MHz	ISA/VL
486DX-based	80486DX	4M to 64M DRAM	256K	1 or 2 3½" 1.44M	540M EIDE	Text, VGA or SVGA	1 or 2	1 or 2	33, 50 or 66MHz	ISA/VL/EISA
Pentium-based	P24T	8M to 32M EDO	512K	1 or 2 3½" 1.44M	1.2G EIDE	Text, VGA or SVGA	1 or 2	1 or 2	66MHz	EISA/PCI
Pentium-based	P150	16M to 128M EDO	512K	1 or 2	1.6G EIDE	Text, VGA or SVGA	1 or 2	1 or 2	150MHz	EISA/PCI
Pentium II-based	Pentium II	64M to 128M EDO	512K	1 or 2 3½" 1.44M	4.3G SCSI	Text, VGA or SVGA	1 or 2	1 or 2	233MHz	EISA/PCI

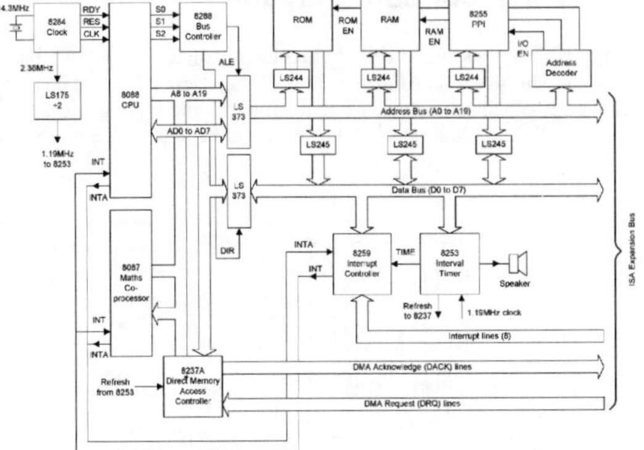

Figure 3.1 System architecture for a generic 8088 (or 8086-based) PC

The CPU bus is extended to the 8087 numeric data processor (maths coprocessor). This device is physically located in close proximity to the CPU in order to simplify the PCB layout.

The original PC required a CPU clock signal of 4.773MHz from a dedicated Intel clock generator chip. The basic timing element for this device is a quartz crystal which oscillates at a fundamental frequency of 14.318MHz. This frequency is internally divided by three in order to produce the CPU clock.

The CPU clock frequency is also further divided by two internally and again by two externally in order to produce a clock signal for the 8253 programmable interrupt timer. This device provides three important timing signals used by the system. One (known appropriately as TIME) controls the 8259 programmable interrupt controller, another (known as REFRESH) provides a timing input for the 8237 DMA controller, whilst the third is used (in conjunction with some extra logic) to produce an audible signal at the loudspeaker.

74LS244 8-bit bus drivers and 74LS245 8-bit bus transceivers link each of the major support devices with the 'system address bus' and 'system data bus' respectively. Address decoding logic (with input signals derived from the system address bus) generates the chip enable lines which activate the respective ROM, RAM and I/O chip select lines.

The basic system board incorporates a CPU, provides a connector for the addition of a maths coprocessor, incorporates bus and DMA control and provides the system clock and timing signals. The system board also houses the BIOS ROM, main system RAM and offers some limited parallel I/O. It does not, however, provide a number of other essential facilities including a video interface, disk and serial I/O. These important functions must normally be provided by means of adapter cards (note that some systems which offer only limited expansion may have some or all of these facilities integrated into the system board).

Adapter cards are connected to the expansion bus by means of a number of expansion slots (see Chapter 9 for further details). The expansion cards are physically placed so that any external connections required are available at the rear (or side) of the unit. Connections to internal sub-systems (such as hard and floppy disk drives) are usually made using lengths of ribbon cables and PCB connectors (see later).

Early system board layout

Figure 3.2 shows the system board layout of an early 8088-based PC-XT. This general layout started with the original PC and has been carried forward with improvements and enhancements into a wide range of PCs (including XT, XT-286, AT and compatible equipment).

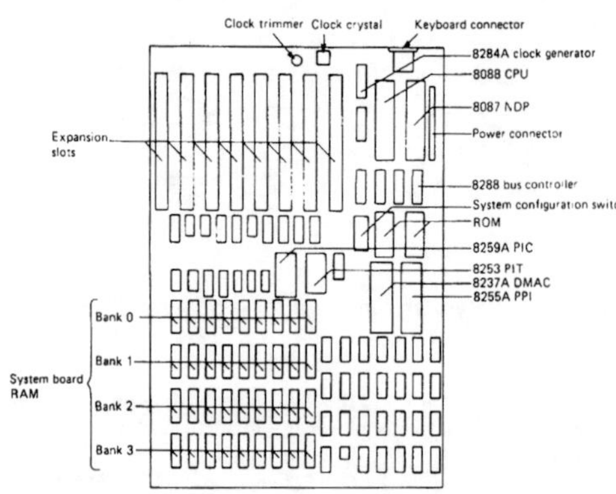

Figure 3.2 Original PC motherboard layout

The original PC's system board RAM was arranged in four banks, each of which provides 64K of memory. This memory is supplied using up to 36 conventional dual-in-line RAM chips. Bank 0 is the lowest 64K of RAM (addresses 00000 to 0FFFF), Bank 1 the next 64K (addresses 10000 to 1FFFF), and so on. The XT uses a similar RAM layout to the original PC but with larger capacity RAM chips (a total of 512K on the system board). Additional memory can only be provided by means of an appropriate adapter card.

The original AT motherboard ('AT Type 1') had its RAM organised in two banks (bank 0 and bank 1). These accommodate up to 36 128K × 1 bit dual-in-line RAM chips. The later AT motherboard ('AT Type 2') and XT-286 machines both use 'memory modules' (rather than individual RAM chips). See Chapter 6 for more information.

The major support devices (8288 bus controller, 8237A direct memory access controller etc.) on all three basic specification machines (PC, XT and AT) are clustered together on the right of the PCB (as viewed from above). More modern machines use integrated support chips and thus there are less (but more complex) devices present on the motherboard. Furthermore, modern system boards invariably use surface mounted components and pin-grid array (PGA) chips (rather than the conventionally soldered dual-in-line chips used in the original specification machines).

Modern system board layouts

Figure 3.3 shows a typical '486 system motherboard layout. This board provides eight EISA slots and two local bus (VL-bus) slots and is typical of early '486-based systems. The board is designed to accept an 80486 CPU (with various 33MHz, 50MHz, 66MHz and 100MHz clock speed options). 256K or 512K of DIL CACHE memory can be fitted. DRAM can be added in two banks (bank 0 and bank 1) using a total of eight single-in-line memory modules (SIMM). Various combinations of DRAM can be fitted, with 4Mbyte, 8Mbyte and 16Mbyte being the most popular (based on 1 × 4Mbyte, 2 × 4Mbyte and 4 × 4Mbyte SIMMs, respectively). Standard IDE hard disk drive and/or CD-ROM ports are provided by means of two 40-way connectors (these are the 'primary' and 'secondary' IDE ports). Note that the floppy disk interface is provided as part of the 'multi-function I/O' adapter card. This card (not shown in Figure 3.3) provides I/O facilities for:

- one or two floppy disk drives (via a 34-way ribbon cable header)
- a first serial port (with its 9-way D-connector fitted to the rear bracket)
- an optional second serial port connector (via an 8-way header)
- a parallel port (with its 25-way D-connector fitted to the rear bracket)
- a game/joystick port (via a 16-way ribbon cable header)
- an optional IDE device (via a 40-way ribbon cable header which is not normally used if IDE facilities are available on the motherboard).

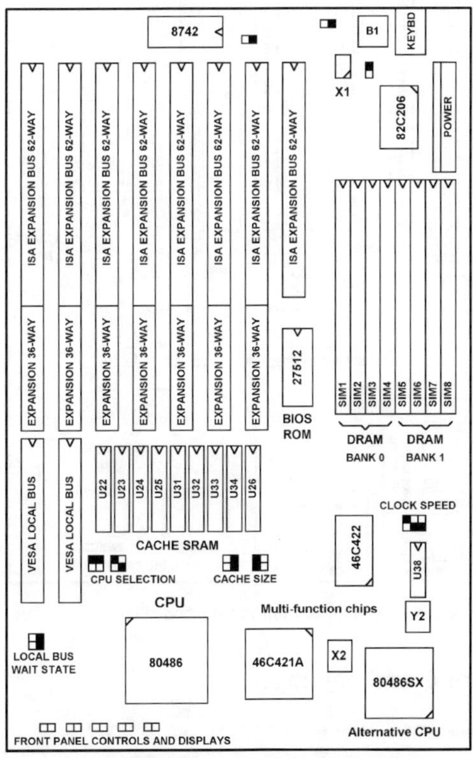

Figure 3.3 Typical '486 motherboard layout

A typical Pentium system motherboard layout is shown in Figure 3.4. This 'MMX-ready' system board provides four PCI slots and two EISA slots. Two three-terminal integrated circuit voltage regulators provide the low-voltage 3.3V supply required by the faster Pentium processors. The 296-pin ZIF socket ('Socket 7') is suitable for a wide variety of devices, including all 6x86 and Pentium chips (including MMX) as well as the AMD K5 and K6. 512K of surface mounted cache memory is fitted. Conventional SIMM DRAM can be added in a single bank of four SIMM modules. In addition, two 168-pin sockets accept up to two dual-in-line memory modules (DIMM) carrying fast (6–7ns) synchronous DRAM or EDO DIMMs. Once again, standard 'primary' and 'secondary' IDE hard disk drive and/or CD-ROM ports are provided by means of two 40-way connectors.

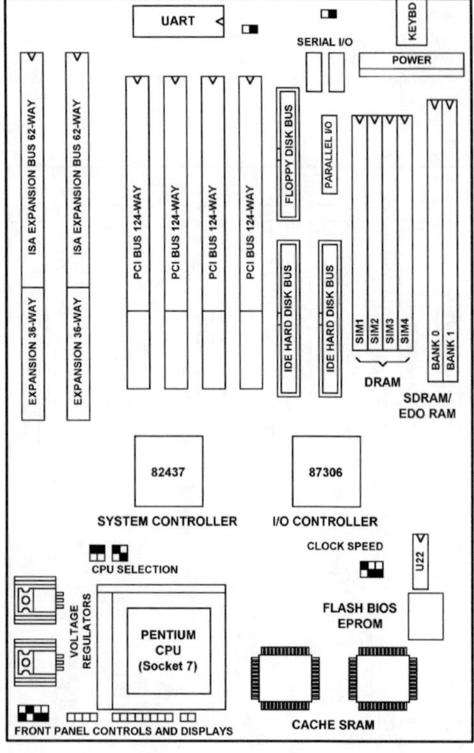

Figure 3.4 Typical Pentium motherboard layout

Wiring and cabling

Internal wiring within a PC tends to take one of three forms:

(a) power connections based on colour coded stranded wires (red, black, yellow etc.)

ribbon cables (flat, multi-core wiring which is often grey or beige in colour)

signal wiring (miniature colour coded wires with stranded conductors) used to connect front panel indicators, switches etc.

TIP

Ribbon cables invariably have a coloured stripe at one end which denotes the position of pin-1 on the connector. Since some connectors are 'non-polarised' (i.e. it is possible to make the connection the 'wrong-way-round') you should always carefully check that the stripe is aligned towards the '1' marked on the PCB. Making the connection the 'wrong-way-round' can sometimes have disastrous consequences.

Colour coding

The power supply wiring is invariably colour coded. The colour coding often obeys the following convention:

Red	+5V	Main system +5V supply rail.
Yellow	+12V	An ancillary supply rail used by disk drives etc.
Black	Ground/ common/0V	This variously named rail links all ground and chassis points and also acts as the negative 'return' connection for the +5V and +12V rails.

Different colours may be used to denote other power supply voltage rails and signals. The colour scheme used by one popular 'clone' manufacturer is shown in Table 3.2.

Table 3.2 Typical colour coding convention for the system power connector in an AT-compatible machine (you should not rely on this being the same in other machines)

Power connector pin number (see Figure 3.3)	Voltage/signal	Colour
1	Power good	Orange
2	+5V d.c.	Red
3	+12V d.c.	Yellow
4	–12V d.c.	Blue
5	0V/common	Black
6	0V/common	Black
7	0V/common	Black
8	0V/common	Black
9	–5V d.c.	White
10	+5V d.c.	Red
11	+5V d.c.	Red
12	+5V d.c.	Red

Making a connection

Several forms of connector are used within PC equipment; including PCB edge connectors (both direct and indirect types), IDC connectors, D-connectors and DIN connectors.

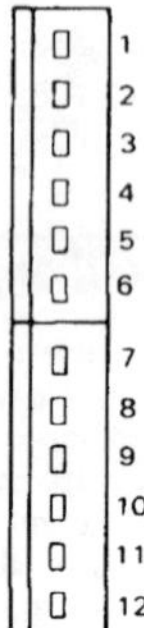

Figure 3.5 System board power connector

PCB edge connectors

PCB edge connectors (usually 34-way) are commonly used with older 5¼" and some 3½" disk drives. This type of connector is also found on older hard disk drives. The connector mates with the edge of the printed circuit board where the PCB tracks are brought out to gold-plated contacts. IDC connectors are generally more reliable than PCB edge connectors and have largely replaced PCB edge connectors for disk drive and CD-ROM connection. PCB edge connectors are also used for the ISA (Industry Standard Architecture) bus and the PCI (Peripheral Component Interconnect) bus (see Chapter 9 for further details).

IDC connectors

IDC (insulation displacement) connectors are commonly used on ribbon cables. These connectors (often 26-way, 34-way or 40-way) use PCB mounted headers. The connector is 'forced' onto the ribbon cable and connection made (without soldering) by means of a special tool. 40-way ribbon cables are used for the IDE bus connection to the hard disk drive(s) and CD-ROM whilst 34-way cables are used for the floppy disk drive(s).

D-type connectors

D-type connectors are invariably used for external connections. Most systems use one or more female 25-way D-connectors for the parallel printer interface together with one or more male 25-way or 9-way D-connectors for serial (RS-232) communications. D-connectors are also commonly used for connecting the display (see Chapter 13 for further information).

TIP

Connectors can be a regular cause of problems on PC equipment. The older style direct contact edge connectors are particularly susceptible to problems which often first manifest themselves as intermittent faults causing random 'crashes' and 'lock-ups'.

TIP

PCB edge connectors benefit from cleaning whenever a system is being overhauled. A PCB cleaning block (e.g. Maplin Electronic Component Supplies order code HX04E) and/or a can of aerosol PCB solvent cleaner (Maplin YJ45Y) is ideal for this purpose. In an emergency, or when no suitable cleaning materials are available, you should disconnect and reconnect the edge connector several times. The action of making and breaking the connection several times will often clear any offending oxide coating.

DIN connectors

The PC's keyboard connection is invariably made using a 5-way DIN connector (see Figure 3.6). Several manufacturers (notably Amstrad) have used DIN connectors for other purposes (including display connection and system board power).

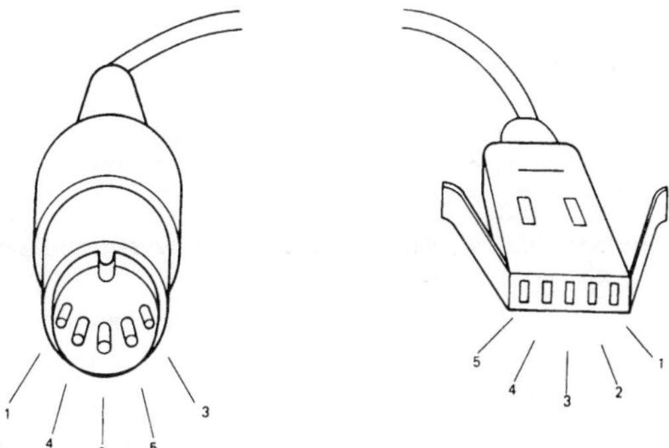

Figure 3.6 Pin-numbering for the standard keyboard connector

Cooling

All PC systems produce heat and some systems produce more heat than others. Adequate ventilation is thus an essential consideration and fans are included within the system unit to ensure that there is adequate air flow. Furthermore, internal air flow must be arranged so that it is unrestricted as modern processors and support chips run at high temperatures. These devices are much more prone to failure when they run excessively hot than when they run cool or merely warm.

If the system unit fan fails to operate (and it is not thermostatically controlled) check the supply to it. If necessary replace the fan. If the unit runs slow or intermittently it should similarly be replaced.

TIP

The '486 and later CPUs produce a considerable amount of heat and often run at an excessive temperature. You can significantly improve the reliability of the processor (and greatly extend its working life) by fitting a miniature CPU. This inexpensive device is available from most PC upgrade suppliers. Note that, other than assisting with some additional air flow within the case of a PC, the fan fitted to the power supply unit actually provides little cooling for the motherboard mounted chips.

TIP

When fitting expansion cards and positioning internal ribbon cables, give some thought to the air flow within the system unit. In particular, it is worth trying to maximise the space between adapter cards (rather than have them sandwiched close together). You should also ensure that the ribbon cables do not impede the flow of air around the motherboard and adapter cards.

Dismantling a system

The procedure for dismantling a system depends upon the type of enclosure. The three examples that follow should at least give you some idea of the main points:

Standard IBM PC, XT and AT desktop system units

1. Exit from any program that may be running.
2. Type PARK to park the hard disk heads (only necessary on older systems).
3. Remove the floppy disk(s) from the drive(s).
4. Switch the system unit power off (using the power switch at the rear of the system unit case).
5. Switch off at the mains outlet and disconnect the mains power lead.
6. Switch off and disconnect any peripherals that may be attached (including keyboard, mouse, printer etc.).
7. Disconnect the display power lead and video signal cable from the rear of the system unit. Remove the display and place safely on one side.
8. Remove the cover retaining screws from the rear of the system unit.
9. Carefully slide the system unit cover away from the rear and towards the front. When the cover will slide no further, tilt the cover upwards, remove the cover from the base and set aside.
10. You will now have access to the system board, power supply, disk drives, and adapter cards.

Tower units

As steps 1–6 for a standard system plus:

7. Disconnect the display power lead and video signal cable from the rear of the system unit.
8. Remove the cover retaining screws from the rear of the system unit.
9. Carefully slide the system unit cover towards the rear until it is clear of the front fascia. Then lift the cover clear of the system unit. It is not usually necessary to remove the fascia.
10. You will now have access to the system board, power supply, disk drives and adapter cards.

Amstrad PC1512, PC1640 (and other non-standard desktop cases)

As steps 1–6 for a standard system plus:

7. Disconnect the display power lead and video signal cable from the rear of the system unit. Lift off the display from the recess in the upper case half and move to one side.
8. Depress the two tabs and then lift off the cover fitted to the expansion area at the rear of the system unit.
9. Remove the four long cross-point screws (two at the rear and two at the front fitted under the two snap-off plastic covers).
10. Remove the three smaller cross-point screws that retain the metal plate which secures the expansion cards.
11. Simultaneously slide the front plastic escutcheon forwards and the upper case half upwards, separating the two plastic mouldings in the process.
12. Remove the two-way PCB connector which links the battery holder with the system unit.
13. Remove the two-way PCB connector which links the front-panel power indicator to the system unit.
14. You will now have access to the system board, power supply, disk drives and adapter cards.

TIP

An egg-box (or similar container) makes an excellent receptacle for screws and small parts removed when you are dismantling a system.

TIP

When a system uses a number of screws of similar size but of differing length, it is important to note the location of each screw so that it can be replaced correctly during re-assembly. A water-based felt-tip pen can be used to mark the screw sizes on the case.

TIP

If you are building or assembling your own system, always start with the largest size enclosure. This will provide you with plenty of scope for expansion and allow you to upgrade more easily.

Reassembly

System unit reassembly is usually the reverse of disassembly. It is, of course, essential to check the orientation of any non-polarised cables and connectors and also to ensure that screws have been correctly located and tightened. Under no circumstances should there be any loose connectors, components or screws left inside a system unit!

Safety first!

The voltages found in mains-operated PC equipment can be lethal. However, high voltages are normally restricted to the power supply and display. The lower voltages present on the system board, disk drives and adapter cards are perfectly safe.

When working inside the power supply or the display it is *essential* to avoid contact with any metal parts or components which may be at a high voltage. This includes all mains wiring, fuses and switches, as well as many of the components associated with the high-voltage a.c. and d.c. circuits in the power supply.

It is always essential to switch-off and allow the capacitors to discharge before attempting to remove or replace components. Occasionally, you may have to test and/or make adjustments on 'live' circuits. In this event you can avoid electric shock hazards by only using tools which are properly insulated, and by using test leads fitted with insulated test prods.

TIP

Another sensible precaution when making high-voltage measurements and adjustments is that of only working with one hand (you should keep the other one safely behind your back or in a pocket). This simple practice will ensure that you never place yourself in a position where electric current will pass from one hand and arm to the other via your heart. In such circumstances an electric shock could be fatal.

Static hazards

Many of the devices used in modern PC equipment are susceptible to damage from stray electrostatic charges. Static is, however, not a problem provided you observe the following simple rules:

1. Ensure that your test equipment is properly earthed.
2. Preserve the anti-static wrapping supplied with boards and components and ensure that it is used for storage and also whenever boards or components have to be returned to suppliers.
3. Invest in an anti-static mat, grounding wire and wrist strap and use them whenever you remove or replace components fitted to a PCB.
4. Check your workshop or work area for potential static hazards (e.g. carpets manufactured from man-made fibres, clothing made from synthetic materials etc.).

TIP

When working within the system unit make sure that you ground yourself by touching any grounded metal part (e.g. the case of the power supply) before removing or replacing any parts or adapter cards.

TIP

When components are mounted on a PCB there are plenty of paths which will allow static charges to drain safely away. Hence you are unlikely to damage components by touching them when they are in their correct locations on a PCB.

4
Processor types and families

This chapter describes the main feature of each type of central processing unit (CPU) used in a PC. It also explains how the CPU operates and how you can identify, remove and replace the device when it fails.

The CPU is crucial in determining the performance of a PC and the 80x86 family (see Table 4.1) has been consistently upgraded. The latest members of the family offer vastly improved performance when compared with their predecessors. Despite this, a core of common features has been retained in order to preserve compatibility, hence all current CPU devices provide a superset of the basic 8086 registers.

Table 4.1 CPU summary

CPU type	Manufacturer	Speed	Data bus	Notes
8088	Intel	5, 8, 10	16-bit	Used in the IBM PC and IBM PC-XT (now obsolete)
8086	Intel	5, 8, 10	8-bit	16-bit data bus version of the 8086 (now obsolete)
80286	Intel	6, 8, 12	16-bit	First used in the IBM PC-AT. Supports only 1M of directly addressable RAM. No internal coprocessor. No internal cache
80386SX (i386SX)	Intel	16, 20, 25, 33	32-bit internal 16-bit external	Cut down and lower cost version of the 386DX
Am386SX	AMD	33	32-bit internal 16-bit external	Faster than Intel's 386SX
80386DX (i386DX)	Intel	16, 20, 25, 33	32-bit	Intel's first 32-bit CPU launched in 1985
Am386DX	AMD	40	32-bit	Faster than Intel's 386DX
486SLC	IBM	20	32-bit internal 16-bit external	Clock-doubled chip. No internal maths coprocessor

Table 4.1 Continued

CPU type	Manufacturer	Speed	Data bus	Notes
486SLC2	IBM	50	32-bit internal 16-bit external	Clock-doubled chip. No internal maths coprocessor
486DLC2	IBM	33/66	32-bit internal	Clock-doubled chip. No internal maths coprocessor
Cx486S	Cyrix	40	32-bit	Replacement for Intel's 486SX; no internal maths coprocessor and only 2Kb of internal cache
Am486DX	AMD	33, 40	32-bit	Similar to Intel's i486DX but faster
Am486DX2	AMD	22/50, 33/66	32-bit	Similar to Intel's i486DX2 but faster. Clock doubled
i486SX2	Intel	50	32-bit	Can offer about 20% faster performance than a 486DX-33 but without the internal maths coprocessor
i486DX	Intel	25, 33, 50	32-bit	Has an internal 8Kb cache and internal maths coprocessor
Cx486S	Cyrix	33, 50	32-bit	Similar to 486DX
i486SX	Intel	16, 20, 25, 33	32-bit	Cut-down version of the 486DX. No internal maths coprocessor
Cx486DRx2	Cyrix	16/32, 20/40, 25/50	32-bit	Replaces an existing 386DX
Cx486SRx2	Cyrix	16/32, 20/40, 25/50	16-bit	Fits over an existing 386SX
OverDrive	Intel	20/40, 25/50, 33/66	16/32-bit	Intel's upgrade processor available in two versions (SX and DX) to plug into the maths coprocessor socket

Table 4.1 Continued

CPU type	Manufacturer	Speed	Data bus	Notes
i486DX2	Intel	25/50, 33/66,	32-bit	Internal clock doubling processor; 33MHz is doubled to 66MHz, and so on
i486DX4	Intel	75, 100	32-bit	Internal clock tripled processor; 25MHz is tripled to 75MHz, and so on
Am5x86	AMD	100, 133	32-bit	Optimised for 32-bit operating systems
6x86	IBM	100, 120, 133	32-bit	Optimised for 32-bit operating systems
Pentium (various)	Intel	60, 66, 75, 90, 100, 120, 132, 150, 200	64-bit	Intel's first 64-bit processor
P24T	Intel	60, 66, 90	32-bit	Pin-compatible Pentium replacement for an Intel '486. Also known as the 'Pentium OverDrive' chip
PowerPC	IBM	60, 66, 80	64-bit	Powerful RISC processor. Requires emulation software to run DOS, Windows and associated applications programs
K5	AMD	166	64-bit	AMD's rival for the Pentium P54C
Pentium II	Intel	233, 266	64-bit	Attached to the motherboard via a slot mounted card interface (known as 'Slot 1'). Card incorporates an external Level 2 cache
K6	AMD	180, 200, 233	64-bit	AMD's answer to the Pentium II. The K6 is optimised for a 32-bit operating system, has a large 64Kb Level 1 cache and includes MMX extensions

8086 and 8088

The original member of the 80x86 family, the 8086, was designed with modular internal architecture. This approach to microprocessor design has allowed Intel to produce a similar microprocessor with identical internal architecture but employing an 8-bit external bus. This device, the 8088, shares the same 16-bit internal architecture as its 16-bit bus counterpart. Both devices are packaged in 40-pin DIL encapsulations, the pin connections for which are shown in Figure 4.1. The CPU signal lines are described in Table 4.2.

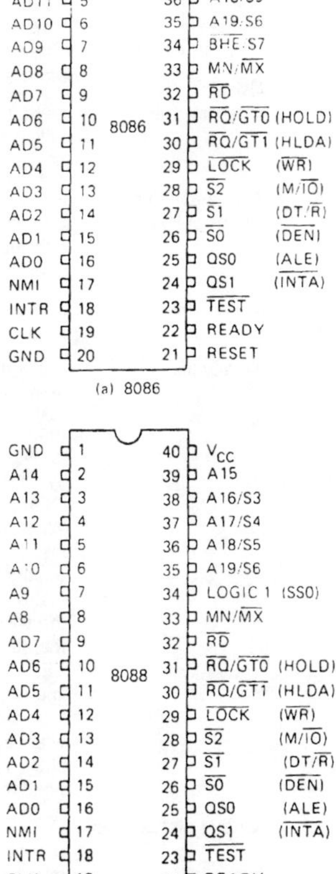

Figure 4.1 Pin connections for the 8086 and 8088 CPU

Table 4.2 8086/8088 signals

Signal	Function	Notes
AD0–AD7	Address/data lines	Multiplexed 8-bit address/data bus
AD0–AD15 (8086)	Address/data lines	Multiplexed 16-bit address/data bus
A8–A19 (8088)	Address lines	Address bus
A16–A19 (8086)	Address lines	Address bus
S0–S7	Status lines	S0–S2 are only available in Maximum Mode and are connected to the 8288 Bus Controller. Note that status lines S3–S7 all share pins with other signals
INTR	Interrupt line	Level-triggered, active high interrupt request input
NMI	Non-maskable interrupt line	Positive edge-triggered non-maskable interrupt input
RESET	Reset line	Active high reset input
READY	Ready line	Active high ready input
TEST	Test	Input used to proivde synchronisation with external processors. When a WAIT instruction is encountered in the instruction stream, the CPU examines the state of the TEST line. If this line is found to be high, the processor waits in an 'idle' state until the signal goes low
QS0, QS1	Queue status lines	Outputs from the processor which may be used to keep track of the internal instruction queue

Table 4.2 Continued

Signal	Function	Notes
LOCK	Bus Lock	Output from the processor which is taken low to indicate that the bus is not currently available to other potential bus masters
RQ/GT0–RQ/GT1	Request/Grant	Used for signalling bus requests and grants placed in the CL register

Architecture

The 8086/8088 can be divided internally into two functional blocks comprising an Execution Unit (EU) and a Bus Interface Unit (BIU), as shown in Figure 4.2. The EU is responsible for decoding and executing instructions whilst the BIU prefetches instructions from memory and places them in an instruction queue where they await decoding and execution by the EU.

The EU comprises a general and special purpose register block, temporary registers, arithmetic logic unit (ALU), a flag (status) register and control logic. It is important to note that the principal elements of the 8086 EU remain essentially common to each of the members of Intel's 80x86 microprocessor family but with additional 32-bit registers in the case of the 80386, 80486 and Pentium.

The BIU architecture varies according to the size of the external data bus. The BIU comprises four segment registers and an instruction pointer, temporary storage for instructions held in the instruction queue and bus control logic.

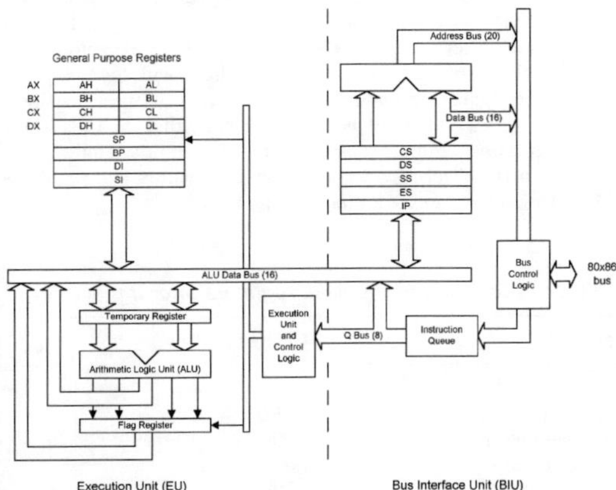

Figure 4.2 Internal architecture of the 8086

Addressing

The 8086 has 20 address lines and thus provides for a physical 1Mbyte memory address range (memory address locations 00000 to FFFFF hex.). The I/O address range is 64Kbytes (I/O address locations 0000 to FFFF hex.).

The actual 20-bit physical memory address is formed by shifting the segment address four zero bits to the left (adding four least significant bits), which effectively multiplies the Segment Register contents by 16. The contents of the Instruction Pointer (IP), Stack Pointer (SP) or other 16-bit memory reference is then added to the result. This process is illustrated in Figure 4.3.

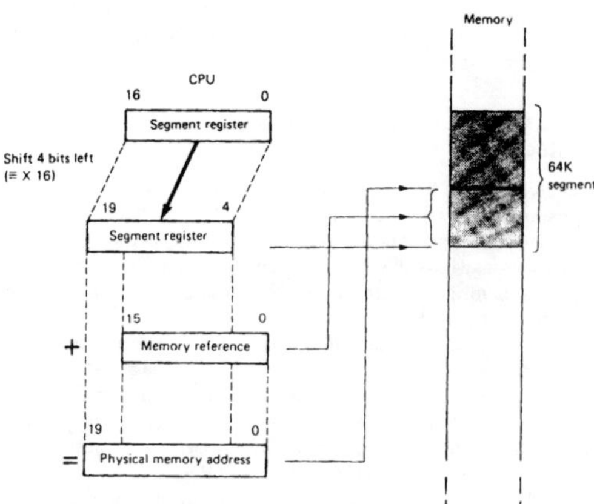

Figure 4.3 Process of forming a 20-bit physical address

As an example of the process of forming a physical address reference, Table 4.2 shows the state of the 8086 registers after the RESET signal is applied. The instruction referenced (i.e. the first instruction to be executed after the RESET signal is applied) will be found by combining the Instruction Pointer (offset address) with the Code Segment register (paragraph address). The location of the instruction referenced is FFFF0 (i.e. F0000 + FFF0). Note that the PC's ROM physically occupies addresses F0000 to FFFFF and that, following a power-on or hardware reset, execution commences from address FFFF0 with a jump to the initial program loader.

Table 4.3 Contents of the 8086 registers after a reset

Register	Contents (hex.)
Flag	0002
Instruction Pointer	FFF0
Code Segment	F000
Data Segment	0000
Extra Segment	0000
Stack Segment	0000

TIP

The NEC V20 and V30 processors are pin-compatible replacements for the Intel 8088 and 8086, respectively. These chips are enhanced versions of their Intel counterparts and they offer an increase in processing speed for certain operations.

80286

Intel's 80286 CPU was first employed in the PC-AT and PS/2 Models 50 and 60. The 80286 offers a 16Mbyte physical addressing range but incorporates memory management capabilities that can map up to a gigabyte of virtual memory. Depending upon the application, the 80286 is up to six times faster than the standard 5MHz 8086 while providing upward software computability with the 8086 and 8088 processors.

The 80286 has 15 16-bit registers of which 14 are identical to those of the 8086. The additional Machine Status Word (MSW) register controls the operating mode of the processor and also records when a task switch takes place.

The bit functions within the MSW are summarised in Table 4.4. The MSW is initialised with a value of FFF0H upon reset, the remainder of the 80286 registers being initialised as shown in Table 4.3. The 80286 is packaged in a 68-pin JEDEC type-A plastic leadless chip carrier (PLCC) as shown in Figure 4.4.

Table 4.4 Bit functions in the 80286 machine status word

Bit	Name	Function
0	Protected mode (PE)	Enables protected mode and can only be cleared by asserting the RESET signal
1	Monitor processor (MP)	Allows WAIT instructions to cause a 'processor extension not present' exception (Exception 7)
2	Emulate processor (EP)	Causes a 'processor extension not present' exception (Exception 7) on ESC instructions to allow emulation of a processor extension
3	Task switched (TS)	Indicates that the next instruction using a procesor extension will cause Exception 7 (allowing software to test whether the current processor extension context belongs to the current task)

Component pad view As viewed from underside of component when mounted on the board

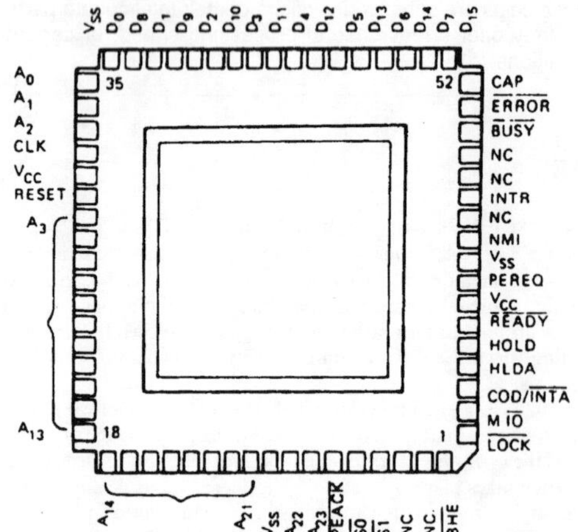

PC Board view As viewed from the component side of the PC board

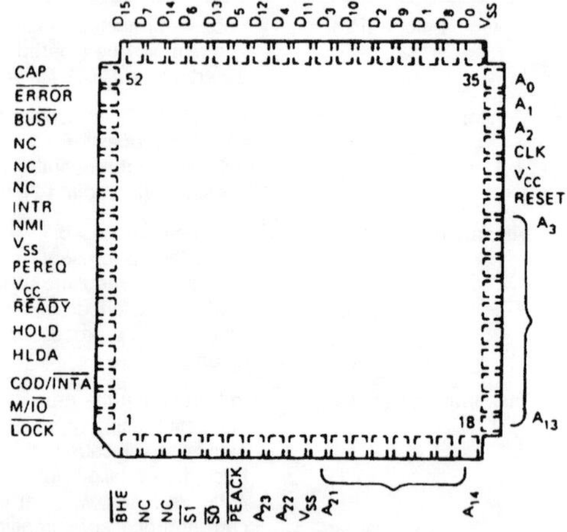

Figure 4.4 Pin connections for the 80286

80386

The 80386 was designed as a full 32-bit device capable of manipulating data 32 bits at a time and communicating with the outside world through a 32-bit address bus. The 80386 offers a 'virtual 8086' mode of operation in which memory can be divided into 1Mbyte chunks with a different program allocated to each partition.

The 80386 is available in two basic versions. The 80386SX operates internally as a 32-bit device but presents itself to the outside world through only 16 data lines. This has made the CPU extremely popular for use in low-cost systems which could still boast the processing power of a '386 (despite the obvious limitation imposed by the reduced number of data lines, the SX version of the 80386 runs at approximately 80% of the speed of its fully fledged counterpart).

Architecture

The 80386 comprises a Bus Interface Unit (BIU), Code Prefetch Unit, Instruction Decode Unit, Execution Unit (EU), Segmentation Unit and Paging Unit. The Code Prefetch Unit performs the program 'lookahead' function.

When the BIU is not performing bus cycles in the execution of an instruction, the Code Prefetch Unit uses the BIU to fetch sequentially the instruction stream. The prefetched instructions are stored in a 16-byte 'code queue' where they await processing by the Instruction Decode Unit.

The prefetch queue is fed to the Instruction Decode Unit which translates the instructions into microcode. These microcoded instructions are then stored in a three-deep instruction queue on a first-in first-out (FIFO) basis. This queue of instructions awaits acceptance by the Execution Unit. Immediate data and opcode offsets are also taken from the prefetch queue.

80486

The 80486 CPU is not merely an upgraded 80386 processor; its redesigned architecture offers significantly faster processing speeds when running at the same clock speed as its predecessor. Enhancements include a built-in maths coprocessor, internal cache memory and cache memory control.

Additional signals and cache operation

The '486 CPU uses a large number of additional signals associated with parity checking (PCHK) and cache operation (AHOLD, FLUSH etc.). The cache comprises a set of four 2K blocks (128 × 16 bytes) of high-speed internal memory. Each 16-byte line of memory has a matching 21-bit 'tag'. This tag comprises a 17-bit linear address together with four protection bits. The cache control block contains 128 sets of seven bits. Three of the bits are used to implement the 'least recently used' (LRU) system for replacement and the remaining four bits are used to indicate valid data.

TIP

The '486's internal cache is responsible for a significant increase in processing speed. For example, a '486 operating at 25MHz can achieve a faster processing speed than a '386 operating at 33MHz!

Pentium

The first Intel Pentium processors were introduced in 1993 and they became widely available fitted into high-performance PC's from 1994 onwards. The Pentium processor contains the equivalent of more than 3.1 million transistors representing a threefold increase when compared with its immediate predecessor. The first production chips offered fairly pedestrian clock speeds of a mere 60 or 66MHz. These chips were, however, quickly joined by 3.3V versions that would operate at 75, 90 and 100MHz. Later still came versions that would operate at 120, 132, 150 and 200MHz.

The Pentium has a 64-bit local data bus (twice the width of its immediate predecessor) and an internal 16Kbyte cache, 8Kbytes of which is used for code with the other 8Kbytes used for data. There are two execution 'pipelines', U and V. These, coupled with the internal 'Level 1' split cache provide a facility for executing two instructions simultaneously (provided, of course, that they do not share the same address references). Note that, since each pipeline is 32-bits wide, the Pentium is, strictly speaking, a 32-bit processor since execution is based on 32-bit chunks of data rather than the 64-bits that the width of the local bus might at first suggest!

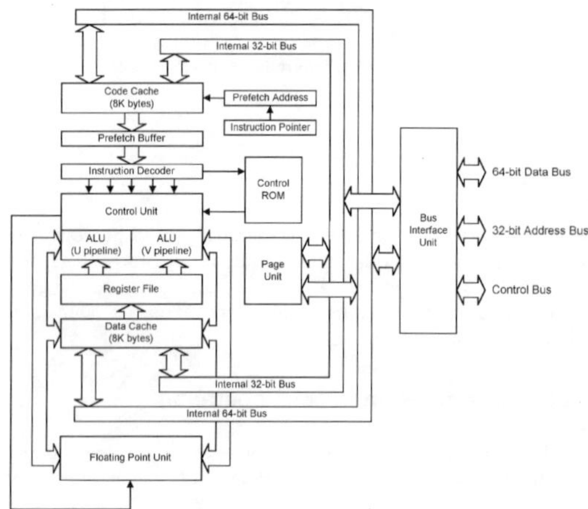

Figure 4.5 Internal architecture of the Pentium

Interrupt handling

Interrupt service routines are sub-programs stored away from the main body of code that are available for execution whenever the relevant interrupt occurs. However, since interrupts may occur at virtually any point in the execution of a main program, the response must be automatic; the processor must suspend its current task and save the return address so that the program can be resumed at the point at which it was left. Note that the programmer must assume responsibility for preserving the state of any registers which may have their contents altered during execution of the interrupt service routine.

The Intel processor family uses a table of 256 four-byte pointers stored in the bottom 1Kbytes of memory (addresses 0000H to 03FFH). Each of the locations in the Interrupt Pointer Table can be loaded with a pointer to a different interrupt service routine. Each pointer contains two bytes for loading into the Code Segment (CS) register and two bytes for loading into the Instruction Pointer (IP). This allows the programmer to place interrupt service routines in any appropriate place within the 1Mbyte physical address space.

Each of the 256 interrupt pointers is allocated a different type number. A Type 0 interrupt has its associated interrupt pointer in the lowest four bytes of memory (0000H to 0003H). A Type 1 interrupt will have its pointer located in the next four bytes of memory (0004H to 0007H), and so on.

The structure of the Interrupt Pointer Table is shown in Figure 4.6. Interrupt Types 0 to 4 have dedicated functions whilst Types 5 to 31 are reserved. Hence there are 224 remaining locations in which interrupt pointers may be stored. The interrupting device places a byte on the data bus in response to an interrupt acknowledgement generated by the CPU. This byte gives the interrupt type and the CPU loads its Code Segment and Instruction Pointer registers with the words stored at the appropriate locations in the Interrupt Pointer Table and then commences execution of the interrupt service routine.

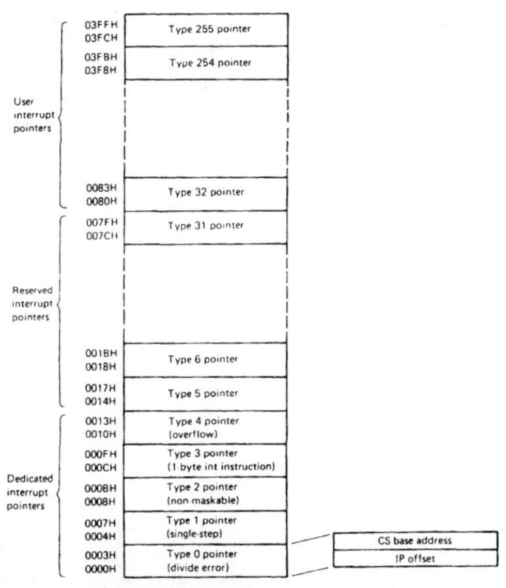

Figure 4.6 Interrupt pointer table

Replacing the CPU

The processor chip (regardless of type) is invariably fitted in a socket and this makes removal and replacement quite straightforward provided that you have the correct tool for the job. Table 4.5 shows the packages and power supply requirements for various members of the 80x86 family.

Table 4.5 Power supply requirements and packages for CPU chips

	CPU type							
	8086	**8088**	**80186**	**80286**	**80386**	**80486 (i386)**	**Pentium (i486)**	**Pentium II**
Supply voltage	5V	5V	5V	5V	5V	5V	3.3V	2.5V, 3.3V, 5V
Supply current	340–360mA	340–360mA	415–550mA	415–550mA	370–550mA	750–900mA	–	–
Supply power (typical)	1.75W	1.75W	2.5W	2.5W	2.5W	5W	15W	25W
Packages	DIP	DIP	PLCC	PLCC, PGA	PGA	PGA	PGA	Slot 1 card
Pins	40	40	68	68	132	168	168, 273, 296	242

Specialised tools will allow you to remove 40-pin DIL packages (8088 and 8086) and PLCC and PGA (80286 and later) chips. An 'extractor' will allow you to grip the chip firmly in its stainless steel jaws whilst an 'inserter' will allow you to replace the chip by simply positioning the device and depressing a plunger or turning a knob. These tools are not cheap but are a worthwhile investment as it is virtually impossible to safely undertake this task by any other means.

The following describes the stages in removing and replacing a CPU chip:

1. Switch 'off', disconnect from the supply and gain access to the system board (as described in Chapter 3).
2. Ensure that you observe the safety and static precautions at all times. Have some anti-static packing available to receive the CPU when it has been removed.
3. Locate the CPU and ensure that there is sufficient room to work all around it (you may have to move ribbon cables or adapter cards to gain sufficient clearance to use the extraction and insertion tools).
4. Check that you have selected the correct extraction tool. Open the jaws of the tool and carefully position it over the chip. Close the jaws and check that the device is gripped firmly (you may need to ease the jaws of the tool gently into place).
5. Lock the jaws into place and ease the chip out of the connector (you should pull straight but firmly but at right angles to the PCB).
6. Immediately deposit the chip in an anti-static container (do not touch any of the pins).
7. Pick up the replacement chip (using the insertion tool) from its anti-static packing. Position the insertion chip over the socket and ensure that it is correctly orientated.
8. Firmly press the plunger (or rotate the knob) on the insertion tool in order to insert the chip into its socket.
9. Re-assemble the system (replacing any adapter cards and cables that may have been removed in order to gain access or clearance around the CPU). Reconnect the system and test.

TIP

In emergency, it is possible to remove and replace a DIL chip without using any specialised tools. The secret is to remove the device by applying firm but even force to each end of the chip.

TIP

Do not attempt to desolder a soldered-in DIL CPU chip unless you are *very* experienced. The system board can be very easily damaged by improper use of soldering tools. If you do attempt this task, make sure that you have a proper extraction tool and desoldering pump to remove the surplus solder from around the CPU pins before you attempt to lever up the chip.

Upgrading the CPU

A relentless increase in the power of the CPU makes this particular component a prime candidate for upgrading a system in order to keep pace with improvements in technology. Figure 4.6 shows how the power of the 80x86 family of Intel processors has increased over the last two decades. Each of the major processor developments is illustrated by a bar on this chart. Notable is the fact that, taken over this 20-year period, it should be noted that there has been an approximate doubling of processor power with the introduction of each new development in technology. What is even more staggering is that this doubling of processor power is now occurring in a time interval of less than 18 months!

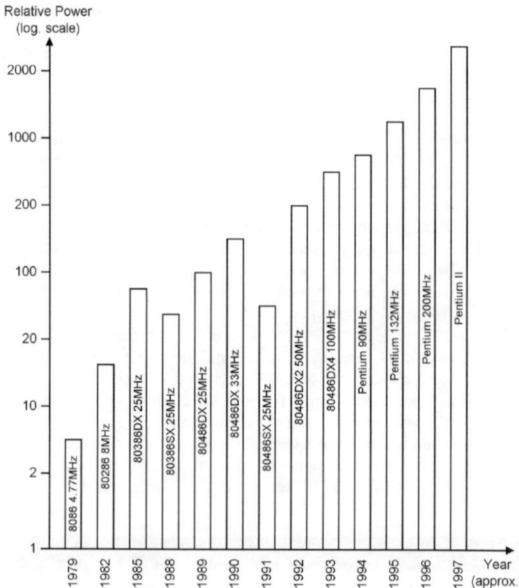

Figure 4.7 Relative power of Intel processors (1979 to 1997)

In the last few years, system manufacturers have begun to recognise the need to provide a means of upgrading the CPU, and motherboards are invariably fitted with a 'zero insertion force' (ZIF) CPU socket (e.g. 'Socket 5' and 'Socket 7') together with the necessary configuration links to set the power supply voltage and clock speed to cope with a variety of upgrade processor options.

Clock doubling (×2) and clock trebling (×3) processors (such as the 486DX2 and 486DX4, respectively) provide an instant means of improving execution speed. Alternatively, the Intel P24T is a Pentium processor designed to be pin-compatible with 486-type processors. This chip will allow you to upgrade the performance of an older '486-based system to something approaching that of a Pentium processor. Figure 4.8 shows a recommended upgrade path for Intel processors.

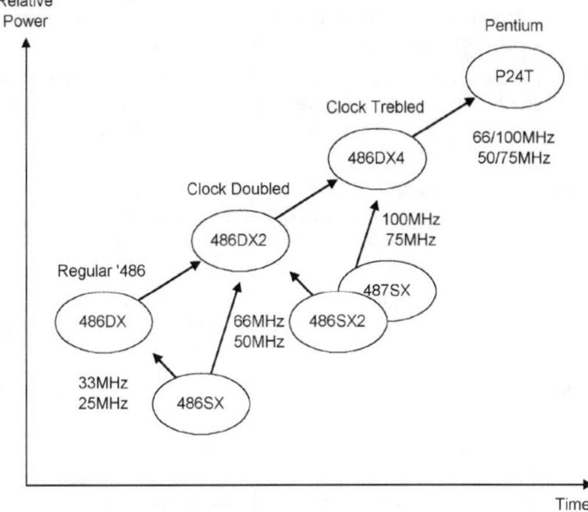

Figure 4.8 Upgrade path for the Intel '486

TIP

It is unwise to expect full 'Pentium-level' performance from a P24T processor fitted in place of your 486DX CPU. The reason for this is simply that the bus width of your system (32-bits) and its Level 2 cache is half that of a comparable Pentium-based motherboard.

TIP

When fitting a P24T (or other significant upgrade chip, for that matter) it is important to be aware of the likely effects of its increased power dissipation compared with the chip that it is replacing. Many systems have grossly inadequate cooling arrangements when presented with a CPU that needs to dissipate two or three times as much power as the device that they were originally designed for. In any event, it is essential to follow the manufacturers' recommendations and built-in processor cooling fans should normally be considered essential.

The stages in upgrading a CPU chip are similar to those used for removing and placing the CPU (see page 45) but with the following additional stages:

1. Check the compatibility of the upgrade CPU with the motherboard manual. If in doubt, contact the motherboard manufacturer's technical support help-line for assistance.
2. Switch 'off', disconnect from the supply and gain access to the system board (as described in Chapter 3).
3. Ensure that you observe the safety and static precautions at all

times. Have some anti-static packing available to receive the CPU when it has been removed. Do not remove the upgrade CPU from its packing at this stage.

(a) Locate the CPU and ensure that there is sufficient room to work all around it (you may have to move ribbon cables or adapter cards to gain sufficient clearance to operate the ZIF socket's lever.

(b) Ensure that the ZIF socket's lever is raised in the 'released' position. Gently grip the chip and ease it upwards, out of and away from, the socket (do not exert too much force, particularly at the corners of the chip).

(c) When the chip has been removed place it in anti-static packaging (do not touch any of the pins) and remove the CPU (where fitted).

(d) Remove the upgrade processor from its anti-static packaging (do not touch any of the pins).

(e) Check that the ZIF socket's lever is still in the 'released' position. Carefully locate the upgrade processor over the socket ensuring that the pins are correctly orientated. Lower the chip into the socket and ease it home (do not exert too much force, particularly at the corners of the chip).

(f) Check that the chip is properly seated before returning the ZIF socket's lever to its 'locked' position.

(g) Replace the CPU fan (or fit a new fan if one was not previously fitted).

(h) Check and adjust correct supply voltage and clock speed settings (you should find the correct settings listed in the motherboard handbook). Note that it is particularly important to check that the supply voltage is set correctly since most upgrade processors will require a 3.3V supply rather than the 5V that may have been provided for an older chip. Applying 5V to a 3.3.V device can have disastrous consequences!

(i) Re-assemble the system (replacing any adapter cards and cables that may have been removed in order to gain access or clearance around the CPU). Reconnect the system and test. If the system does not boot up normally switch off and check the configuration links again – do not allow the system to run for any length of time if you suspect that the configuration settings are incorrect.

TIP

Before attempting a CPU upgrade it is well worth giving careful attention to the cost-effectiveness of the upgrade – in many cases there may be other ways of improving its performance for less outlay. In particular, if you are operating on a limited budget it may be worth considering a RAM or hard disk upgrade *before* attempting to upgrade the CPU. In both cases, significant improvements in performance can usually be achieved at moderate cost.

5
Support devices

Each of the major support devices present within a PC has a key role to play in off-loading a number of routine tasks that would otherwise have to be performed by the CPU. This chapter provides a brief introduction to each generic device together with internal architecture and pin connecting details. Table 5.1 provides details of Intel's recommended support devices for CPUs up to, and including the 80386. In recent years, from the '286 onwards, PC motherboard manufacturers have taken steps to reduce the number of individual support devices and now prefer to make use of VLSI devices that replicate the function of several of the generic devices and provide additional functionality, such as cache memory control, VL-bus control, PCI control etc. Such devices are often referred to as 'chip sets' and they are manufactured by several well-known companies.

Locating and identifying the support devices

The support devices are usually easy to identify as they occupy much larger packages than the cache RAM devices and other (smaller) logic circuits. In older computers, many of the support devices may be

Table 5.1 Intel support chips used with 80x86 processors

	CPU type				
	8086	**8088**	**80186**	**80286**	**80386**
Clock generator	8284A	8284A	On-chip	82284	82384
Bus controller	8288	8288	On-chip	82288	82288
Integrated support chips				82230/ 82231, 82335	82230/ 82231, 82335
Interrupt controller	8259A	8259A	On-chip	8259A	8259A
DMA controller	8089/ 82258	8089/ 8237/ 82258	On-chip/ 82258	8089/ 82258	8237/ 82258
Timer/counter	8253/ 8254	8253/ 8254	On-chip	82543/ 8254	8253/ 8254
Maths coprocessor	8087	8087	8087	80287	80287/ 80387
Chip select/wait state logic	TTL	TTL	On-chip	TTL	TTL

mounted in sockets, however, in today's PCs they are almost invariably soldered directly to the motherboard (without a socket). To aid identification, support devices are usually marked with the manufacturer's name (or logo), the device coding and the date of manufacture.

The procedure for removing and replacing conventional DIL packaged support devices is the same as that described in Chapter 4. Where the functions of several support devices have been integrated into a single device, the chip will generally be surface mounted and specialised handling techniques will be required if the chip is to be removed and replaced.

Coprocessors, such as the '387 and '487SX chips, generally make use of pin-grid arrays (PGA) and are mounted in sockets. The most popular 'chip-sets' designed for use in the latest generation of Pentium-based machines employ surface mounted 100 and 208 pin quad-flat packs (QFP).

TIP

Integrated circuits are usually clearly marked with their device code. However, you can sometimes be confused by the four digit date code which is also marked on the chip. For example, a chip marked '8288 8806' is an 8288 chip manufactured in the sixth week of 1988.

TIP

You must carefully check the orientation of a chip whenever you remove and replace it. Pin-1 is often marked with a small circular indentation on the package. In addition, the end of a DIL package adjacent to the lowest and highest numbered pins (e.g. 1 and 40) is invariably marked with a rectangular or semicircular notch. To make things even easier, DIL i.c. holders also carry a notch which should align with the notch on the chip's package. PGA mounted chips have a flattened corner placed adjacent to pin reference 'A1'.

TIP

Like the CPU, support chips can be very susceptible to damage from stray electrostatic charges. It is, therefore, essential to observe the correct anti-static handling procedures whenever handling such devices.

Maths Coprocessors

Maths coprocessors, 'numeric data processors' (NDP) or 'floating point units' (FPU) as they are variously called, provide a means of carrying out mathematical operations on large, 'floating point' numbers. A floating point number comprises three parts; the *sign* which may be positive or negative, the significant digits (or *mantissa*) and an *exponent* (which effectively fixes the position of the decimal point within the number). Hence, floating point numbers are essentially numbers in which the decimal point 'floats' rather than occupies a fixed position. The manipulation of floating point numbers is exclusively the province of the maths coprocessor – the ALU of a normal CPU is not equipped to operate with such numbers.

TIP

The addition of a maths coprocessor is likely to be most effective if you have software that actually takes advantage of floating point instructions. Without such software, very little benefit may be noticed. Most software companies will clearly state in their hardware requirements that the software they supply is able to make use of a coprocessor. In some extreme cases, the presence of a coprocessor may be *essential* to the correct operation of the software and programs may refuse to run without such a device fitted.

8087 maths coprocessor

The 8087 was the original maths coprocessor which was designed to be active when mathematics related instructions were encountered in the instruction stream of an 8086 or 8088 CPU. The 8087, which is effectively wired in parallel with the 8086 or 8088 CPU, adds eight 80-bit floating point registers to the CPU register set. The 8087 maintains its own instruction queue and executes only those instructions which are specifically intended for it. The internal architecture of the 8087 is shown in Figure 5.1. The 8087 is supplied in a 40-pin DIL package, the pin connections for which are shown in Figure 5.2.

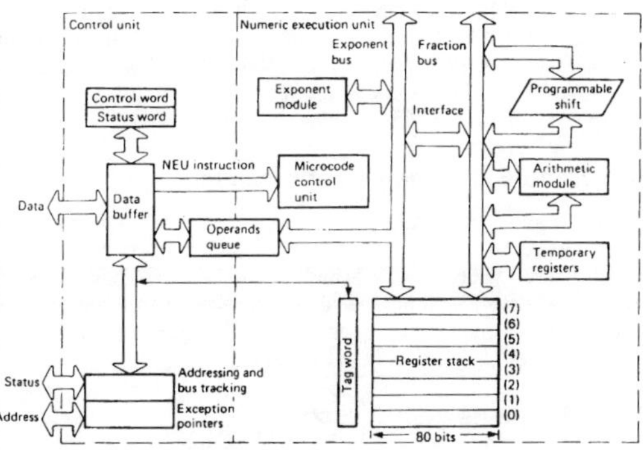

Figure 5.1 Internal architecture of the 8087

The active-low TEST input of the 8086/8088 CPU is driven from the BUSY output of the 8087 NDP. This allows the CPU to respond to the WAIT instruction (inserted by the assembler/compiler) which occurs before each coprocessor instruction. An FWAIT instruction follows each coprocessor instruction which deposits data in memory for immediate use by the CPU. The instruction is then translated to the requisite 8087 operation (with the preceding WAIT) and the FWAIT instruction is translated as a CPU WAIT instruction.

Signal	Pin		Pin	Signal
GND	1		40	V_{CC}
(A14) AD14	2		39	AD15
(A13) AD13	3		38	A16/S3
(A12) AD12	4		37	A17/S4
(A11) AD11	5		36	A18/S5
(A10) AD10	6		35	A19/S6
(A9) AD9	7		34	$\overline{BHE}$/S7
(A8) AD8	8		33	$\overline{RQ}/\overline{GT1}$
AD7	9		32	INT
AD6	10	8087	31	$\overline{RQ}/\overline{GT0}$
AD5	11		30	NC
AD4	12		29	NC
AD3	13		28	$\overline{S2}$
AD2	14		27	$\overline{S1}$
AD1	15		26	$\overline{S0}$
AD0	16		25	QS0
NC	17		24	QS1
NC	18		23	BUSY
CLK	19		22	READY
GND	20		21	RESET

Figure 5.2 Pin connections for the 8087

During coprocessor execution, the BUSY line is taken high and the CPU (responding to the WAIT instruction) halts its activity until the line goes low. The two Queue Status (QS0 and QS1) signals are used to synchronise the instruction queues of the two processing devices.

80287 and 80387 chips provide maths co-processing facilities within AT and '386-based PCs, respectively. In '486DX and later systems there is no need for a maths coprocessor as these facilities have been incorporated within the CPU itself.

80287 and 80387 maths coprocessors

The 80287 and 80387 maths coprocessors operate in conjunction with 80286 and 80386 CPUs, respectively. The '287 coprocessor was introduced in 1985 whilst the '387 made its debut in 1987. Each device represented a significant upgrade on its predecessor – the most notable factor being an increase in speed from 5MHz (the original 8087) to 33MHz (the fastest version of the 80387).

80487SX maths coprocessors

With the advent of the 80486, Intel placed the floating point unit *inside* the CPU (the floating point unit was actually based on the 33MHz version of the 80387). Since not all applications demand the power of a maths coprocessor, Intel developed a 'cut down' version of the '486 CPU *without* the internal floating point unit. This processor was designated the '486SX (to upgrade a system based on such a device so that it can take advantage of maths coprocessor instructions it is merely necessary to add a '487 coprocessor). The logic behind Intel's approach was apparently that users could later upgrade their systems if they found that the addition of a maths coprocessor was necessary for the software that they intended to run. This approach could hardly be described as cost-effective since the falling cost of CPUs meant that a full '486DX soon cost less than the two chips it could replace (i.e. a '486SX plus a '487SX). That said, there are doubtless many '486SX systems chugging along out there that could potentially see some benefit from the addition of a '487SX chip. However, if you do find yourself having to upgrade such a system, do check the prices of the chips first!

TIP

A maths coprocessor can perform certain operations between 10 and 100 times faster than the main processor. A '386- or '486SX-based system can greatly benefit from the addition of such a device if you regularly make use of 'maths-intensive' applications (e.g. CAD, spreadsheet, maths and statistical packages).

TIP

You can find out whether a coprocessor is fitted to a system without dismantling it. If bit 1 of the byte stored at address 0410 hex. is set, a maths coprocessor is present. If bit 1 is reset, no coprocessor is fitted. You can check the bit in question using Debug (see Chapter 14) or by using the following fragment of QuickBASIC code:

```
DEF SEG = 0
byte = PEEK(&H410)
IF byte AND 2 THEN
  PRINT "Coprocessor fitted"
ELSE
  PRINT "No coprocessor present"
END IF
```

8237A direct memory access controller

The 8237A DMA Controller (DMAC) can provide service for up to four independent DMA channels, each with separate registers for Mode Control, Current Address, Base Address, Current Word Count and Base Word Count (see Figure 5.3). The DMAC is designed to improve system performance by allowing external devices to directly transfer information to and from the system memory. The 8237A offers a variety of programmable control features to enhance data throughput and allow dynamic reconfiguration under software control.

The 8237A provides four basic modes of transfer: Block, Demand, Single Word and Cascade. These modes may be programmed as required, however, channels may be autoinitialised to their original condition following an End Of Process (EOP) signal.

The 8237A is designed for use with an external octal address latch such as the 74LS373. A system's DMA capability may be extended by cascading further 8237A DMAC chips and this feature is exploited in the PC-AT which has two such devices.

The least significant four address lines of the 8237A are bi-directional: when functioning as inputs, they are used to select one of the DMA controller's 16 internal registers. When functioning as outputs, on the other hand, a 16-bit address is formed by taking the eight address lines (A0–A7) to form the least significant address byte whilst the most

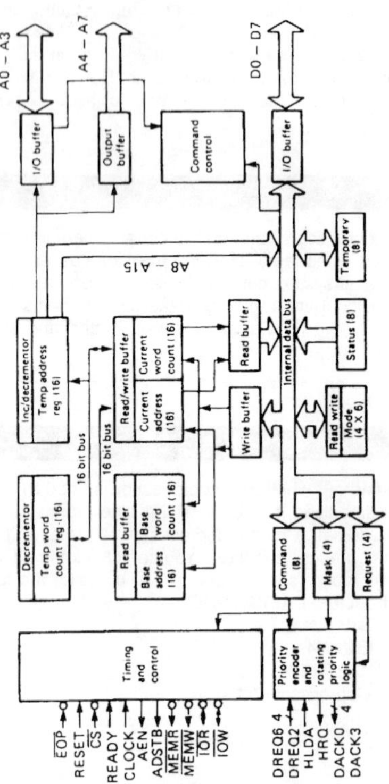

Figure 5.3 Internal architecture of the 8237A

significant address byte (A8–A15) is multiplexed onto the data bus lines (D0–D7). The requisite address latch enable signal (ADSTB) is available from pin-8. The upper four address bits (A16–A19) are typically supplied by a 74LS670 4 × 4 register file. The requisite bits are placed in this device (effectively a static RAM) by the processor before the DMA transfer is completed.

DMA channel 0 (highest priority) is used in conjunction with the 8253 Programmable Interval Timer (PIT) in order to provide a memory refresh facility for the PC's dynamic RAM. DMA channels 1–3 are connected to the expansion slots for use by option cards.

The refresh process involves channel 1 of the PIT producing a negative going pulse with a period of approximately 15μs. This pulse sets a bistable which, in turn, generates a DMA request at the channel-0 input of the DMAC (pin-19). The processor is then forced into a wait state and the address and data bus buffers assume a tri-state (high impedance) condition. The DMAC then outputs a row refresh address and the row address strobe (RAS) is asserted. The 8237 increments its refresh count register and control is then returned to the processor. The process then continues such that all 256 rows are refreshed within a time interval of 4ms. The pin connections for the 8237A are shown in Figure 5.4.

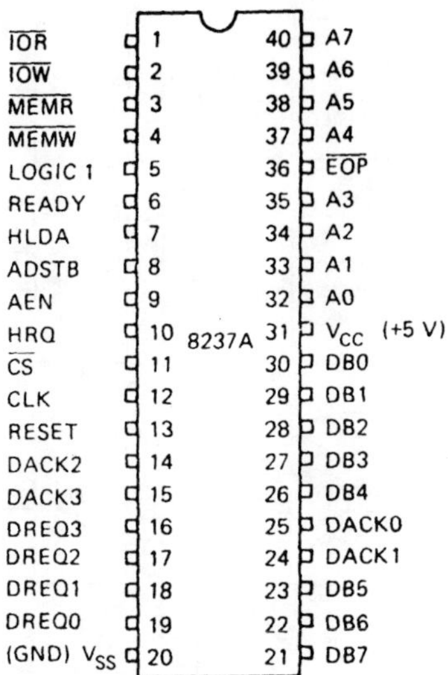

Figure 5.4 Pin connections for the 8237A

8253 programmable interval timer

The 8253 is a Programmable Interval Timer (PIT) which has three independent pre-settable 16-bit counters each offering a count rate of up to 2.6MHz. The internal architecture and pin connections for the 8253 are shown in Figures 5.5 and 5.6, respectively. Each counter consists of a single 16-bit presettable down counter. The counter can function in binary or BCD and its input, gate and output are configured by the data held in the Control Word Register. The down counters are negative edge triggered such that, on a falling clock edge, the contents of the respective counter is decremented.

The three counters are fully independent and each can have separate mode configuration and counting operation, binary or BCD. The contents of each 16-bit count register can be loaded or read using simple software referencing the relevant port addresses shown in Table 5.3. The truth table for the chip's active-low chip select (CS), read (RD), write (WR) and address lines (A1 and A0) is shown in Table 5.2.

8255A programmable peripheral interface

The 8255A Programmable Peripheral Interface (PPI) is a general purpose I/O device which provides no less than 24 I/O lines arranged as three 8-bit I/O ports. The internal architecture and pin connections of the 8255A are shown in Figures 5.7 and 5.8, respectively. The Read/Write and Control Logic block manages all internal and external data transfers. The port addresses used by the 8255A are given in Table 5.3.

The functional configuration of each of the 8255's three I/O ports is fully programmable. Each of the control groups accepts commands

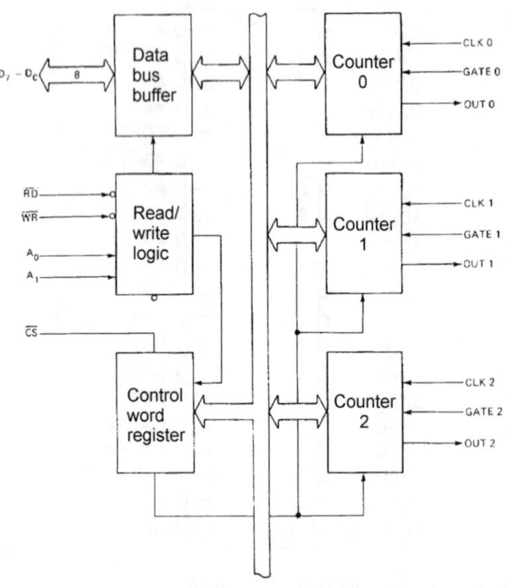

Figure 5.5 Internal architecture of the 8253

from the Read/Write Control Logic, receives Control Words via the internal data bus and issues the requisite commands to each of the ports. At this point, it is important to note that the 24 I/O lines are, for control purposes, divided into two logical groups (A and B). Group A comprises the entire eight lines of Port A together with the four upper (most significant) lines of Port B. Group B, on the other hand, takes in all eight lines from Port B together with the four lower (least significant) lines of Port C. The upshot of all this is simply that Port C can be split into two in order to allow its lines to be used for status and control (handshaking) when data is transferred to or from Ports A or B.

Signal	Pin	8253	Pin	Signal
D_7	1		24	V_{CC}
D_6	2		23	$\overline{WR}$
D_5	3		22	$\overline{RD}$
D_4	4		21	$\overline{CS}$
D_3	5		20	A_1
D_2	6		19	A_0
D_1	7		18	CLK 2
D_0	8		17	OUT 2
CLK 0	9		16	GATE 2
OUT 0	10		15	CLK 1
GATE 0	11		14	GATE 1
GND	12		13	OUT 1

Figure 5.6 Pin connections for the 8253

Table 5.2 Truth table for the 8253

CS	RD	WR	A1	A0	Function
0	1	0	0	0	Load counter 0
0	1	0	0	1	Load counter 1
0	1	0	1	0	Load counter 2
0	1	0	1	1	Write mode word
0	0	1	0	0	Read counter 0
0	0	1	0	1	Read counter 1
0	0	1	1	0	Read counter 2
0	0	1	1	1	No-operation (tri-state)
1	x	x	x	x	Disable tri-state
0	1	1	x	x	No-operation (tri-state)

8259A programmable interrupt controller

The 8259A Programmable Interrupt Controller (PIC) was designed specifically for use in real-time interrupt driven microcomputer systems. The device manages eight levels of request and can be expanded using further 8259A devices.

The sequence of events which occurs when an 8259A device is used in conjunction with an 8086 or 8088 processor is as follows:

(a) One or more of the interrupt request lines (IR0–IR7) are asserted (note that these lines are active-high) by the interrupting device(s).

(b) The corresponding bits in the IRR register become set.

(c) The 8259A evaluates the requests on the following basis:
  (i) If more than one request is currently present, determine which of the requests has the highest priority.

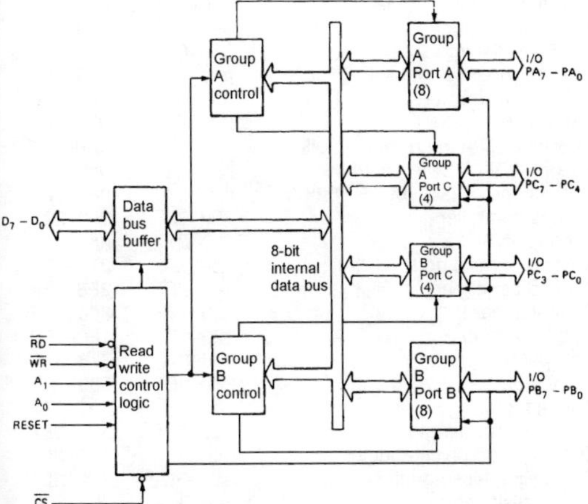

Figure 5.7 Internal architecture of the 8255A

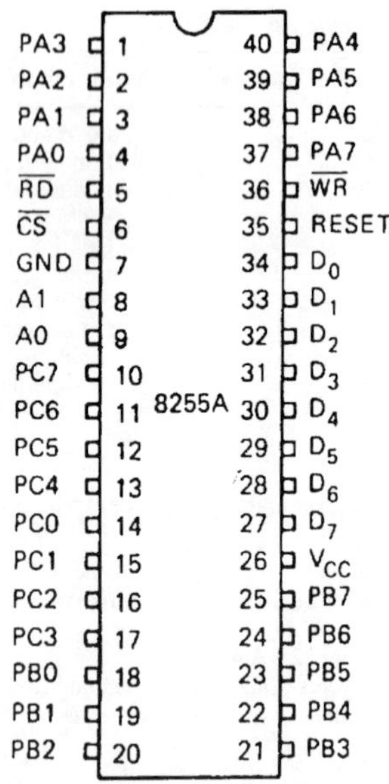

Figure 5.8 Pin connections for the 8255A

Table 5.3 Port addresses used in the PC family

Device	PC-XT	PC-AT etc
8237A DMA controller	000–00F	000–01F
8259A interrupt controller	020–021	020–03F
8253/8254 timer	040–043	040–05F
8255 parallel interface	060–063	n/a
8042 keyboard controller	n/a	060–06F
DMA page register	080–083	080–09F
NMI mask register	0A0–0A7	070–07F
Second 8259A interrupt controller	n/a	0A0–0BF
Second 8237A DMA controller	n/a	0C0–0DF
Maths coprocessor (8087, 80287)	n/a	0F0–0FF
Games controller	200–20F	200–207
Expansion unit	210–217	n/a
Second parallel port	n/a	278–27F
Second serial port	2F8–2FF	2F8–2FF
Prototype card	300–31F	300–31F
Fixed (hard) disk	320–32F	1F0–1F8
First parallel printer	378–37F	378–37F
SDLC adapter	380–38F	380–38F
BSC adapter	n/a	3A0–3AF
Monochrome adapter	3B0–3BF	3B0–3BF
Enhanced graphics adapter	n/a	3C0–3CF
Colour graphics adapter	3D0–3DF	3D0–3DF
Floppy disk controller	3F0–3F7	3F0–3F7
First serial port	3F8–3FF	3F8–3FF

1. Ascertain whether the successful request has a higher priority than the level currently being serviced.
2. If the condition in (ii) is satisfied, issue an interrupt to the processor by asserting the active-high INT line.

(d) The processor acknowledges the interrupt signal and responds by pulsing the interrupt acknowledge (INTA) line.

(e) Upon receiving the INTA pulse from the processor, the highest priority ISR bit is set and the corresponding IRR bit is reset.

(f) The processor then initiates a second interrupt acknowledge (INTA) pulse. During this second period for which the INTA line is taken low, the 8259 outputs a pointer on the data bus which is then read by the processor.

The internal architecture and pin connections for the 8259A are shown in Figures 5.9 and 5.10, respectively.

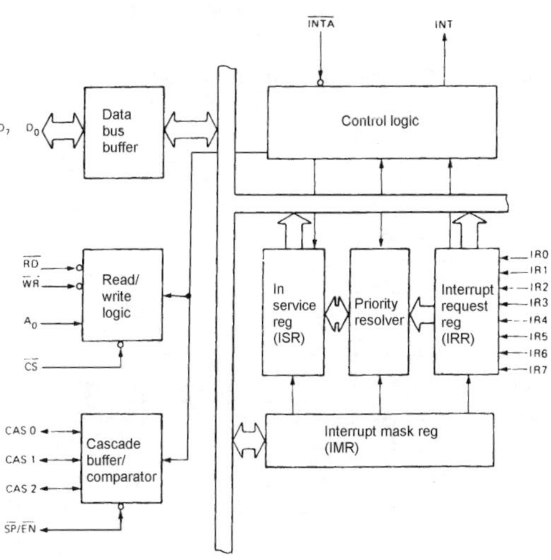

Figure 5.9 Internal architecture of the 8259A

8284A clock generator

The 8284A is a single chip clock generator/driver designed specifically for use by the 8086 family of devices. The chip contains a crystal oscillator, divide-by-3 counter, ready and reset logic as shown in Figure 5.11. On the original PC, the quartz crystal is a series mode fundamental device which operates at a frequency of 14.312818MHz. The output of the divide-by-3 counter takes the form of a 33% duty cycle square wave at precisely one-third of the fundamental frequency (i.e. 4.77MHz). This signal is then applied to the processor's clock (CLK) input. The clock generator also produces a signal at 2.38MHz which is externally divided to provide a 5.193MHz 50% duty cycle clock signal for the 8253 Programmable Interval Timer (PIT), as shown in Figure 5.13.

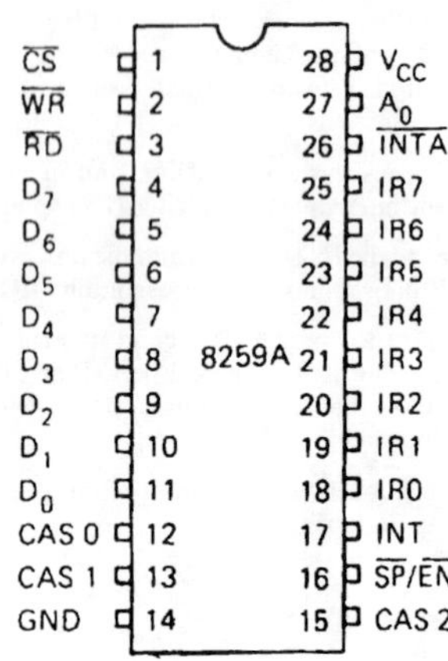

Figure 5.10 Pin connections for the 8259A

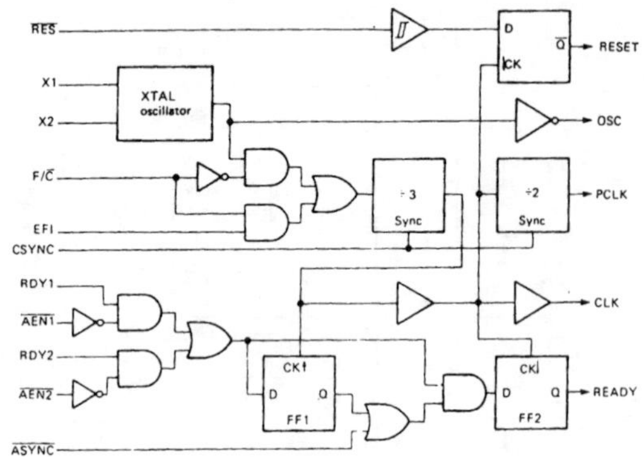

Figure 5.11 Internal architecture of the 8284A

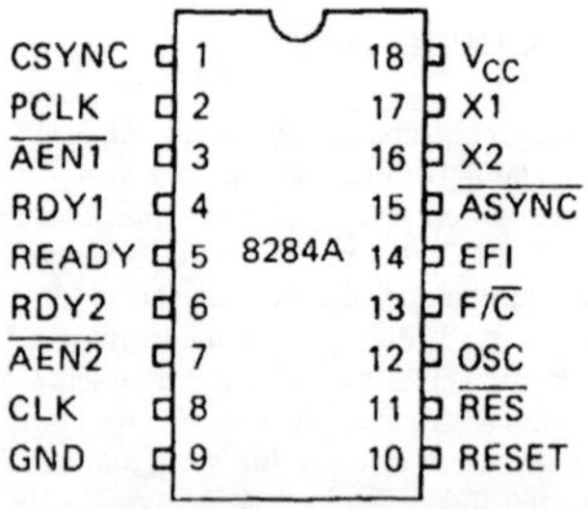

CSYNC 1
PCLK 2
AEN1 3
RDY1 4
READY 5
RDY2 6
AEN2 7
CLK 8
GND 9
8284A
18 V_{CC}
17 X1
16 X2
15 ASYNC
14 EFI
13 F/C
12 OSC
11 RES
10 RESET

Figure 5.12 Pin connections for the 8284A

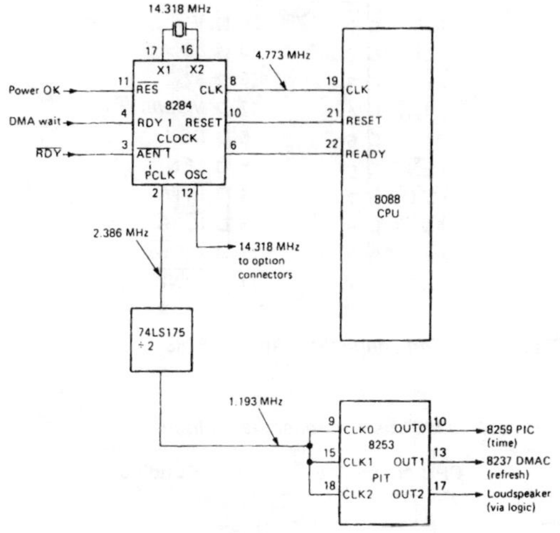

Figure 5.13 Clock signals in the PC

8288 bus controller

The 8288 bus controller decodes the status outputs from the CPU (S0 and S1) in order to generate the requisite bus command and control signals. These signals are used as shown in Table 5.4.

The 8288 issues signals to the system to strobe addresses into the address latches, to enable data onto the buses and to determine the direction of data flow through the data buffers. The internal architecture and pin connections for the 8288 are shown in Figures 5.14 and 5.15, respectively.

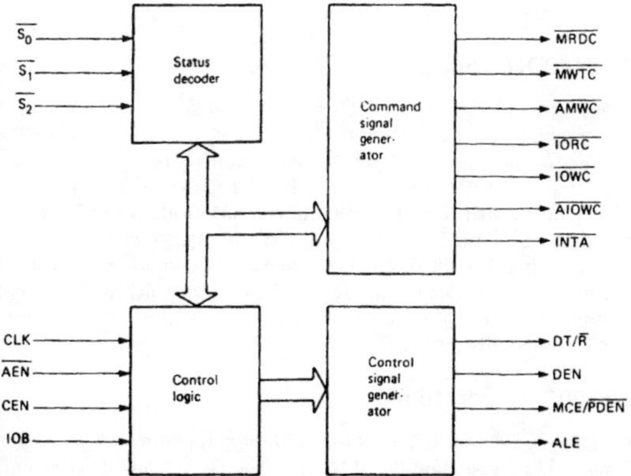

Figure 5.14 Internal architecture of the 8288

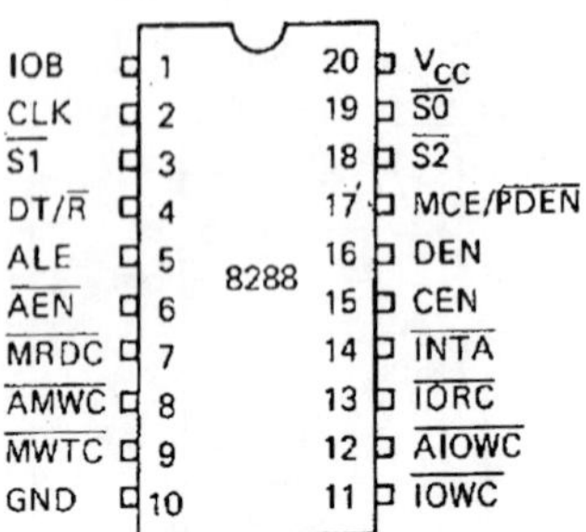

Figure 5.15 Pin connections for the 8288

Table 5.4 8288 bus controller status inputs

CPU status line			Condition
S2	S1	S0	
0	0	0	Interrupt acknowledge
0	0	1	I/O read
0	1	0	I/O write
0	1	1	Halt
1	0	0	Memory read
1	0	1	Memory read
1	1	0	Memory write
1	1	1	Inactive

Integrated support devices

In modern PCs, the overall device count has been significantly reduced by integrating several of the functions associated with the original PC chip set within a single VLSI device or within the CPU itself. The following are examples of such devices.

82C100 XT controller

The Chips and Technology 82C100 XT Controller found in older 'XT compatible systems', provides the functionality associated with no less than six of the original XT chip set and effectively replaces the following devices: one 8237 DMA Controller, one 8253 Counter/Timer, one 8255 Parallel Interface, one 8259 Interrupt Controller, one 8284 Clock Generator and one 8288 Bus Controller. In order to ensure software compatibility with the original PC, the 82C100 contains a superset of the registers associated with each of the devices which it is designed to replace. The use of the chip is thus completely transparent as far as applications software is concerned.

82C206 AT controller

OPTi's 82C206 and 82C495XLC chip set is found in many modern '486, P24T and Pentium-based systems. The 82C206 provides the functions of two 82437 DMA Controllers, two 8259 Interrupt Controllers, one 8254 Counter/Timer, one 146818-compatible Real Time Clock

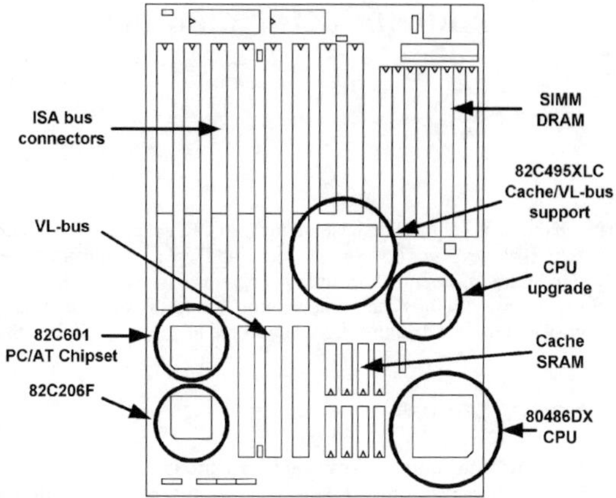

Figure 5.16 Motherboard layout for a '486-based system using the OPTi chip set

and one 74LS612 Memory Mapper. In addition, the chip provides 114 bytes of CMOS RAM (used for storing the BIOS configuration settings). The matching 82C495XLC device provides cache memory control and shadow RAM support for system, video and adapter card BIOS. The chip also contains on-chip hardware that provides direct support for up to two VL-bus master devices. Finally, Figure 5.16 shows the functional and elegant layout of a typical system motherboard based on this popular OPTi chip set.

6
Semiconductor memory

This chapter will help you understand the use of RAM and ROM within your PC. It also explains how you can locate and replace a faulty memory chip. In addition, several short utility programs have been included to help you locate useful system information stored in your computer's memory and protect the important data stored in your CMOS RAM.

Memory basics

Semiconductor memory devices tend to fall into two main categories: 'read/write' and 'read-only'. Read/write memory is simply memory which can be read from and written to. In other words, the contents of the memory can be modified at will. Read-only memory, on the other hand, can only be read from; an attempt to write data to such a memory will have no effect on its contents.

Obvious examples of read-only and read/write memories with which the man in the street will be familiar are, respectively, compact disks and audio cassette tapes. Once recorded, compact disks cannot be modified whereas a pre-recorded audio tape cassette can be erased and re-recorded many times.

Memory organisation

Each location in semiconductor ROM and RAM has its own unique address. At each address a byte (comprising eight bits) is stored. Each ROM, RAM (or bank of RAM devices) accounts for a particular block of memory, its size depending upon the capacity of the ROM or RAM in question.

As an example, an original XT system may have had a 'base memory' arranged in two blocks, each of nine 256K × 1-bit DRAM devices (the ninth chip provides a parity checking bit for each memory location). The total capacity of this memory is 512Kbytes (there are 256Kbytes in each block, not counting the parity bits). The organisation of this memory (which occupies the address range from 00000 to 9FFFF) is shown in Table 6.1 where 'U1', 'U2' etc. are the component designations for the individual RAM chips.

Now consider a more modern but minimal '386- or '486-based system with 4Mbyte of RAM arranged in four blocks of 1Mbyte. Each 1Mbyte of RAM is provided by a single-in-line memory module (SIMM) fitted with nine DRAM chips. Each DRAM chip has a capacity of 1,048,576 bits. The organisation of this memory (which occupies the address range from 000000 to 3FFFFF) is shown in Table 6.2 where 'U1', 'U2' etc. are once again the component designations for the individual RAM chips (note that a total of 36 chips are fitted).

BIOS ROM

The BIOS ROM that contains the low-level code required to control the system's hardware is programmed during chip manufacture. The programming data is supplied to the semiconductor manufacturer by

Table 6.1 512Kbyte DIL memory example

Block	Address range	D7	D6	D5	D4	D3	D2	D1	D0	Parity bit
0	00000–3FFFF	U8	U7	U6	U5	U4	U3	U2	U1	U9
1	40000–7FFFF	U17	U16	U15	U14	U13	U12	U11	U10	U18

Table 6.2 4 × 1Mbyte SIMM memory example (total 4Mbyte)

Block	Address range	D7	D6	D5	D4	D3	D2	D1	D0	Parity bit
0	000000–0FFFFF	U8	U7	U6	U5	U4	U3	U2	U1	U9
1	100000–1FFFFF	U17	U16	U15	U14	U13	U12	U11	U10	U18
2	200000–2FFFFF	U26	U25	U24	U23	U22	U21	U20	U19	U27
3	300000–3FFFFF	U35	U34	U33	U32	U31	U30	U29	U28	U36

the BIOS originator. This process is cost-effective for large-scale production, however, programming of the ROM is irreversible; once programmed, devices cannot be erased in preparation for fresh programming. Hence, the only way of upgrading the BIOS is to remove and discard the existing chips and replace them with new ones. This procedure is fraught with problems, not least of which is compatibility of the BIOS upgrade with existing DOS software.

The BIOS ROM invariably occupies the last 64Kbytes or 128Kbytes of memory (from F0000 to FFFFF or E0000 to FFFFF, respectively). It is sometimes based on two chips; one for the data stored at the odd addresses and one for the data stored at the even addresses.

BIOS variations

Several manufacturers (e.g. Compaq) have produced ROM BIOS code for use in their own equipment. This code must, of course, be compatible with IBM's BIOS code. Several other companies (e.g. American Megatrends (AMI), Award Software and Phoenix Software) have developed generic versions of the BIOS code which has been incorporated into numerous clones and compatibles.

There are, of course, minor differences between these BIOS versions. Notably these exist within the power-on self-test (POST), the set up routines and the range of hard disk types supported.

TIP

Some users of the AMI BIOS dated 04/09/90 (or earlier) have reported problems with the keyboard controller when running Windows or OS/2. If you have difficulties check the BIOS date and, if necessary, upgrade the BIOS ROMs to a later version.

Upgrading your BIOS ROM

At some point, you may find it necessary to upgrade the BIOS ROM on a machine. There are various reasons for doing this but most centre on the need to make your software recognise significant hardware upgrades (e.g. to make use of an IDE hard drive or when replacing the 360Kbytes or 720Kbytes floppy drives on an older machine with newer 1.44Mbytes or 2.88Mbytes drives).

With a DIL packaged BIOS ROM (either socketed or soldered in) the following stages are required:

1. As far as possible, make sure that the new BIOS is compatible with your system (it might be wise to ask the supplier if they will offer a refund if you have any problems).
2. Note down your existing CMOS configuration (using your 'set-up' program).
3. Power-down your system as described in Chapter 3 (page 28).
4. Locate the BIOS ROM chips (note their position and orientation).
5. Remove and replace the BIOS ROM chips (follow the procedure described in Chapter 5 (page 45).
6. Re-assemble the system and run the 'set up' program, making any changes necessary.

TIP

In a two-chip BIOS ROM set, the chips are usually marked 'Low' and 'High' (or 'Odd' and 'Even') in order to distinguish them from one another. Always make sure that you replace them in the correct sockets (i.e. locate the new 'Low' chip in the socket vacated by the old 'L' chip).

Some of the latest generation of motherboards have their BIOS stored in electrically erasable read-only memory (EEPROM). This memory can be easily reprogrammed *without* having to remove the BIOS chip(s) from the motherboard. As an example, the Intel 28F001BXT 'flash' memory device has a capacity of 128Kbytes, 64Kbytes of which is used for the main BIOS (from addresses F0000 to FFFFF) and the remainder is used for 'plug-and-play' data and for storing data.

Flash memory

Flash memory makes upgrading your BIOS easy. A new version can be installed from a disk supplied by the manufacturer. Alternatively, BIOS upgrades can be distributed through the Internet (simply download them from the OEM's site and then run the executable file). The Intel disk-based flash upgrade utility (FMUP.EXE) has three options:

- the flash BIOS can be upgraded from the disk
- the current BIOS code can be copied from flash memory onto the disk (for backup purposes)
- the data in the flash memory can be compared with that on the disk to determine whether or not the current version is installed.

Before operation, the upgrade utility must first check that the system's hardware (the 'target system') is fully compatible with the BIOS upgrade. This helps to avoid the danger of installing a BIOS upgrade intended for a different hardware configuration!

Random access memory (RAM)

The PC system board's read/write memory provides storage for the DOS and BIOS as well as transient user programs and data. In addition, read/write memory is also used to store data which is displayed on the screen. Depending upon the nature of the applications software, this memory may be either character mapped (text) or bit-mapped (graphics). The former technique involves dividing the screen into a number of character-sized cells.

Each displayed character cell requires one byte of memory for storage of the character plus a further byte for 'attributes' (see Chapter 13). Hence a screen having 80 columns × 25 lines (corresponding to the IBM's basic text mode) will require 2000 bytes; 1000 for storage of the characters and a further 1000 for the attributes.

Bit-mapped graphic displays require a very much larger amount of storage. Each display pixel is mapped to a particular bit in memory and the bit may be a 1 or a 0 depending upon whether it is to be light or dark. Where a colour display is to be produced, several colour planes must be implemented and consequently an even larger amount of memory is required. A VGA graphics adapter, for example, may be fitted with up to 1Mbyte of video RAM. Chapter 13 provides more information on the size and organisation of video memory.

Static versus dynamic memories

Semiconductor random access memories are divided into 'static' and 'dynamic' types. Static types are generally CMOS types (for low power consumption) and are based on bistable memory cells. Each cell will retain a stored bit (logic 1 or logic 0) for as long as the power is left connected.

Dynamic memories (DRAM) are generally NMOS types which utilise charge storage within a semiconductor junction (effectively a tiny capacitor). To prevent the stored charge leaking away (in which case the memory would lose its contents) the charge is periodically 'refreshed' by a continuous process of reading and writing. This process takes place automatically.

DIL packaged DRAM

The data in Table 6.3 refers to a range of the most popular dual-in-line (DIL) packaged DRAM chips whilst Table 6.4 shows equivalent 64K × 1 bit and 256K × 1 bit devices. The pin connections for the most common DIL packaged DRAMs are shown in Figure 6.1. Note that access times are often included within a chip's coding. A chip marked TMS4164–15, for example, has an access time of 150ns whilst one marked MSM41256–10 has an access time of 100ns.

Table 6.3 DRAM data

Type	Size (bits)	Organisation	Package
4116	16384	16K words × 1 bit	16-pin DIL
4164	65536	64K words × 1 bit	16-pin DIL
4256	262144	256K words × 1 bit	16-pin DIL
4716	16384	16K words × 1 bit	16-pin DIL
4816	16384	16K words × 1 bit	16-pin DIL
4864	65536	64K words × 1 bit	16-pin DIL
4865	65536	64K words × 1 bit	16-pin DIL
41256	262144	256K words × 1 bit	16-pin DIL

Table 6.3 Continued

Type	Size (bits)	Organisation	Package
41257	262144	256K words × 1 bit	16-pin DIL
41416	65536	16K words × 4 bit	18-pin DIL
48416	65536	16K words × 4 bit	18-pin DIL
50256	262144	256K words × 1 bit	16-pin DIL
50257	262144	256K words × 1 bit	16-pin DIL
50464	262144	64K words × 4 bit	18-pin DIL
51256	262144	256K words × 1 bit	16-pin DIL

Table 6.4 DRAM equivalents

Organisation	Manufacturer	Part number
64K × 1 bit	AMD	AM9064
	Fairchild	F64K
	Fujitsu	MB8264A/MB8265A
	Hitachi	HM4864/HM4864A
	Inmos	IMS2600
	Intel	2164A
	Matsushita	MN4164
	Micron Tech.	MT4264
	Mitsubishi	MSK4164
	Mostek	MK4564
	Motorola	MCM66665A
	National Semi.	NMC4164
	NEC	uPD4164
	Oki	MSM3764
	Siemens	HYB4164
	Texas Instr.	TMS4164
	Toshiba	TMM4164
	Tristar	KM4164A
256K × 1	Fujitsu	MB81256/MB81257
	Hitachi	HM50256/HM50257
	Micron Tech.	MT1256
	Mitsubishi	MSM4256
	Motorola	MCM6256
	NEC	uPD41256/uPD41257
	Oki	MSM37256
	Texas Instr.	TMS4256/TMS4257
	Toshiba	TMM41256
	Western Elec.	WCM41256

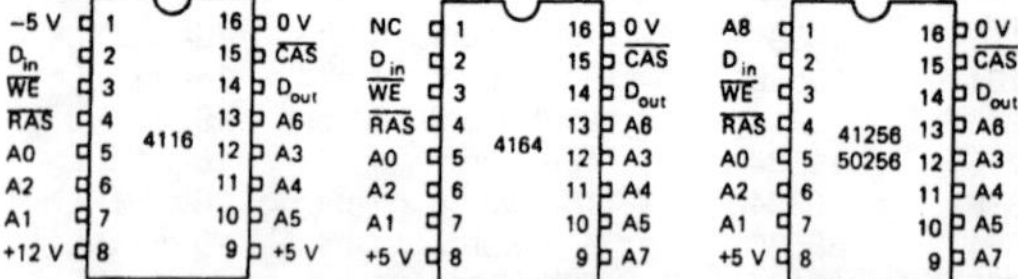

Figure 6.1 DRAM pin connections

TIP

'Zero-wait' state memory offers the fastest access time. Slower memory devices may require between 1 and 5 'wait states' (i.e. do-nothing cycles) to slow the CPU down to match the access time of the RAM. You can often adjust the number of wait states by means of a system board jumper if you suspect that your RAM is too slow for your CPU.

SIMMs

In modern machines, DIL packaged DRAM devices have been replaced by single in-line memory modules (SIMMs). These units are small cards which usually contain surface-mounted DRAM chips and which simply plug into the system board.

SIMMs are available in various sizes including 1M, 2M, 4M, 8M, 16M and 32Mbyte. Older (and smaller capacity) SIMMs (up to 4Mbyte) are supplied in 30-pin packages whilst most modern SIMMs are supplied in 72-pin packages. SIMMs are usually inserted into their motherboard 'headers' at an angle of about 45 degrees and then simply snapped into place by standing them upright. To remove a SIMM, you must first open the locking tabs and gently release the module from its header.

TIP

It is essential to observe correct anti-static procedures whenever you handle memory chips and modules. Chips and modules are actually safer when they are PCB mounted or placed in their sockets since even the highest resistance present on a PCB card will help to provide a discharge path for stray static charges. Anti-static packaging should be used whenever a memory device is not in a socket.

TIP

Memory access times can be important if you have to replace DRAM chips or modules. Access times vary from 150ns (or even 200ns) in some of the older devices to as little as 60ns with the latest generation of SIMM modules. Check the supplier or manufacturer's data when replacing your DRAM or SIMM. When in doubt, the last two digits of the chip's device code (often separated by a dash or hyphen) usually denote the access time. Examples are '-10' for 100 ns, '-8' for 80ns, and '-6' for 60ns.

DIMMs

To further improve the capacity of memories, dual in-line memory modules (DIMMs) are replacing SIMMs in the latest generation machines. DIMMs are based on a double-sided connector having a total of 168-pins and typical capacities are 8M, 16M, 32M and 64Mbytes.

Memory terminology

Conventional RAM

The PC's RAM extending from 00000 to 9FFFF is referred to as 'conventional memory' or 'base memory'. This 640K of read/write memory provides storage for user programs and data as well as regions reserved for DOS and BIOS use.

Upper memory area

The remaining memory within the 1Mbyte direct addressing space (i.e. that which extends from A0000 to FFFFF is referred to as the 'upper memory area' (UMA). The UMA itself is divided into various regions (depending upon the machine's configuration) including that which provides storage used by video adapters.

Video RAM

As its name implies, video RAM is associated with the video/graphics adapter. The video RAM occupies the lower part of the upper memory area and its precise configuration will depend upon the type of adapter fitted.

Extended memory

Memory beyond the basic 1Mbyte direct addressing space is referred to as 'extended memory'. This memory can be accessed by a '286 or later CPU operating in 'protected mode'. In this mode, the CPU is able to generate 24-bit addresses (instead of the real mode's 20-bit addresses) by multipying the segment register contents by 256 (instead of 16). This scheme allows the CPU to access addresses ranging from 000000 to FFFFFF (a total of 16Mbyte). When the CPU runs in protected mode, a program can only access the designated region of memory. A processor exception will occur if an attempt is made to write to a region of memory that is outside of the currently allocated block.

Expanded memory

Expanded memory was originally developed for machines based on the 8088 and 8086 CPU which could not take advantage of the protected mode provide by the '286 and later processors. Expanded memory is accessed through a 64K 'page frame' located within the upper memory area. This page frame acts as a window into a much larger area of memory.

Expanded memory systems are based on a standard developed by three manufacturers (Lotus, Intel and Microsoft). This 'LIM standard' is also known as the Expanded Memory Standard (EMS). In order to make use of EMS, a special expanded memory driver is required. EMS has largely been superseded by the advanced memory management facilities provided by the '386 and '486 CPU chips.

CMOS RAM

The PC-AT and later machine's CMOS memory is 64 bytes of battery-backed memory contained within the real-time clock chip (a Motorola

MC146818). Sixteen bytes of this memory are used to retain the real-time clock settings (date and time information) whilst the remainder contains important information on the configuration of your system. When the CMOS battery fails or when power is inadvertently removed from the real-time clock chip, all data will become invalid and you will have to use your set up program to restore the settings for your system. As mentioned in Chapter 2, this can be a real problem unless you know what the settings should be.

The organisation of the CMOS memory is shown in Table 6.5 (note that locations marked 'reserved' may have different functions in some non-IBM systems).

Table 6.5 CMOS memory organisation

Offset (Hex)	Contents
00	Seconds
01	Seconds alarm
02	Minutes
03	Minutes alarm
04	Hours
05	Hours alarm
06	Day of the week
07	Day of the month
08	Month
09	Year
0A	Status register A
0B	Status register B
0C	Status register C
0D	Status register D
0E	Diagnostic status byte
0F	Shutdown status byte
10	Floppy disk type (drives A and B)
11	Reserved
12	Fixed disk type (drives 0 and 1)
13	Reserved
14	Equipment byte
15	Base memory (low byte)
16	Base memory (high byte)
17	Extended memory (low byte)
18	Extended memory (high byte)
19	Hard disk 0 extended type
1A	Hard disk 1 extended type
1B-2D	Reserved
2E-2F	Checksum for bytes 10 to 1F
30	Actual extended memory (low byte)
31	Actual extended memory (high byte)
32	Date century byte (in BCD format)
33–3F	Reserved

The QuickBASIC program shown in Figure 6.2 will reveal the contents of the second 16 bytes of CMOS RAM (offset addresses 10 to 1F inclusive). These 16 bytes will tell you how the system has been configured (i.e. how much base and extended memory is present and the types of floppy and hard drive). A typical set of CMOS data for these locations is shown in Figure 6.3.

```
DIM cmos%(32)
CLS
PRINT "Offset", "Value"
PRINT "(hex)", "(hex)"
PRINT
FOR i% = 16 TO 31
  OUT &H70, i%
  cmos%(i%) = INP(&H71)
  PRINT HEX$(i%), HEX$(cmos%(i%))
NEXT i%
```

Figure 6.2 QuickBASIC program to reveal the contents of the second 16 bytes of CMOS RAM

Offset (hex)	Value (hex)	*Comment*
10	44	*Both drives are 1.44M (type 4)*
11	EB	
12	F0	*Hard drive 0 is type 15, no hard drive 1*
13	9C	
14	4F	*2 floppy drives, use display adapter's BIOS*
15	80	
16	2	*640K of base memory*
17	0	
18	D	*3328K of extended memory (4M total)*
19	2F	*Hard drive 0 extended type 47*
1A	0	*No hard drive 1*
1B	68	
1C	3	
1D	8	
1E	0	
1F	0	

Figure 6.3 Output produced by the program shown in Figure 6.2

TIP

The QuickBASIC program shown in Figure 6.4 will allow you to backup and restore your CMOS RAM data. The source code together with a fully compiled (.EXE) version of the program is available for downloading from the Web site listed in Chapter 18.

FPM, HPM and EDO RAM

In recent years and with the advent of faster processors, several attempts have been made to reduce the data access times of RAM devices. Fast Page Mode (FPM) is often used on fast 60ns chips whilst Hyper Page Mode (HPM) or Extended Data Output (EDO) RAM provides even faster access times.

TIP

Improvements in performance from fitting HPM or EDO RAM can only be fully realised if your chip-set can take advantage of such devices. If in doubt, you should consult the motherboard handbook which will usually specify the types of RAM that are supported by the chip-set (note that the immensely popular Intel Triton chip-set currently provides support for HPM RAM).

```
REM ** PC Troubleshooting CMOS memory backup **
ON ERROR GOTO warning
DIM cmos%(64)
main:
DO
  CLS
  PRINT "CMOS memory utility"
  PRINT "[B] = backup"
  PRINT "[R] = restore"
  PRINT "[Q] = exit to DOS"
  DO
    r$ = UCASE$(INKEY$)
  LOOP UNTIL r$ <> "" AND INSTR("BRQ", r$)
  IF r$ = "Q" THEN CLS : END
  IF r$ = "B" THEN
    ' user has selected backup
    PRINT "Backing up CMOS data, please wait..."
    OPEN "A:\CMOS.DAT" FOR OUTPUT AS #1
    FOR i% = 16 TO 63
      OUT &H70, i%
      cmos%(i%) = INP(&H71)
      PRINT #1, cmos%(i%)
    NEXT i%
    CLOSE #1
    PRINT "Done!"
    GOSUB waitkey
  END IF
  IF r$ = "R" THEN
    ' user has selected restore
    PRINT "Restoring CMOS data, please wait..."
    OPEN "A:\CMOS.DAT" FOR INPUT AS #1
    FOR i% = 16 TO 63
      INPUT #1, cmos%(i%)
      OUT &H70, i%
      OUT (&H71), cmos%(i%)
    NEXT i%
    CLOSE #1
  PRINT "Done!"
  GOSUB waitkey
  END IF
LOOP
'
waitkey:
PRINT "Press any key to continue..."
DO
  r$ = INKEY$
LOOP UNTIL r$ <> ""
RETURN
'
warning:
PRINT "An error has occurred!"
GOSUB waitkey
DO
  r$ = INKEY$
LOOP UNTIL r$ <> ""
RESUME main
```

Figure 6.4 QuickBASIC program to backup and restore the CMOS RAM

Down memory lane (finding your way around)

The allocation of memory space within a PC can be usefully illustrated by means of a 'memory map'. An 8086 microprocessor can address any one of 1,048,576 different memory locations with its 20 address lines. It thus has a memory which ranges from 00000 (the lowest address) to FFFFF (the highest address). We can illustrate the use of memory using a diagram known as a 'memory map'. Figure 6.5 shows a representative memory map for a PC in which the memory is allocated as shown in Table 6.6.

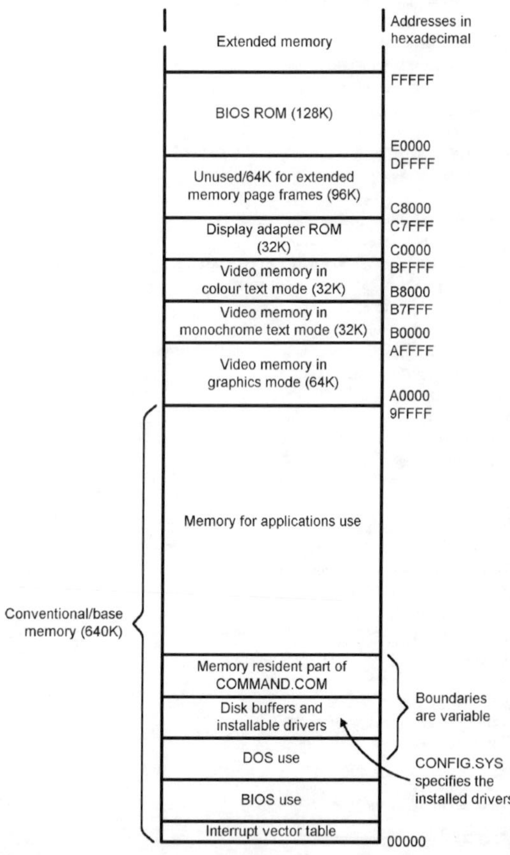

Figure 6.5

Table 6.6 Memory allocation in a basic specification PC

Address range (hex)	Size (bytes)	Use
00000–9FFFF	640K	Conventional (base) memory
A0000–AFFFF	64K	Video memory (graphics mode)
B0000–B7FFF	32K	Video memory (monochrome text mode)
B8000–BFFFF	32K	Video memory (colour text mode)
C0000–C7FFF	32K	Display adapter ROM (EGA, VGA etc.)
C8000–DFFFF	96K	Unused (page frame for extended memory etc.)
E0000–FFFFF	128K	BIOS ROM

TIP

Microsoft's Windows 3.1 provides you with an excellent utility called MSD (Microsoft Diagnostics). You will find this program in your WINDOWS directory (see Chapter 14 if you need to know how to change the directory and run a DOS program). MSD will provide you with a great deal of useful information on your system, including a complete 'on-screen' memory map. A sample memory map produced by MSD is shown in Figure 6.6.

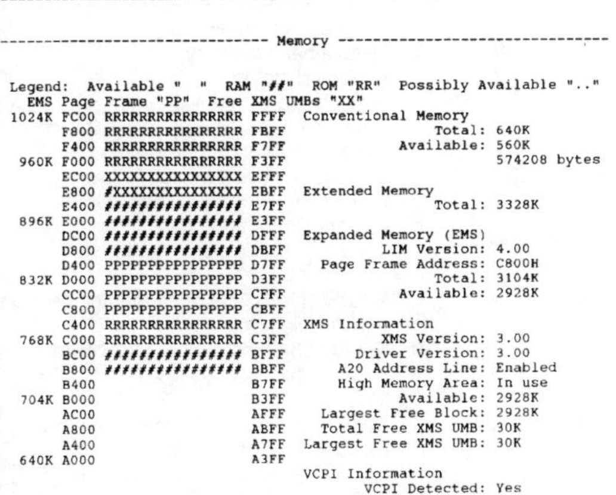

```
  Microsoft Diagnostics version 2.00    6/27/93   11:10pm    Page  2
======================================================================

------------------------------ Memory ------------------------------

Legend:  Available "  "  RAM "##"  ROM "RR"  Possibly Available ".."
  EMS Page Frame "PP"  Free XMS UMBs "XX"
1024K FC00 RRRRRRRRRRRRRRRR FFFF  Conventional Memory
      F800 RRRRRRRRRRRRRRRR FBFF                 Total: 640K
      F400 RRRRRRRRRRRRRRRR F7FF             Available: 560K
 960K F000 RRRRRRRRRRRRRRRR F3FF                        574208 bytes
      EC00 XXXXXXXXXXXXXXXX EFFF
      E800 #XXXXXXXXXXXXXXX EBFF  Extended Memory
      E400 ################ E7FF                 Total: 3328K
 896K E000 ################ E3FF
      DC00 ################ DFFF  Expanded Memory (EMS)
      D800 ################ DBFF           LIM Version: 4.00
      D400 PPPPPPPPPPPPPPPP D7FF    Page Frame Address: C800H
 832K D000 PPPPPPPPPPPPPPPP D3FF                 Total: 3104K
      CC00 PPPPPPPPPPPPPPPP CFFF             Available: 2928K
      C800 PPPPPPPPPPPPPPPP CBFF
      C400 RRRRRRRRRRRRRRRR C7FF  XMS Information
 768K C000 RRRRRRRRRRRRRRRR C3FF           XMS Version: 3.00
      BC00 ################ BFFF        Driver Version: 3.00
      B800 ################ BBFF     A20 Address Line: Enabled
      B400                  B7FF     High Memory Area: In use
 704K B000                  B3FF             Available: 2928K
      AC00                  AFFF    Largest Free Block: 2928K
      A800                  ABFF    Total Free XMS UMB: 30K
      A400                  A7FF  Largest Free XMS UMB: 30K
 640K A000                  A3FF
                                  VCPI Information
                                        VCPI Detected: Yes
                                              Version: 1.00
                                     Available Memory: 2928K
```

Figure 6.6 A sample memory map produced by MSD

TIP

The DOS MEM command will let you know which programs and drivers are present in memory at any time. The command will also tell you how much extended memory you have available. Use the /CLASSIFY or /DEBUG switches with the MEM command (see page 76).

TIP

If you have a '386 or later system, you can use the EMM386 driver to tell you what is happening in your expanded memory. Just enter the command EMM386 (you must have EMM386.EXE for this to work) to view the LIM/EMS version, the size of your expanded memory and the segment address of its page frame.

Using RAM and ROM to find out about your system

A number of memory locations can be useful in determining the current state of a PC or PC-compatible microcomputer. You can display the contents of these memory locations (summarised in Table 6.7) using the MS-DOS DEBUG utility (see Chapter 14) or using a short routine written in QuickBASIC.

Table 6.7 Useful RAM locations

Address (hex)	Number of bytes	Function
0410	2	Installed equipment list
0413	2	Usable base memory
0417	2	Keyboard status
043E	1	Disk calibration (see Chapter 10)
043F	1	Disk drive motor status (see Chapter 10)
0440	1	Drive motor count (see Chapter 10)
0441	2	Disk status (see Chapter 10)
0442	2	Disk controller status (see Chapter 10)
0449	1	Current video mode (see Chapter 13)
044A	2	Current screen column width (see Chapter 13)
046C	4	Master clock count (incremented by 1 on each clock 'tick')
0472	2	Set to 1234 hex. during a keyboard re-boot (this requires <CTRL- ALT-DEL> keys)
0500	1	Screen print byte (00 indicates normal ready status, 01 indicates that a screen print is in operation, FF indicates that an error has occurred during the screen print operation)

As an example, the following DEBUG command can be used to display the contents of 10 bytes of RAM starting at memory location 0410:

D0:0410L0A

(N.B. the equivalent command using the DR-DOS SID utility is: D0:410,419.)

A rather more user-friendly method of displaying the contents of RAM is shown in Figure 6.7. This QuickBASIC program prompts the user for a start address (expressed in hexadecimal) and the number of bytes to display.

Figure 6.8 shows a typical example of running the program in Figure 6.7 on a '486-based computer. The program has been used to display the contents of 10 bytes of RAM from address 0410 onwards.

```
DEF SEG = 0
CLS
INPUT "Start address (in hex)"; address$
address$ = "&H" + address$
address = VAL(address$)
INPUT "Number of bytes to display"; number
PRINT
PRINT "Address", "Byte"
PRINT "(hex)", "(hex)"
PRINT
FOR i% = 0 TO number - 1
  v = PEEK(address + i%)
  PRINT HEX$(address + i%), HEX$(v)
NEXT i%
PRINT
END
```

Figure 6.7 QuckBASIC program to display RAM contents

```
Start address (in hex)? 410
Number of bytes to display? 10

Address          Byte
(hex)            (hex)

410              63
411              44
412              BF
413              80
414              2
415              0
416              18
417              20
418              0
419              0
```

Figure 6.8 Output produced by the program in Figure 6.7

What equipment's installed?

The machine's Installed Equipment List (see Table 6.8) can tell you what hardware devices are currently installed in your system. The equipment list is held in the word (two bytes) starting address 0410. Figure 6.9 and Table 6.9 show you how to decipher the Equipment List word.

Table 6.8 Equipment list word at address 0410

Bit Number	Meaning		
0	Set if disk drives are present		
1	Unused		
2 and 3	System Board RAM size:		
	Bit 3	**Bit 2**	**RAM size**
	0	0	16K
	0	1	32K
	1	1	64K/256K
	(NB: on modern systems this coding does not apply)		
4 and 5	Initial video mode:		
	Bit 5	**Bit 4**	**Mode**
	0	1	40 column colour
	1	0	80 column colour
	1	1	80 column monochrome
6 and 7	Number of disk drives plus 1:		
	Bit 7	**Bit 6**	**Number of drives**
	0	0	1
	0	1	2
	1	0	3
	1	1	4
8	Reset if DMA chip installed (standard)		
9 to 11	Number of serial ports installed		
12	Set if an IBM Games Adapter is installed		
13	Set if a serial printer is installed		
14 and 15	Number of printers installed		

```
Address:  (hex)          0411              0410

Contents: (hex)         4     2           2     D

          (binary)   0100  0010        0010  1101
                     |        |        |        |
Bit position:        15       8        7        0
```

Figure 6.9 Deciphering the equipment list

Table 6.9 Example equipment list

Bit position	Status	Comment
0	1 = set	Disk drives are present
1	1 = set	This bit is not used
2	0 = reset	These bits have no meaning with
3	0 = reset	Systems having greater than 256K RAM
4	0 = reset	Initial video mode is 80 column
5	1 = set	Colour
6	1 = set	Two disk drives installed
7	0 = reset	
8	0 = reset	DMA controller fitted (standard)
9	0 = reset	Two serial ports installed
10	1 = set	
11	0 = reset	
12	0 = reset	No IBM Games Adapter installed
13	0 = reset	No serial printer installed
14	1 = set	One printer attached
15	0 = reset	

How much base memory is available?

The amount of usable base memory can be determined from the two bytes starting at address 0413. The extent of memory is found by simply adding the binary weighted values of each set bit position. Figure 6.10 and Table 6.10 show how this works.

```
Address:  (hex)          0414                 0413
Contents: (hex)         0     2              8     0
          (binary)    0000   0010          1000   0000
                      |         |          |         |
Bit position:         15        8          7         0
```

Figure 6.10 Determining the usable base memory

What ROM is fitted?

The BIOS ROM release date and machine ID can be found by examining the area of read-only memory extending between absolute locations FFFF5 and FFFFC. The ROM release information (not found in all compatibles) is presented in American date format using ASCII characters. Various ROM release dates for various IBM models are shown in Table 6.11.

Table 6.10 Determining the base memory

Bit position	Status	Value
9	Set	512K
8	Reset	256K
7	Set	128K
6	Reset	64K
5	Reset	32K
4	Reset	16K
3	Reset	8K
2	Reset	4K
1	Reset	2K
0	Reset	1K

Adding together the values associated with each of the set bits gives (512+128) = 640K.

Table 6.11 IBM major ROM release dates

ROM date	PC version
04/24/81	Original PC
10/19/81	Revised PC
08/16/82	Original XT
10/27/82	PC upgrade to XT BIOS level
11/08/82	PC-XT
06/01/83	Original PC Junior
01/10/84	Original AT
06/10/85	Revised PC-AT
09/13/85	PC Convertible
11/15/85	Revised PC-AT
01/10/86	Revised PC-XT
04/10/86	XT 286
06/26/87	PS/2 Model 25
09/02/86	PS/2 Model 30
12/12/86	Revised PS/2 Model 30
02/13/87	PS/2 Models 50 and 60
12/05/87	Revised PS/2 Model 30
03/30/87	PS/2 Model 80 (16MHz)
10/07/87	PS/2 Model 80 (20MHz)
01/29/88	PS/2 Model 70
12/01/89	PS/1
11/21/89	PS/2 Model 80 (25MHz)
02/08/90	PS/2 Model 65SX
02/08/90	PS/2 Model 55LS
02/15/90	PS/2 Model 80
03/15/91	PS/2 Model 35SX/40SX
04/24/91	PS/2 Model 95

What kind of machine is it?

The type of machine (whether PC-XT, AT etc.) is encoded in the form of an identification (ID) byte which is stored at address FFFFE. Table 6.12 gives the ID bytes for each member of the PC family (non-IBM machines may have ID bytes which differ from those listed).

Table 6.12 ID bytes for various IBM machines

ID Byte (hex)	Machine
F8	PS/2 Models 35, 40, 65, 70, 80 and 90 ('386 and '486 CPU)
F9	PC Convertible
FA	PS/2 Models 25, 30 ('8086 CPU)
FB	PC-XT (revised versions, post 1986)
FC	AT, PS/2 Models 50 and 60 ('286 CPU)
FD	PC Junior
FE	XT and Portable PC
FF	Original PC

Getting into the BIOS ROM

You can display the ROM release date and machine ID byte by using the MS-DOS DEBUG utility or by using the simple QuickBASIC program shown in Figure 6.11. An example of the output produced by this program is shown in Figure 6.12 (the machine in question has an ID byte of FC and a ROM release date of 06/06/92).

```
DEF SEG = &HFFF0
CLS
PRINT "ROM address", "Byte", "ASCII"
PRINT "(hex)", "(hex)"
PRINT
FOR i% = &HF0 TO &HFF
  v = PEEK(i%)
  PRINT HEX$(i%), HEX$(v), ;
  IF v > 31 AND v < 128 THEN
    PRINT CHR$(v)
  ELSE
    PRINT ""
  END IF
NEXT i%
PRINT
END
```

Figure 6.11 QuickBASIC program to display the last 16 bytes of BIOS ROM

ROM address (hex)	Byte (hex)	ASCII	*Comment*
F0	EA		
F1	5B	[	
F2	E0		
F3	0		
F4	F0		
F5	30	0	*ROM release date*
F6	36	6	*06/06/92*
F7	2F	/	
F8	30	0	
F9	36	6	
FA	2F	/	
FB	39	9	
FC	32	2	
FD	0		
FE	FC		*Machine ID byte*
FF	0		

Figure 6.12 Output produced by the program shown in Figure 6.11

TIP

If you have limited RAM fitted in your system, utilities like Quarterdeck's excellent MagnaRAM2 can help you squeeze more out of your existing memory. In particular, they will let you run larger programs, increase speed and reduce hard-disk wear (by reducing the number of hard disk accesses). They will also allow you to run multiple applications in Windows. Memory compression utilities work by compressing the data present in your RAM as well as that present in 'virtual memory' (this is actually a file that Windows writes to your hard disk when your *phsyical* RAM becomes full) and they can be particularly cost-effective on laptop computers where RAM may be expensive or difficult to upgrade.

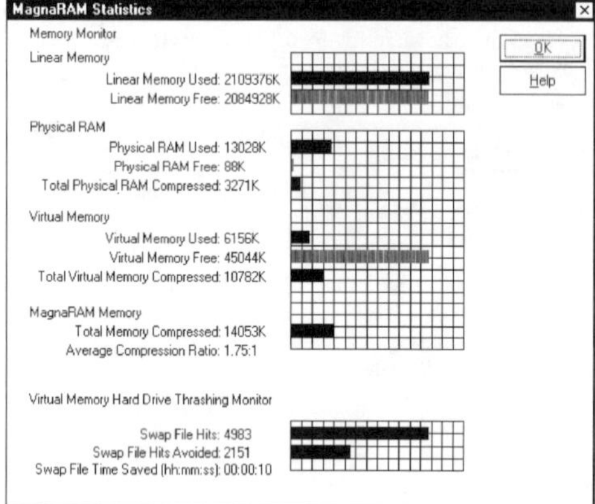

Figure 6.13

Memory diagnostics

ROM diagnostics

The PC's BIOS ROM incorporates some basic diagnostic software which checks the BIOS ROM and DRAM during the initialisation process. The ROM diagnostic is based upon a known 'checksum' for the device. Each byte of ROM is successively read and a checksum is generated. This checksum is then compared with a stored checksum or is adjusted by padding the ROM with bytes which make the checksum amount to zero (neglecting overflow). If any difference is detected an error message is produced and the bootstrap routine is aborted.

RAM diagnostics

In the case of RAM diagnostics the technique is quite different and usually involves writing and reading each byte of RAM in turn. Various algorithms have been developed which make this process more reliable (e.g. 'walking ones'). Where a particular bit is 'stuck' (i.e. refuses to be changed), the bootstrap routine is aborted and an error code is displayed. This error code will normally allow you to identify the particular device that has failed.

The power-on self-test (POST) code within the BIOS ROM checks the system (including system board ROM and RAM) during initialisation. The POST reports any errors detected using a numeric code (see Chapter 17 for a full list).

More complex RAM diagnostics involve continuously writing and reading complex bit patterns. These tests are more comprehensive than simple read/write checks. RAM diagnostics can also be carried out on a non-destructive basis. In such cases, the byte read from RAM is replaced immediately after each byte has been tested. It is thus possible to perform a diagnostic check some time after the system has been initialised and without destroying any programs and data which may be resident in memory at the time.

TIP

You can usually bypass the BIOS POST memory check by pressing the <ESC> key. This will abandon the memory self-test and continue initialising the system in the normal way.

Parity checking

The integrity of stored data integrity can be checked by adding an extra 'parity bit'. This bit is either set or reset according to whether the number of 1's present within the byte are even or odd (i.e. 'even parity' and 'odd parity').

Parity bits are automatically written to memory during a memory write cycle and read from memory during a memory read cycle. A non-maskable interrupt (NMI) is generated if a parity error is detected and thus users are notified if RAM faults develop during normal system operation.

TIP

Parity errors can very occasionally occur due to the spontaneous passage of stray radioactive particles through a RAM chip. If this phenomenon does occur and your system reports a 'parity error' and then shuts down it will usually reboot. This type of error is often referred to as a 'soft error' and it will not normally recur. Repeated or permanent parity errors, on the other hand, usually indicate a failed (or failing) RAM chip. These 'hard errors' usually mean that you must replace a chip or module to restore normal operation.

The last resort . . .

Fault finding on DIL-packaged memory devices (e.g. BIOS ROM or cache RAM) is relatively simple when software diagnostic routines are available. In some cases (e.g. failure of the BIOS ROM or a bus failure within a DRAM device), a faulty chip may prevent normal system initialisation. In such cases, a failed device may consume excessive power and run very warm. The following procedure will normally allow you to identify the defective chip:

(i) Leave the system running for 10 minutes, or more, then touch the centre of each chip in turn in order to ascertain its working temperature. If a device is running distinctly hot (i.e. so warm that it is too hot to touch or noticeably warmer than other similar devices) it should be considered a prime suspect. (If possible compare with the heat produced by an identical chip fitted in the same machine.)

(ii) Where the boot ROM or DRAM chips have been fitted in sockets, carefully remove and replace each suspected device in turn (disconnecting the power and observing the static precautions mentioned in Chapter 3). Replace each device with a known functional device.

(iii) Where the boot ROM or DRAM chips are soldered directly to the PCB, a current tracer (see Chapter 16) can be usefully employed to pinpoint a failed device. The current tracer should be applied to the copper PCB at strategic points along the +5V supply rail to each device in turn.

Finally, if you do have to desolder a suspect BIOS ROM, it is well worth fitting the PCB with a socket before replacing the chip. A low-profile DIL socket with the appropriate number of pins will only cost a few pence but it could save much aggravation in the event of another failure!

TIP

It is relatively easy to locate a failed SIMM module by simply swapping them around within your system and noting the error message and total RAM size displayed. After one or two swaps you should be in a position to identify the failed module.

TIP

A SIMM module may apparently fail simply because of a poor contact between the pins of the module and its header. If you suspect that this may be the case (the symptom is usually an intermittent memory problem that occurs with increasing frequency) you should release each SIMM in turn from its header and simply re-seat it. Momentarily breaking and making the SIMM's contacts will usually help to break through any oxide coating and restore normal operation. In extreme cases, you might have to clean the PCB contacts using a cotton bud and an isopropyl cleaning solution. This will invariably provide you with a permanent cure!

7
The parallel printer interface

The PC's parallel ports (LPT1 and LPT2) provide a very simple and effective interface which can be used to link your PC to a wide range of printers and other devices such as external tape and disk drives. This chapter explains the principles of parallel I/O and describes the Centronics interface standard before discussing basic fault finding and troubleshooting procedures which can be applied to the parallel interface.

Parallel I/O

Parallel I/O is used to transfer bytes of data at a time between a microcomputer and a peripheral device (such as a printer). This method of I/O requires a minimum of hardware (e.g. a single 8255 parallel I/O device) and it is thus relatively easy and inexpensive to implement.

The 8255 (or equivalent) is used to interface the PC's system data bus to the external 8-bit data lines that link the computer to the printer. In addition, several other control signals are present in order to achieve 'handshaking', the aptly named process which controls the exchange of data between the computer system and the printer.

A basic handshake sequence is as follows:

(a) the PC indicates that it is ready to output data to the printer by asserting the STROBE line

(b) the PC then waits for the printer to respond by asserting the ACK (acknowledge) line

(c) when ACK is received by the PC, it places the outgoing data on the eight data lines

(d) the cycle is then repeated until the printer's internal buffer is full of data.

The buffer may have to be filled several times during the printing of a large document. Each time, the port will output data at a fast rate but the printer will takes an appreciable amount of time to print each character and thus will operate at a very much slower rate. Clearly, your PC will be 'tied up' for less time if you have a larger printer buffer!

> **TIP**
>
> You can read the status of the PC's parallel printer ports using a few QuickBASIC statements. As an example, the code in Figure 7.1 will let you determine the status of LPT1 and also give you some idea of what is happening at the printer.

The Centronics interface standard

The Centronics interface has become established as the most commonly used interface standard for the transfer of data between a PC

```
DEF SEG = &H40
DO
  status& = PEEK(9) * 256 + PEEK(8) + 1
  stat% = INP(status&)
  IF stat% = &H57 THEN PRINT "Printer not ready"
  IF stat% = &H77 THEN PRINT "Printer out of paper"
  IF stat% = &HF7 THEN PRINT "Printer off-line"
  GOSUB waitkey
LOOP UNTIL stat% = &HDF
PRINT "Printer ready"
DEF SEG
```

Figure 7.1 Checking the printer's status

and a printer. The standard employs parallel data transmission (a byte is transferred at a time).

The standard is based on a 36-way Amphenol connector (see Figure 7.2 and Table 7.1). The interface is generally suitable for transfer of data at distances of up to 4m, or so. At greater distances, an RS-232 serial data link is usually more effective. Note that, whilst an Amphenol connector is usually fitted at the printer, the PC invariably has a standard female 25-way female D-type connector.

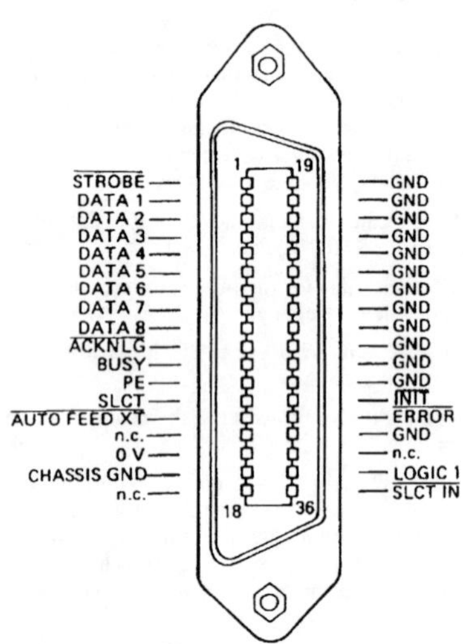

Figure 7.2 36-way Centronics printer interface connector

It is also worth noting that data transfer is essentially in one direction only (from the microcomputer to the printer). Indeed, some early PC's have printer ports which can only be configured in one direction (i.e. output only).

Handshaking between the microcomputer and printer is accomplished by means of the strobe (STROBE), acknowledge (ACK) and busy (BUSY) lines. The BUSY line is asserted when an 'error' condition occurs (e.g. 'printer off-line' or 'paper out').

Table 7.1 The Centronics printer interface signals and pin connections

Pin no. 36-way Amphenol connector	Pin no. 25-way female PC connector	Signal	Function
1	1	STROBE	Strobe. Pulsed low to initiate data transfer.
2	2	DATA1	Data line 1 (bit 0)
3	3	DATA2	Data line 2 (bit 1)
4	4	DATA3	Data line 3 (bit 2)
5	5	DATA4	Data line 4 (bit 3)
6	6	DATA5	Data line 5 (bit 4)
7	7	DATA6	Data line 6 (bit 5)
8	8	DATA7	Data line 7 (bit 6)
9	9	DATA8	Data line 8 (bit 7)
10	10	ACK	Acknowledge. Pulsed low to indicate that data has been received.
11	11	BUSY	Busy. Usually taken high under the following conditions: (a) during data entry (b) during a printing operation (c) when the printer is 'off-line' (d) when an error condition exists.
12	12	PE	Paper end. Taken high to indicate that the printer is out of paper.
13	13	SLCT	Select. Taken high to indicate that the printer is in the selected state.
14	14	AUTO FEEDXT	Automatic feed. When this input is taken low, the printer is instructed to produce an automatic line feed after printing. This function can normally also be selected by means of an internal DIP switch.
15		n.c.	Not connected (unused)
16		0V	Logic ground
17		CHASSIS GND	Printer chassis (usually isolated from logic ground).
18		n.c.	Not connected (unused)
19 to 30	18 to 25	GND	Signal ground. Originally defined as 'twisted pair earth returns' for each of the data lines, pins 1 to 12 respectively, these lines are just simply connected to the common ground.

Table 7.1 Contined

Pin no. 36-way Amphenol connector	Pin no. 25-way female PC connector	Signal	Function
31	16	INIT	Initialise. Pulsed low to reset the printer controller.
32	15	ERROR	Taken low by the printer to indicate: (a) Paper-end status (b) Off-line status (c) Error status.
33		GND	Signal ground
34		n.c.	Not connected (unused)
35		LOGIC1	Logic 1 (usually pulled to +5V by a fixed resistor)
36	17	SLCTIN	Select input. Data entry to the printer is only possible when this line is taken low. The function can normally be disabled using a DIP switch.

Notes:
1. Signals, pin numbers, and signal directions are as seen by the printer.
2. The PC end of the interface is fitted with a 25-way D-connector (rather than a 36-way Amphenol connector).
3. All signals employ standard TTL levels and are 'TTL compatible'.
4. The ERROR and ACK are not supported on a number of machines.

Printer types and emulations

A vast selection of different types of printer is available to the PC user including laser, thermal, ink-jet, and impact dot matrix types. Whatever the actual printing technology, printers tend to fall into one of two main categories; 'line printers' and 'page printers'. In the former case each line of text is built up in turn whilst in the later the full image of a page is received and processed before printing.

Most printers nowadays support a number of different standards or 'emulations'. These include the following:

1. The Diablo standard used with early daisy-wheel printers which only offer text printing capability.
2. The Epson standard which is widely used with impact dot-matrix printers and which offers a number of variants including FX, RX, LQ, GQ, etc.
3. As its name implies, the Hewlett-Packard LaserJet standard was designed for laser printers. The standard uses a simple language based on escape sequences (known as 'printer control language'). Printer control language (PCL) has been progressively enhanced as shown in Table 7.2.

Table 7.2 Printer control language

Language	Machines supported
PCL3	Original LaserJet printers.
PCL4	LaserJet Plus and LaserJet II printers.
PCL5	LaserJet III printers (this version supports 'scalable fonts').

In addition, many printers now support the increasingly popular PostScript emulation. This will allow you to incorporate a vast range of scalable typefaces into your documents.

Troubleshooting the parallel printer interface

Fault finding on a PC printer interface is usually quite straightforward and generally involves checking first that the printer is operating correctly (by using the printer 'self-test'), and that no error condition exists (e.g. 'paper out' or incorrect DIP switch setting). Printer cables and connectors often prove to be troublesome (particularly when they are regularly connected and disconnected) and it is always worth checking the cable first.

It will usually be a fairly easy matter to decide which part of the interface (printer, cable or the PC's parallel port) is at fault. Where text is printed but characters appear to be translated resulting in garbled output, one or more of the data line signals may be missing. In this case it is worth checking individual signal lines (D1 to D8) at each end of the cable.

Where the handshake signals are missing, you will usually be warned by an on-screen error message (such as 'printer not responding' or 'printer off-line'). Handshake lines (and, where appropriate, individual data lines) can be easily checked using a logic probe. An output line which is 'stuck' (i.e. permanently at logic 1 or logic 0) or is 'floating' (i.e. takes neither logical state) can be easily located.

It is always worth checking that you have selected the correct printer emulation and print options (e.g. paper size, lines per page etc.). Many software packages are supplied with printer configuration files or 'printer driver' files which ensure that the control codes generated by the software match those required by the printer.

TIP

Standard printer output routines direct their output to the parallel printer port (LPT1). You can use the DOS MODE command (see Chapter 14) to redirect the output to an alternative output device (e.g. COM1).

TIP

You can use the DOS PRINT command to redirect printing. Suppose, for example, that you need to send all your printed output to LPT2 whenever you use your system. All you need to do is include the following statement in your AUTOEXEC.BAT file:

```
PRINT /D:LPT2
```

TIP

The DOS MODE command allows you to configure your printer. When used to configure the printer the MODE command syntax (DOS 3.3) is as follows:
MODE LPTn: c,l
The equivalent syntax for DOS 4 (and higher) is:
MODE LPTn: COLS=n LINES=l
where n = printer port number (1, 2 etc.)
c = columns (80 or 132)
l = vertical spacing (6 or 8 lines per inch)

TIP

The DOS PRINT command lets you establish a print buffer in memory. The default size of the buffer is a mere 512 bytes (about eight lines of average text). You can increase the size of the buffer (and speed things up a bit when using the PRINT command to output files to your printer) by increasing the buffer size. If you have sufficient memory available, try incorporating the following line in your AUTOEXEC.BAT file:
PRINT /B:8192
The command establishes an 8K buffer (enough for two pages of normal text).

Printer control codes

Special codes can be sent to a printer in order to determine the type style and page format. These codes can take the form of single byte characters (ASCII characters in the range 0 to 1F hex.) or a sequence of characters preceded by the ASCII Escape character (27 decimal or 1B hex.). In addition, dot matrix printers are normally capable of operating in text (character based) or graphics (bit image) modes. You can switch modes by means of escape sequences.

Table 7.3 QuickBASIC commands that will allow you to control print styles on Epson-compatible printers

Command	Effect
LPRINT CHR$ (15);	Condensed mode
LPRINT CHR$ (27); “G”;	Double strike mode
LPRINT CHR$ (27); “E”;	Emphasised mode
LPRINT CHR$ (27); “4”;	Italic mode
LPRINT CHR$ (27); “S”; “0”;	Subscript mode
LPRINT CHR$ (27); “S”; “1”;	Superscript mode
LPRINT CHR$ (18);	Cancel condensed mode
LPRINT CHR$ (27); “F”;	Cancel emphasised mode
LPRINT CHR$ (27); “H”;	Cancel double strike mode
LPRINT CHR$ (27); “5”;	Cancel italic mode
LPRINT CHR$ (27); “T”;	Cancel subscript/superscript mode

TIP

You can configure an Epson-compatible printer using the simple QuickBASIC commands shown in Table 7.3. These commands can be entered in immediate mode or incorporated into a configuration program (don't forget to reset the printer when you have finished!).

TIP

When printing text on a LaserJet-compatible printer, it is often useful to be able to change the number of characters printed on each line. The simple QuickBASIC commands shown in Table 7.4 will let you select printing using either 80, 96 or 132 characters per line.

Printing from Windows

When you wish to use a printer with Windows applications, you need to do the following:

1. Install the printer driver file for the printer in question (this file will normally be present on one of your installation disks and Windows will copy it to the hard disk).
2. Select the port you wish to assign to the printer (e.g. LPT1, LPT2, COM1, or COM2).
3. Choose the printer and print options that you wish to use with the installed printer.
4. Select the 'active' printer for each port (you can have more than one printer installed but only one can be active on each port at any time).
5. Select the 'default printer' (i.e. the printer driver that is loaded automatically when Windows starts up).

Windows lets you select a 'default printer' and an 'active printer' via the Control Panel window. You can also install further printer drivers or set up various options to use with your existing printer (select the 'Configure' option).

Finally, the Windows Print Manager allows you to establish a 'print queue'. This lets your system carry out its printing as a 'background operation' (you can carry on using the application whilst files in the print queue are 'spooled' to your printer). Note that you can change the order of this queue, pause the printing and also delete files that are currently waiting in the queue.

Table 7.4 QuickBASIC commands that will allow you to select the number of characters per line on LaserJet compatible printers

Command	Effect
LPRINT CHR$ (27); "E";	Reset the printer (80 chars/line)
LPRINT CHR$ (27); "(s0p12H)";	Select 96 chars/line
LPRINT CHR$ (27); (s16.66H);	Select 132 chars/line

TIP

Microsoft's Windows 3.1 provides you with an excellent DOS utility called MSD (Microsoft Diagnostics). You will find this program in your WINDOWS directory (see Chapter 14 if you need to know how to change the directory and run a DOS program). MSD includes a printer test routine which will allow you to select a printer type and port before putting your printer through its paces.

8
The serial communications ports

The PC's serial communication ports (COM1, COM2 etc.) provide a means of linking your PC with the rest of the world. Data can be exchanged with remote host computers, 'bulletin boards' and a vast number of other PC users world-wide. This chapter explains the basic principles of serial I/O and describes the RS-232 interface standard before providing you with some useful fault finding and troubleshooting information.

Serial I/O devices

Serial I/O involves transmitting a stream of bits, one after another, from a PC to a peripheral device and vice versa. Since parallel (8, 16 or 32-bit) data is present on the system bus, serial I/O is somewhat more complex than parallel I/O.

Serial input data must be converted to parallel (byte wide) data which can be presented to the system data bus. Conversely, the parallel data on the bus must be converted into serial data before it can be output from the port. In the first case, conversion can be performed with a serial-input parallel-output (SIPO) shift register whilst in the second case a parallel-input serial-output (PISO) shift register is required.

Serial data may be transferred in either 'synchronous' or 'asynchronous' mode. In the former case, transfers are carried out in accordance with a common clock signal (the clock must be available at both ends of the transmission path). Asynchronous operation, on the other hand, involves transmission of data in small 'packets'; each packet containing the necessary information required to decode the data which it contains. Clearly this technique is more complex but it has the considerable advantage that a separate clock signal is not required.

As with programmable parallel I/O devices, a variety of different names are used to describe programmable serial I/O devices including 'asynchronous communications interface adaptor' (ACIA) and 'universal asynchronous receiver/transmitter' (UART). Both types of device have common internal features including registers for buffering the transmit and receive data and controlling the format of each data word. The most notable input and output signals used with serial I/O devices are shown in Table 8.1.

Signals produced directly by serial I/O devices are invariably TTL compatible. Furthermore, such signals are unsuitable for anything other than the shortest of data transmission paths (e.g. between a keyboard and a system enclosure). Serial data transmission over any appreciable distance requires additional 'line drivers' to provide buffering and level shifting between the serial I/O device and the physical medium. Additionally, 'line receivers' are required to condition and modify the incoming signal to TTL levels.

The RS-232 standard

The RS-232/CCITT V.24 interface is currently the most widely-used standard for serial communication between microcomputers, peripheral devices, and remote host computers. Unfortunately, the standard is not generally well understood and end-users of

Table 8.1 Signals produced by a serial I/O device

Signal	Function
D0 to D7	Data input/output lines connected directly to the system data bus
RXD (or RD)	Received (incoming) serial data
TXD (or TD)	Transmitted (outgoing) serial data
CTS	Clear to send. This signal is taken low by the peripheral when it is ready to accept data from the computer system
RTS	Request to send. This signal is taken low by the UART when it wishes to send data to the peripheral

microcomputers often experience considerable difficulty in connecting together equipment using the RS-232 interface.

The RS-232 standard was first defined by the Electronic Industries Association (EIA) in 1962 as a recommended standard (RS) for modem interfacing. The latest revision of the RS-232 standard (RS-232D, January 1987) brings it in-line with international standards CCITT V24, V28 and ISO IS2110. The RS-232D standard includes facilities for 'loop-back' testing which were not defined under the previous RS-232C standard.

Terminology

The standard relates essentially to two types of equipment; Data Terminal Equipment (DTE) and Data Circuit Terminating Equipment (DCE). Data Terminal Equipment (i.e. a PC) is capable of sending and/or receiving data via the COM1 or COM2 serial interface. It is thus said to 'terminate' the serial link. Data Circuit Terminating Equipment (formerly known as Data Communications Equipment), on the other hand, facilitates data communications. A typical example is that of a 'modem' (modulator-demodulator) which forms an essential link in the serial path between a PC and a telephone line.

TIP

You can normally distinguish a DTE device from a DCE device by examining the type of connector fitted. A DTE device is normally fitted with a male connector whilst a DCE device is invariably fitted with a female connector.

TIP

There is a subtle difference between the 'bit rate' as perceived by the computer and the 'baud rate' (i.e. the signalling rate in the transmission medium. The reason is simply that additional start, stop and parity bits must accompany the data so that it can be recovered from the *asynchronous* data stream. For example, a typical PC serial configuration might use a total of 11 bits to convey each 7-bit ASCII character. In this case, a line baud rate of 600 baud implies a useful data transfer rate of a mere 382 bits per second.

The RS-232 connector

A PC serial interface is usually implemented using a standard 25-way D connector (see Figure 8.1). The PC (the DTE) is fitted with a male connector and the peripheral device (the DCE) normally uses a female connector. When you need to link two PC's together, they must *both* adopt the role of DTE whilst thinking that the other is a DCE. This little bit of trickery is enabled by means of a 'null-modem'. The null-modem works by swapping over the TXD and RXD, CTS and RTS, DTR and DSR signals.

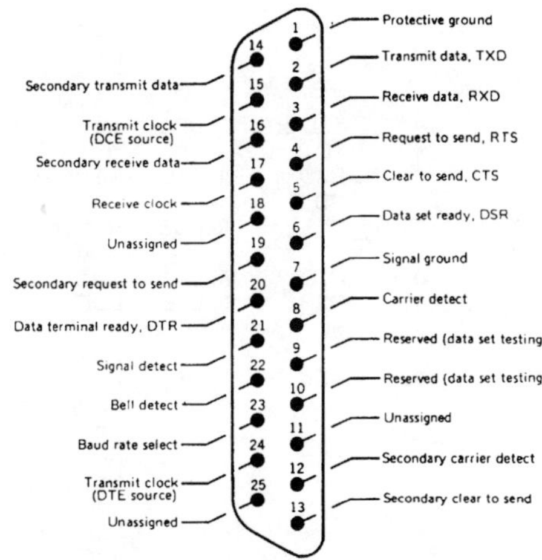

Figure 8.1 Standard 25-way RS-232 D-connector

RS-232 signals

The signals present within the RS-232 interface fall into one of the following three categories:

(a) **Data** (e.g. TXD, RXD)
RS-232 provides for two independent serial data channels (described as 'primary' and 'secondary'). Both of these channels provide for full duplex operation (i.e. simultaneous transmission and reception).

(b) **Handshake control** (e.g. RTS, CTS)
Handshake signals provide the means by which the flow of serial data is controlled allowing, for example, a DTE to open a dialogue with the DCE prior to actually transmitting data over the serial data path.

(c) **Timing** (e.g. TC, RC)
For synchronous (rather than the more usual asynchronous) mode of operation, it is necessary to pass clock signals between the devices. These timing signals provide a means of synchronising the received signal to allow successful decoding.

The *complete* set of RS-232D signals is summarised in Table 8.2, together with EIA and CCITT designations and commonly used signal line abbreviations.

Table 8.2 The complete set of RS-232 signals and pin connections

Pin	EIA interchange circuit	CCITT equiv.	Common abbrev.	Direction	Signal/function
1	–	–	FG	–	Frame or protective ground
2	BA	103	TXD or TD	To DCE	Transmitted data
3	BB	104	RXD or RD	To DTE	Received data
4	CA	105	RTS	To DCE	Request to send
5	CB	106	CTS	To DTE	Clear to send
6	CC	107	DSR	To DTE	DCE ready
7	AB	102	SG	–	Signal ground/common
8	CF	109	DCD	To DTE	Received line signal detector (carrier detect)
9	–	–	–	–	Reserved for testing (positive test voltage)
10	–	–	–	–	Reserved for testing (negative test voltage)
11	–	–	(QM)	–	(Equaliser mode)
12	SCF/CI	122/112	SDCD	To DTE	Secondary received line signal detector/ Data rate select (DCE source)
13	SCB	121	SCTS	To DTE	Secondary clear to send
14	SBA	118	STD	To DCE	Secondary transmitted data
15	DB	114	TC	To DTE	Transmitter signal element timing (DCE source)
16	SBB	119	SRD	To DTE	Secondary received data
17	DD	115	RC	To DTE	Receiver signal element timing (DCE source)
18	LL	141	(DCR)	To DCE	Local loopback (Divided receive clock)

Table 8.2 Continued

Pin	EIA interchange circuit	CCITT equiv.	Common abbrev.	Direction	Signal/function
19	SCA	120	SRTS	To DCE	Secondary request to send
20	CD	108.2	DTR	To DCE	Data terminal ready
21	RL/CG	140/ 110	SQ	To DCE/ To DTE	Remote loopback/ Signal quality detector
22	CE	125	RI	To DTE	Ring indicator
23	CH/CI	111/112	–	To DCE/ To DTE	Data signal rate selector (DTE) Data signal rate selector (DCE)
24	DA	113	TC	To DCE	Transmit signal element timing
25	TM	142	–	To DTE	Test mode

Notes:
1. The functions given in brackets for lines 11 and 18 relate to the Bell 113B and 208A specifications.
2. Lines 9 and 10 are normally reserved for testing. A typical use for these lines is testing of the positive and negative voltage levels used to represent the MARK and SPACE levels.
3. For new designs using EIA interchange circuit SCF, CH and CI are assigned to pin-23. If SCF is not used, CI is assigned to pin-12.
4. Some manufacturers use spare RS-232 lines for testing and/or special functions peculiar to particular hardware (some equipment even feeds power and analogue signals along unused RS-232C lines!).

In practice, few RS-232 implementations make use of the secondary channel and, since asynchronous (non-clocked) operation is almost invariably used with microcomputer systems, only eight or nine of the 25 RS-232 signals are used in the PC. These signals present on the PC's 9-way serial port connector are described in Table 8.3.

TIP

There are various types of RS-232 data cable. Some may have as few as four connections, many have nine or fifteen, and some have all 25. When you purchase a cable it is worth checking how many connections are present within the cable. A cheaper 9-way cable will *usually* work provided your software does not make use of the 'ring indicator' facility. Figure 8.2 shows some of the possibilities for data cable wiring.

Table 8.3 Subset of RS-232 signals used on the PC's 9-pin connector

Pin no:	EIA interchange circuit	Signal	Function
1	CF	DCD	Active when a data carrier is detected.
2	BB	RXD	Serial data received by the PC from the DCE.
3	BA	TXD	Serial data transmitted from PC to DCE.
4	CD	DTR	When active, the DTE is signalling that it is operational and that the PC may be connected to the communications channel.
5	AB	SG	Common signal return path.
6	CC	DSR	When active, the DCE is signalling that a communications path has been properly established.
7	CA	RTS	When active, the PC is signalling that it wishes to send data to the DCE.
8	CB	CTS	When active, the DCE is signalling that it is ready to accept data from the PC.

(a) 4-way cable for dumb terminals

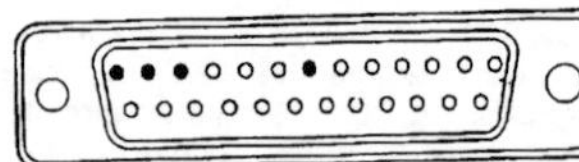

Pins used: 1-3 and 7 (pins 8 and 20 are jumpered)

(b) 9-way cable for asynchronous communications

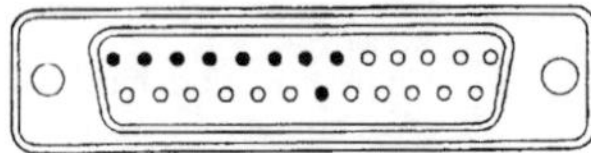

Pins used: 1-8 and 20

(c) 15-way cable for synchronous communications

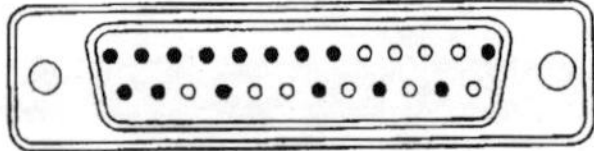

Pins used: 1–8, 13, 15, 17, 20, 22 and 24

(d) 25-way cable for universal applications

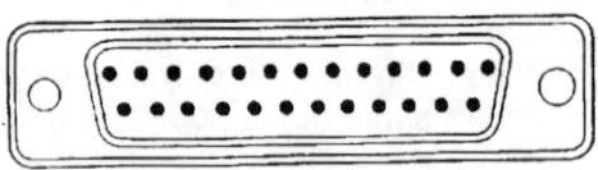

Pins used: 1-25

Figure 8.2 Various possibilities for RS-232 data cables

Line signals and voltages

In most RS-232 systems, data is transmitted asynchronously as a series of small 'packets' each of which represents a single ASCII (or control) character.

ASCII characters are represented by seven bits. The upper case letter 'A', for example, is represented by the seven-bit binary word; 1000001. In order to send the letter 'A' via an RS-232 system, extra bits must be added to signal the start and end of the data packet. These are known as the 'start bit' and 'stop bits' respectively. In addition, you can include a further bit to provide a simple 'parity' error detecting facility.

One of the most commonly used schemes involves the use of one start bit, one parity bit, and two stop bits. The commencement of the data packet is signalled by the start bit which is always low irrespective of the contents of the packet. The start bit is followed by the seven data bits representing the ASCII character concerned. A parity bit is added to make the resulting number of 1's in the group either odd ('odd parity') or even ('even parity'). Finally, two stop bits are added. These are both high. The TTL representation of this character is shown in Figure 8.3.

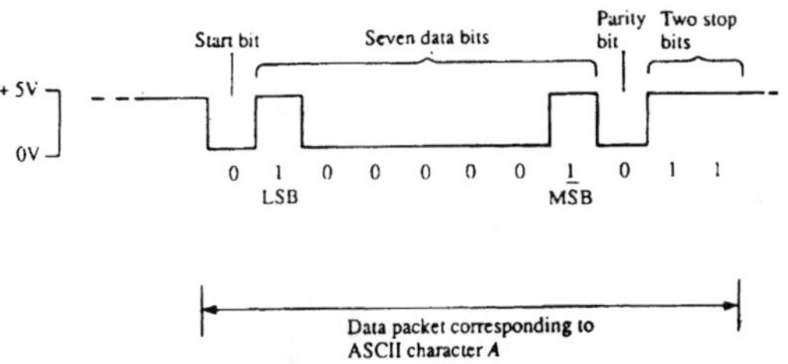

Figure 8.3 Representation of ASCII character 'A' using TTL levels (1 start bit, 1 parity bit and 2 stop bits)

> **TIP**
>
> You can configure the serial ports using the DOS MODE command. MODE allows you to set up the baud rate, the number of data bits, the number of stop bits, and the type of parity checking (even, odd or none).

The complete asynchronously transmitted data word thus comprises eleven bits (note that only seven of these actually contain data). In binary the word can be represented as: 01000001011. In this case, even parity has been used and thus the ninth (parity bit) is reset (0).

The voltage levels employed in an RS-232 interface are markedly different from those used within a microcomputer system. A positive voltage (of between +3V and +25V) is used to represent a logic 0 (or 'SPACE') whilst a negative voltage (of between –3V and –25V) is used to represent a logic 1 (or 'MARK'). The line signal corresponding to the ASCII character 'A' is shown in Figure 8.4.

The level shifting (from TTL to RS-232 signal levels and vice versa)

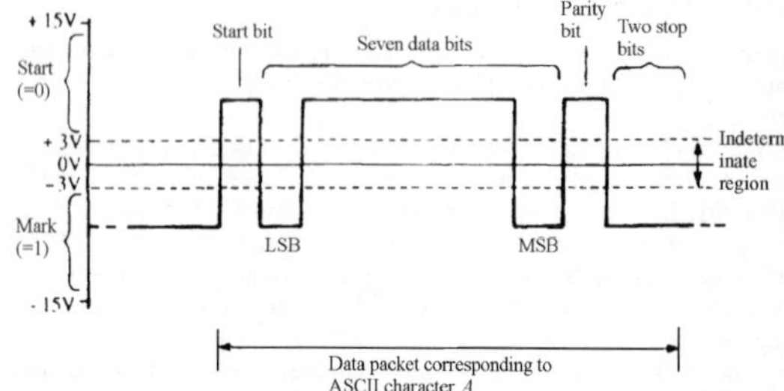

Figure 8.4 Representation of ASCII character 'A' at standard RS-232 line voltage levels (compare this diagram with Figure 8.3)

is invariably accomplished using 'line driver' and 'line receiver' chips, the most common examples being the 1488 and 1489 devices (see Figures 8.5 and 8.6, respectively).

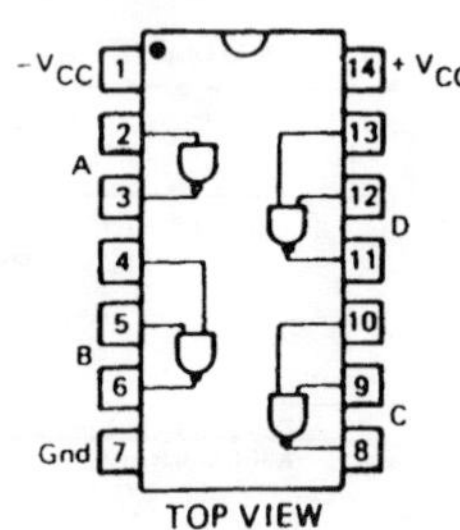

Figure 8.5 1488 RS-232 line receiver pin connections

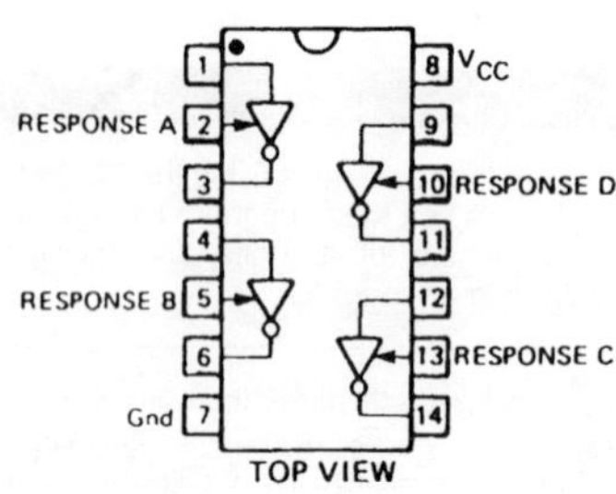

Figure 8.6 1489 RS-232 line receiver pin connections

RS-232 electrical characteristics

Table 8.4 summarises the principal electrical specification for the RS-232 standard whilst Figure 8.7 shows the normally acceptable range of RS-232 line voltage levels:

Table 8.4 Electrical characteristics of the RS-232 interface

Maximum line driver output voltage (open circuit):	±25V
Maximum line driver output current (short circuit):	±500mA
Minimum line impedance:	3k (in parallel with 2.5nF)
Line driver SPACE output voltage (3k $\leq R_L \leq$ 7k):	+5V to +15V
Line driver MARK output voltage (3k $\leq R_L \leq$ 7k):	–5V to –15V
Line driver output (idle state):	MARK
Line receiver output with open circuit input:	logic 1
Line receiver output with input ≥ 3V:	logic 0
Line receiver output with input ≥ –3V:	logic 1

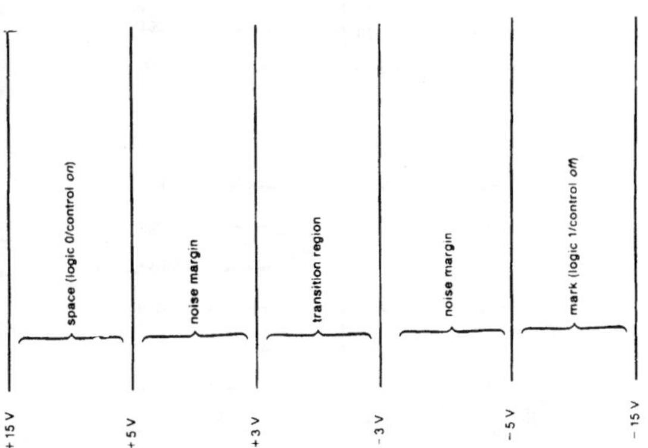

Figure 8.7 Normally accepted range of voltages used in an RS-232 interface

Troubleshooting the communications ports

Troubleshooting the communications ports usually involves the following basic steps:

(a) Check the physical connection between the PC (the 'DTE') and the DCE (e.g. the modem). Where both devices are PCs (i.e. both configured as DTE) a patch box or null modem (see Figure 8.8) should be inserted for correct operation.

(b) Check that the correct cable has been used. Note that RS-232 cables are provided in a variety of forms; 4-way (for 'dumb' terminals), 9-way (for normal asynchronous data communications) 15-way (for synchronous communications) and 25-way (for 'universal' applications) – see Figure 8.2. If in doubt, use a full 25-way cable.

(c) Check that the same data word format and baud rate has been selected at each end of the serial link (note that this is most important and it often explains why an RS-232 link fails to operate even though the hardware and cables have been checked).

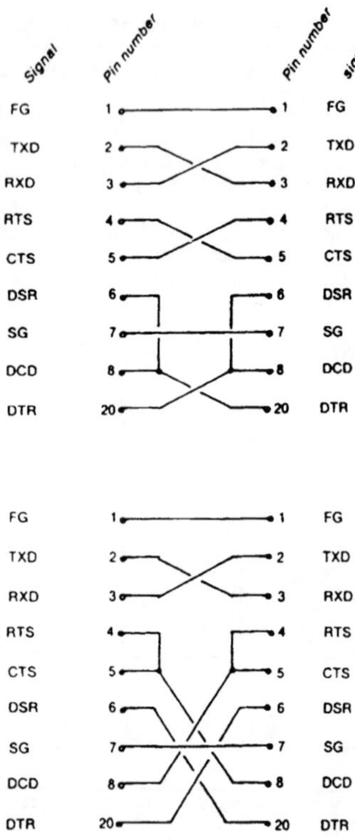

Figure 8.8 Two forms of null-modem

Activate the link and investigate the logical state of the data (TXD and RXD) and handshaking (RTS, CTS etc.) signal lines using a line monitor, breakout box or interface tester. Lines may be looped back to test each end of the link.

If in any doubt, refer to the equipment manufacturer's data in order to ascertain whether any special connections are required and to ensure that the interfaces are truly compatible. Note that some manufacturers have implemented quasi-RS-232 interfaces which make use of TTL signals. These are NOT electrically compatible with the normal RS-232 system even though they may obey the same communication protocols. They will also NOT interface directly with a standard PC COM port!

The communications software should be initially configured for the 'least complex' protocol (e.g. basic 7-bit ASCII character transfer at 1200 baud). When a successful link has been established, more complex protocols may be attempted in order to increase the data transfer rate or improve upon data checking.

Table 8.5 Loopback plug wiring

Signals	Pins linked (9-way)	Pins linked (25-way)
RXD and TXD	2 to 3	3 to 2
RTS and CTS	7 to 8	4 to 5
DTR and DSR	4 to 6	20 to 6

```
' Loopback test routine using COM1 serial port
CLS
PRINT "Keyboard characters will be output to COM1"
PRINT "Screen shows from characters received from COM1"
PRINT "Press <ESC> to end the test..."
PRINT
OPEN "COM1:9600,E,7,1" FOR RANDOM AS #1
'
getkey:
K$ = INKEY$
IF K$ = "" THEN GOTO waitin
IF K$ = CHR$(3) OR K$ = CHR$(27) THEN GOTO finish
PRINT #1, K$;
'
waitin:
IF EOF(1) THEN GOTO getkey
C$ = INPUT$(LOC(1), #1)
PRINT C$;
GOTO getkey
'
finish:
CLOSE #1
CLS
END
```

Figure 8.9 QuickBASIC loopback test program

TIP

You can easily check your serial COM ports using a simple loopback test. You will need a female 25-pin or 9-pin D connector with three links soldered, as shown in Table 8.5. Connect the loopback plug to the port that you wish to test and then run the QuickBASIC program shown in Figure 8.9. The program reads consecutive keypresses and outputs them to the serial port. It then reads them from the serial port and displays the received characters on the screen.

9
The PC expansion bus

The availability of a versatile expansion bus system within the PC must surely be one of the major factors in ensuring its continuing success. The bus is the key to expansion. It allows you to painlessly upgrade your system and configure it for almost any conceivable application.

A number of standards are employed in conventional PC expansion bus schemes, ranging from the original 'Industry Standard Architecture' (ISA) to the latest 'Peripheral Component Interconnect' (PCI). This chapter introduces you to the ISA, EISA, MCA, VESA and PCI bus standards and explains some of the pitfalls that can occur when you make use of the expansion bus.

PC expansion systems

ISA bus

The PC's ISA bus is based upon a number of expansion 'slots' each of which is fitted with a 62-way direct edge connector together with an optional subsidiary 36-way direct edge connector. The first ISA connector (62-way) provides access to the 8-bit data bus and the majority of control bus signals and power rails whilst the second connector (36-way) gives access to the remaining data bus lines together with some additional control bus signals. Applications which require only an 8-bit data path and a subset of the PC's standard control signals can make use of only the first connector. Applications which require access to a full 16-bit data path (not available in the early original PC and PC-XT machines) must make use of both connectors.

Expansion (or option) cards may be designed to connect only to the 62-way connector or may, alternatively, mate with both the 62-way and 36-way connectors. Since only the 62-way connector was fitted on early machines (which then had an 8-bit data bus), cards designed for use with this connector are sometimes known as '8-bit expansion cards' or 'XT expansion cards'. The AT machine, however, provides access to a full 16-bit data bus together with additional control signals and hence requires the additional 36-way connector. Cards which are designed to make use of *both* connectors are generally known as '16-bit expansion cards' or 'AT expansion cards'.

The original PC was fitted with only five expansion slots (spaced approximately 25mm apart). The standard XT provided a further three slots to make a total of eight (spaced approximately 19mm apart). Some cards, particularly those providing hard disk storage, require the width occupied by two expansion slot positions on the XT. This is unfortunate, particularly where the number of free slots may be at a premium!

All of the XT expansion slots provide identical signals with one notable exception; the slot nearest to the power supply was employed in a particular IBM configuration (the IBM 3270 PC) to accept a Keyboard/Timer Adapter. This particular configuration employs a dedicated 'card select' signal (B8 on the connector) which is required by the system motherboard. Other cards that *will* operate in this position include the IBM 3270 Asynchronous Communications Adapter.

Like the XT, the standard AT also provides eight expansion slots. Six of these slots are fitted with two connectors (62-way and 36-way) whilst two positions (slots one and seven) only have 62-way connectors. Slot positions one and seven are designed to accept earlier 8-bit expansion cards which make use of the maximum allowable height throughout their length. If a 36-way connector had been fitted to the system motherboard, this would only foul the lower edge of the card and prevent effective insertion of the card in question.

Finally, it should be noted that boards designed for AT systems (i.e. those specifically designed to take advantage of the availability of the full 16-bit data bus) will offer a considerable speed advantage over those which are based upon the 8-bit PC-XT data bus provided by the original XT expansion connector. In some applications, this speed advantage can be critical.

EISA bus

'Extended Industry Standard Architecture' (EISA) is an extension of the ISA bus which has been, and still is, widely supported by a large number of manufacturers. Unlike the ISA bus, EISA provides access to a full 32-bit data bus. To make the system compatible with ISA expansion cards, the standard is based on a two-level connector. The lowest level contacts (used by EISA cards) make connection with the extended 32-bit bus whilst the upper level contacts (used by ISA cards) provide the 8- and 16-bit connections.

MCA bus

With the advent of PS/2, a more advanced expansion scheme has become available. This expansion standard is known as 'Micro Channel Architecture' (MCA) and it provides access to the 16-bit DATA bus in the IBM PS/2 Models 50 and 60 whereas access to a full 32-bit data bus is available in the Model 80 which has an 80386 CPU.

An important advantage of MCA is that it permits data transfer at a significantly faster rate than is possible with ISA. In fairness, the increase in data transfer rate may be unimportant in many applications and also tends to vary somewhat from machine to machine. As a rough guide, when a standard ISA bus AT machine is compared with an MCA PS/2 Model 50, data transfer rates can be expected to increase by around 25% for conventional memory transfers and by 100% (or more) for DMA transfers.

Since MCA interrupt signals are shared between expansion cards, MCA interrupt structure tends to differ from that employed within ISA where interrupt signals tend to remain exclusive to a particular expansion card. More importantly, MCA provides a scheme of bus arbitration in order to decide which of the 'feature cards' has rights to exercise control of the MCA bus at any particular time.

MCA's arbitration mechanism provides for up to 15 bus masters, each one able to exercise control of the bus. As a further bonus, MCA provides an auxiliary video connector and programmable option configuration to relieve the tedium of setting DIP switches on system boards and expansion cards.

VESA (or VL) bus

The Video Electronics Standards Association (VESA), a consortium of over 120 companies, produced the VL-bus specification as a solution to the bottleneck imposed by the ISA bus. The VL-bus (VESA Local Bus) allows data to be transferred at much higher speeds than those supported by the ISA and EISA bus standards.

VL-bus supports up to three local bus masters. Each can take control of the bus and use it to move data to and from memory or to any I/O board present on the bus. The standard was initially popular with graphics card manufacturers because it allowed systems based on faster '486 processors to run graphic-intensive applications at reasonable speeds free from the constraints imposed by the ISA bus.

The VL-bus specification supports low-voltage (3.3V) logic devices (provided that they can withstand the +5V upper logic level limit associated with a conventional +5V powered CPU). The 3.3V logic design is instrumental in permitting faster clock speeds by reducing the power dissipated in the CPU. The upper limit for the VL-bus is about 130Mbyte/s (based on 32-bit transfers). The standard ISA bus, on the other hand, is only capable of supporting data transfer rates of up to 5Mbyte/s.

The VL-bus connector is arranged in-line with existing ISA connectors (up to three VL-bus slots may be provided). This arrangement allows manufacturers to produce cards which will operate with either bus. Table 9.4 (at the end of this chapter) provides pin connecting details for the VL-bus.

The VL-bus has 32 data bus lines (and thus supports 32-bit data transfers). The connector has a total of 116 ways. VESA has also defined a 64-bit extension to the basic 32-bit VL-bus standard 32 address bus. This bus is capable of supporting data transfer of up to 250Mbyte/s.

PCI bus

Initially devised by Intel and subsequently supported by the PCI Special Interest Group (PCI-SIG), the Peripheral Component Interconnect bus has become established as arguably the most popular and 'future proof' bus standard available today.

Because the PCI bus is not connected *directly* to the CPU (it is separated by an interface formed by a dedicated 'PCI chipset') the bus is sometimes referred to as a 'mezzanine bus'. This technique offers two advantages over the earlier VL-bus specification:

- reduced loading of the bus lines on the CPU (permitting a longer data path and allowing more bus cards to be connected to it)
- making the bus 'processor independent'.

PCI bus is designed for operation at clock speeds of 33MHz (although it is probably capable of speeds of up to about 50MHz). With a 32-bit data path, the 33MHz clock rate implies a maximum data transfer rate of around 130Mbyte/s (about the same as VL-bus). Like the VL-bus, the PCI bus connector is similar to that used for MCA. To cater for both 32 and 64-bit operation, PCI bus cards may have either 62 or 94-pins (see Table 9.5).

Concurrent PCI (supported by modern chipsets) allows for more efficient use of the PCI bus and helps prevent conflicts between PCI and CPU bus mastering devices.

TIP

The PCI bus operates under the control of a separate PCI bus controller (a device within the 'PCI chipset'). The PCI bus thus operates independently of the CPU clock. Thus, when you upgrade your CPU you need not have any concerns about whether your existing PCI cards will cope with the higher clock speed!

Expansion cards and connectors

Expansion cards for PC systems tend to vary slightly in their outline and dimensions (see Figure 9.1). However, the maximum allowable

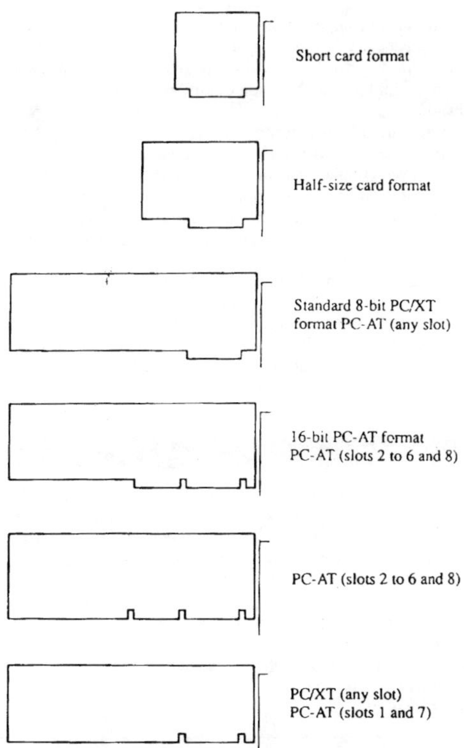

Figure 9.1 Outlines for various types of PC expansion card

dimensions for the adapter and expansion cards fitted to PC (and PS/2) equipment are shown in Table 9.1.

It is important to note that, although the XT-286 is based on an AT motherboard, it is fitted in an XT enclosure and thus expansion and

Table 9.1 Expansion card dimensions

Bus	Standard	Maximum card dimensions (approx.)					
		Height		Length		Width	
		(inches)	(mm)	(inches)	(mm)	(inches)	(mm)
EISA	AT	5.0	127	13.2	334	0.5	12.7
ISA	XT	4.2	107	13.2	334	0.5	12.7
ISA	AT	4.8	122	13.2	334	0.5	12.7
MCA	PS/2	3.8	96	13.2	334	0.5	12.7
PCI	AT	4.2	107	7.0	178	0.5	12.7
VL	AT	4.8	122	12.3	312	0.5	12.7

adapter cards used in this machine *must* conform with the general height restriction imposed on XT cards (i.e. 4.2 inches maximum). Whilst many expansion card manufacturers are very conscious of this requirement, 4.8 inch height cards are still commonly available and XT users should thus exercise some caution when selecting expansion hardware.

Another difficulty is that some XT cards may fail to operate in AT equipment due to interrupt, DMA, addressing or other problems. In fairness, most manufacturers of adapters and expansion cards provide very clear indications of the systems with which their products are compatible. In any event, it is always wise to check with a manufacturer or distributor concerning compatibility of a card with a particular microcomputer system.

With the exception of the eighth slot in the XT, the position in which an adapter or expansion card is placed should be unimportant. In most cases, this does hold true, however, in certain circumstances it is worth considering in which slot one should place a card. The most important factor that should be taken into account is ventilation.

TIP

Where cards are tightly packed together (particularly where ribbon cables may reduce airflow in the space between expansion cards) it is wise to optimise arrangements for cooling. Boards which are tightly packed with heat producing components should be located in the positions around which air flow can be expected to be the greatest. This generally applies to the sixth, seventh or eighth slot in a system fitted with a fan. Furthermore, when introducing a new card to a system, it may be worth rearranging those cards which are already fitted in order to promote the unimpeded flow of air.

TIP

To minimise noise and glitches on the supply rails, it is usually beneficial to place boards which make large current demands or switch rapidly, in close proximity to the power supply (i.e. in slots six, seven and eight). This precaution can be instrumental in reducing supply borne disturbances (glitches) and can also help to improve overall system integrity and reliability.

TIP

Whilst timing is rarely a critical issue, some advantages can accrue from placing cards as close to the CPU (and coprocessor) as possible. Expansion memory cards should, therefore, be fitted in slot positions six, seven and eight in preference to positions one, two and three. In some cases this precaution may be instrumental in improving overall memory access times and avoiding parity errors.

The 62-way ISA expansion bus connector

The 62-way PC expansion bus connector is a direct edge-type fitted to the system motherboard. One side of the connector is referred to as A (lines are numbered A1 to A31) whilst the other is referred to as B (lines are numbered B1 to B31). The address and data bus lines are grouped together on the A-side of the connector whilst the control bus and power rails occupy the B-side (see Figure 9.2).

TIP

It is important to be aware that some early PC expansion bus pin numbering systems did not use letters A and B to distinguish the two sides of the expansion bus connector. In such cases odd numbered lines (1 to 61) formed one side of the connector whilst even numbered lines (2 to 62) formed the other.

Table 9.2 describes each of the signals present on the 62-way expansion bus connector.

Table 9.2 Signals present on the 62-way ISA bus connector

Pin No.	Abbrev.	Direction	Signal	Function
A1	IOCHK	I	I/O Channel check	Taken low to indicate a parity error in a memory or I/O device
A2	D7	I/O	Data line 7	Data bus line
A3	D6	I/O	Data line 6	Data bus line
A4	D5	I/O	Data line 5	Data bus line
A5	D4	I/O	Data line 4	Data bus line
A6	D3	I/O	Data line 3	Data bus line
A7	D2	I/O	Data line 2	Data bus line
A8	D1	I/O	Data line 1	Data bus line
A9	D0	I/O	Data line 0	Data bus line
A10	IOCHRDY	I	I/O channel ready	Pulsed low by a slow memory or I/O device to signal that it is not ready for data transfer
A11	AEN	O	Address enable	Issued by the DMA controller to indicate that a DMA cycle is in progress. Disables port I/O during a DMA operation in which IOR AND IOW may be asserted

Table 9.2 Continued

Pin No.	Abbrev.	Direction	Signal	Function
A12	A19	I/O	Address line 19	Address bus line
A13	A18	I/O	Address line 18	Address bus line
A14	A17	I/O	Address line 17	Address bus line
A15	A16	I/O	Address line 16	Address bus line
A16	A15	I/O	Address line 15	Address bus line
A17	A14	I/O	Address line 14	Address bus line
A18	A13	I/O	Address line 13	Address bus line
A19	A12	I/O	Address line 12	Address bus line
A20	A11	I/O	Address line 11	Address bus line
A21	A10	I/O	Address line 10	Address bus line
A22	A9	I/O	Address line 9	Address bus line
A23	A8	I/O	Address line 8	Address bus line
A24	A7	I/O	Address line 7	Address bus line
A25	A6	I/O	Address line 6	Address bus line
A26	A5	I/O	Address line 5	Address bus line
A27	A4	I/O	Address line 4	Address bus line
A28	A3	I/O	Address line 3	Address bus line
A29	A2	I/O	Address line 2	Address bus line
A30	A1	I/O	Address line 1	Address bus line
A31	A0	I/O	Address line 0	Address bus line
B1	GND	n.a.	Ground	Ground/common 0V
B2	RESET	O	Reset	When taken high this signal resets all expansion cards
B3	+5V	n.a.	+5V d.c.	Supply voltage rail
B4	IRQ2	I	Interrupt request level 2	Interrupt request (highest priority)
B5	–5V	n.a.	–5V d.c.	Supply voltage rail
B6	DRQ2	I	Direct memory accress request level 2	Taken high when a DMA transfer is required. The signal remains high until the corresponding DACK line goes low
B7	–12V	n.a.	–12V d.c.	Supply voltage rail
B8	0WS	I	Zero wait state	Indicates to the CPU that the present bus cycle can be completed without inserting any additional wait cycles
B9	+12V	n.a.	+12V d.c.	Supply voltage rail
B10	GND	n.a.	Ground	Ground/common 0V

Table 9.2 Continued

Pin No.	Abbrev.	Direction	Signal	Function
B11	MEMW	O	Memory write	Taken low to signal a memory write operation
B12	MEMR	O	Memory read	Taken low to signal a memory read operation
B13	IOW	O	I/O write	Taken low to signal an I/O write operation
B14	IOR	O	I/O read	Taken low to signal an I/O read operation
B15	DACK3	O	Direct memory access acknowledge level 3	Taken low to acknowledge a DMA request on the corres-ponding level (see notes)
B16	DRQ3	I	Direct memory access request level 3	Taken high when a DMA transfer is required. The signal remains high until the corresponding DACK line goes low
B17	DACK1	O	Direct memory access acknowledge level 1	Taken low to acknowledge a DMA request on the corres-ponding level (see notes)
B18	DRQ1	I	Direct memory access request level 1	Taken high when a DMA transfer is required. The signal remains high until the corresponding DACK line goes low
B19	DACK0	O	Direct memory access acknowledge level 0	Taken low to acknowledge a DMA request on the corres-ponding level (see notes)
B20	CLK4	O	4.77MHz clock	CPU clock divided by 3, 210ns period, 33% duty cycle
B21	IRQ7	I	Interrupt request level 7	Asserted by an I/O device when it requires service (see notes)

Table 9.2 Continued

Pin No.	Abbrev.	Direction	Signal	Function
B22	IRQ6	I	Interrupt request level 6	Asserted by an I/O device when it requires service (see notes)
B23	IRQ5	I	Interrupt request level 5	Asserted by an I/O device when it requires service (see notes)
B24	IRQ4	I	Interrupt request level 4	Asserted by an I/O device when it requires service (see notes)
B25	IRQ3	I	Interrupt request level 3	Asserted by an I/O device when it requires service (see notes)
B26	DACK2	O	Direct memory access acknowledge level 2	Taken low to acknowledge a DMA request on the corres-ponding level (see notes)
B27	TC	O	Terminal count	Pulsed high to indicate that a DMA transfer terminal count has been reached
B28	ALE	O	Address latch enable	A falling edge indicates that the address latch is to be enabled. The signal is taken high during DMA transfers
B29	+5V	n.a.	+5V d.c.	Supply voltage rail
B30	OSC	O	14.31818MHz clock	Fast clock with 70 ns period, 50% duty cycle
B31	GND	n.a.	Ground	Ground/common 0V

Notes:
(a) Signal directions are quoted relative to the system mother-board; I represents input, O represents output, and I/O represents a bi-directional signal used both for input and also for output (n.a. indicates not applicable).
(b) IRQ4, IRQ6 and IRQ7 are generated by the motherboard serial, disk and parallel interfaces respectively.
(c) DACK0 (sometimes labelled REFRESH) is used to refresh dynamic memory whilst DACK1 to DACK3 are used to acknowledge other DMA requests.

The 36-way ISA bus connector

The PC-AT and later machines are fitted with an additional expansion bus connector which provides access to the upper eight data lines, D8 to D15, as well as further control bus lines. The ISA AT-bus employs an additional 36-way direct edge-type connector. One side of the connector is referred to as C (lines are numbered C1 to C18) whilst the other is referred to as D (lines are numbered D1 to D18), as shown in Figure 9.2. The upper eight data bus lines and latched upper address lines are grouped together on the C-side of the connector (together with memory read and write lines) whilst additional interrupt request, DMA request and DMA acknowledge lines occupy the D-side.

Table 9.3 describes each of the signals present on the 32-way expansion bus.

Table 9.3 Signals present on the 36-way ISA bus connector

Pin No.	Abbrev.	Direction	Signal	Function
C1	SBHE	I/O	System bus high enable	When asserted this signal indicates that the high byte (D8 to D15) is present on the DATA bus.
C2	LA23	I/O	Latched address line 23	Address bus line
C3	LA22	I/O	Latched address line 22	Address bus line
C4	LA21	I/O	Latched address line 21	Address bus line
C5	LA20	I/O	Latched address line 20	Address bus line
C6	LA23	I/O	Latched address line 19	Address bus line
C7	LA22	I/O	Latched address line 18	Address bus line
C8	LA23	I/O	Latched address line 17	Address bus line
C9	MEMW	I/O	Memory write	Taken low to signal a memory write operation
C10	MEMR	I/O	Memory read	Taken low to signal a memory read operation
C11	D8	I/O	Data line 8	Data bus line
C12	D9	I/O	Data line 9	Data bus line
C13	D10	I/O	Data line 10	Data bus line
C14	D11	I/O	Data line 11	Data bus line
C15	D12	I/O	Data line 12	Data bus line
C16	D13	I/O	Data line 13	Data bus line
C17	D14	I/O	Data line 14	Data bus line
C18	D15	I/O	Data line 15	Data bus line

Table 9.3 Continued

Pin No.	Abbrev.	Direction	Signal	Function
D1	MEMCS16	I	Memory chip-select 16	Taken low to indicate that the current data transfer is a 16-bit (single wait state) memory operation
D2	IOCS16	I	I/O chip-select 16	Taken low to indicate that the current data transfer is a 16-bit (single wait state) I/O operation
D3	IRQ10	I	Interrupt request level 10	Asserted by an I/O device when it requires service
D4	IRQ11	I	Interrupt request level 11	Asserted by an I/O Device when it requires service
D5	IRQ12	I	Interrupt request level 12	Asserted by an I/O device when it requires service
D6	IRQ13	I	Interrupt request level 13	Asserted by an I/O device when it requires service
D7	IRQ14	I	Interrupt request level 14	Asserted by an I/O device when it requires service
D8	DACK0	O	Direct memory access acknowledge level 0	Taken low to acknowledge a DMA request on the corres-ponding level
D9	DRQ0	I	Direct memory access request level 0	Taken high when a DMA transfer is required. The signal remains high until the corresponding DACK line goes low
D10	DACK5	O	Direct memory access acknowledge level 5	Taken low to acknowledge a DMA request on the corres-ponding level

Table 9.3 Continued

Pin No.	Abbrev.	Direction	Signal	Function
D11	DRQ5	I	Direct memory access request level 5	Taken high when a DMA transfer is required. The signal remains high until the corresponding DACK line goes low
D12	DACK6	O	Direct memory access acknowledge level 6	Taken low to acknowledge a DMA request on the corres-ponding level
D13	DRQ6	I	Direct memory access request level 6	Taken high when a DMA transfer is required. The signal remains high until the corresponding DACK line goes low
D14	DACK7	O	Direct memory access acknowledge level 7	Taken low to acknowledge a DMA request on the corres-ponding level
D15	DRQ7	I	Direct memory access request level 7	Taken high when a DMA transfer is required. The signal remains high until the corresponding DACK line goes low
D16	+5V	n.a.	+5V d.c.	Supply voltage rail
D17	MASTER	I	Master	Taken low by the I/O processor when controlling the system address, data and control bus lines
D18	GND	n.a.	Ground	Ground/common 0V

Electrical characteristics

All of the signals lines present on the expansion connector(s) are TTL-compatible. In the case of output signals from the system mother-board, the maximum loading imposed by an expansion card adapter

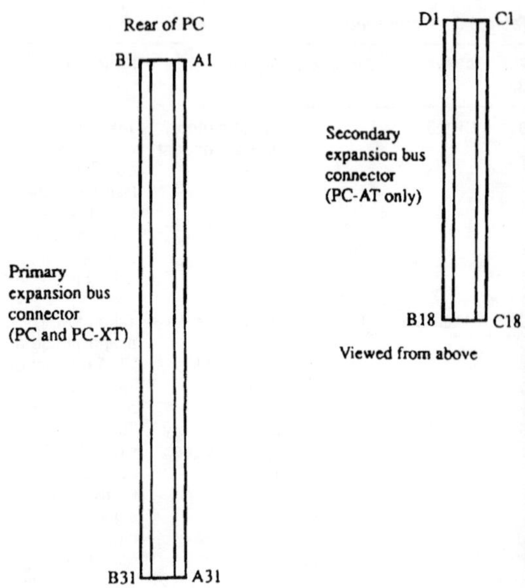

Figure 9.2 ISA expansion bus connectors

should be limited to no more than two low-power (LS) TTL devices. The following expansion bus lines are open-collector; MEMCS16, IOCS16 and 0WS.

The IOCHRDY line is available for interfacing slow memory or I/O devices. Normal processor generated read and write cycles use four clock (CLK) cycles per byte transferred. The standard PC clock frequency of 4.77MHz results in a single clock cycle of 210ns. Thus each processor read or write cycle requires 840ns at the standard clock rate. DMA transfers, I/O read and write cycles, on the other hand, require five clock cycles (1050µs). When the IOCHRDY line is asserted, the processor machine cycle is extended for an integral number of clock cycles.

Finally, when an I/O processor wishes to take control of the bus, it must assert the MASTER line. This signal should not be asserted for more than 15µs as it may otherwise impair the refreshing of system memory.

A word about power . . .

Problems sometimes arise when systems have been upgraded or expanded, often caused by excessive loading on the power supply. Under marginal conditions the system will *appear* to operate satisfactorily but it may crash or lock-up at some later time when the system temperature builds up or when one or more of the power rail voltages momentarily falls outside its tolerance limits.

As an example, consider a 'power audit' of a fairly typical system fitted with a CD-ROM drive and an internal modem:

The Intel Advanced/AS motherboard consumes 2.7A from the +5V supply rail, 0.12A from the –5V supply rail, 0.8A from the +12V supply rail, and 0.1A from the –12V supply rail. The total motherboard power (P_m) is thus:

$$P_m = (2.7 \times 5) + (0.12 \times 5) + (0.8 \times 12) + (0.1 \times 12) = 24.9W$$

A Western Digital Caviar hard disk drive consumes 1.1A from the +12V rail (at spin-up) and 0.2A from the +5V rail. The total hard disk power (P_{hd}) is thus:

$$P_{hd} = (1.1 \times 12) + (0.2 \times 5) = 14.2W$$

A Goldstar R580 CD-ROM drive consumes 1.5A from the +12V rail and 0.3A at +5V. The total CD-ROM power (P_{cd}) is thus:

$$P_{cd} = (1.5 \times 12) + (0.3 \times 5) = 19.5W$$

A standard 1.44Mbyte DSHD floppy disk drive consumes 0.4A from the +5V rail and 1A at +12W. The total floppy disk drive power (P_{fdd}) is thus:

$$P_{fdd} = (0.4 \times 5) + (1 \times 12) = 14W$$

An SVGA graphics card consumes 1A from the +5V rail, the power required being:

$$P_{svga} = (1 \times 5) = 5W$$

The internal modem consumes 0.5A from the +5V rail and 0.4A from the +12V supply. The total modem power (P_{mdm}) is thus:

$$P_{mdm} = (0.5 \times 5) + (0.4 \times 12) = 7.3W$$

Finally, a CPU fan is fitted. This fan consumes 0.2A from the +5V supply, the power required being:

$$P_{fan} = (0.2 \times 5) = 1W$$

The total demand on the power supply will thus be:

$$P_{tot} = P_m + P_{hd} + P_{cd} + P_{fdd} + P_{svga} + P_{mdm} + P_{fan} = 85.9W$$

The power supply must be rated at more than 85.9W. How much more remains debatable, however, it would be senseless to operate too close to the maximum rating. A sensible margin for safety would be to allow for a minimum of 15%, thus a supply with an output power rating of 100W should be considered as the smallest acceptable for use with this system.

Note that, as well as checking the *total* power, it is important to check that the current rating is not exceeded for any of the individual supply rails. For example, the system described earlier must have a +5V rail rated at more than 5.3A and a +12V rail rated at more than 4.8A.

TIP

Never attempt to connect or remove an expansion card (or anything else for that matter!) when the power is connected and the system is switched on. If this sounds rather obvious, I make no apologies for repeating it. In the heat of the moment it is all too easy to forget that a system is 'live'. Like me, you are only likely to make this mistake once – the cost and frustration will have a profound effect!

TIP

When planning a major upgrade to your system it is worth carrying out a 'power audit'. This can be done quite simply by noting the maximum rating of your power supply (in Watts) before comparing this with the sum of the products of current and voltage required by each individual system component (including motherboard, expansion cards, floppy disk drive, hard disk drive, CD-ROM and any backup device that may be fitted). You should consider upgrading the power supply in the event that the total loading imposed on it approaches (or exceeds) 85% of its rated power.

Resolving conflict . . .

When you add an expansion card to a system, potential conflicts must be avoided. This is because the existing hardware will be configured into I/O space with interrupt request (IRQ) and direct memory access (DMA) channels already established. It is vitally important that any new card does not disturb the existing configuration by attempting to use the same memory space, IRQ or DMA channels.

TIP

When fitting expansion cards you should always carefully check the I/O address, IRQ and DMA settings of your *existing* cards before you accept the manufacturer's default settings. In many cases the default settings will prove satisfactory but in others they won't!

Table 9.4 Signals present on the 116-way VESA VL-bus connectors

Pin No.	Signal	Pin No.	Signal	Pin No.	Signal	Pin No.	Signal
B1	DAT00	A1	DAT01	B30	ADR17	A30	ADR16
B2	DAT02	A2	DAT03	B31	ADR15	A31	ADR14
B3	DAT04	A3	GND	B32	Vcc	A32	ADR12
B4	DAT06	A4	DAT05	B33	ADR13	A33	ADR10
B5	DAT08	A5	DAT07	B34	ADR11	A34	ADR08
B6	GND	A6	DAT09	B35	ADR09	A35	GND
B7	DAT10	A7	DAT11	B36	ADR07	A36	ADR06
B8	DAT12	A8	DAT13	B37	ADR05	A37	ADR04
B9	Vcc	A9	DAT15	B38	GND	A38	WBACK#
B10	DAT14	A10	GND	B39	ADR03	A39	BEO#
B11	DAT16	A11	DAT17	B40	ADR02	A40	Vcc
B12	DAT18	A12	Vcc	B41	n/c	A41	BE1#
B13	DAT20	A13	DAT19	B42	RESET#	A42	BE2#
B14	GND	A14	DAT21	B43	DC#	A43	GND
B15	DAT22	A15	DAT23	B44	M/ID#	A44	BE3#
B16	DAT24	A16	DAT25	B45	W/R#	A45	ADS#
B17	DAT26	A17	GND	B46		A46	
B18	DAT28	A18	DAT27	B47		A47	
B19	DAT30	A19	DAT29	B48	RDYRTN#	A48	LRDY#

Table 9.4 Continued

Pin No. Signal	Pin No. Signal	Pin No. Signal	Pin No. Signal
B20 Vcc	A20 DAT31	B49 GND	A49 LDEV#
B21 ADR31	A21 ADR30	B50 IRQ9	A50 LREQ#
B22 GND	A22 ADR28	B51 BRDY#	A51 GND
B23 ADR29	A23 ADR26	B52 BLAST#	A52 LGNT#
B24 ADR27	A24 GND	B53 ID0	A53 Vcc
B25 ADR25	A25 ADR24	B54 ID1	A54 ID2
B26 ADR23	A26 ADR22	B55 GND	A55 ID3
B27 ADR21	A27 Vcc	B56 LCLK	A56 ID4
B28 ADR19	A28 ADR20	B57 Vcc	A57 LKEN#
B29 GND	A29 ADR18	B58 LBS16#	A58 LEAD5#

Notes:
(a) The B-side is the PCB track side.
(b) The A-side is the component side.
(b) # indicates an active low (asserted low) signal line.

Table 9.5 Signals present on the 62 and 94-way PCI bus connectors

Pin No. Signal	Pin No. Signal	Pin No. Signal	Pin No. Signal
B1 –12V	A1 TRST#	B48 AD10	A48 Ground
B2 TCK	A2 +12V	B49 Ground	A49 AD09
B3 Ground	A3 TMS	B50 Keyway2	A50 Keyway2
B4 TDO	A4 TDI	B51 Keyway2	A51 Keyway2
B5 +5V	A5 +5V	B52 AD08	A52 C/BE0#
B6 +5V	A6 INTA#	B53 AD07	A53 +3.3V
B7 INTB#	A7 INTC#	B54 +3.3V	A54 AD06
B8 INTD#	A8 +5V	B55 AD05	A55 AD04
B9 PRSNT1#	A9 reserved	B56 AD03	A56 Ground
B10 reserved	A10 +Vi/o	B57 Ground	A57 AD02
B11 PRSNT2#	A11 reserved	B58 AD01	A58 AD00
B12 Keyway1	A12 Keyway1	B59 Vi/o	A59 +Vi/o
B13 Keyway1	A13 Keyway1	B60 ACK64#	A60 REQ64#
B14 reserved	A14 reserved	B61 +5V	A61 +5V
B15 Ground	A15 RST#	B62 +5V	A62 +5V
B16 CLK	A16 Vi/o	B63 reserved	A63 Ground
B17 Ground	A17 VNT#	B64 Ground	A64 C/BE7#
B18 REQ#	A18 Ground	B65 C/BE6#	A65 C/BE5#
B19 +Vi/o	A19 reserved	B66 C/BE4#	A66 +Vi/o
B20 AD31	A20 AD30	B67 Ground	A67 PAR64
B21 AD29	A21 +3.3V	B68 AD63	A68 AD62
B22 Ground	A22 AD28	B69 AD61	A69 Ground
B23 AD27	A23 AD26	B70 +Vi/o	A70 AD60
B24 AD25	A24 Ground	B71 AD59	A71 AD58
B25 +3.3V	A25 AD24	B72 AD57	A72 Ground
B26 C/BE3#	A26 IDSEL	B73 Ground	A73 AD56
B27 AD23	A27 +3.3V	B74 AD55	A74 AD54
B28 Ground	A28 AD22	B75 AD53	A75 +Vi/o
B29 AD21	A29 AD20	B76 Ground	A76 AD52
B30 AD19	A30 Ground	B77 AD51	A77 AD50
B31 +3.3V	A31 AD18	B78 AD49	A78 Ground
B32 AD17	A32 AD16	B79 +Vi/o	A79 AD48
B33 C/BE2#	A33 +3.3V	B80 AD47	A80 AD46

Table 9.5 Continued

Pin No.	Signal	Pin No.	Signal	Pin No.	Signal	Pin No.	Signal
B34	Ground	A34	FRAME#	B81	AD45	A81	Ground
B35	IRDY#	A35	Ground	B82	Ground	A82	AD44
B36	+3.3V	A36	TRDY#	B83	AD43	A83	AD42
B37	DEVSEL#	A37	Ground	B84	AD41	A84	+Vi/o
B38	Ground	A38	STOP#	B85	Ground	A85	AD40
B39	LOCK#	A39	+3.3V	B86	AD39	A86	AD38
B40	PERR#	A40	SDONE	B87	AD37	A87	Ground
B41	+3.3V	A41	SBO#	B88	+Vi/o	A88	AD36
B42	SERR#	A42	Ground	B89	AD35	A89	AD34
B43	+3.3V	A43	PAR	B90	AD33	A90	Ground
B44	C/BE1#	A44	AD15	B91	Ground	A91	AD32
B45	AD14	A45	+3.3V	B92	reserved	A92	reserved
B46	Ground	A46	AD13	B93	reserved	A93	Ground
B47	AD12	A47	AD11	B94	Ground	A94	reserved

Notes:

(a) Pins 63 to 94 exist on the 64-bit PCI implementation only.
(b) Keyway1 exists on Universal and 3.3V boards but are Ground on 5V boards.
(c) Keyway2 exists on Universal and 5V boards but are Ground on 3.3V boards.
(d) +Vi/o is 3.3V on 3.3V boards, 5V on 5V boards, and define signal rails on the Universal board.
(e) # indicates an active low (asserted low) signal line.

10
Floppy disk drives

Floppy disks provide you with a means of installing programs on your hard disk, exchanging data between computers and backing-up the data stored on your hard disk. This chapter begins by introducing the most commonly used floppy disk formats and the structure of boot records and file allocation tables (FAT). It also describes the floppy disk interface and the functions of the PC's floppy disk controller (FDC). The chapter also explains how to remove and replace a floppy disk drive.

Floppy disk formats

A variety of different floppy disk formats are supported by PCs (see Table 10.1 and Figure 10.1). To help you select the correct type of disks for your drive, they are generally marked 'DSDD', 'DSHD', 'HD', 'ED' etc. If there are no markings, the presence of additional notches and windows (on 5¼" and 3½" disks, respectively) will give you some clue as to the media type. As an example, a 'high density' 1.44Mbyte 3½" disk has two small square windows on each side of the plastic housing. One window (fitted with a sliding shutter) is used to make the disk 'read-only' (i.e. it disables writing). The other window is used to indicate that the disk is a high density DSHD type. Optical sensors within the disk drive are used to detect the presence of the windows and configure the system accordingly.

When a disk is formatted, DOS writes a magnetic pattern on the surface of the disk. The pattern normally comprises 80 concentric 'tracks', each of which is divided into a number of 'sectors' depending upon the type of disk (see Table 10.1). The magnetic pattern is repeated on both sides of the disk (note that some obsolete disk formats are designed for 'single-sided' disks). In order to locate the data stored on the disk, DOS allocates numbers to the sides, tracks and sectors. In addition, DOS employs a basic unit of disk storage space known as a 'cluster'. Note that there are two sectors per cluster on a standard double-sided floppy disk formatted by DOS.

Table 10.1 PC floppy disk formats

Size	Formatted capacity	Media type	Number of tracks	Number of sectors	DOS support (from version)
5¼"	360Kbyte	DSDD	40	9	2.0
5¼"	1.2Mbyte	HD	80	15	3.0
3½"	720Kbyte	DSDD	80	9	3.2
3½"	1.44Mbyte	HD	80	18	3.2
3½"	2.88Mbyte	ED	80	36	5.0

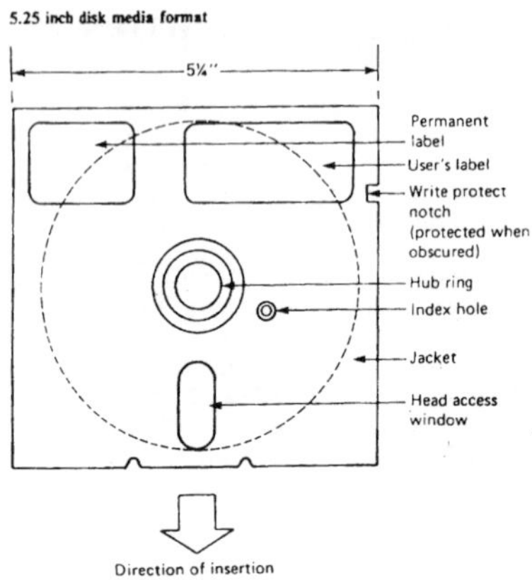

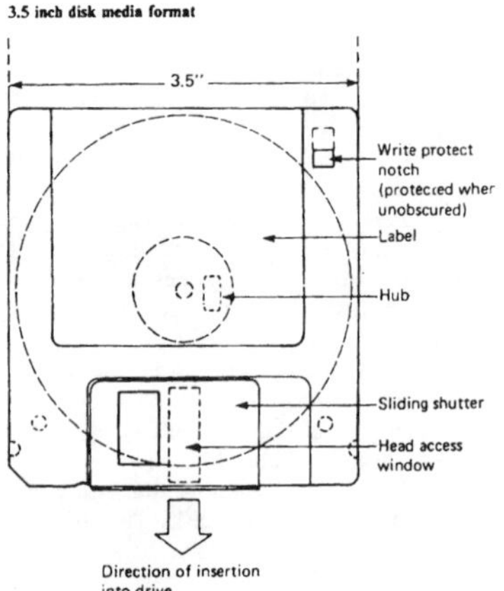

Figure 10.1 5.25" and 3.5" disks

TIP

Don't be tempted to buy cheap un-branded floppy disks. Such disks are often of indeterminate quality and may have been rejected as part of a reputable manufacturer's production test procedures. If you do need a source of inexpensive disks you are actually better off using 'second-hand' branded disks. These are available from various sources and simply require reformatting before use. Another source of cheap disks is out of date magazine cover disks. These can usually be purchased in quantity at reasonable cost from computer fairs.

TIP

Floppy disks sometimes become contaminated with surface films (e.g. due to liquid spills). If you need to recover the data stored on such a disk, you should first carefully remove the disk by prizing apart its plastic housing, and then rinse it under a tap with warm running water. Do not use cleansers or detergents. When the surface of the disk has been thoroughly rinsed, you should dry the disk in warm (but not hot) air before replacing it in its plastic housing. During the cleaning process it is important to hold the disk by the edges or by the central hub ring. You should avoid touching the surface of the disk. Once the disk has been reassembled, you should immediately attempt to copy the data to another disk or to a temporary directory on the hard drive (use **XCOPY *.* /S,** see page 194).

TIP

Problems often occur when you attempt to read a high capacity disk on an obsolete drive in an older machine which only supports lower density media (e.g. when reading data from a 1.2Mbyte 5¼" disk in a 360Kbyte drive). DOS will usually report an error as the drive will not be able to differentiate the data from several tracks at once. If you do need to transfer data from a PC with a 1.2Mbyte drive to another with only a 360Kbyte drive it is essential to ensure that you format your disks to the media capacity format of the smaller drives. The DOS FORMAT command provides you with the necessary 'switches' to do this. For example: **FORMAT A: /4** formats a 5¼" disk in a 1.2Mbyte drive A: to the 360Kbyte 5¼" disk format. Similarly, **FORMAT A: /N:9 /T:80** will format a 3½" disk to 720Kbyte when placed in a 1.44Mbyte drive.

TIP

During disk formatting, you may occasionally notice that the drive spends some considerable time towards the end of the process (the heads may appear to be stepping erratically). This is a sure sign that DOS has discovered some 'bad tracks' on the surface of your disk. If the problem is severe, the formatting will be aborted (this also happens if track 00 is found to be bad). However, if it is not severe, the format will eventually be completed but the disk may not deliver the capacity that you expect. In such a case, it is worth formatting the disk a second time. You should also use the DOS **CHKDSK** utility to reveal the number of bad sectors and the total amount of free space on the disk. Never be tempted to use a disk that is in any way dubious – throw it away and format another one!

The boot record

A floppy disk's 'boot record' (or 'master boot record') occupies the very first sector of a disk. The boot record contains a number of useful parameters as well as code which will load *and* run (i.e. 'boot'). Boot disks must also contain two other programs, IBMIO.COM and IBMDOS.COM (or IO.SYS and MSDOS.SYS). These, in turn, are responsible for locating, loading and running the command interpreter (COMMAND.COM).

The parameters contained in the boot record (see Table 10.2) include details of the disk format (e.g. the number of bytes per sector and the number of sectors per cluster).

Table 10.2 Contents of the boot record

Offset (dec.)	(hex.)	Length	Contents
0	00	3 bytes	Jump instruction
3	03	8 bytes	System identification
11	0B	1 word	Number of bytes per sector
13	0D	1 byte	Number of sectors per cluster
14	0E	1 word	Number of reserved sectors at beginning
16	10	1 byte	Number of copies of the FAT
17	11	1 word	Number of root directory entries
19	13	1 word	Total number of sectors on disk
21	15	1 byte	Media descriptor (see Table 10.4)
22	16	1 word	Number of sectors per FAT
24	18	1 word	Number of sectors per track
26	1A	1 word	Number of sides
28	1C	1 word	Number of reserved sectors

Booting the system

When a PC performs a 'warm boot' or 'cold boot' (using the <CTRL><ALT><DEL> keys or by pressing the 'reset' button, respectively), the ROM BIOS code initialises the system and then attempts to read the boot sector of the floppy disk in drive A:. If no disk is present in drive A:, the ROM BIOS reads the first sector of the hard drive, C:. Note that many BIOS set up programs actually give you the option of ignoring any operating system code that may be present on a disk placed in drive A: at boot-up time. In such cases, the system will only boot from the hard drive (i.e. drive C:). Disabling the drive A: boot facility has the advantage that any disk containing a boot sector virus (see page 160) will be ignored. Unfortunately, there is also a downside to this – having disabled booting from drive A: you will have problems when drive C: eventually fails and the system refuses to boot because it cannot locate the DOS system files! However, if (or when) this eventually happens there is no need for panic as all you need do is enter the BIOS set up routine to once again enable booting from drive A:.

The 512 byte boot sector is read into memory starting at absolute address location 0000:7C00. The BIOS code then checks the last two bytes of data (loaded at address 0000:7DFE and 0000:7DFF, respectively). If these two locations contain 55 and AA, respectively, the boot program jumps to 0000:7C00 (i.e. the start of the *image* of the boot sector in RAM). The CPU then continues by executing the boot code which has been loaded from the floppy disk.

On a 'system disk' (i.e. disks formatted using the DOS command **FORMAT A: /S**) the first three bytes of the boot sector are a jump instruction (EB 34 90 in Figure 10.2). This instruction is needed in order to branch forward, avoiding the disk parameters stored at the beginning of the sector (which do not, of course, constitute executable code).

Using Debug to display the boot record

Fortunately DOS provides you with a handy means of examining (and, if necessary, editing) the boot sectors of your disks. The MS-DOS Debug utility (see page 213) can be used to read any part of the disk into memory and then Debug will let you display the contents of the block of memory in question. You are thus able to examine an *image* of the disk's tracks and sectors.

This isn't quite so complicated as it may sound. As an example, suppose that you have placed a floppy disk in drive A: and you wish to examine the boot sector of the disk. The following Debug commands will load the boot sector and display the first 256 bytes of the boot record (see Chapter 14 for information on using Debug):

```
10001     (loads the boot sector into memory)
d01100    (displays the first 256 bytes of the boot sector)
```

(Note that, when entering these commands it is important to distinguish 'l' (for 'load') and '1' for 'one').

A typical result of using these commands (in this case revealing the boot record of a standard 1.44Mbyte floppy disk formatted using MS-DOS 5.0) is shown in Figure 10.2.

It is worth taking a close look at Figure 10.2. The 'offset' addresses are the rightmost four hex characters in the left hand column (i.e. 0000, 0010, 0020 etc.). The bytes of data (shown in hex. format in the 16 columns of data) are EB, 3C, 90 etc. The ASCII representation of this data is shown in the rightmost column (note that non-printing ASCII characters are represented by a '.').

The contents of the first three bytes are thus:

Offset:	0000	0001	0002
Contents:	EB	3C	90

These three bytes constitute the 80x86 jump instruction to the start of the DOS boot code (mentioned earlier). The next eight bytes identify the operating system that was used to format the disk. As this information is 'ASCII-encoded' you will find the ASCII display in Figure 10.2 somewhat more useful than the hex data! This will tell you that the disk was formatted under MS-DOS 5.0.

The number of bytes per sector is contained in the word at offset 11 (0B hex). The word (two bytes) is thus:

Offset:	000B	000C
Contents:	00	02

Don't be too surprised if this is not what you might at first expect; an 80x86 processor stores data in memory in 'low-byte-first' format. We need to reverse the data values to express them in 'conventional human' format. Hence the number of bytes per sector is 0200 hex (not 0002!). In other words, the disk uses the standard 512 bytes per sector.

If you continue deciphering the boot record you will find that the disk in question is formatted according to the parameters shown in Table 10.3.

```
C:\DOS>debug
-l 0 0 0 1
-d 0 1 100
1DD1:0000  EB 3C 90 4D 53 44 4F 53-35 2E 30 00 02 01 01 00   .<.MSDOS5.0.....
1DD1:0010  02 E0 00 40 0B F0 09 00-12 00 02 00 00 00 00 00   ...@............
1DD1:0020  00 00 00 00 00 00 29 F2-12 19 28 4E 4F 20 4E 41   ......)...(NO NA
1DD1:0030  4D 45 20 20 20 20 46 41-54 31 32 20 20 20 FA 33   ME    FAT12   .3
1DD1:0040  C0 8E D0 BC 00 7C 16 07-BB 78 00 36 C5 37 1E 56   .....¦...x.6.7.V
1DD1:0050  16 53 BF 3E 7C B9 0B 00-FC F3 A4 06 1F C6 45 FE   .S.>¦.........E.
1DD1:0060  0F 8B 0E 18 7C 88 4D F9-89 47 02 C7 07 3E 7C FB   ....¦.M..G...>¦.
1DD1:0070  CD 13 72 79 33 C0 39 06-13 7C 74 08 8B 0E 13 7C   ..ry3.9..¦t....¦
1DD1:0080  89 0E 20 7C A0 10 7C F7-26 16 7C 03 06 1C 7C 13   .. ¦..¦.&.¦...¦.
1DD1:0090  16 1E 7C 03 06 0E 7C 83-D2 00 A3 50 7C 89 16 52   ..¦...¦....P¦..R
1DD1:00A0  7C A3 49 7C 89 16 4B 7C-B8 20 00 F7 26 11 7C 8B   ¦.I¦..K¦.  ..&.¦.
1DD1:00B0  1E 0B 7C 03 C3 48 F7 F3-01 06 49 7C 83 16 4B 7C   ..¦..H....I¦..K¦
1DD1:00C0  00 BB 00 05 8B 16 52 7C-A1 50 7C E8 92 00 72 1D   ......R¦.P¦...r.
1DD1:00D0  B0 01 E8 AC 00 72 16 8B-FB B9 0B 00 BE E6 7D F3   .....r.........}.
1DD1:00E0  A6 75 0A 8D 7F 20 B9 0B-00 F3 A6 74 18 BE 9E 7D   .u.. .....t...}
1DD1:00F0  E8 5F 00 33 C0 CD 16 5E-1F 8F 04 8F 44 02 CD 19   ._.3...^....D...
-
```

Figure 10.2 Boot record displayed using Debug

TIP

The ability to load, examine (and modify) the boot sector of a floppy disk can be extremely useful. If you wish to modify the contents of a boot sector (or a FAT) it is *essential* to make a backup copy of the disk *before* you make any changes. The penalty for ignoring this advice is that you might find that you can no longer access the information stored on the disk in question – DOS can be an extremely efficient policeman!

Table 10.3 Typical boot sector parameters for a 1.44Mbyte floppy disk

Operating system	MS-DOS 5.0
Bytes per sector	512
Sectors per cluster	1
Number of reserved sectors	1
Number of FAT copies	2
Number of root directory entries	224
Total number of sectors	2880
Media descriptor	F0 (i.e. 1.44Mbyte)
Sectors per FAT	9
Sectors per track	18
Number of sides	2
Reserved sectors	0

The file allocation table

Each disk contains a 'file allocation table' (or FAT) which keeps a record of where the data is stored on the surface of the disk. As the FAT is crucial to being able to successfully locate the data stored on the disk, DOS keeps more than one copy of it. If one copy of the FAT is damaged or corrupted, the other may still be readable.

There are two different types of FAT distinguished by the length of the entries. The more common 12-bit format used on floppy disks and some older (and smaller) hard disks, uses three nibbles (three 4-bit hex characters) to identify the cluster numbers whilst the 16-bit format (used by larger hard disks) employs a single 16-bit word (four 4-bit hex characters) to represent the cluster numbers.

Special characters are used in the FAT to denote features such as unusable clusters (sectors which have been identified as 'bad tracks' during formatting), available clusters, and the last cluster in each file.

Media descriptors

DOS recognises the type of disk and drive by means of a single byte code known as a 'media descriptor' (see Table 10.4). The media descriptor is placed in the first byte of the disk's FAT.

Table 10.4 DOS media descriptors

Disk capacity	**DOS media descriptor**
160Kbyte	FE
180Kbyte	FC
320Kbyte	FF
360Kbyte	FD
720Kbyte or 1.2Mbyte	F9
1.44Mbyte or 2.88Mbyte	F0
Hard disk	F8

Using Debug to display the FAT

You can use the MS-DOS Debug utility to display the contents of a disk's FAT in just the same way as you can show the boot record.

Assuming that the disk is placed in drive A:, the following Debug commands will load and display the FAT (see Chapter 14 for information on using Debug):

```
l100011       (loads the FAT into memory)
d1001100      (displays 256 bytes of the FAT)
```

(Once again it is worth noting that, when entering these commands it is important to distinguish 'l' (for 'load') and '1' for 'one').

A typical result of using these commands to display the FAT from that of a 1.44Mbyte floppy disk formatted using MS-DOS 5.0 is shown in Figure 10.3.

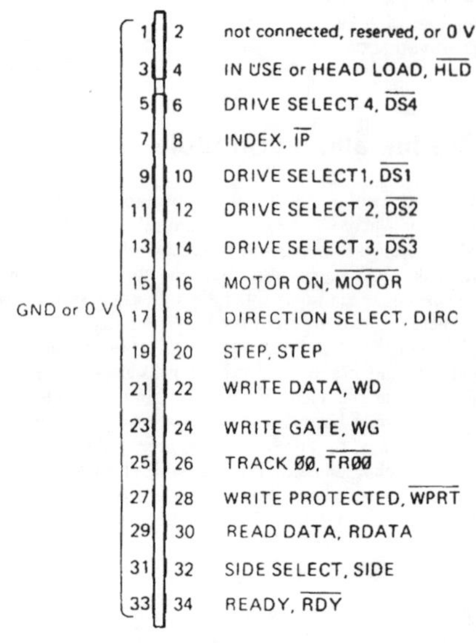

Figure 10.3 Disk drive pin connectors

Floppy disk controllers

The floppy disk interface is managed by a dedicated VLSI device, the floppy disk controller (FDC). This chip manages the storage and retrieval of data in the sectors and tracks which are written to the disk during the formatting process. The FDC is thus an extremely complex device, being capable of both formatting the disk (acting upon instructions from the DOS FORMAT utility, see page 192) and then writing/reading the data on it.

The DOS and FDC act in concert to translate requests for logical files into physical tracks and sectors and also to maintain the FAT and disk directory. The FDC has various dedicated functions, which include:

1. Formatting the disk with the required number of tracks and sectors as determined by the DOS.
2. Accepting commands issued by DOS and translating these to appropriate actions within the disk drive, such as positioning the read/write head.
3. Maintaining various internal registers that:

   (a) reflect the current status of the controller

   (b) indicate the current track over which the read/write head is positioned

   (c) hold the address of the desired sector position.

   Note that copies of the FDC status are held within the system RAM area (see page 135).

4. Providing an interface to the system bus so that:

   (a) during the write process, incoming parallel data from the bus is converted into a serial self-clocking data stream for writing to the floppy disk

   (b) during the read process, incoming serial data from the floppy disk is separated from the accompanying clock, and fed to a serial-to-parallel shift register before outputting to the data bus.

5. Generating the necessary cyclic redundancy check (CRC) characters and appending these to the write data stream at the appropriate time.

The floppy disk bus

Each disk drive contains its own interface to the bus, which links all the drives in a system to the disk adapter and its FDC. The floppy disk bus uses a 34-way connector, the 17 odd-numbered lines of which are common ground. The typical designation and function of the signal lines are shown in Table 10.5. It should be noted that since the drive requires an appreciable current, the +12V and +5V power lines employ a separate 4-way connector.

Table 10.5 Floppy disk bus pin connections

Pin no.	Designation	Meaning	Function
2	n.c.	Not connected	
4	HEADLOAD	Head Load	Output from FDC, active low, when asserted it activates the head load solenoid
6	DS4	Drive Select 4	Output from FDC, active low, when asserted it activates the fourth drive
8	INDEX	Index	Input to FDC, active low, when asserted it indicates that the index hole has been detected by the appropriate sensor

Table 10.5 Continued

Pin no.	Designation	Meaning	Function
10	DS1	Drive Select 1	Output from FDC, active low, when asserted it activates the first drive
12	DS2	Drive Select 2	Output from FDC, active low, when asserted it activates the second drive
14	DS3	Drive Select 3	Output from FDC, active low, when asserted it activates the third drive
16	MOTOR ON	Motor on	Output from FDC, active low, when asserted it turns the drive motor on
18	DIRC	Direction	Output from FDC, selects direction of head stepping, the head steps outwards when high and inwards when low
20	STEP	Step	Output from FDC, steps the head on a rising edge pulse
22	WRITE DATA	Write data	Output from FDC, inactive high, pulsed low when data is written to the disk
24	WRITE GATE	Write gate	Output from FDC, write when low and read when high
26	TRACK 00	Track zero	Input to FDC, low when the head is positioned over track zero (the outermost track)
28	WRITE PROT	Write protect	Input to FDC, active low
30	READ DATA	Read data	Input to FDC, inactive high, pulsed low when data is read from the disk
32	SIDE SELECT	Side select	Output from FDC, side select 0 or 1
34	READY	Ready	Input to FDC, active low, when asserted indicates that the drive is ready for a read or write operation

Note: There are some minor variations in the names given to the various lines and, in particular, drive selects are often numbered DS0 to DS3 rather than DS1 to DS4, HEAD LOAD and READY signals are not always provided.

Disk drive troubleshooting

Troubleshooting disk drives can be just a complex a task as that associated with the system board. In addition, it must be recognised that the drive contains highly sophisticated electronic and mechanical components which require both careful and sympathetic handling. Hence it is recommended that, at least for the inexperienced reader, consideration be given to returning drives for overhaul and service by the manufacturer or importer as this may be more cost-effective in the long run. In any event, fault diagnosis within drives should only be carried out when one is certain that the disk interface and controller can be absolved from blame. Thus, whenever the drive in a single-drive system is suspect, it should first be replaced by a unit that is known to be good. In a two drive system it will, of course, be relatively easy to recognise a failure within one or other of the drives. Even so, it is worth interchanging the two drives before attempting to dismantle the suspect unit.

TIP

Floppy disk drives have links, jumpers or selectors which identify them as a particular drive in the system (i.e. A: or B:). The jumpers are usually located in a fairly obvious position at the rear of the drive close to the PCB edge connector. On 5.25" floppy drives, the jumpers are variously marked 'DS0, DS1, DS2, DS3', 'D1, D2, D3, D4', or 'DS1, DS2, DS3, DS4'. On 3½" disk drives the jumpers will usually be marked 'DS0, DS1' or 'D0, D1' (this is simply because the PC normally supports up to two floppy drives, A: and B:). The lowest numbered link position will correspond to drive A: and so on. Note that only one of these links should be in place on any particular drive. Furthermore, if you have a two-drive system, the drive select links must identify the two drives differently, i.e. one drive must be configured as drive A: (with the *lowest* numbered link fitted) while the other should be drive B: (with the *next lowest* number link fitted). If you ever have to swap drives around for test purposes don't forget to also change over the drive select links. There is, however, a notable exception to all of this which relates to IBM AT-systems and compatibles which use the so-called 'twisted' floppy cable. This cable can easily be recognised as part of the ribbon will have been cut, then separated and twisted in order to swap several of the connections over. The result is simply that the cable makes the two drives *appear* different to the system even if they both use the same drive select links. The furthermost drive will normally be A: whilst the drive on the other side of the twist will be B:. Both may be fitted with their drive select links in the second lowest numbered position.

The read/write heads

Great care should be exercised whenever operating on or near the read/write heads. These are the single most expensive component within the drive and are easily damaged. Fortunately, head adjustment is normally only required when either:

(a) the head itself, or

(b) the assembly on which the head is mounted, is replaced, or a particular drive is found to be incompatible with others when disks are exchanged.

Alignment requires the use of a special tool in conjunction with an analogue alignment disk and an oscilloscope. The alignment disk usually contains both continuous tones and bursts of tones which are used respectively to adjust radial alignment and azimuth. Fortunately, alignment disks are normally supplied with full instructions showing typical display patterns. These disks will normally allow you to perform the following operations:

(a) accurately locate track 00

(b) adjust the index timing and hence check motor speed

(c) check the skew error of the head positioning mechanism

(d) align the head positioning mechanism with the track centre line

(e) verify read output for correct head-to-disk compliance

(f) check the head azimuth.

TIP

Modern 3½" disk drives are so inexpensive that it is not usually cost-effective to carry out any repairs or head adjustments on them and many floppy disk drives are discarded when they first begin to cause problems. That said, the most frequent cause of problems is simply an accumulation of dust, dirt and oxide on the read/write heads. Thorough cleaning is all that is required to put this right!

The read/write heads of disk units require regular cleaning to ensure trouble-free operation. In use, the disk surface is prone to environmental contaminants such as smoke, airborne dust, oils and fingerprints, and these can be transferred to the read/write heads along with oxide particles from the coating of the disk itself. Periodic cleaning is thus essential and, although this can easily be carried out by untrained personnel using one of several excellent head cleaning kits currently available, head cleaning is rarely given the priority it deserves. Thus, whenever a PC is being overhauled, routine cleaning of the heads may be instrumental in helping to avoid future problems.

TIP

The read/write heads of a floppy disk drive are permanently in contact with the disk surface when the disk is in use. The heads can thus easily become contaminated with particles of dust and magnetic oxide. You can avoid this problem by cleaning your read/write heads regularly using a proprietary head cleaning disk and cleaning fluid. As a rough guide, you should clean the heads every month if you use your system for two, or more hours each day.

Replacing a floppy disk drive

The procedure for removing and replacing a floppy disk drive is quite straightforward. You should adopt the following procedure:

1. Power-down and gain access to the interior of the system unit (as described in Chapter 3).
2. Locate the drive in question and remove the disk-drive power and floppy disk bus connectors from the rear of the drive.
3. Remove the retaining screws from the sides of the drive (four screws are usually fitted). In the case of the older AT-style system units in which the drives are mounted using plastic guides, you should remove the two retaining screws and metal tabs at the front of the system chassis.
4. Once the drive chassis is free, it can be gently withdrawn from the system unit. Any metal screening can now be removed in order to permit inspection. The majority of the drive electronics (read/write amplifiers, bus buffers and drivers) normally occupies a single PCB on one side of the drive.
5. The head load solenoid, head assembly and mechanical parts should now be clearly visible and can be inspected for signs of damage or wear. Before reassembly, the heads should be thoroughly inspected and cleaned using a cotton bud and proprietary alcohol-based cleaning solvent.
6. Re-assemble the system (replacing the drive, if necessary) and ensure that the disk bus and power cables are correctly connected before restoring power to the system.

TIP

Take special care when replacing machined screws which locate directly with the diecast chassis of a disk drive. These screws can sometimes become cross-threaded in the relatively soft diecast material used to manufacture the exterior chassis of some drives (particularly older 5¼" drives). If you are fitting a new drive, you *must* also ensure that you use screws of the correct length. A screw that is too long can sometimes foul the PCB mounted components.

TIP

A 34-way male PCB header is usually fitted to 3½" drives. Unfortunately, the matching female IDC connector can easily be attached the wrong way round. You should thus check that the connector has been aligned correctly when replacing or adding a disk drive to your system. Pin-1 (and/or pin-34) is usually clearly marked on the PCB. You should also notice a stripe along one edge of the ribbon cable. This stripe must be aligned with pin-1 on the connector.

Diagnostic/alignment disks

For all but the most obvious mechanical faults in disk drives, software diagnostics quickly become essential. It is rarely possible to make meaningful assessments of the performance of drives without such an aid. Disk diagnostics vary widely in sophistication. As a minimum they should be capable of:

(a) Selecting a particular drive and verifying the operation of the disk controller by reading the status register.

(b) Performing step-in and step-out operations and testing for track 00.

(c) Reading and displaying the contents of a selected track.

(d) Writing a particular byte pattern in a selected track (or tracks), then reading and verifying the result.

(e) Measuring, and displaying, the rotational speed of the disk.

With some of the older types of drive it is wise to check the drive motor speed when a system is being overhauled since this can be instrumental in avoiding future problems. With older drives, motor speed adjustment is invariably provided by means of a small preset potentiometer mounted on the motor control PCB. Access to this control is often arranged so that speed adjustment can be carried out without having to dismantle, or even remove, the drive. The drive speed should be within ±3rpm of 300rpm and should always be adjusted whenever it is outside this range. With care, it should be possible to adjust the speed to within ±0.5rpm of the nominal 300rpm.

You can display the disk controller's status using a simple QuickBASIC program along the lines shown in Figure 10.4. This program displays the individual bits that indicate the status of the FDC (see Figure 10.5 and Table 10.6). A somewhat more comprehensive QuickBASIC disk drive test program has been included in Chapter 18.

```
DEF SEG = 0
CLS
PRINT "Disk controller status"
PRINT "Address", "Byte", " Status"
PRINT "(hex)", "(hex)", ;
FOR i = 7 TO 0 STEP -1
  PRINT i;
NEXT i
PRINT
PRINT
FOR address = &H43E TO &H443
  v = PEEK(address)
  GOSUB convert
  PRINT HEX$(address), HEX$(v), ;
  FOR i = 7 TO 0 STEP -1
    PRINT b(i);
  NEXT i
  PRINT
NEXT address
PRINT
END
'
convert:
x = v
FOR n = 0 TO 7
  b(n) = x - INT(x / 2) * 2
  x = INT(x / 2)
NEXT n
RETURN
```

Figure 10.4 QuickBASIC program that displays the FDC status

```
Disk controller status
Address         Byte          Status
(hex)           (hex)         7  6  5  4  3  2  1  0

43E             1             0  0  0  0  0  0  0  1
43F             81            1  0  0  0  0  0  0  1
440             25            0  0  1  0  0  1  0  1
441             0             0  0  0  0  0  0  0  0
442             4             0  0  0  0  0  1  0  0
443             0             0  0  0  0  0  0  0  0
```

Figure 10.5 Typical output produced by the program of Figure 10.4

Table 10.6 Disk status byte at address 0441

Bit number	Meaning
0	Set if an invalid disk command has been requested
1	Set if address mark on disk is not found
2	Set if sector is not found (this error occurs if the disk is damaged or has not been formatted)
3	Set if a DMA error has occurred
4	Set if a CRC error has occurred
5	Set if the disk controller is not responding
6	Set if a track seek operation has failed
7	Set if the disk has 'timed out' (i.e. failed to respond in a preset time)

TIP

Diagnostic programs, such as AMI's diagnostic software (sometimes supplied with a new system), will allow you to check the speed of a disk drive from DOS. The drive speed is displayed on screen as the drive is exercised – changes in speed can easily be detected.

Data compression utilities – zipping and unzipping

The 1.44Mbyte limitation imposed by the standard DSHD 3½" disk can be overcome by using a file compression program such PKZIP or WINZIP. Depending upon the type of file, such utilities will often reduce the size of a file by between 40% and 70% with a consequent saving in disk space. Typical facilities offered by a disk compression program (in this case PKZIP for Windows) are as follows:

Zipping (compression)

- create, open and extract from .ZIP archived or compressed files (PKZIP will also allow files to be added to an existing zipped archive)
- create self-extracting files and directories storing all attribute and sub-directory information within the .ZIP file
- select different levels of compression.

Unzipping (decompression)

- view files within .ZIP files
- unzip files by size, date, name or file type

- check data integrity by means of a cyclic redundancy check (CRC)
- extract files from .ZIP files that have been spanned over multiple disks.

TIP

Use PKZIP and PKUNZIP (or equivalent) to save files in excess of 1.44Mbyte to a standard DSHD 3½" disk. You can also use these utilities to group a number of smaller files into a single zipped file for archive storage.

Zip disk drives

Iomega's popular Zip disk standard provides a means of storing up to 100Mbyte of data in a removable disk which is only slightly larger than a conventional DSHD 3½" disk. A Zip disk drive can be added internally (in a vacant drive bay) or externally (different versions are available for connection to a parallel or a SCSI connector). Internal drives are connected to the EIDE interface in just the same way as modern floppy or CD-ROM drives. External drives are connected via a multi-way cable and a through-port facility is provided which allows a parallel printer to be connected at the same time as a parallel port Zip drive. Iomega are to be congratulated on the simplicity and versatility of this system which looks set to eclipse other low-cost backup and archiving systems.

11
Hard disk drives

Your hard disk drive provides a means of storing a very large amount of data which can be accessed virtually instantaneously. Not only does a hard disk drive provide more storage than a large quantity of high-density floppy disks, but it also transfers the data approximately 10 times faster. Unfortunately, the failure of a hard drive can be catastrophic – in many cases you may find that your precious data is totally irretrievable.

This chapter begins by introducing each of the most commonly used types of hard disk. It continues by explaining the process of formatting a hard disk and describing the structure of master boot records and partition tables. The chapter also explains how to remove and replace a hard disk drive.

Hard disk basics

Like floppy disks, the data stored on a hard disk takes the form of a magnetic pattern stored in the oxide coated surface of a disk. Unlike floppy disks, hard disk drives are sealed in order to prevent the ingress of dust, smoke and dirt particles. This is important since hard disks work to much finer tolerances (track spacing etc.) than do floppy drives. Furthermore, the read/write heads of a hard disk 'fly' above the surface of the disk when the platters are turning. Due to the high speed of rotation (typically 3,600 to 9,000rpm) it is essential that none of the read/write heads comes into direct contact with the area of the disk surface used for data storage.

A typical Western Digital 340Mbyte Caviar hard disk drive has two platters which provide four data surfaces. The drive is thus fitted with four read/write heads (one for each data surface). The read/write heads are all operated from the same 'voice coil' actuator so that they step in and out together across the surface of the disk. In addition, the innermost cylinder is designated as a 'landing zone'. No data is stored in this region and thus it provides a safe place for the heads to 'land' and make contact with the disk surface.

Sectors, tracks and cylinders

The physical parameters of the 340Mbyte Caviar drive are such that its innermost track has 56 sectors whilst the outer track has 96 sectors (each of 512 bytes). Since there are four heads, we can think of the data being stored in a number of concentric cylinders each comprising four vertically stacked tracks. The number of sectors per cylinder will be $4 \times 56 = 224$ for the innermost track and $4 \times 96 = 384$ for the outermost track. The total number of cylinders present is 2,233 whilst the total number of sectors is 666,600. Since there are 512 bytes of data stored in each sector the capacity of the disk will be $666{,}600 \times 512 = 341{,}299{,}200$ bytes. Dividing this figure by 1,024 gives the capacity in Mbytes. Thus the formatted capacity of the drive will be 341,299 /1,024 = 325Mbytes.

TIP

Considerable confusion is caused by hard disk manufacturers who insist in defining a megabyte (Mbyte) as 1,000,000 bytes (i.e. a decimal megabyte). In computing, a Mbyte is more usually defined as 1,048,576 (i.e. a binary megabyte). This fact explains why a nominal 2.1Gbyte hard disk might have a specified capacity of 2,035.6Mbyte whilst the DOS CHKDSK utility reports a size of 2,111.8Mbyte.

Unfortunately, the fact that the number of sectors varies according to the cylinder number poses problems as far as the system's BIOS is concerned. In fact, the BIOS would find it impossible to recognise every conceivable arrangement of cylinders, tracks and sectors. Instead, the BIOS recognises a 'logical' drive which has different parameters from the real 'physical' drive to which it relates. All that is needed is a table which performs the required translation from the 'logical' to the 'physical' drive and vice versa. This type of BIOS (prevalent in most recent computers) is known as a 'translating BIOS'. We shall explain how this works later in this chapter.

Seek time and latency

Seek time is the time taken for the heads to move to the cylinder in which the target data are stored. Obviously, this will depend upon which track the heads are positioned over before the seek command is received and which track they end up over. The fastest seek time corresponds to a moving from one track to next inner or outer track whereas the slowest seek time results from moving from the innermost track to the outermost track (or vice versa). This is sometimes referred to as the drive's 'full stroke'. The seek time quoted by the manufacturer or supplier is, in fact, an average time for a large number of requests to position the heads over a randomly chosen cylinder.

Once the head has been positioned above the desired cylinder it has to wait for the desired sector to appear before the data can be read. The time take for this to happen is called the 'rotational latency' and it should be obvious that this depends on the speed at which the drive rotates (on average, it will be equal to one-half the time required for one complete rotation of the disk platter). As an example, a rotational speed of 5,400rpm produces a rotational latency of about 5.5ms whilst a drive rotating at 7,200rpm exhibits a latency of about 4ms.

TIP

The time required to access data stored on a hard disk drive will be the sum of the seek time and rotational latency plus any additional time required to switch heads (i.e. the 'controller overhead'). In practice, the head switching time is very much smaller than either the seek time or the rotational latency and thus it can usually be ignored. For a modern drive, an average seek time of 14ms and a rotational latency of 4ms add together to produce a typical data access time of 18ms. The head switching of the controller adds only a mere 0.3ms, or so, to this figure.

Cache memory

All modern hard disk drives incorporate their own cache memory. This is usually used both when writing to the hard disk and when reading from it. The idea of cache memory is that it acts as a buffer between the relatively fast IDE (or EIDE) bus data and the relatively slow speed at which it is transferred to and from the magnetic surface of the disk. The organisation of the cache is crucial in optimising the performance of the hard disk drive.

Parking

When a drive is static or coming up to speed, the heads remain in the landing zone (note that it may take 5s or more for a hard disk to spin up to speed). When sufficient rotational speed has been achieved, the heads leave the surface of the disk and are then stepped across to the active part of the disk surface where reading and writing takes place. Finally, when the disk becomes inactive, the motor ceases to rotate and the heads return to the landing zone where they are 'parked'.

TIP

Some obsolete hard disk drives do not park their read/write heads automatically. You can, however, park the heads using a simple program that steps the heads to the innermost track. Thereafter, it is safe to switch the power off. A hard disk park utility (e.g. PARK.COM) can still be obtained from most shareware libraries.

TIP

You can have your read/write heads parked automatically after a predetermined period of inactivity by means of an automatic parking utility (e.g. AUTOPARK.COM from Sydex). This memory-resident program will park the heads after a period which can be set from 1 to 60 minutes (5 minutes is the default).

TIP

Never attempt to move a PC when the power is on and the system is active. A bump or knock can easily cause your drive's read/write heads to 'crash' against the oxide coated surface of the disk platters. If this happens, you may be unlucky enough to remove part of one or more of the tracks and your precious data will be forever lost!

Hard disk types

A variety of different hard disk types are supported by PCs including ST506 (MFM), RLL, ESDI and SCSI types. Since they all have different interfacing requirements, it is important to know which type you are dealing with. Typical data transfer rates and capacities for various types of hard disk drive are shown in Table 11.1.

Table 11.1 Typical data transfer rates and capacities for various types of hard disk drive

Interface	Data transfer rate (bit/s)	Capacity (byte)
ST506	0.1–1M	10M–20M
ESDI	1.2–1.8M	40M–320M
IDE	2–12M	80M–680M
EIDE	8–30M	540M–4.2G
SCSI	20–80M	1G–9G

ST506

Now well and truly obsolete, the Shugart ST506 interface standard was popular in the late '70s and early '80s and it became the hard disk standard to be used in the first generation of PCs that were fitted with hard disk drives.

The ST506 used 'modified frequency modulation' (MFM) to digitally encode its data. This method of recording digital information has now been superseded by 'run-length-limited' (RLL) encoding which uses the available disk space more efficiently. Note that MFM ST506 drives are normally formatted with 17 sectors per track whilst RLL drives generally use 26 sectors per track.

When RLL encoding is used, a limit is imposed on the number of consecutive 0 bits that can be recorded before a 1 bit is included. '2,7 RLL' uses strings of between 2 and 7 consecutive 0 bits whilst '3,9 RLL' is based on sequences of between 3 and 9 consecutive 0 bits before a 1 bit is inserted. 2,7 RLL and 3,9 RLL, respectively, offer a 50% and 100% increase in drive capacity.

ST506 drives, whether MFM or RLL types, require a complex hard disk controller card. Drives are connected to the card by means of two separate ribbon cables; a 34-way cable for control signals and a 20-way cable for data. Tables 11.2 and 11.3, respectively, show the pin control and data connections for RLL/MFM drives.

Table 11.2 RLL/MFM 34-way control connection

Pin No.	Signal	Pin No.	Signal
1	GND	2	Head Sel 8
3	GND	4	Head Sel 4
5	GND	6	Write Gate
7	GND	8	Seek Complete
9	GND	10	Track 0
11	GND	12	Write Fault
13	GND	14	Head Sel 1
15	GND	16	(Reserved)
17	GND	18	Head Sel 2
19	GND	20	Index
21	GND	22	Ready
23	GND	24	Step
25	GND	26	Drive Sel 1
27	GND	28	Drive Sel 2
29	GND	30	Drive Sel 3
31	GND	32	Drive Sel 4
33	GND	34	Direction In

Table 11.3 RLL/MFM 20-way data connection

Pin No.	Signal	Pin No.	Signal
1	Drive Selected	2	GND
3	(Reserved)	4	GND
5	(Reserved)	6	GND
7	(Reserved)	8	GND
9	(Reserved)	10	(Reserved)
11	GND	12	GND
13	Write Data+	14	Write Data
15	GND	16	GND
17	Read Data+	18	NRZ Read Data
19	GND	20	GND

ESDI

The 'enhanced small device interface' (ESDI) is an updated and improved standard based on the original ST506 interface. ESDI was first introduced by Maxtor in 1983 and its BIOS code is generally software-compatible with the earlier standard. You should note, however, that most ESDI drives are formatted to 32 sectors per track. Like ST506 drives, ESDI units require the services of a separate hard disk controller card. Both the ESDI and ST506 interface standards support up to four physical drives though usually no more than two drives are actually fitted. Tables 11.2 and 11.3, respectively, show the pin control and data connections for ESDI drives.

Table 11.4 ESDI 34-way control connection

Pin No.	Signal	Pin No.	Signal
1	GND	2	Head Sel 3
3	GND	4	Head Sel 2
5	GND	6	Write Gate
7	GND	8	Config/Stat Data
9	GND	10	Transfer Ack
11	GND	12	Attn
13	GND	14	Head Sel 0
15	GND	16	Sect/Add Mark Found
17	GND	18	Head Sel 1
19	GND	20	Index
21	GND	22	Ready
23	GND	24	Trans Req
25	GND	26	Drive Sel 1
27	GND	28	Drive Sel 2
29	GND	30	Drive Sel 3
31	GND	32	Read Gate
33	GND	34	Command Data

IDE

'Integrated drive electronics' (IDE) drives are designed to interface very easily with the ISA bus. The interface can either make use of a simple adapter card (without the complex controller associated with ST506

Table 11.5 ESDI 20-way data connection

Pin No.	Signal	Pin No.	Signal
1	Drive Selected	2	Sect/Add MK Found
3	Seek Complete	4	Addr Mark Enable
5	(Reserved)	6	GND
7	Write Clk+	8	Write Clk
9	Cartridge Chng	10	Read Ref Clk+
11	Read Ref Clk	12	GND
13	NRZ Write Data+	14	NRZ Write Data
15	GND	16	GND
17	NRZ Read Data+	18	NRZ Read Data
19	GND	20	GND

and ESDI drives) or can be connected directly to the system motherboard where the requisite 40-way IDC connector has been made available by the manufacturer.

In either case, the 40-way ISA bus extension is sometimes known as an 'AT Attachment' (ATA). This interface is simply a subset of the standard ISA bus signals and it can support up to two IDE drives in a 'daisy-chain' fashion (i.e. similar to that used for floppy disk drives). This makes IDE drives extremely cost-effective since they dispense with the complex hard disk controller/adapter card required by their predecessors.

IDE drives are 'low-level formatted' with a pattern of tracks and sectors that are already in-place when they reach you. This allows them to be formatted much more efficiently; the actual physical layout of the disk is hidden from BIOS which only sees the logical format presented to it by the integrated drive electronics. This means that the disk can have a much larger number of sectors on the outer tracks than on the inner tracks. Consequently, a much greater proportion of the disk space is available for data storage. Table 11.6 shows the pin connections for IDE and EIDE drives.

Table 11.6 IDE/EIDE bus connection

Pin No.	Signal
1	RESET
2	GND
3	HD7
4	HD8
5	HD6
6	HD9
7	HD5
8	HD10
9	HD4
10	HD11
11	HD3
12	HD12
13	HD2
14	HD13
15	HD1
16	HD14
17	HD0
18	HD15

Table 11.6 Continued

Pin No.	Signal
19	GND
20	KEY
21	RESVD
22	GND
23	IOW#
24	GND
25	IOR#
26	GND
27	IORDY#
28	ALE
29	RESVD
30	GND
31	IRQ14
32	IO16#
33	HA1
34	RESVD#
35	HA0
36	HA2
37	CS0#
38	CS1#
39	DRAC#
40	GND
41	+5V Logic
42	+5V Motor
43	GND
44	TYPE (0=ATA)

Notes:

1. Pins 37 and 38 are used for the cable select option. If this option is enabled the drive number will be determined by whether the drive is attached to the first or second connector on the cable. A special cable is needed to utilise the cable select option.
2. If the cable does not have pin-20 keyed then pin-1 on the cable is determined by the red stripe on the edge of the cable. Many IDE cables have an insert in pin-20 of the cable connector to orient the connector correctly.
3. The control signals are the same for the 40 and 44-pin cables.
4. The 44-pin socket is often a 50-pin connector with two pins removed to clear the wall of the connector socket. The additional pins (A to D) at the drive end are reserved for manufacturers' use and are not connected to the host through the cable.
5. Signals marked # are active low (asserted low).

TIP

If you are fitting two IDE drives in a system, one drive must be designated the 'master' and the other must be the 'slave'. You can do this simply by setting a jumper (in one of three positions) at the rear of the drive. The jumper is not usually fitted when there is only one IDE drive present in a system.

EIDE

The enhanced IDE (or EIDE) interface takes the IDE interface one step further. EIDE is based on ATA-2 (a refinement of the original AT-Attachment standard). ATA-2 adds several features to the original standard, including faster PIO and DMA modes as well as an improved 'Identify Drive' facility. The ATA Packet Interface (ATAPI) adds further functionality to the ATA standard so that it can cater for other devices (such as CD-ROM and tape drives), not just hard disk drives. In addition, Logical Block Addressing (LBA) provides an improved method of addressing sectors on the hard disk. It is worth explaining how this works.

LBA is a method of linearly addressing the sectors on a hard disk. LBA addresses begin at cylinder 0, head 0, sector 1 (i.e. CHS 0,0,1). This is equivalent to LBA 0. Cylinder 0, head 0, sector 2 (i.e. CHS 0,0,2) occupies LBA 1 and so on.

Breaking the 504Mbyte barrier

A vast amount of confusing and often contradictory information has appeared in print concerning the so-called 504Mbyte barrier. This is often (incorrectly) attributed to MS-DOS. You need to understand how this problem has arisen and what actually imposes the limitation of hard disk size.

BIOS traditionally uses CHS addressing to specify the location of data on a hard disk. In itself this is not a problem, however, the size of the fields used to hold CHS data in the disk's partition table does imposes some limitations on the ultimate size of the hard disk that DOS can recognise. To put this into perspective, BIOS uses the following fields to specify the hard disk geometry:

- 10 bits to hold the total number of cylinders (maximum possible = 1,024 cylinders)
- 8 bits for the number of heads (maximum possible = 256 heads)
- 6 bits for the number of sectors (since sector numbering starts from 1 and not 0, the maximum possible = 63 sectors.

The maximum possible number of sectors recognised by BIOS will thus be 1,024 × 256 × 63 = 16,515,072. Since each sector can hold 512 bytes the maximum storage capacity of a hard disk under BIOS will be 8,455,716,864 bytes (or 8 Gbytes).

Unfortunately, that is not the end of the story. IDE hard disks have their own particular limitations. Once again, these arise from the way that CHS information is stored. The following fields are employed for CHS data for an ATA, IDE or EIDE hard disk drive:

- 16 bits for the cylinder number (maximum possible = 65,536 cylinders)
- 4 bits for the head number (maximum possible = 16 heads)
- 6 bits for the sector number (maximum possible = 63 sectors as for the BIOS).

Combining the two sets of restrictions (i.e. that imposed by BIOS together with that set by the IDE/ATA standard) leaves us with the following limitation on cylinders, heads and sectors:

- cylinders = 1,024 (upper limit imposed by BIOS)
- heads = 16 (upper limit imposed by IDE/ATA standards)
- sectors = 63 (no difference between BIOS and IDE/ATA).

The practical limitation on sectors is thus 1,024 × 16 × 63 = 1,032,192. With 512 bytes of data contained in each sector this implies a maximum storage capacity of 528,482,304 bytes (or 504 Mbytes).

In order to overcome the 504Mbyte barrier with CHS enabled in a modern hard disk (i.e. one with more than 1,024 cylinders) the 'translating BIOS' divides the cylinder number by an appropriate factor and then multiplies the head number by the same factor. This keeps the number of 'logical' cylinders within BIOS limitations but increases the number of 'logical' heads by the same amount. With LBA enabled, an appropriate LBA sector address is generated instead.

Having effectively overcome the 504Mbyte barrier we are still faced with the 8Gbyte upper limit imposed by BIOS. Unfortunately, this can only be overcome using extensions to a system's BIOS. Using a BIOS supporting 'extended INT 13 calls', logical block addressing can be made to handle hard disk capacities that are currently unheard of. Doubtless, advances in technology will eventually prove this last statement to be ridiculous!

SCSI

The only practical alternative to IDE and EIDE drives are those based on the 'small computer systems interface' (SCSI). This interface standard is not particularly new (it originated with the 'small minicomputers' of the late 1970's and early 1980's) but it does offer a powerful and highly flexible method of expansion which is particularly suited to mass storage applications.

SCSI is a local I/O bus which is commonly used to interface peripheral devices (such as hard disk and tape drives) to a host computer system. The SCSI bus supports a total of eight devices (including the host computer). Communication is allowed between two devices at any one time. Each device present must have its own unique SCSI ID (invariably selected by means of links or DIP switch settings).

When two devices communicate on the SCSI bus, the unit originating the operation is designated as the 'initiator'. The unit performing the operation, on the other hand, is known as the 'target'. Any desired combination of initiators and targets may be present in an SCSI bus system (provided, of course, that the total number of devices present does not exceed eight). Data transfers on the SCSI bus are asynchronous and follow a defined handshake protocol in which signals are exchanged on the Request (REQ) and Acknowledge (ACK) lines. The SCSI interface employs a total of nine control signals and nine data signals (including an optional parity bit).

TIP

With most SCSI drives, you will find an 8-pin SCSI ID selector fitted at the rear of the drive. You should fit jumpers to this selector in order to establish the ID for the drive in question. If you have more than one SCSI drive fitted they *must* have different IDs!

The SCSI connector

The SCSI interface uses a 50-way connector arranged in two rows, each of 25-ways. The connector pin assignment is shown in Table 11.7.

Table 11.7 SCSI bus connection

Signal	Pin No.
DB(0)	2
DB(1)	4
DB(2)	6
DB(3)	8
DB(4)	10
DB(5)	12
DB(6)	14
DB(7)	16
DB(P)	18
GND	20
GND	22
GND	24
Terminator power	26
GND	28
GND	30
ATN	32
GND	34
BSY	36
ACK	38
RST	40
MSG	42
SEL	44
C/D	46
REQ	48
I/O	50

Note:
1. All odd numbered pins, with the exception of pin-25, are connected to ground (GND). Pin-25 is not connected.
2. Pin-1 is marked by a triangle indentation on the 50-way connector.

Formatting hard disks

Formatting a hard disk is essentially a three-stage process but you do not always have to perform all three stages. The first stage of the process, a 'low-level' or 'physical' format, allows the drive to be configured for a particular hard disk controller card. The low-level format writes tracks and sectors on the magnetic surface and allocates numbers to identify their *physical* position on the disk. At this stage, the sectors may be 'interleaved'.

Interleaving

Although the 17 sectors of an ST-506 compatible hard disk are numbered 1 to 17, there is no reason why the sectors should be numbered *consecutively*. Indeed, there is a very good reason for *not* numbering them in a strict numerical sequence. It is worth attempting to explain this particular point.

A considerable improvement in data transfer rate can be achieved by not attempting to read the sectors of a hard disk in strict physical sequence. This is because the controller transfers one sector at a time and, when it is ready to read the next physical sector it is quite likely that the sector will have already passed under the read/write head. In this case it will be necessary to wait until the disk has completed a further revolution before it is possible to read the next wanted sector. A far better scheme would be to arrange the sectors so that the next wanted sector is one or two sectors further on.

In 1:1 interleaving (i.e. no interleaving) the sectors are numbered consecutively around the circumference of the disk. 2:1 interleaving numbers the sectors 1, 10, 2, 11, 3, 12 etc., and 3:1 interleaving uses the sequence 1, 7, 13, 2, 8, etc. Whilst 3:1 interleaving was once very commonplace, most modern hard disk drives are usually able to support an interleave of 1:1.

Performing a low-level format

There are three methods of performing a low-level format on an older non-IDE/EIDE hard disk drive:

(a) using formatting software supplied on disk and shipped with a drive and/or controller

(b) using the BIOS set up program when it includes a hard disk utility

(c) using a formatting program resident within the hard disk controller's ROM.

In the first case, you need only insert the disk in drive A:, run the program and follow the on-screen instructions. In the last case, you may have to use Debug (using a command of the form G=C800:5, or equivalent) in order to execute the code stored in the disk controller's ROM.

In all three cases you will have to specify information on your drive including its type, number of heads, cylinders, landing zone etc. You can usually also specify the interleaving that you wish to use.

With modern IDE/EIDE hard disk drives there is no need to perform a low-level format. Such disks are supplied with the low-level format already in place. Indeed, any attempt to impose a low-level format on such a disk can render it useless under a 'translating BIOS'.

Partitioning

Once a low-level format has been completed, you can partition a non-IDE/EIDE disk so that it behaves as several *logical* drives. Partitioning was originally invented to work around one of DOS's early limitations. This was simply that, by virtue of the 16-bit sector numbering system, early versions of DOS could only support a hard disk of up to 32Mbyte.

To put this into context, assume that you had a fairly average 80Mbyte capacity drive in a system operating under MS-DOS 3.3. You could arrange this drive with a 'primary partition' (C:) of 32Mbyte plus two further 'extended partitions' (D: and E:) of 24Mbyte each. Note that, whilst the extended partitions can be of different sizes, neither of the extended partitions should exceed 32Mbyte in size.

With the advent of MS-DOS 5.0 there was no longer any need to partition a large drive into several smaller logical drives. Subject to the '504Mbyte barrier' described earlier, you can have a single 'primary DOS partition' and no 'extended DOS partitions' (note that MS-DOS 5.0 and later allow you to have up to 23 logical drives within the extended DOS partition). The primary DOS partition can occupy the entire drive

TIP

In order to start DOS from a hard disk, the disk must have a primary DOS partition that contains the three system files; IO.SYS, MSDOS.SYS and COMMAND.COM. This partition must be made the 'active partition'. You can have up to 23 logical drives (D: to Z:) in the remaining 'extended DOS partition'.

TIP

DriveSpace, Stacker and SuperStor (and other popular disk compression programs) create a single very large compressed *file* which appears to DOS to be a logical drive (the *real* drive is renamed using another drive letter). For example, if you have a single drive with a limited physical capacity of, say, 120Mbytes, SuperStor will provide you with a logical drive C: of about 230Mbyte capacity. A small amount of uncompressed space must be retained on the original 'host' disk. It is important to note that the fake drive is actually a compressed data file, not a disk partition. DriveSpace operates in a similar manner, however, with modern hard disks it is often better to upgrade the entire drive rather than attempt to use data compression to gain more space.

Using FDISK

The DOS FDISK utility creates and displays information about partitions and logical drives. It also sets the active partition and allows you to delete partitions and logical drives. FDISK provides simple on-screen instructions. If the drive has been used before, it is worth displaying the existing partition information before you make any changes.

When you exit FDISK the system will restart and the new options will then take effect. If you have changed the size of your primary DOS partition, FDISK will prompt you to insert an MS-DOS system disk in drive A: (you can use the emergency boot disk described on page 154 for this).

After using FDISK you should use the DOS FORMAT command (see page 192) to format any partition that you have created or changed. If you fail to do this DOS will display an 'invalid media' error message.

TIP

FDISK destroys all existing files in the partitions that you modify. If you intend to use FDISK to change the partitions on your hard disk you must first backup your files to floppy disk.

TIP

If you are formatting the primary DOS partition of your hard disk, don't forget to transfer the DOS system files by using the /S switch within the FORMAT command. If, for example, you have created a primary DOS partition (C:) with two logical drives (D: and E:) in the extended partition, you should use the following three DOS commands:
FORMAT C: /S
FORMAT D:
FORMAT E:

The master boot record

Hard disk drives, like floppy disks, have a boot record which occupies the very first sector of the disk. On hard disks, this is known as the 'master boot record'. Apart from the basic parameter table, the structure of the boot sector is somewhat different from that used for a floppy disk.

You can examine the master boot record in the same way as for a floppy disk (see page 125). Note, however, that the Debug command to load the master boot sector for drive C: into RAM is:

1 0 2 0 1 (not 1 0 0 0 1 which applies to drive A:).

Booting the system

The master boot program (starting at byte 0) copies itself to a different location in memory and then inspects the partition table looking for a startable partition. If more than one startable partition exists or any Boot Indicator is not 80 or 0 then DOS will display an 'Invalid Partition Table' error message.

When the partition table has been successfully validated, the boot program obtains the Begin Head, Sector and Cylinder for the startable partition and reads it from the hard disk to absolute memory location 0000:7C00. It checks the last two bytes of the master boot record (55 AA) and then jumps to location 0000:7C00. From this point on startup is identical to booting from a floppy (see page 124).

The partition table

The 'partition table' starts at location 0000:01BE. This structure contains entries which have the format shown in Table 11.3. Like the master boot record, the partition table can be examined using simple Debug commands.

Hard drive troubleshooting

Failure of one or more of the read/write heads, the drive electronics, the voice coil actuator, or a major problem with one or more of the disk surfaces can render a hard disk drive inoperable. Furthermore, whilst many of these faults are actually quite simple, specialist tools, test facilities and a 'clean area' are essential if a hard drive is to be successfully repaired.

For this reason, it is wise not to attempt to carry out an internal

Table 11.8 The partition table

Offset	Size	Field	Purpose		
+0	1	Boot Indicator	Indicates if partition is startable, as follows:		
				Contents (hex)	**Meaning**
				00	Non-startable partition
				80	Startable partition
+1	1	Begin Head	Side on which partition starts		
+2	1	Begin Sector	Sector at which partition starts		
+3	1	Begin Cylinder	Cylinder at which partition starts		
+4	1	System ID	Identifies partition type, as follows:		
				Contents (hex)	**Meaning**
				00	Empty partition entry
				01	DOS FAT12
				02	XENIX
				04	DOS FAT16
				05	Extended partition
				06	DOS > 32M
				07	HPFS
				64	Novell
				75	PCIX
				DB	CP/M
				FF	BBT
+5	1	End Head	Side on which partition ends		
+6	1	End Sector	Sector at which partition ends		
+7	1	End Cylinder	Cylinder at which partition ends		
+8	4	Relative Sectors	Number of sectors before start of partition		
+12	4	Number Sectors	Number of sectors in partition		

repair unless you are *completely* confident that you can dismantle inspect, repair, align *and* reassemble the unit without a hitch. If you have any doubts about this it is better to return the unit for specialist attention.

Furthermore, modern drives offer significantly greater amounts of data storage and better overall performance than their predecessors and thus, in many cases, you will not wish to replace an older hard drive with an identical unit. On a 'cost-per-Mbyte' basis, modern drives are considerably cheaper than their predecessors!

TIP

Modern applications packages make considerable demands on your precious hard disk space. As an example, many Windows applications require more than 20Mbytes of storage and may require as much as 50–120Mbytes. Hence, as a general rule, you should consider *doubling* the hard disk space on any system that you have to repair. A failed 270Mbyte hard drive should be upgraded to at least 540Mbyte, a 540Mbyte drive by a 1.2Gbyte unit, and so on. If you (or the user) needs to further increase the storage then you could consider the use of a disk compression program. As a rule of thumb, this will roughly double the *unused* storage space again. Note, however, that disk compression is nowadays becoming less cost effective than purchasing a larger hard disk – the difference in cost between comparable 1.2Gbyte and 2.1Gbyte drives is now less than £40. Note also that the Windows 95 disk compression utility, Drive Space, will not compress a disk with more than 500Mbytes of data present.

TIP

In addition to compressing an entire drive, DriveSpace can use the free space on an uncompressed drive to create a new, empty compressed drive. For example, instead of compressing the entire drive C:, you could use 100Mbytes of free space on drive C: to create a new drive with approximately 200Mbytes of free space. Note that this 'drive' is actually a single compressed file (a 'compressed volume file' or CVF file).

Installing, replacing or upgrading a hard disk drive

The procedure for installing or replacing a hard disk is very similar to that which applies to a floppy disk drive (see page 132). The following procedure is recommended:

1. Power-down and gain access to the interior of the system unit (as described in Chapter 3).
2. Remove the hard disk's power and data connectors from the rear of the drive.
3. Remove the retaining screws from the sides of the drive (four screws are usually fitted).
4. Once the drive chassis is free, it can be gently withdrawn from the system unit (you may have to move cables around to clear enough space at the rear of the drive).
5. Verify the jumper configurations at the rear of the new drive. In particular, check the Master/Slave jumper settings (a Master setting will be required if the hard disk is to be the bootable drive – the Slave is not bootable and would normally be the second drive in a system fitted with two drives). If you are fitting the new drive as a second drive (not as a replacement for the first drive) you will also have to ensure that the original drive has its jumpers configured for operation as a Master.

6. Fit the new drive and ensure that the data and power cables are correctly connected before restoring power to the system.
7. Apply power to the system and, when the memory check has been completed, enter the CMOS set-up routine (on most systems you need only press the Delete key to do this). If the system BIOS supports a user programmable drive type you can enter the default parameters of the new drive (you will find the information in the handbook supplied with the drive or printed on the drive's label). If the BIOS does not support a user programmable drive type you should select parameters that most closely match those of your new drive. If you have a recent BIOS you may be offered the option of using the program to automatically detect the drive's parameters. This is usually quicker and more reliable than attempting to enter the information manually. Whatever method is used, once the parameters have been accepted you should ensure that the new data is written to the CMOS memory before you exit from the set-up program (the drive's parameters will not be stored and your drive will not be recognised if you fail to save this information).
8. Boot the system from a DOS disk boot disk that contains FDISK.EXE and FORMAT.COM. If you are installing a second hard drive you can boot from the existing C: drive (provided that it has been configured as a Master and then use the FDISK.EXE and FORMAT.COM utilities from the DOS (or other directory) on the existing hard disk.
9. Next you must use the DOS FDISK utility to set-up the partitions and prepare the disk for DOS. Then you must the DOS FORMAT command to prepare the disk for data. The procedure is slightly different depending upon whether the hard disk is the only disk present or whether it is the second hard disk in a system with two hard disk drives.

The following stages are required if the hard disk is to be *the only drive* in a system (in which case DOS will identify the drive as drive C:):

10. You will have booted from drive A: (C: will not be recognised at this stage). At the A:> prompt, type FDISK followed by <Enter>. At the menu options, select option 1 to create a DOS Partition. A second menu will now appear. From the new set of options select 1 to create a Primary DOS Partition. Select 'Yes' to make 1 large partition and it will automatically become active. Then quit out of FDISK.
11. At the A:> prompt, type FORMAT C: /S followed by <Enter>. This command will perform a high-level format on the drive and it will also transfer the system files in order to make the drive bootable. (Note that all modern IDE and EIDE drives are low-level formatted by the manufacturer and they *only* require a high-level format.)
12. When the format has been completed the new hard disk drive is ready for use. Remove the DOS disk from drive A: and press the reset button. If all is well, the computer should perform its full boot routine and you should be rewarded with a C:> prompt when the process completes. If not, check each of the stages from 5 to 11.

The following stages are required if the hard disk is to be the *second drive* in a system (in which case DOS will identify the drive as drive D:):

10. You may have booted from drive A: or from drive C: (D: will not be recognised at this stage). At the A:> (or C:>) prompt (assuming that FDISK.EXE and FORMAT.COM are located

in a directory listed in the PATH statement), type FDISK followed by <Enter>. At the menu options, select option 5 to switch to the second then enter Fixed Disk Drive Number 2. Next choose option 1 to create a DOS Partition, then select option 1 again to create a Primary DOS partition to option 2 to create an Extended DOS partition. Then quit out of FDISK.

11. At the DOS prompt, type FORMAT D: followed by <Enter>. This command will perform a high-level format on the drive and it will also transfer the system files in order to make the drive bootable. (Note that all modern IDE and EIDE drives are low-level formatted by the manufacturer and they *only* require a high-level format.)

TIP

One of the most common problems with hard disks is related to temperature. If you use your PC in an unheated room on a cold morning you may find that the hard disk does not operate correctly. You may also encounter similar problems when it is very hot. Problems can often be reduced by ensuring that the hard disk is formatted at the normal working temperature of the machine. In other words, before you attempt to carry out a hard disk format, you should wait for between 15 and 20 minutes for the machine's internal temperature to stabilise. Never attempt a format first thing on a cold and frosty morning or last thing in the afternoon where the temperature has been building up all day. The difference in these two extremes can be greater than 20°C and, like you, your hard disk may well not perform consistently over the whole of this range!

TIP

Never turn off your computer when it is performing a hard disk access (you should *always* check the hard disk indicator before switching off). Failure to observe this simple rule can cause many hours of frustration and may even require drastic action on your part to recover lost or corrupt data. If you are unlucky enough to be presented with a system which boots up with an error message relating to the hard disk or that tells you that there is no space available on the disk or that directories are missing or corrupt, it is worth trying to recall what happened when you *last used* the system. If you do suspect that something was not right when the PC was switched off (e.g. the user switched off while Windows was manipulating a giant swap file) it is worth running the DOS **CHKDSK** utility. If you discover a number of 'lost clusters' use **CHKDSK** again with the **/F** switch (see page 189) in order to convert the lost clusters to files and to update the disk accordingly. Having done this, you can examine the files (FELE0000.CHK, FILE0001.CHK etc.) using an ASCII text editor or word processor. If they contain nothing that is recognisable then you can delete them otherwise they can be renamed, saved and used to reconstruct the lost data file.

TIP

If your hard disk fails don't immediately rush to reformat the disk. There are several things that you can do before you resort to this course of action. If DOS does not recognise the existence of your drive you should use the BIOS set-up routine and check the CMOS RAM settings. If DOS recognises your drive but you are not able to either write to or read from it, you should use the DOS **CHKDSK** utility (see page 189) to gain some insight into the structure of the disk (or at least how DOS currently perceives it). It is also worth examining the master boot record and partition table for further clues.

TIP

It is well worth having an 'emergency boot' disk available in the event that your PC may one day fail to boot from the hard disk. Assuming that you have placed a blank disk in drive A:, you should enter the command **FORMAT A:/S**. This command will format the disk and copy the system files to it. If your DOS version does not copy COMMAND.COM to the disk when the **/S** switch is used, you should use the **COPY** command (see page 183) to copy COMMAND.COM to the disk. In addition, you may find it useful to also copy the following files (or their equivalents) to your emergency boot disk:

FORMAT.COM	(the first seven files will be found in your DOS directory)
XCOPY.EXE	
EDITOR.EXE	
FDISK.COM	
DEBUG.EXE	
DISKCOPY.COM	
CHKDSK.COM	
CONFIG.SYS	(your existing system configuration file)
AUTOEXEC.BAT	(your existing auto-execute batch file)

Armed with the above, you should be able to reformat and partition the hard disk (using **FDISK** and **FORMAT**), transfer files to the hard disk (using **XCOPY**), check the disk (using **CHKDSK**) and create/edit CONFIG.SYS and AUTOEXEC.BAT files). For good measure, **DEBUG** will allow you to examine the master boot record and partition table.

TIP

Windows 95 gives you an option to create a boot disk. This takes much of the effort out of having to perform this task manually. Place a blank, formatted disk in the floppy disk drive and select 'Settings', 'Control Panel' and 'Add/Remove Programs'. Then select 'Startup Disk' tab and click on 'Create Disk'. Windows will then copy the necessary files to the disk (starting with COMMAND.COM). If necessary, Windows 95 will prompt you to insert the original Windows 95 disk from which the required file can be obtained. Alternatively, Windows will ask you to specify an alternative location where the required file can be found. Once the process has been completed, you will have a floppy disk that can be used to boot the system when and if the hard disk fails.

TIP

You can improve file access times by using a 'disk optimiser' or 'defragmenter' utility. Within a DOS environment, DR-DOS 6.0 provides a useful tool (DISKOPT) that will perform this task. DISKOPT makes all files contiguous, moves all free space to the end of the disk and sorts all directories (if required). In Windows 95, the Defrag utility (DEFRAG.EXE) will perform the same task. Defrag will even operate in the background, leaving you to continue with your applications whilst it carries out the process of defragmentation. Before starting, however, Defrag will advise you if it is actually worth defragmenting the disk! Furthermore, if Defrag detects errors in the file structure on the hard disk, it will halt and invite you to run ScanDisk. ScanDisk will check the file structure on your disk and can automatically fix any errors that it encounters. ScanDisk is usually run before Defrag when performing a routine check on a hard disk drive. Both ScanDisk and Defrag can usually be found in the Windows directory of drive C:.

TIP

Windows 98 takes the art of disk optimisation one stage further with its 'Defragmenter Optimisation Wizard'. This utility tracks the programs that you run most often, then clusters these programs on the fastest part of your hard disk. To use the utility, you must close down all applications before launching the wizard. Once activated, the wizard asks you to specify the programs that you run most frequently. It then launches these programs and notes which files are accessed before moving them to their new location on the hard drive. Grouping files together minimises the seek time and ensures that your applications launch and run in the fastest possible time.

TIP

Take special care when replacing the screws used for mounting a hard disk drive. It is *very* important to use the correct length of screw. Internal damage can easily be caused by screws that are too long!

Recovering from disaster

Not only is it important to have a backup strategy but it is also important to be fully aware of the implications of that strategy. The secret of having an effective backup strategy is being able to accurately assess the risks that you might be subject to. Remember, too, that you are not just protecting against hard disk failure – other disasters can also render your data inaccessible!

Risk assessment

Consider each of the following possible scenarios:

(a) your hard disk suddenly fails and all the data stored on it becomes inaccessible

(b) your laptop computer is stolen and the police are unable to recover it

(c) your office, and all its contents, are destroyed by fire

(d) you discover that a virus has corrupted most of the files on your hard disk drive

In case (a) you would be adequately protected by a recent backup kept locally. Simply replace the hard disk drive and restore its contents from the backup device. Likewise in case (b). Case (c) is rather different – you will only be able to recover from this type of disaster if you keep a remote backup (or have a totally fire-proof safe!). Case (d) requires an effective virus recovery program – simply restoring your files from your most recent backup may only serve to re-infect your system!

Scenarios (a)–(d) are all examples of risks that you might have to face one day. There may be others that apply to your own individual situation. Only *you* can make a realistic assessment of these risks and how likely they are to occur!

Backup strategy

A backup strategy involves answering the following questions:

- what to backup?
- when to back it up?
- where to back it up?
- how to back it up?

What to backup? could include:

- all files (including hidden and system files)
- all data files
- all files in the My Documents directory
- all files created or modified since 1st June 1998
- all files modified or added since the last backup (i.e. an *incremental* backup).

When to back it up? could include:

- at the end of each working day
- at the end of each working week
- on the first and third Fridays of each month
- at the end of each month
- overnight, after close of business each Saturday
- after each new report has been completed.

Where to back it up? could include:

- to a set of floppy disks kept in the bottom drawer
- to a QIC tape stored in the IT department's fire safe
- to a Zip disk kept at the branch office
- to a network server in the company's computer centre
- to an FTP Internet site.

How to back it up? could include:

- using a single floppy disk drive and Winzip or PKzip to combine and compress files
- using floppy disks in drive C: and the DOS BACKUP or MSBACKUP utilities
- using an internal Zip disk drive and Iomega's proprietary Zip tools
- using an external Jaz tape drive and Iomega's proprietary Jaz tools
- using an integral QIC tape drive and Central Point's Backup
- using an external hard disk drive and Windows File Manager
- using a Travan or DAT external SCSI tape drive
- using Netware to upload compressed files to an Internet site.

TIP

An effective backup strategy for most users is to perform an incremental backup on a regular basis (daily or weekly) with a full backup (i.e. all files) performed on a less regular basis (weekly, fortnightly or monthly). It might also be worth considering the use of different types of media for these two operations (e.g. Zip disks for incremental backup and Travan or DAT tape for full backups). If you then store at least one of these backups off-site (together with an earlier 'Grandfather' or 'Father' copy of the backup made using the *other* media) you will have a very high degree of protection. If you do adopt a mixed strategy like this it is, of course, essential to label all of your backups so that you know which one is the most recent!

TIP

It can take some time to perform a dull backup during which your system may be unavailable for normal use. If this is a problem you should consider automating your backup so that it will be performed when you are out of the office (most good backup software will allow you to do this). Alternatively, you should make time in your working routine so that your system is able to perform the required backup operation on a regular basis.

12
Viruses

A virus is simply a program that has been designed to replicate itself in every system that it comes into contact with. It is more or less successful in this goal depending on several factors including the sophistication of the virus, the level of anti-virus protection present, and the 'habits' of the user.

Sooner or later all computer users have to come to terms with this particular nuisance. Don't think that it can't happen to you; just like hard disk failure it can and will happen to you sometime!

This chapter explain what a virus is and briefly describes the most common types of virus. It explains how your system can become infected by a virus as well as the simple steps that you can take to avoid infection. The chapter also describes the procedure for detecting and removing a virus from your system.

TIP

When your hard disk fails to boot or your system locks up for no apparent reason, don't always jump to the conclusion that you have a virus. In most cases you won't have!

Types of virus

Opinions differ, but conservative estimates would suggest that there are currently well over 2,000 known viruses in existence and many of these exist in a number of different strains. Some viruses originated more than a decade ago but may appear with monotonous regularity in a variety of new disguises. In addition, completely new (and often highly sophisticated) viruses appear from time to time. Table 12.1 describes the characteristics of some of the most common types.

Table 12.1 Some common virus types

Virus name	Virus type	Type of damage	Notes
AIDS	Trojan	Corrupts COM and EXE files and affects system operation	Several strains exist
Bad Boy	File	Self-installs in memory, infects COMMAND.COM, affects program and data files	Several strains exist

Table 12.1 Continued

Virus name	Virus type	Type of damage	Notes
Concept	Macro	A document infected with the Concept virus contains the macros: AAAZAO AutoOpen AAAZFS Payload When an infected file is run opened, the AutoOpen macro is run and it copies the virus files to the global macro file. During the copying process it changes the name of AAAZFS to FileSaveAs. Thereafter, whenever a file is saved, FileSaveAs copies the virus macros into the saved file	This is a demonstration showing how a macro virus can be created (also known as the Prank macro virus)
Darth Vader	Trojan	Self-installs in memory, infects COMMAND.COM, affects program and data files	
Dir2	Stealth	Self-installs in memory, infects COMMAND.COM and COM files	Programs increase in size by 1024 bytes
Form	Boot	Infects the boot sector of a hard disk when the system is booted from an infected disk placed in drive A:. Thereafter, the virus is loaded into memory whenever the system is booted and the virus code is then written to the boot sector of any floppy disk when that disk is accessed	Many variations exist – some causing other effects on set dates
Friday 13th	File	Infects COM files	Several strains exist
Gotcha	File	Self-installs in memory, infects COM, EXE and overlay files	Several strains exist
Jerusalem	File	Self-installs in memory, affects COM, EXE and overlay files	Programs increase in size by approx. 1700 bytes

Table 12.1 Continued

Virus name	Virus type	Type of damage	Notes
Michelangelo	Boot	Self-installs in memory, corrupts boot sectors	
Stoned	Boot	Self-installs in memory, corrupts boot sectors and then infects any floppy disks during subsequent disk accesses	Other variants include the Volga family of viruses. Also exists in stealth form
Tequila	Stealth	Self-installs in memory, infects EXE files	Programs increase in size by 2468 bytes
USSR	File	Affects COMMAND.COM, COM and EXE files	Various strains exist
Vienna	File	When executed, they search for .COM files in the current directory and the directories listed in the PATH statement, then write themselves to the end of each file	Various strains exist – some check the file's date stamp before infecting the file

Viruses tend to fall into one of several main categories depending upon their mode of operation (i.e. whether they attach themselves to files, overwrite boot sectors or pretend to be something they are not). The following main types exist.

Boot sector viruses

A boot sector virus copies itself to the boot sector of a hard disk or floppy disk. Boot sector viruses overwrite the original boot code and replace it with their own code. The virus thus becomes active every time the system is booted from an infected disk. The virus will then usually attempt to make copies of itself in the boot sectors of other disks.

Companion viruses

Companion viruses masquerade as an original program. They run before the program that acts as their companion – executing that program when they complete. This is sometimes referred to as a 'spawning' virus.

Software bombs

Software bombs are not really viruses. They are, however, a rather unpleasant form of malicious coding designed to cripple a program (or a system!) under a given set of circumstances (e.g. elapsed time, failure to enter a password). Unlike a virus, a software bomb does not attempt to replicate itself. It is simply embedded in the code to disable the software and/or the system on which it runs.

Software bombs can produce a variety of undesirable effects, some more unpleasant than others. The least problematic type simply erases itself from memory (together with any data that you were working on at the time). Others are liable to lock up your system (often until a cryptic password is entered) and some will delete programs and data files from your hard disk. The most extreme form of software bomb will effectively 'trash' your hard disk – yet another reason for making a regular backup!

Trojan horses

Trojan horses are destructive programs disguised as legitimate software. Sometimes these programs may purport to add some extra features to your system (e.g. additional graphics capability) or they may appear to be copies of commercial software packages.

The unwitting user simply loads the program (the user is often asked to boot the system from the floppy disk on which the trojan horse is distributed) and then some time later finds that things are not what they should be!

Stealth viruses

A stealth virus is designed to hide itself from any virus scanning protection that might be present. In an extreme case, the virus may be 'armoured' against the virus researcher trying to find out how it works and replicates itself.

Polymorphic viruses

A polymorphic virus is one which mutates each time it successfully invades a system. The changing nature of this type of virus makes them much harder to detect.

TIP

Beware the unsolicited disk that arrives in your mail. There has been at least one major case of a trojan horse distributed by an unscrupulous software company. Once installed this extremely unfriendly 'evaluation program' disabled your system and then invited you to pay for the privilege of purchasing an antidote. Until you did this, your system was unusable. The (very) small print that accompanied the disk did, in fact, warn users that they would be committing themselves to a very large cash outlay when they installed the software. This is one reason why I immediately trash any unsolicited disks that arrive in my mail and I strongly advise that you do the same!

Sources of viruses

Viruses can find their way into your system in a number of ways and from a variety of sources, including:

Bulletin boards

Unless managed correctly, an open-access bulletin board can be an environment in which a virus can thrive. Most good system operators arrange for regular or automatic virus checks. These can be instrumental in reducing the incidence of infection.

The Internet and World Wide Web

When you download software from the World Wide Web (or receive an executable file along with an e-mail communication) you run the risk of transferring a virus into your computer.

Networks

Like bulletin boards, networks must also be considered a 'public place' in which viruses can potentially thrive. Most network managers take steps to implement reliable anti-virus measures.

Magazine cover disks

Even the magazine cover disk that proclaims that it has been 'tested for all known viruses' is not always what it seems. There have been several cases of viruses spread by cover disks even though the disk was 'checked' before duplication. So how did this happen? The important phrase is 'all known' – no scanning software can protect you from a virus strain that it doesn't know about!

Pirated software

It should go without saying that pirate copies of commercial software passed from person to person carry a significant risk of being infected with viruses. Many viruses are spread this way.

TIP

It is illegal to make copies of commercial software and distribute these to others. People who indulge in this practice put themselves at risk not only of infecting their systems with viruses but also of prosecution for what amounts to theft. It just isn't worth it!

Virus prevention

Fortunately, there are plenty of things that you can do to safeguard yourself from virus infection and avoid the frustration of having to 'clean up' when disaster strikes. A few basic precautions will help you to avoid the vast majority of virus infections but if you do find that your system has been invaded by one of these 'nasties' you can usually destroy them quickly and easily using one of several proprietary 'virus killers'.

You can prevent viruses infecting your system by adopting 'clean habits', notably:

- **(a)** Only download software from reputable bulletin board systems. If you are unsure about downloaded software you should scan it (using a proprietary anti-virus package) before you run any of the downloaded programs.
- **(b)** Never use pirated copies of games and commercial software (these carry a very high risk of virus infection).
- **(c)** Don't install or copy files onto your system from any unsolicited disk.
- **(d)** Never install programs on your system from anything other than original distribution disks (or your own personally made backup copies of them).

Make sure that other users of your system do not import their own software or install any software onto your system that you don't know about. Make them adhere to your 'clean habits'! Purchase a reputable anti-virus package. Use this to periodically scan your system and also to check any new disks that you are uncertain of.

TIP

You should ensure that your anti-virus software is regularly updated to take account of any new virus strains that have appeared. Most anti-virus producers provide such a service at nominal cost.

TIP

In severe cases of virus infection you may find it necessary to reformat your hard disk and replace the programs and data stored on it in just the same way as you would if the hard disk itself had failed. This 'last resort' will eradicate an existing virus completely and should serve to further emphasise the need to make regular backups of the data stored on your hard disk. You can use the DOS BACKUP command (see page 189) or one of several excellent proprietary backup packages to help you perform this task. Note, however, that if one (or more) of your backup files has been infected the problem will eventually recur when the file in question is executed.

Detecting and eliminating viruses

Detecting a virus

Some viruses will forcibly announce their presence by displaying messages, corrupting screen data or simply by 'dissolving' your screen. Others are a little more subtle in operation. In such cases you should look for the following 'tell-tale' signs:

1. Has your hard disk increased in size for no apparent reason?
2. Have you noticed an increase (albeit small) in the size of individual programs?
3. Is hard disk activity occurring when you don't expect it?
4. Has your system become noticeably slower recently?
5. When your system accesses the floppy drive, does it take longer than before?

Next you should ask yourself what you have done recently that could have been responsible for importing a virus:

6. Have you installed any new software recently?
7. Have you recently downloaded software from the Web?
8. Have you transferred any programs from someone else's disks to your machine?
9. Has anyone else had access to your machine?
10. Has anyone recently sent you an e-mail with an executable file attached?

If you are sure that you are suffering a virus infection and not a hardware fault (you can confirm this using proprietary anti-virus software) the next stage is to eradicate the virus before it spreads.

Eliminating a virus

To prevent the virus present on your hard disk becoming active when you boot your system, you will need a 'clean boot' disk. This is simply an emergency boot disk (see page 154) which must, of course, have been produced before your system was infected.

You should boot from this disk (in which case your system will be 'clean' when the DOS prompt appears). You can then run a proprietary virus detection program to scan the complete system.

Scanning software will first check memory for any viruses that may have installed themselves into RAM. It will then check boot sectors, COM, EXE, overlay and data files for any viruses that may have attached themselves to your existing software.

This process may take some time as the scanning software works through the entire contents of your hard disk. When the scan has been completed, the anti-virus package will display a report on the types of virus (if any) that it has detected. If a virus is found, the scanning software may suggest the remedy. Alternatively, you may have to refer to a printed table in order to decide upon the best method for removing the virus. The technique will vary with the type of virus and, in particular, whether it invades boot sectors or attaches itself to files. In some cases (e.g. where the virus has overwritten some of your program code) you may have to re-install applications software in order to restore the code to its original state.

Anti-virus software – six of the best

A reliable anti-virus package is an essential purchase, particularly if you regularly exchange disks with other users or download software from the World Wide Web. There are currently more than a dozen anti-virus software packages to choose from – the six listed here are the current market leaders and any one of them will satisfy the needs of most users:

Dr Solomon's Anti-Virus Toolkit: This highly effective package provides a very comprehensive range of features and it works under Windows 3.1, Windows 95 and DOS. The success rate of this package (in terms of detecting viruses) is extremely high. A scheduler is provided for automatic scanning at predetermined intervals.

F-Prot Professional: This highly effective package provides a very comprehensive range of features and it works under Windows 3.1, Windows 95 and DOS. The success rate of this package (in terms of detecting viruses) is extremely high. The package comprises two main programs; a scanner and disinfector and a scheduler. A 'gatekeeper' provides on-access virus checking. Virus recognition rates are very high.

IBM Anti-Virus: This is a reasonably priced program that offers a high degree of protection. During installation, the software provides you with an opportunity to create a bootable rescue disk. The performance of this package is good at a very moderate price.

McAfee Virus Scan: McAfee's anti-virus suite is one of the most popular of today's anti-virus packages. The package is available in various versions and at reasonable cost. The software includes VirusScan (an on-demand scanner) and Vshield (an on-access scanner). The package is highly effective and it can be strongly recommended.

Norton Anti-Virus: Like McAfee's package, the Norton anti-virus programs have earned a well-deserved reputation for simplicity in use coupled with a wide range of features. In comparison with some of the other packages, the Norton anti-virus software is not particularly fast and the current version (for Windows 95) is not suitable for use with DOS (this could be a problem if you have to recover a system from scratch).

Thunderbyte Anti-Virus: Reflex Magnetic's Thunderbyte software is currently the fastest anti-virus software available. It also offers remarkably high detection rates. Different versions are available for Windows 95 and Windows 3.1/DOS (the latter version does not currently provide on-access protection although this is available with the Windows 95 version).

TIP

Not all anti-virus programs provide the same range facilities and it is important to check the features that you need before you commit to a particular product. As a minimum, you should consider on-access and on-demand scanning to be essential features. The ability to scan zipped files (i.e. files with a .ZIP extension) is highly desirable if you regularly download or exchange compressed files whilst the ability to detect macro viruses is essential if you regularly work with Microsoft Word and Excel files.

TIP

It is wise not to rely on cheap anti-virus programs as they may have unacceptably low recognition rates and may thus not detect all types of virus. It is also wise to ensure that your anti-virus software supplier will support the product with regular updates including the latest virus signatures. For this reason, it is wise to consider only purchasing well-known and well-supported programs from established suppliers.

TIP

When downloading software from the World Wide Web it is important to be aware that viruses may be present on any executable files (including those incorporated within zipped files) that you download. Viruses may also be present on executable macros (such as those available for Microsoft Word for Windows and Excel). When downloading *any* files from the Web, it is wise not to take any chances and ensure that each file is downloaded into a purpose created download directory and subsequently scanned before execution. Some, *but not all*, anti-virus packages are effective when used to scan zipped (.ZIP) files. If you do not have such a package, it is essential to unzip and then scan each file before the installation or set up procedure is started. You should also note that graphics files (e.g. .JPG and .GIF files) are non-executable and therefore they are not prone to virus infection.

Getting help via the Internet and World Wide Web

In the event that you might need information and support in tracking down a virus, a connection to the World Wide Web can be invaluable. Some of the most useful sources of anti-virus information are listed below:

Anti-Viral Toolkit Pro Virus Encyclopaedia
http://www.metro.co/avpe/findex.stm

This is an on-line encyclopaedia of computer viruses. The encyclopaedia can be searched using an intelligent keyword facility.

Computer Information Centre (CompInfo)
http://www.compinfo.co.uk

This UK-based Web site contains a large number of useful links including several to the sites of anti-virus software suppliers.

Dr Solomon's Software Virus Encyclopaedia
http://www.drsolomon.com.vircen/enc/

This is another excellent on-line encyclopaedia of computer viruses which incorporates an alphabetic selection as well as a keyword search facility.

IBM Anti-Virus On-line
http://www.av.ibm.com/current/frontpage/

IBM's Web pages include a number of useful articles dealing with anti-virus issues.

McAfee Virus Information
http://www.mcafee.com/support/techdocs/vinfo/

McAfee's Web site contains a great deal of information on a large number of known viruses.

Microsoft Office Macro Virus Tools
http://www.microsoft.com/msoffice/freestuf/msword/download/mvtool/

This Web site currently contains a tool for detecting Macro viruses (mvtool10.exe) together with a document describing its use (mvtool2.htm).

Symantec Anti-Virus Research Centre
http://www.symantec.com/avcenter/vinfodb.html

Symantec's Anti-Virus Research Centre provides an excellent database of virus information.

Finally, it is worth noting that several of the leading anti-virus companies provide virus scanning software that can be downloaded from the World Wide Web for evaluation purposes. In many cases, this software is fully functional and it will allow you to tackle an immediate virus problem. Furthermore, when you become a registered user, you can also use the Web to periodically update your anti-virus software.

13
Displays

The PC supports a wide variety of different types of display. This chapter explains the most commonly used display standards and video modes. It also tells you how to get and set the current video mode and provides some basic information on how the PC produces a colour display.

PC display standards

The video capability of a PC will depend not only upon the display used but also upon the type of 'graphics adapter' fitted. Most PCs will operate in a number of video modes which can be selected from DOS or from within an application.

The earliest PC display standards were those associated with the Monochrome Display Adapter (MDA) and Colour Graphics Adapter (CGA). Both of these standards are now obsolete although they are both emulated in a number of laptop PCs that use LCD displays.

MDA and CGA were followed by a number of other much enhanced graphics standards. These include Enhanced Graphics Adapter (EGA), Multi-Colour Graphics Array (MCGA), Video Graphics Array (VGA) and the 8514 standard used on IBM PS/2 machines.

The EGA standard was followed by VGA and now SVGA ('super VGA'). The first generation of VGA displays (1987) were based on 8-bit controllers and only supported a resolution of 640 × 480 pixels. These were followed (in 1989) by second generation controllers and displays capable of a resolution of 800 × 600 pixels. At the same time, architecture moved from 8-bits to 16-bits.

The third generation of SVGA controllers and displays appeared in 1991. These systems supported display resolutions of up to 1024 × 768 pixels. At the same time, video cache memories became commonplace together with the VL-bus interface which provides a vast increase in display speed and overall performance.

Today's SVGA controllers – fourth generation controllers – provide even more acceleration with wider video ports and much larger display memories (e.g. 8 Mbyte). In addition '3-D' shading and texturing is provided by many controllers to enhance multimedia and games programs. A very high degree of integration is now provided in the controller chip-sets which move graphic data around in 32 or 64-bit chunks.

Table 13.1 Display adapter summary

Display standard	Approx. year of intro-duction	Text capability (columns × lines)	Graphics capability (horiz. × vert. pixels)
MDA	1981	80 × 25 monochrome	None
HGA	1982	80 × 25 monochrome	720 × 320 monochrome

Table 13.1 Display adapter summary

Display standard	Approx. year of intro-duction	Text capability (columns × lines)	Graphics capability (horiz. × vert. pixels)
CGA	1983	80 × 25 in 16 colours	320 × 200 in two sets of 4 colours
EGA	1984	80 × 40 in 16 colours	640 × 350 in 16 colours
MCGA	1987	80 × 30 in 16 colours	640 × 480 in 2 colours, 320 × 200 in 256 colours
8514/A (PS/2)	1987	80 × 60 in 16 colours	1024 × 768 in 256 colours
VGA	1987	80 × 50 in 16 colours	640 × 480 in 16 colours, 320 × 200 in 256 colours
SVGA (XGA)	1991	132 × 60 in 16 colours	1024 × 768 in 256 colours, 640 × 480 in 32,768 colours

TIP

As the resolution is increased, the size of individual pixels displayed, and therefore the 'step' between them, is reduced. As the pixel and step size is reduced, the jagged edges become less jagged and therefore less noticeable. For this reason, you should always use the highest resolution available on your system but note that this will depend upon the capability of your graphics controller *as well as* your display. To put this into perspective, it is worth comparing some of the most popular video standards for both computers with those used in television:

Standard	Horizontal resolution	Vertical resolution
CGA	640	200
EGA	640	350
VGA	640	480
NTSC TV	672	525
PAL TV	767	575
SVGA	800	600
VHR	1280	1024
HDTV	1920	1080
UHR	2048	1536

TIP

When purchasing or upgrading a display and/or a graphics adapter there are a number of important questions that you should put to the supplier. These include:

(a) How many and what video standards and resolutions supported?
(b) How much RAM is supplied on the adapter card? (1Mbyte should now be considered the minimum with 2Mbyte or 4Mbyte preferable)
(c) What type of RAM is supplied on the adapter card? (high-speed VRAM and EDO RAM will result in faster video throughput)
(d) What card format (ISA or PCI) is supplied?
(e) Do I need a Windows accelerator (i.e. a card that is optimised for faster Windows graphics performance)? (this will cost more)
(f) Do I need an MPEG compatible card? (useful for multimedia video playback)
(g) Are drivers supplied for particular applications? (most suppliers will provide software drivers that are optimised for popular applications including Windows, AutoCAD, Ventura, OS/2 Presentation Manager, WordPerfect etc.)

TIP

When purchasing a display, it is important to check that it will cope with a range of different vertical and horizontal scanning frequencies. Most 'multi-sync' compatible monitors will operate with vertical scanning frequencies between 50Hz and 100Hz and horizontal scanning frequencies between 30kHz and 38kHz. If your chosen display cannot accept this range of scanning frequencies you will be unable to make use of the higher resolution text and graphics modes.

TIP

When operating in a high resolution mode, a 'multi-sync' display may occasionally suffer a loss of synchronisation which will usually result in a series of jagged lines across the screen. Sometimes, a display will regain 'lock' after a few seconds. However in a severe case, the display may completely fail to synchronise. If this is the case, you can usually cure the problem by making adjustments to the 'h-sync' or 'hold' control. This control may be adjusted externally in some cases but in others you may have to disassemble the monitor in order to locate the requisite preset adjustment on the display's printed circuit board. The same applies to vertical synchronisation (in which case the display will 'roll'). If you do have to dismantle the display, it is vitally important that you follow the high-voltage safety precautions described on page 30.

Video modes

It is important to realise at the outset that graphics adapters normally operate in one of several different modes. A VGA card will, for example, operate in 'text mode' using either 80 or 40 columns, and in 'graphics mode' using 4, 16 or 256 colours.

The graphics adapter contains one or more VLSI devices that organise the data which produces the screen display. You should recall that a conventional cathode ray tube (CRT) display is essentially a serial device (screen data is built up using a beam of electrons which continuously scans the screen). Hence the graphics adapter must store the screen image whilst the scanning process takes place.

Getting and setting the video mode

To determine the current video mode, you can simply read the machine's video mode byte stored in RAM at address 0449 (see Chapter 6). This byte indicates the current video mode (using the hex. values shown in Table 13.2). You can examine the byte at this address using the Debug command D0:0449L1 (the equivalent SID command is D0:449,44A). Alternatively, you can make use of the QuickBASIC program shown in Figure 6.7.

If you need to change the video mode for DOS applications, you can make use of the **MODE** command.

TIP

In DOS, you can easily give your PC a 40 (rather than 80) column screen by using the command, **MODE CO40**. This command can be handy if the user suffers from impaired vision or when a screen has to be viewed from a distance. If you have a monochrome monitor you may find the command **MODE BW80** useful when running certain DOS applications. Of course, either of these two **MODE** commands can be included in your AUTOEXEC.BAT file so that the required video mode will then become active whenever the system is switched on (see page 204). Note that DOS applications can override the current graphics mode when they initialise thus your 40 column screen may revert to an 80 column screen when your favourite DOS text editor is running!

Graphics adapter memory

The amount of memory required to display a screen in text mode is determined by the number of character columns and lines and also on the number of colours displayed. In modes 0 to 6 and 8, a total of 16Kbytes is reserved for display memory whilst in mode 7 (monochrome 80 × 25 characters) the requirement is for only 4Kbytes (colours are not displayed).

In modes 0 to 3, less than 16Kbytes is used by the screen at any one time. For these modes, the available memory is divided into pages. Note that only one page can be displayed at any particular time. Displayed pages are numbered 0 to 7 in modes 0 and 1 and 0 to 3 in modes 2 and 3.

The extent of display memory required in a graphics mode depends upon the number of pixels displayed (horizontal × vertical) and also on the number of colours displayed. Provided that a

Table 13.2 Video display modes and graphics adapter standards

Mode	Display Type	Colours	Screen resolution (note 1)	Display adapters supporting this mode					
				MDA	CGA	EGA	MCGA	VGA	HGA (Note 3)
00	Text	16	40 × 25		*	*	*	*	*
01	Text	16	40 × 25		*	*	*	*	*
02	Text	16	80 × 25		*	*	*	*	*
03	Text	16	80 × 25		*	*	*	*	*
04	Graphics	4	320 × 200		*	*	*	*	*
05	Graphics	4	320 × 200		*	*	*	*	*
06	Graphics	2	640 × 200		*	*	*	*	*
07	Text	Mono	80 × 25	*		*		*	*
08	Graphics	16	160 × 200	(Note 2)					
09	Graphics	16	320 × 200	(Note 2)					
0A	Graphics	4	640 × 200	(Note 2)					
0B	(Note 4)								
0C	(Note 4)								
0D	Graphics	16	320 × 200		*		*		
0E	Graphics	16	640 × 200			*		*	
0F	Graphics	Mono	640 × 350			*		*	
10	Graphics	16	640 × 350			*		*	
11	Graphics	2	640 × 480				*	*	
12	Graphics	16	640 × 480				*	*	
13	Graphics	256	320 × 200				*		

Notes:
1. Resolutions are quoted in (columns × lines) for text displays and (horizontal × vertical) pixels for graphics displays.
2. Applies only to the PC Junior (now obsolete).
3. The Hercules Graphics Adapter card combines the graphics (but NOT colour) capabilities of the CGA adapter with the high quality text display of the MDA adapter.
4. Reserved mode.

display adapter has sufficient RAM fitted, the concept of screen pages also applies to graphics modes. Again, it is only possible to display one page at a time.

Colour

The basic 16-colour palette for a PC used in the vast majority of basic DOS applications is based on a 4-bit 'intensity plus RGB' code (see Table 13.3). This simple method generates colours by switching on and off the individual red, green and blue electron beams. The intensity signal simply serves to brighten up or darken the display at the particular screen location. The result is the 16 basic PC colours that we have all grown to know and love!

Table 13.3 The PC's 16 colour palette

Hex. code	Binary code I R G B	Colour produced
00	0 0 0 0	Black
01	0 0 0 1	Blue
02	0 0 1 0	Green
03	0 0 1 1	Cyan
04	0 1 0 0	Red
05	0 1 0 1	Magenta
06	0 1 1 0	Yellow
07	0 1 1 1	White
08	1 0 0 0	Grey
09	1 0 0 1	Bright blue
0A	1 0 1 0	Bright green
0B	1 0 1 1	Bright cyan
0C	1 1 0 0	Bright red
0D	1 1 0 1	Bright magenta
0E	1 1 1 0	Bright yellow
0F	1 1 1 1	Bright white

Note:
I = intensity, R = red, B = blue, G = green.

The 16-colour palette is adequate for most text applications, however, to produce more intermediate shades of colour, we need a larger palette. One way of doing this is to make use of a 6-bit code where each of the three basic colours (red, green and blue) is represented by two bits (one corresponding to bright and the other to normal). This allows each colour to have four levels and produces 64 possible colour combinations.

A better method (which generates a virtually unlimited colour palette) is to use 'analogue RGB' rather than 'digital RGB' signals. In this system (used in VGA, SVGA and XGA), the three basic colour signals (red, green and blue) are each represented by analogue voltages in the range 0V to 0.7V (at the video connector). The number of colours displayed using such an arrangement depends upon the number of bits used to represent the intensity of each colour before its conversion to an analogue signal.

TIP

The Display Check program (see page 304) will allow you to carry out a variety of checks and display adjustments. This program allows you to change the video mode between CGA, EGA, and VGA and examine the effect on both text and colour screen displays.

TIP

A screen saver will help to protect your system against the long-term effects of phosphor burn. It will not, however, eliminate the effects of constant power-on since the cathode ray tube heater will still be energised even when the screen saver is operational. Tube emission slowly deteriorates due to removal of the active material at the heater/cathode – a screen saver will not protect against this.

TIP

Certain screen savers have been known to crash a system when left for long periods. For this reason, you should always save your work before leaving the system and the screen saver to do its work. Indeed, there is no real reason to have a screen saver at all – just reducing the setting of the display's brightness control will have the same effect, at no cost and with less risk!

TIP

There has been some debate recently about whether it is better to leave a computer system (and its display) operational 24-hours a day rather than to switch it on and off (the act of switching on and off places additional electrical strain on a system). Calculations of mean-time-to-failure (MTTF) show that MTTF is reduced significantly if a system is left permanently on. Similarly, MTTF is reduced if a system is switched on and off several times each day (e.g. when taking breaks). The best compromise (and longest MTTF) can be obtained by switching on and off *once* each working day and leaving the system off at night and at weekends. In addition, when the user leaves the work station he, or she, should either turn the brightness control down to a low setting or should ensure that a reliable screen saver becomes operational after a few minutes of non-use.

TIP

Modern SVGA controller cards and their drivers offer you a choice of colour definition and resolution. To adjust these values from within Windows 95 you need to select Settings, then Control Panel, then Display and then choose the Settings tab. From here you can select the number of colours that will be displayed on the screen as well as the screen resolution (note that you may have to accept a trade-off between these two parameters depending upon the amount of graphics memory available). The colours settings available with most controllers include:

- 16 colours
- 256 colours (selected from a palette of 262,144 colours)
- 'High-colour' (16-bit – 32,768 on-screen colours)
- 'True-colour' (24-bit – 16,777,216 on-screen colours).

Some experimentation will be required if you want to get the best out of your system. Much will depend upon the type of applications that you run. For example, 16 or 256 colours will be perfectly adequate for word processing and spreadsheet applications but can be woefully inadequate for graphics and digital photography.

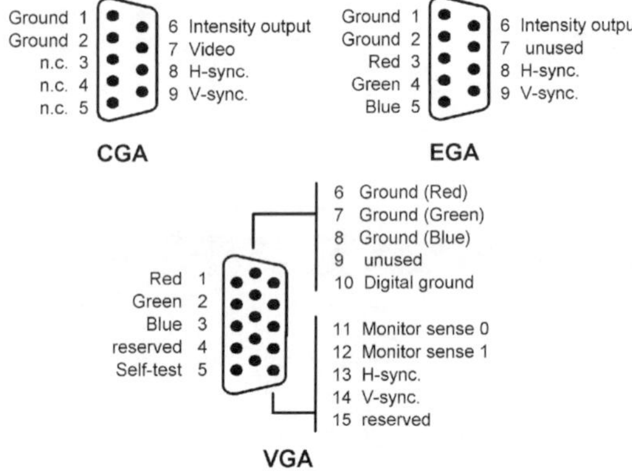

Figure 13.1 Pin numbering for standard CGA, EGA and VGA displays

14

DOS system configuration

DOS provides you with various methods for configuring your system; individual DOS commands entered from the DOS command processor, batch files, hardware device drivers and two vitally important files; CONFIG.SYS and AUTOEXEC.BAT. All of these can be instrumental in helping you to get the best out of your system.

This chapter is designed to give you a good understanding of the resources provided by your DOS. It begins by explaining some of the basic facilities provided, including how to make backup copies of disks and how DOS uses I/O channels and file specifications. The chapter continues with a detailed description of each of the standard internal and external DOS commands and numerous examples have been included for you to follow.

The chapter includes a section on creating and using batch files as well as the CONFIG.SYS and AUTOEXEC.BAT files which are used to initialise your system. The chapter also shows you how to use some of the most popular device drivers, including how to set up a disk cache, a RAM drive, make use of extended and/or expanded memory, and how to configure the display and printer for international characters and fonts. The chapter concludes with an introduction to the powerful debug utility provided as part of your DOS package.

DOS basics

Booting the system

DOS is automatically loaded from the hard disk (drive C:) or the floppy disk placed in drive A: whenever the system is 'booted' (i.e. whenever the power is applied and the CPU executes the BIOS code stored in the ROM). After successful loading, the title and version of the operating system is displayed on the screen. The message is then followed by a prompt that gives the currently selected drive (usually C:\> in a system fitted with a hard disk drive). This prompt shows that the system is ready to receive a command from the user.

If an AUTOEXEC batch file is present, the commands that it contains are executed before control is passed to the user. Furthermore, if such a file contains the name of an executable program (i.e. a file with a COM or EXE extension) then this program will be loaded from disk and executed. The program may take one of several forms including a program that simply performs its function and is then cleared from memory, a 'terminate and stay resident' (TSR) program, or a fully-blown application.

In any event, it is important to remember that the currently selected drive remains the default drive unless explicitly changed by the user. As an example, consider a system that is booted with a system disk (floppy) placed in drive A:. The default drive will then be A: (unless an AUTOEXEC file is present that contains commands to change the current drive). The system prompt will indicate that A is the current drive. Thereafter, it is implicit that all commands which do not specify a drive refer, by default, to that drive. The SET PATH command (see page 185) can, however, be used to specify a directory path which will be searched if a command or filename does not appear in the current directory.

TIP

To return to the root directory from within any level of sub-directory you need only type **CD** (followed, of course, by the <ENTER> key). To return to just one level of sub-directory towards the root you can simply type **CD..** . To help you navigate the system use the **PROMPT pg** command (see page 185).

Making back up copies of disks

It is often necessary to make back up copies of software supplied on distribution disks. Indeed, it should be considered essential to make at least one back up copy of every disk in current use. This simple precaution can help to save much agonising when a disk becomes corrupt or is inadvertently subjected to a **FORMAT** command!

Having made a back up copy, the distribution or master disk should be safely stored away and the working copy clearly labelled with the program name, version number and creation date, where appropriate. Assuming that a hard disk-based system is in use and that the DOS command utilities are placed in a sub-directory named DOS on drive C:, the procedure for backing-up a floppy disk is as follows:

1. Boot the system from the hard disk in the normal way.
2. When the system prompt (usually C:\>) appears, enter the command:
   SET PATH=C:\DOS
   The command may be entered in either upper or lower case and should be immediately followed by the <ENTER> key.
   An alternative to using the **SET PATH** command is to make the DOS directory the current directory by entering the command:
   CD DOS
   Note, however, that this step can be omitted if the DOS command utilities are present in the root directory of drive C or if the SET PATH command has been included in the AUTOEXEC.BAT file.
3. Now enter the command:
   DISKCOPY A: A: (or **DISKCOPY A: B:** if you have two disk drives of similar size and capacity)
   The system will respond with a message of the form:
   Insert SOURCE diskette in drive A:
   Press any key when ready . . .
4. Insert the distribution or master disk in drive A: and press a key. The system will read information from the master disk and transfer the contents of the disk to memory. At the start of this process a message of the form:
   Copying 80 tracks, 18 sectors/track, 2 side(s)
   will be displayed.
5. When all data has been transferred from the disk to memory, the system will prompt for insertion of the destination or Target disk. The following message (or its equivalent) will appear:
   Insert DESTINATION diskette in drive A:
   Press any key when ready . . .
   The destination disk should then be inserted. This disk may be a blank (unformatted) disk or may be a disk which has been

previously written to. In the latter case, the disk write protection should be removed. If the disk is blank (unformatted) it will be formatted during the process. In this case the following message will appear:
Formatting while copying

6. When the copying process has been completed (several disk swaps may be necessary on systems with limited RAM available) you will be prompted with the following message:
   Copy another diskette (Y/N)?
   Further disks may then be copied or the user may choose to exit from the **DISKCOPY** utility and return to the command prompt. In the latter case, the contents of the target disk may be checked by issuing the following command from the system prompt:
   DIR A:
7. If it is necessary to abort the copying process at any stage, the user should use the <CTRL-C> key combination (see page 178). It should also be noted that early versions of DOS require the user to format disks before using **DISKCOPY**.

I/O channels

In order to simplify the way in which DOS handles input and output, the system recognises the names of its various I/O devices (see Table 14.1). This may, at first, appear to be unnecessarily cumbersome but it is instrumental in allowing DOS to redirect data. This feature can be extremely useful when, for example, output normally destined for the printer is to be redirected to an auxiliary serial port.

Table 14.1 DOS I/O channels

Channel	Meaning	Function	Notes
COM1: and COM2:	Communications	Serial I/O	Via RS-232 ports
CON:	Console	Keyboard (input) and screen (output)	This channel combines the functions associated with the keyboard and the display (i.e. a 'terminal').
LPT1: LPT2: and LPT3:	Line printer	Parallel printer (output)	This interface conforms to the Centronics standard.
PRN:	Printer	Serial or parallel printer (output)	
NUL:	Null device	Simulated I/O	Provides a means of simulating a physical I/O channel without data transfer taking place.

TIP

The COPY command (see page 183) can be used to transfer data from one device to another. As an example, the command **COPY CON: PRN:** copies data from the keyboard (console input device) to the printer, **COPY CON: COM1** copies data from the keyboard to the serial port. In either case, the end-of-file character, <CTRL-Z> or <F6>, must be entered to terminate input.

DOS commands

DOS responds to command lines typed at the console and terminated with a <RETURN> or <ENTER> keystroke. A command line is thus composed of a command keyword, an optional command tail, and <RETURN>. The command keyword identifies the command (or program) to be executed. The command tail can contain extra information relevant to the command, such as a filename or other parameters. Each command line must be terminated using <RETURN> or <ENTER> (not shown in the examples which follow).

As an example, the following command can be used to display a directory of all bit-mapped picture files (i.e. those with a BMP extension) within a directory named GALLERY in drive C:, indicating the size of each:

DIR C:\GALLERY*.BMP

Note that, in this example and the examples which follow, we have omitted the prompt generated by the system (indicating the current drive).

It should be noted that the command line can be entered in any combination of upper-case or lower-case characters. DOS converts all letters in the command line to upper-case before interpreting them. Furthermore, whilst a command line generally immediately follows the system prompt, DOS permits spaces between the prompt (e.g. C:\>) and the command word.

As characters are typed at the keyboard, the cursor moves to the right in order to indicate the position of the next character to be typed. Depending upon the keyboard used, a <BACKSPACE>, or <DELETE> key can be used to delete the last entered character and move the cursor backwards one character position. Alternatively, a combination of the CONTROL and H keys (i.e. <CTRL-H>) may be used instead. Various other control characters are significant in DOS and these are shown in Table 14.2.

Table 14.2 DOS control characters

Control character	Hex.	Function
<CTRL-C>	03	Terminates the current program (if possible) and returns control to the user
<CTRL-G>	07	Sounds the audible warning device (bell) but can only be used as part of a program of batch file
<CTRL-H>	08	Moves the cursor back by one space (i.e. the same as the <BACKSPACE> key) and deletes the character present at that position

Table 14.2 Continued

Control character	Hex.	Function
<CTRL-I>	09	Tabs the cursor right by a fixed number of columns (usually eight). Performs the same function as the <TAB> key
<CTRL-J>	10	Issues a line feed and carriage return, effectively moving the cursor to the start of the next line
<CTRL-L>	12	Issues a form feed instruction to the printer
<CTRL-M>	13	Produces a carriage return (i.e. has the same effect as <RETURN>)
<CTRL-P>	16	Toggles screen output to the printer (i.e. after the first <CTRL-P> is issued, all screen output will be simultaneously echoed to the printer. A subsequent <CTRL-P> will disable the simultaneous printing of the screen output). Note that <CTRL-PRT.SC.> has the same effect as <CTRL-P>
<CTRL-S>	19	Pauses screen output during execution of the TYPE command (<CTRL-NUM.LOCK> has the same effect)
<CTRL-Z>	26	Indicates the end of a file (can also be entered using <F6>)

TIP

<CTRL-ALT-DEL> can be used to perform a 'warm' system reset. This particular combination should only be used in the last resort as it will clear system memory. Any program or data present in RAM will be lost!

Repeating or editing DOS commands

If it is necessary to repeat or edit the previous command, the <F1> (or right-arrow) key may be used to reproduce the command line, character by character, on the screen. The left-arrow key permits backwards movement through the command line for editing purposes. The <F3> key simply repeats the last command in its entirety.

File specifications

Many of the DOS commands make explicit reference to files. A file is simply a collection of related information stored on a disk. Program files comprise a series of instructions to be executed by the processor whereas data files simply contain a collection of records. A complete file specification has four distinct parts; a drive and directory specifier (known as a 'pathname'), a filename and a filetype.

The drive specifier is a single letter followed by a colon (e.g. C:). This is then followed by the directory and sub-directory names (if applicable) and the filename and filetype. The filename comprises 1 to 8 characters whilst the filetype takes the form of a 1 to 3 character extension separated from the filename by means of a full stop ('.'). A complete file specification (or 'filespec') thus takes the form:

[pathname]:[filename].[filetype]

As an example, the following file specification refers to a file named MOUSE and having a COM filetype found in the root directory of the disk in drive A:

A\:MOUSE.COM

DOS allows files to be grouped together within directories and sub-directories. Directory and sub-directory names are separated by means of the backslash (\) character. Directories and sub-directories are organised in an heirarchical (tree) structure and thus complete file specifications must include directory information.

The 'root' or base directory (i.e. that which exists at the lowest level in the heirarchical structure) is accessed by default when we simply specify a drive name without further reference to a directory. Thus:

C:\MOUSE.COM

refers to a file in the root directory whilst:

C:\DOS\MOUSE.COM

refers to an identically named file resident in a sub-directory called 'DOS'.

Sub-directories can be extended to any practicable level. As an example:

C:\DOS\UTILS\MOUSE\MOUSE.COM

refers to a file named MOUSE.COM present in the MOUSE sub-directory which itself is contained within the UTILS sub-directory found within a directory named DOS.

When it is necessary to make explicit reference to the root directory, we can simply use a single backslash character as follows:

C:

File extensions

The filetype extension provides a convenient mechanism for distinguishing different types of file and DOS provides various methods for manipulating groups of files having the same filetype extension. We could, for example, delete all of the backup (BAK) present in the root directory of the hard disk (drive C:) using a single command of the form:

ERA C:*.BAK

Alternatively, we could copy all of the executable (EXE) files from the root directory of the disk in drive A: to the root directory on drive C: using the command:

COPY A:*.EXE C:

Commonly used filetype extensions are shown in Table 14.3.

Table 14.3 Common file extensions

Extension	Type of file
ASC	An ASCII text file
ASM	An assembly language source code file
BAK	A back up file (often created automatically by a text editor which renames the source file with this extension and the revised file assumes the original file specification)
BAS	A BASIC program source file
BAT	A batch file which contains a sequence of operating system commands
BIN	A binary file (comprising instructions and data in binary format)
BMP	A bit-mapped picture file
C	A source code file written in the C language
CLP	A Windows 'clipboard' file

Table 14.3 Continued

Extension	Type of file
COM	An executable program file in small memory format (i.e. confined to a single 64Kbyte memory segment)
CPI	A 'code page information' file
CRD	A Windows 'card index' file
DAT	A data file (usually presented in either binary or ASCII format)
DBG	A DEBUG text file
DOC	A document file (not necessarily presented in standard ASCII format)
EXE	An executable program file in large memory format (i.e. not confined to a 64Kbyte memory model)
GIF	A graphics image file
HEX	A file presented in hexadecimal (an intermediate format sometimes used for object code)
INI	An initialisation file which may contain a set of inference rules and/or environment variables
LIB	A library file (containing multiple object code files)
LST	A listing file (usually showing the assembly code corresponding to each source code instruction together with a complete list of symbols)
OBJ	An object code file
OLD	A back up file (replaced by a more recent version of the file)
PAS	A source code file written in Pascal
PCX	A picture file
PIF	A Windows 'program interchange file'
SCR	A DEBUG script file
SYS	A system file
TIF	A tagged image file
TMP	A temporary file
TXT	A text file (usually in ASCII format)
WRI	A document file produced by Windows 'Write'
$$$	A temporary file

Wildcard characters

DOS allows the user to employ wildcard characters when specifying files. The characters, '*' and '?', can be used to replace complete fields and individual characters, respectively, within a file specification. DOS will search then carry out the required operation on all files for which a match is obtained.

The following examples illustrate the use of wildcard characters:

A:*.COM

refers to all files having a COM extension present in the root directory of drive A:.

C:\TOOLS*.*

refers to all files (regardless of name or extension) present in the directory named TOOLS on drive C:.

B:\TURBO\PROG?.C

refers to all files having a C extension present in the TURBO directory on the disk in drive B: which have PROG as their first three letters and any alphanumeric character in the fourth character place. A match will occur for each of the following files:

PROG1.C PROG2.C PROG3.C PROGA.C PROGB.C etc.

Internal and external commands

It is worth making a distinction between DOS commands which form part the resident portion of the operating system (internal commands) and those which involve other utility programs (external commands). Intrinsic commands are executed immediately whereas extrinsic commands require the loading of transient utility programs from disk and hence there is a short delay before the command is acted upon.

In the case of external commands, DOS checks only the command keyword. Any parameters which follow are passed to the utility program without checking.

At this point we should perhaps mention that DOS only recognises command keywords which are correctly spelled! Even an obvious typing error will result in the non-acceptance of the command and the system will respond with an appropriate error message.

As an example, suppose you attempt to format a disk but type **FORMATT** instead of **FORMAT**. Your system will respond with this message:

Bad command or file name

indicating that the command is unknown and that no file of that name (with a COM, BAT, or EXE extension) is present in the current directory.

TIP

To get on-line help from within MS-DOS 5.0 and DR-DOS 6.0 (and later operating systems) you can simply type the command name followed by **/?**. Hence **DIR /?** will bring you help before using the directory command. With MS-DOS 5.0 (and later) you can also type **HELP** followed by the command name (e.g. **HELP DIR**). In DR-DOS 6.0 you can type **DIR /H**.

Internal DOS commands

We shall now briefly examine the function of each of the most commonly used internal DOS commands. Examples have been included wherever they can help to clarify the action of a particular command. The examples relate to the most commonly used versions of MS-DOS, PC-DOS, and DR-DOS.

Command	**Function**
BREAK	The **BREAK** command disables the means by which it is possible to abort a running program. This facility is provided by means of the <CTRL-C> or <CTRL-BREAK> key combinations and it normally only occurs when output is being directed to the screen or the printer. **BREAK** accepts two parameters, **ON** and **OFF**. Examples: **BREAK ON** enables full <CTRL-C> or <CTRL-BREAK> key checking (it is important to note that this will normally produce a dramatic reduction in the speed of execution of a program). **BREAK OFF** restores normal <CTRL-C> or <CTRL-BREAK> operation (i.e. the default condition).

TIP

BREAK ON will often result in a significant reduction in the speed of execution of a program. You should only use this command when strictly necessary!

CD — See **CHDIR**.

CHDIR — The **CHDIR** command allows users to display or change the current directory. **CHDIR** may be abbreviated to **CD**.
Examples:
CHDIR A:
displays the current directory path for the disk in drive A:.
CHDIR C:\APPS
changes the directory path to APPS on drive C:.
CD D:\DEV\PROCESS
changes the directory path to the sub-directory PROCESS within the directory named DEV on drive D:.
CD
changes the directory path to the root directory of the *current* drive.
CD..
changes the directory path one level back towards the root directory of the *current* drive.

CLS — **CLS** clears the screen and restores the cursor position to the top left-hand corner of the screen.

COPY — The **COPY** command can be used to transfer a file from one disk to another using the same or a different filename. The **COPY** command is effective when the user has only a single drive. The **COPY** command must be followed by one or two file specifications. When only a single file specification is given, the command makes a single drive copy of a file. The copied file takes the same filename as the original and the user is prompted to insert the source and destination disks at the appropriate point. Where both source and destination file specifications are included, the file is copied to the specified drive and the copy takes the specified name. Where only a destination drive is specified (i.e. the destination filename is omitted) the **COPY** command copies the file to the specified drive without altering the filename. **COPY** may be used with the * and ? wildcard characters in order to copy all files for which a match is found.
Examples:
COPY A\:ED.COM B:
copies the file ED.COM present in the root directory of the disk in drive A: to the disk present in drive B:. The copy will be given the name ED.COM.

TIP

On a single drive system the only available floppy drive can be used as both the source and destination when the **COPY** command is used. The single physical drive will operate as both drive A: and drive B: and you will be prompted to insert the source and destination disks when required.

TIP

COPY is unable to make copies of files located within sub-directories. If you need this facility use **XCOPY** with the **/s** switch (see page 194).

DATE The **DATE** command allows the date to be set or displayed.
Examples:
DATE
displays the date on the screen and also prompts the user to make any desired changes. The user may press <RETURN> to leave the settings unchanged.
DATE 12–27–99
sets the date to 27th December 1999.

DEL See **ERASE**.

DIR The **DIR** command displays the names of files present within a directory. Variations of the command allow the user to specify the drive to be searched and the types of files to be displayed. Further options govern the format of the directory display.
Examples:
DIR
displays all files in the current default directory.
A:\ DIR
changes the default drive to A: (root directory) and then displays the contents of the root directory of the disk in drive A:.
DIR *.BAS
displays all files with a BAS extension present in the current default directory drive.
DIR C:\DEV.*
displays all files named DEV (regardless of their type or extension) present in the root directory of drive C: (the hard disk).
DIR C:\MC*.BIN
displays all files having a BIN extension present in the sub-directory named MC on drive C: (the hard disk).
DIR/W
displays a directory listing in 'wide' format (excluding size and creation date/time information) of the current default directory.

TIP

To prevent directory listings scrolling off the screen use **DIR/P** or **DIR/ MORE**. These commands will pause the listing at the end of each screen and wait for you to press a key before continuing.

TIP

MS-DOS 5.0 (and later) includes many options for use with the **DIR** command including sorting the directory listing and displaying hidden system files.

ERASE

The **ERASE** command is used to erase a filename from the directory and release the storage space occupied by a file. The **ERASE** command is identical to the **DEL** command and the two may be used interchangeably. **ERASE** may be used with the * and **?** wildcard characters in order to erase all files for which a match occurs.

Examples:

ERASE PROG1.ASM

erases the file named PROG1.ASM from the disk placed in the current (default) directory.

ERASE B:\TEMP.DAT

erases the file named TEMP.DAT from the root directory of the disk in drive B:.

ERASE C:*.COM

erases all files having a COM extension present in the root directory of the hard disk (drive C:).

ERASE A:\PROG1.*

erases all files named PROG1 (regardless of their type extension) present in the root directory of the disk currently in drive A:.

MD

See **MKDIR**.

MKDIR

The **MKDIR** command is used to make a new directory or sub-directory. The command may be abbreviated to **MD**.

Examples:

MKDIR APPS

creates a sub-directory named APPS within the *current* directory (note that the **CHDIR** command is often used after **MKDIR** – having created a new directory you will probably want to move to make it the current directory before doing something with it!).

MD C:\DOS\BACKUP

creates a sub-directory named BACKUP within the DOS directory of drive C:.

PATH

The **PATH** command may be used to display the current directory path. Alternatively, a new directory path may be established using the **SET PATH** command.

Examples:

PATH

displays the current directory path (a typical response would be **PATH=C:\WINDOWS**).

SET PATH=C:\DOS

makes the directory path C:\DOS.

PROMPT

The **PROMPT** command allows the user to change the system prompt. The **PROMPT** command is followed by a text string which replaces the system prompt. Special characters may be inserted within the string, as follows:

$d	current date
$e	escape character
$g	>
$h	backspace and erase
$l	<
$n	current drive
$p	current directory path
$q	=
$t	current time
$v	DOS version number
$$	$
$	newline

Examples:
PROMPT tg
changes the prompt to the current time followed by a >.
PROMPT Howard Associates PLC $?
changes the prompt to Howard Associates PLC followed by a carriage return and newline on which a ? is displayed.
PROMPT
restores the default system prompt (e.g. C:\>).

TIP

The most usual version of the **PROMPT** command is **PROMPT pg** which displays the current directory/sub-directory and helps to avoid confusion when navigating within DOS directories.

RD — See **RMDIR**.

RENAME — The **RENAME** command allows the user to rename a disk file. **RENAME** may be used with the * and **?** wild-card characters in order to rename all files for which a match occurs. **RENAME** may be abbreviated to **REN**.
Examples:
RENAME PROG2.ASM PROG1.ASM
renames PROG1.ASM to PROG2.ASM on the disk placed in the current (default) directory.
REN A:\HELP.DOC HELP.TXT
renames the file HELP.DOC to HELP.TXT in the root directory of the disk in drive A:.
REN B:\CONTROL.* PROG1.*
renames all files with name PROG1 (regardless of type extension) to CONTROL (with identical extensions) found in the root directory of the disk in drive B:.

RMDIR — The **RMDIR** command is used to remove a directory. **RMDIR** may be abbreviated to **RD**. The command cannot be used to remove the current directory and any directory to be removed must be empty and must not contain further sub-directories.
Example:
RMDIR ASSEM
removes the directory ASSEM from the current directory (note that DOS will warn you if the named directory is *not* empty!).
RD C:\DOS\BACKUP
removes the directory ASSEM from the current directory (once again, DOS will warn you if the named directory is *not* empty!).

SET — The **SET** command is used to set the environment variables (see **PATH**).

TIME — The **TIME** command allows the time to be set or displayed.
Examples:
TIME
displays the time on the screen and also prompts the user to make any desired changes. The user may press <RETURN> to leave the settings unchanged.
TIME 14:30
sets the time to 2.30 p.m.

TYPE — This useful command allows you to display the contents of an ASCII (text) file on the console screen. The **TYPE** command can be used with options which enable or disable paged mode displays. The <PAUSE> key or <CTRL-S> combination may be used to halt the display. You can press any key or use the <CTRL-Q> combination respectively to restart. <CTRL-C> may be used to abort the execution of the **TYPE** command and exit to the system.

Examples:

TYPE C\:AUTOEXEC.BAT

will display the contents of the AUOTEXEC.BAT file stored in the root directory of drive C:. The file will be sent to the screen.

TYPE B\:PROG1.ASM

will display the contents of a file called PROG1.ASM stored in the root directory of the disk in drive B. The file will be sent to the screen.

TYPE C:\WORK*.DOC

will display the contents of *all* the files with a DOC extension present in the WORK directory of the hard disk (drive C:).

TIP

You can use the **TYPE** command to send the contents of a file to the printer at the same time as viewing it on the screen. If you need to do this, press <CTRL-P> before you issue the **TYPE** command (but do make sure that the printer is 'on-line' and ready to go!). To disable the printer output you can use the <CTRL-P> combination a second time.

TIP

The ability to redirect data is an extremely useful facility. DOS uses the < and > characters in conjunction with certain commands to redirect files. As an example:

TYPE A:\README.DOC >PRN

will redirect normal screen output produced by the **TYPE** command to the printer. This is usually more satisfactory than using the <PRT.SCREEN> key.

VER — The **VER** command displays the current DOS version.

VERIFY — The **VERIFY** command can be used to enable or disable disk file verification. **VERIFY ON** enables verification whilst **VERIFY OFF** disables verification. If **VERIFY** is used without **ON** or **OFF**, the system will display the state of verification (either 'on' or 'off').

VOL — The **VOL** command may be used to display the volume label of a disk.

External DOS commands

Unlike internal commands, these commands will not function unless the appropriate DOS utility program is resident in the current (default) directory. External commands are simply the names of utility programs (normally resident in the DOS sub-directory). If you need to gain access to these utilities from any directory or sub-directory, then the following lines should be included in your AUTOEXEC.BAT file (see page 205):

SET PATH=C:\DOS

The foregoing assumes that you have created a sub-directory called DOS on the hard disk and that this sub-directory contains the DOS utility programs. As with the internal DOS commands, the examples given apply to the majority of DOS versions.

Command	**Function**
APPEND	The **APPEND** command allows the user to specify drives, directories and sub-directories which will be searched through when a reference is made to a particular data file. The **APPEND** command follows the same syntax as the **PATH** command.
ASSIGN	The **ASSIGN** command allows users to re-direct files between drives. **ASSIGN** is particularly useful when a RAM disk is used to replace a conventional disk drive. Examples: **ASSIGN A=D** results in drive D: being searched for a file whenever a reference is made to drive A:. The command may be countermanded by issuing a command of the form: **ASSIGN A=A** Alternatively, all current drive assignments may be overridden by simply using: **ASSIGN**

TIP

ASSIGN A=B followed by **ASSIGN B=A** can be used to swap the drives over in a system which has two floppy drives. The original drive assignment can be restored using **ASSIGN**.

ATTRIB	The **ATTRIB** command allows the user to examine and/or set the attributes of a single file or a group of files. The **ATTRIB** command alters the file attribute byte (which appears within a disk directory) and which determines the status of the file. (e.g. read-only). Examples: **ATTRIB A:\PROCESS.DOC** displays the attribute status of copies the file PROCESS.DOC contained in the root directory of the disk in drive A:. **ATTRIB +R A:\PROCESS.DOC** changes the status of the file PROCESS.DOC contained in the root directory of the disk in drive A: so that is a read-only file. This command may be countermanded by issuing a command of the form: **ATTRIB -R A:\PROCESS.DOC**

TIP

A crude but effective alternative to password protection is that of using **ATTRIB** to make all the files within a sub-directory hidden. As an example, **ATTRIB +H C:\PERSONAL** will hide all of the files in the PERSONAL sub-directory. **ATTRIB -H C:\PERSONAL** will make them visible once again.

BACKUP The **BACKUP** command may be used to copy one or more files present on a hard disk to a number of floppy disks for security purposes. It is important to note that the **BACKUP** command stores files in a compressed format (i.e. not in the same format as that used by the **COPY** command). The **BACKUP** command may be used selectively with various options including those which allow files to be archived by date. The **BACKUP** command usually requires that the target disks have been previously formatted however, from MS-DOS 3.3 onwards, an option to format disks has been included.

Examples:

BACKUP C:*.* A:

backs up all of the files present on the hard disk. This command usually requires that a large number of (formatted) disks are available for use in drive A:. Disks should be numbered so that the data can later be restored in the correct sequence.

BACKUP C:\DEV*.C A:

Backs up all of the files with a C: extension present within the DEV sub-directory on drive C:.

BACKUP C:\PROCESS*.BAS A:/D:01–01–99

Backs up all of the files with a BAS extension present within the PROCESS sub-directory of drive C: that were created or altered on or after 1st January 1999.

BACKUP C:\COMMS*.* A:/F

Backs up all of the files present in the COMMS subdirectory of drive C: and formats each disk as it is used.

CHKDSK The **CHKDSK** command reports on disk utilisation and provides information on total disk space, hidden files, directories, and user files. **CHKDSK** also gives the total memory and free memory available. **CHKDSK** incorporates options which can be used to enable reporting and to repair damaged files.

CHKDSK provides two useful switches; **/F** fixes errors on the disk and **/V** displays the name of each file in every directory as the disk is checked. Note that if you use the **/F** switch, **CHKDSK** will ask you to confirm that you actually wish to make changes to the disk's file allocation table (FAT).

Examples:

CHKDSK A:

Checks the disk placed in the A: drive and displays a status report on the screen.

CHKDSK C:\DEV*.ASM/F/V

checks the specified disk and directory, examining all files with an ASM extension, reporting errors and attempting to correct them.

TIP

If you make use of the /**F** switch, **CHKDSK** will ask you to confirm that you actually wish to correct the errors. If you do go ahead **CHKDSK** will usually change the disk's file allocation table (FAT). In some cases this may result in loss of data!

TIP

The **CHKDSK** command has a nasty bug in certain versions of MS-DOS and PC-DOS. The affected versions are:

DOS version	File name	File size	Data
PC-DOS 4.01	CHKDSK.COM	17771 bytes	17 Jun 88
MS-DOS 4.01	CHKDSK.COM	17787 bytes	30 Nov 88
PC-DOS 5.0	CHKDSK.EXE	16200 bytes	09 Apr 91
MS-DOS 5.0	CHKDSK.EXE	16184 bytes	09 May 91

The bug destroys the directory structure when **CHKDSK** is used with the **/F** switch and the total allocation units on disk is greater than 65,278. The bug was corrected in maintenance release 5.0A dated 11 Nov 91 however the problem does not arise if the hard disk partition is less than 128Mbytes. If you have an affected DOS version it is well worth upgrading to avoid the disastrous consequences of this bug!

COMP The **COMP** command may be used to compare two files on a line by line or character by character basis. The following options are available:

- **/A** use . . . to indicate differences
- **/B** perform comparison on a character basis
- **/C** do not report character differences
- **/L** perform line comparison for program files
- **/N** add line numbers
- **/T** leave tab characters
- **/W** ignore white space at beginning and end of lines

Example:

COMP /B PROC1.ASM PROC2.ASM

carries out a comparison of the files PROC1.ASM and PROC2.ASM on a character by character basis.

DISKCOMP The **DISKCOMP** command provides a means of comparing two (floppy) disks. **DISKCOMP** accepts drive names as parameters and the necessary prompts are generated when a single-drive disk comparison is made.

Example:

DISKCOMP A: B:

compares the disk in drive A: with that placed in drive B:.

EXE2BIN The **EXE2BIN** utility converts, where possible, an EXE program file to a COM program file (which loads faster and makes less demands on memory space).

Example:

EXE2BIN PROCESS

will search for the program PROCESS.EXE and generate a program PROCESS.COM.

TIP

EXE2BIN will not operate on EXE files that require more than 64Kbytes of memory (including space for the stack and data storage) and/or those that make reference to other memory segments (CS, DS, ES and SS *must* all remain the same during program execution).

FASTOPEN The **FASTOPEN** command provides a means of rapidly accessing files. The command is only effective when a hard disk is fitted and should ideally be used when the system is initialised (e.g. from within the AUTOEXEC-.BAT file).

Example:

FASTOPEN C:32

enables fast opening of files and provides for the details of up to 32 files to be retained in RAM.

TIP

FASTOPEN retains details of files within RAM and must not be used concurrently with **ASSIGN**, **JOIN** and **SUBST**.

FDISK The **FDISK** utility allows users to format a hard (fixed) disk. Since the command will render any existing data stored on the disk inaccessible, **FDISK** should be used with extreme caution. Furthermore, improved hard disk partitioning and formatting utilities are normally supplied when a hard disk is purchased. These should be used in preference to **FDISK** whenever possible.

TIP

To ensure that **FDISK** is not used in error, copy **FDISK** to a sub-directory that is not included in the **PATH** statement then erase the original version using the following commands:

CD
MD XDOS
COPY C:\DOS\FDISK.COM C:\XDOS
ERASE C:\DOS\FDISK.COM

Finally, create a batch file, FDISK.BAT, along the following lines and place it in the DOS directory:

ECHO OFF
CLS
ECHO *** You are about to format the hard disk! *******
ECHO All data will be lost - if you do wish to continue
ECHO change to the XDOS directory and type FDISK again.

FIND The **FIND** command can be used to search for a character string within a file. Options include:

- **/C** display the line number(s) where the search string has been located
- **/N** number the lines to show the position within the file
- **/V** display all lines which do not contain the search string

Example:

FIND/C "output" C:/DEV/PROCESS.C

searches the file PROCESS.C present in the DEV sub-directory for occurrences of output. When the search string is located, the command displays the appropriate line number.

FORMAT The **FORMAT** command is used to initialise a floppy or hard disk. The command should be used with caution since it will generally not be possible to recover any data which was previously present. Various options are available including:

/1 single-sided format
/8 format with 8 sectors per track
/B leave space for system tracks to be added (using the **SYS** command)
/N:8 format with 8 sectors per track
/S write system tracks during formatting (note that this must be the last option specified when more than one option is required)
/T:80 format with 80 tracks
/V format and then prompt for a volume label

Examples:
FORMAT A:
formats the disk placed in drive A:.
FORMAT B:/S
formats the disk placed in drive B: as a system disk.

TIP

When you format a disk using the **/S** option there will be less space on the disk for user programs and data. As an example, the system files for DR-DOS 6.0 consume over 100Kbytes of disk space!

JOIN The **JOIN** command provides a means of associating a drive with a particular directory path. The command must be used with care and must not be used with **ASSIGN**, **BACKUP**, **DISKCOPY**, **FORMAT** etc.

KEYB The **KEYB** command invokes the DOS keyboard driver. **KEYB** replaces earlier utilities (such as **KEYBUK**) which were provided with DOS versions prior to MS-DOS 3.3. The command is usually incorporated in an AUTOEXEC.BAT file and must specify the country letters required.
Example:
KEYB UK
selects the UK keyboard layout.

LABEL The **LABEL** command allows a volume label (maximum 11 characters) to be placed in the disk directory.
Example:
LABEL A: TOOLS
will label the disk present in drive A: as TOOLS. This label will subsequently appear when the directory is displayed.

MODE The **MODE** command can be used to select a range of screen and printer options. **MODE** is an extremely versatile command and offers a wide variety of options.
Examples:
MODE LPT1: 120,6
initialises the parallel printer LPT1 for printing 120 columns at 6 lines per inch.
MODE LPT2: 60,8
initialises the parallel printer LPT2 for printing 60 columns at 8 lines per inch.

MODE COM1: 1200,N,8,1
initialises the COM1 serial port for 1200 baud operation with no parity, eight data bits and one stop bit.
MODE COM2: 9600,N,7,2
initialises the COM2 serial port for 9600 baud operation with no parity, seven data bits and two stop bits.
MODE 40
sets the screen to 40 column text mode.
MODE 80
sets the screen to 80 column mode.
MODE BW80
sets the screen to monochrome 40 column text mode.
MODE CO80
sets the screen to colour 80 column mode.
MODE CON CODEPAGE PREPARE= ((850)C:\DOS\EGA.CPI)
loads codepage 850 into memory from the file EGA.CPI located within the DOS directory.

TIP

The **MODE** command can be used to redirect printer output from the parallel port to the serial port using **MODE LPT1:=COM1:**. Normal operation can be restored using **MODE LPT1:**.

PRINT — The **PRINT** command sends the contents of an ASCII text file to the printer. Printing is carried out as a background operation and data is buffered in memory. The default buffer size is 512 bytes however the size of the buffer can be specified using **/B:** (followed by required buffer size in bytes). When the utility is first entered, the user is presented with the opportunity to redirect printing to the serial port (COM1:). A list of files (held in a queue) can also be specified.
Examples:
PRINT README.DOC
prints the file README.DOC from the current directory.
PRINT /B:4096 HELP1.TXT HELP2.TXT HELP3.TXT
establishes a print queue with the files HELP1.TXT, HELP2.TXT, and HELP3.TXT and also sets the print buffer to 4Kbytes. The files are sent to the printer in the specified sequence.

RESTORE — The **RESTORE** command is used to replace files on the hard disk which were previously saved on floppy disk(s) using the **BACKUP** command. Various options are provided (including restoration of files created before or after a specified date.
Examples:
RESTORE C:\DEV\PROCESS.COM
restores the files PROCESS.COM in the sub-directory named DEV on the hard disk partition, C:. The user is prompted to insert the appropriate floppy disk (in drive A:).
RESTORE C:\BASIC /M

restores all modified (altered or deleted) files present in the sub-directory named BASIC on the hard disk partition, C:.

SYS — The **SYS** command creates a new boot disk by copying the hidden DOS system files. **SYS** is normally used to transfer system files to a disk which has been formatted with the **/S** or **/B** option. **SYS** cannot be used on a disk which has had data written to it after initial formatting.

TREE — The **TREE** command may be used to display a complete directory listing for a given drive. The listing starts with the root directory.

XCOPY — The **XCOPY** utility provides a means of selectively copying files. The utility creates a copy which has the same directory structure as the original. Various options are provided:

- **/A** only copy files which have their archive bit set (but do not reset the archive bits).
- **/D** only files which have been created (or that have been changed) after the specified date.
- **/M** copy files which have their archive bit set but reset the archive bits (to avoid copying files unnecessarily at a later date).
- **/P** prompt for confirmation of each copy.
- **/S** copy files from sub-directories.
- **/V** verify each copy.
- **/W** prompt for disk swaps when using a single drive machine

Example:

XCOPY C:\DOCS*.* A:/M

copy all files present in the DOCS sub-directory of drive C:. Files will be copied to the disk in drive A:. Only those files which have been modified (i.e. had their archive bits set) will be copied.

TIP

Always use XCOPY in preference to COPY when sub-directories exist. As an example, XCOPY C:\DOS*.* A:\ /S will copy all files present in the DOS directory on drive C: together with all files present in any sub-directories, to the root directory of the disk in A:.

Using batch files

Batch files provide a means of avoiding the tedium of repeating a sequence of operating system commands many times over. Batch files are nothing more than straightforward ASCII text files which contain the commands which are to be executed when the name of the batch is entered. Execution of a batch file is automatic; the commands are executed just as if they had been typed in at the keyboard. Batch files may also contain the names of executable program files (i.e. those with a COM or EXE extension), in which case the specified program is executed and, provided the program makes a conventional exit to DOS upon termination, execution of the batch file will resume upon termination.

Batch file commands

DOS provides a number of commands which are specifically intended for inclusion within batch files.

Command	Function
ECHO	The **ECHO** command may be used to control screen output during execution of a batch file. **ECHO** may be followed by **ON** or **OFF** or by a text string which will be displayed when the command line is executed. Examples: **ECHO OFF** disables the echoing (to the screen) of commands contained within the batch file. **ECHO ON** re-enables the echoing (to the screen) of commands contained within the batch file. (Note that there is no need to use this command at the end of a batch file as the reinstatement of screen echo of keyboard generated commands is automatic.) **ECHO Sorting data – please wait!** displays the message: **Sorting data – please wait!** on the screen.

TIP

You can use **@ECHO OFF** to disable printing of the ECHO command itself. You will normally want to use this command instead of **ECHO OFF**.

FOR	**FOR** is used with **IN** and **DO** to implement a series of repeated commands. Examples: **FOR %A IN (IN.DOC OUT.DOC MAIN.DOC) DO COPY %A LPT1:** copies the files IN.DOC, OUT.DOC, and MAIN.DOC in the current directory to the printer. **FOR %A IN (*.DOC) DO COPY %A LPT1:** copies all the files having a DOC extension in the current directory to the printer. The command has the same effect as **COPY *.DOC LPT1:**.
IF	If is used with **GOTO** to provide a means of branching within a batch file. **GOTO** must be followed by a label (which must begin with :). Example: **IF NOT EXIST SYSTEM.INI GOTO :EXIT** transfers control to the label **:EXIT** if the file SYSTEM.INI cannot be found in the current directory.
PAUSE	the pause command suspends execution of a batch file until the user presses any key. The message: **Press any key when ready . . .** is displayed on the screen.
REM	The **REM** command is used to precede lines of text which will constitute remarks. Example: **REM Check that the file exists before copying**

Creating batch files

Batch files may be created using an ASCII text editor or a word processor (operating in ASCII mode). Alternatively, if the batch file comprises only a few lines, the file may be created using the DOS COPY command. As an example, let us suppose that we wish to create a batch file which will:

1. Erase all of the files present on the disk placed in drive B:.
2. Copy all of the files in drive A: having a TXT extension to produce an identically named set of files on the disk placed in drive B:.
3. Rename all of the files having a TXT extension in drive A: so that they have a BAK extension.

The required operating system commands are thus:

```
ERASE B:\*.*
COPY A:\*.TXT B:\
RENAME A:\*.TXT A:\*.BAK
```

The following keystrokes may be used to create a batch file named ARCHIVE.BAT containing the above commands (note that <ENTER> is used to terminate each line of input):

```
COPY CON: ARCHIVE.BAT
ERASE B:\*.*
COPY A:\*.TXT B:\
RENAME A:\*.TXT A:\*.BAK
<CTRL-Z>
```

If you wish to view the batch file which you have just created simply enter the command:

```
TYPE ARCHIVE.BAT
```

Whenever you wish to execute the batch file simply type:

```
ARCHIVE
```

Note that, if necessary, the sequence of commands contained within a batch file may be interrupted by typing:

```
<CTRL-C>
```

(i.e. press and hold down the CTRL key and then press the C key).

The system will respond by asking you to confirm that you wish to terminate the batch job. Respond with **Y** to terminate the batch process or **N** if you wish to continue with it.

Additional commands can easily be appended to an existing batch file. Assume that we wish to view the directory of the disk in drive A: after running the archive batch file. We can simply append the extra commands to the batch files by entering:

```
COPY ARCHIVE.BAT + CON:
```

The system displays the filename followed by the CON prompt. The extra line of text can now be entered using the following keystrokes (again with each line terminated by <ENTER>):

```
DIR A:\
<CTRL-Z>
```

Passing parameters

Parameters may be passed to batch files by including the % character to act as a place holder for each parameter passed. The parameters are numbered strictly in the sequence in which they appear after the name of the batch file. As an example, suppose that we have created a batch file called REBUILD, and this file requires two file specifications to be passed as parameters. Within the text of the batch file, these parameters will be represented by %1 and %2. The first file specification following the name of the batch file will be %1 and the second will be %2. Hence, if we enter the command:

```
REBUILD PROC1.DAT PROC2.DAT
```

During execution of the batch file, %1 will be replaced by PROC1.DAT whilst %2 will be replaced by PROC2.DAT.

It is also possible to implement simple testing and branching within a batch file. Labels used for branching should preferably be stated in lower case (to avoid confusion with operating systems commands) and should be preceded by a colon when they are the first (or only) statement in a line. The following example, which produces a sorted list of directories, illustrates these points:

```
@ECHO OFF
IF EXIST %1 GOTO valid
ECHO Missing or invalid parameter
GOTO end
:valid
ECHO Index of Directories in %1
DIR %1 | FIND "<DIR>" | SORT
:end
```

The first line disables the echoing of subsequent commands contained within the batch file. The second line determines whether, or not, a valid parameter has been entered. If the parameter is invalid (or missing) the **ECHO** command is used to print an error message on the screen.

TIP

Simple menus can be created with batch files. As an example, the following batch files make a very simple 'front-end' for three well-known DOS applications:

```
MENU.BAT    ECHO OFF
            CLS
            CD\
            ECHO **** MENU ****
            ECHO [1] = ASEASY
            ECHO [2] = DBASE
            ECHO [3] = QBASIC
            ECHO **************
1.BAT       CD ASEASY
            ASEASY
2.BAT       CD DBASE
            DBASE
3.BAT       CD QBASIC
            QBASIC
```

Note that all four batch files must be present in the root directory.

Using CONFIG.SYS

When DOS starts, but before the commands within the AUTOEXEC-.BAT file are executed, DOS searches the root directory of the boot disk for a file called CONFIG.SYS. If this file exists, DOS will attempt to carry out the commands in the file. As with any batch file, the configuration sequence can be abandoned by means of <CTRL-C> or <CTRL-BREAK>. CONFIG.SYS is a plain ASCII text file with commands on separate lines. The file can be created using any text editor or word processor operating in ASCII mode (CONFIG.SYS can also be created using **COPY CON:** as described earlier for the creation of batch files).

Only the following subset of DOS commands are valid within CONFIG.SYS:

Command	**Function**
BREAK	Determines the response to a <CTRL-BREAK> sequence. If you set **BREAK ON** in CONFIG.SYS, DOS checks to see whether you have requested a break whenever a DOS call is made. If you set **BREAK OFF**, DOS checks for a break only when it is working with the video display, keyboard, printer or a serial port.
BUFFERS	Sets the number of file buffers which DOS uses. This command can be used to significantly improve disk performance with early versions of DOS and when a disk cache (accessed via IBMCACHE.SYS or SMARTDRV.SYS) is not available. The use of buffers can greatly reduce the number of disk accesses that DOS performs (DOS only reads and writes full sectors). Data is held within a buffer until it is full. Furthermore, by reusing the least-recently used buffers, DOS retains information more likely to be needed next. It is worth noting that each buffer occupies 512 bytes of RAM (plus 16 additional bytes overhead). Hence, the number of buffers may have to be traded-off against the amount of conventional RAM available (particularly in the case of machines with less than the standard 640K RAM). In general, **BUFFERS=20** will prove adequate for most applications. **BUFFERS=40** (or greater) may be necessary for database or other applications which make intensive use of disk files. DOS uses a default value for **BUFFERS** of between 2 and 15 (depending upon the disk and RAM configuration). Later versions of DOS (e.g. MS-DOS 4.1) provide a much improved **BUFFERS** command which includes support for expanded memory and look-ahead buffers which can store sectors ahead of those requested by a DOS read operation. The number of look-ahead buffers must be specified (in the range 0 to 8) and each buffer requires 512 bytes of memory and corresponds exactly to one disk sector. The use of expanded memory can be enabled by means of a /X switch. Example: **BUFFERS=100,8 /X** sets the number of buffers to 100 (requiring approximately 52Kbytes of expanded memory) and also enables eight look-ahead buffers (requiring a further 4Kbytes of expanded memory).
COUNTRY	Sets the country-dependent information.
DEVICE	Set the hardware device drivers to be used with DOS. Examples: **DEVICE=C:\MOUSE\MOUSE.SYS** enables the mouse driver (MOUSE.SYS) which contained in a sub-directory called MOUSE. **DEVICE=C:\DOS\ANSI.SYS** selects the ANSI.SYS screen driver (the ANSI.SYS file must be present in the DOS directory). **DEVICE=C:\WINDOWS\HIMEM.SYS** selects the Windows extended memory manager HIMEM.SYS (the HIMEM.SYS file must be present

in the WINDOWS directory).
DEVICE=C:\DOS\DISPLAY.SYS CON=(EGA,850,2) selects the DOS display driver and switches it to multilingual EGA mode (code page 850) with up to two code pages.

TIP

Drivers often provide a number of 'switches' which allow you to optimise them for a particular hardware configuration. Always consult the hardware supplier's documentation to ensure that you have the correct configuration for your system.

TIP

You may find it handy to locate all of your drivers in a common directory called DRIVERS, DEVICE or SYS. This will keep them separate from applications and help you to find them at some later date.

Finally, note that you can load as many device drivers as you need, but you must use a separate DEVICE line for each driver.
Example:
DEVICE = C:\DRIVERS\ANSI.SYS
DEVICE = C:\DRIVERS\CDROM.SYS

FCBS — Set the number of file control blocks that DOS can have open at any time (note that this command is now obsolete).

FILES — Sets the maximum number of files that DOS can access at any time.

INSTALL — Installs memory-resident programs.
Example:
INSTALL = C:\DOS\FASTOPEN.EXE C:=100
installs the DOS **FASTOPEN** utility and configures it to track the opening of up to 100 files and directories on drive C:.

TIP

Slightly less memory is used when memory-resident programs are loaded with this command than with AUTOEXEC.BAT. Do not, however, use INSTALL to load programs that use environment variables or shortcut keys or that require COMMAND.COM to be present to handle critical errors.

LASTDRIVE — Specifies the highest disk drive on the computer.

REM — Treats a line as a comment/remark.

SHELL — Determines the DOS command processor (e.g. COMMAND.COM).

STACKS — Sets the number of stacks that DOS uses.

SWITCHES — Disables extended keyboard functions.

Using device drivers

DOS provides a number of device drivers and utility programs which can be installed from CONFIG.SYS. The following drivers will allow you to make the most of your own particular hardware configuration and to modify it to cater for hardware upgrades:

Function	**Device driver (generic name)**
Disk caches	IBMCACHE.SYS, SMARTDRV.SYS
RAM drives	RAMDRIVE.SYS, VDISK.SYS
Additional disk drives	DRIVER.SYS
Memory management	XMAEM.SYS, EMM386.SYS, EMM386.EXE
Display adapter configuration	DISPLAY.SYS
Printer configuration	PRINTER.SYS

Note: The names of device drivers tend to vary with different versions of DOS.

Disk caching

A disk cache provides improved file access times and helps to reduce the number of physical disk accesses made by a program which makes regular use of disk files. Data is initially read from the disk into the cache. Subsequent file accesses make use of the cache rather than the disk itself. At some later time, data is written back to the disk. Generally a cache will hold more information than is likely to be requested at any one time by the program. Redundant disk accesses are eliminated as data in the cache can be manipulated directly without having to access data on the disk.

A disk cache remembers what sections of the disk have been used most frequently. When the cache must be recycled, the program keeps the more frequently used areas and discards those less frequently used. Some experimentation will normally be required in order to obtain the optimum size of a disk cache. This also varies according to the requirements of a particular application program.

TIP

Because of its 'intelligent' features, a disk cache will normally outperform a disk buffer (created using the **BUFFERS** directive). Furthermore, a disk cache offers some advantages over a RAM drive since its operation is 'transparent' and you are less likely to lose all your data due to power failure. If your applications program makes frequent use of disk files, it is well worth setting up a cache.

Using IBMCACHE.SYS

IBMCACHE.SYS is a file that accompanies any IBM PS/2 machine that uses extended memory (this excludes Models 25 and 30). The program is installed by inserting from the Reference Disk. The cache can be changed after installation either by re-running **IBMCACHE** or by editing the reference to **IBMCACHE** in CONFIG.SYS.

Example:

DEVICE = C:\IBMDOS\IBMCACHE.SYS 32 /E /P4

configures the cache size to 32Kbytes using extended memory and allows four sectors to be read at a time. IBMCACHE.SYS is resident in the IBMDOS directory.

Using SMARTDRV.SYS

MS-DOS, DR-DOS and Novell DOS offer an alternative disk-caching utility called SMARTDRV.SYS which is installed by means of an appropriate directive within CONFIG.SYS.

Example:

DEVICE = C:\WINDOWS\SMARTDRV.SYS 512 /A

configures the cache size to 512Kbytes using expanded memory with SMARTDRV.SYS resident in the WINDOWS directory.

(Note that 256Kbytes is the default cache size for SMARTDRV.)

Using RAMDRIVE.SYS (or VDISK.SYS)

RAMDRIVE.SYS (or VDISK.SYS) is used to simulate a disk drive in RAM. The simulated drive behaves exactly like a conventional drive but with vastly improved access time. RAMDRIVE.SYS is installed using the **DEVICE** command from within CONFIG.SYS. A RAM drive can be established in conventional memory, extended memory or expanded memory as appropriate.

Examples:

DEVICE = C:\DOS\VDISK.SYS

establishes a RAM drive of 642Kbytes (the default size) with 128 bytes per sector (the default sector size) and 64 directory entries (the default number of directory entries) within conventional base memory.

DEVICE = C:\DOS\RAMDRIVE.SYS 128 512 96 /X

establishes a RAM drive of 1282Kbytes with 512 bytes per sector and 96 directory entries within expanded memory.

DEVICE = C:\DOS\VDISK.SYS 256 256 128 /E

establishes a RAM drive of 256Kbytes with 256 bytes per sector and 128 directory entries within extended memory.

DEVICE = C:\DRIVERS\RAMDRIVE.SYS 512 256 96 /A

creates a 512Kbytes RAM disk with 256 byte sectors and 96 directory entries in expanded memory.

DEVICE = C:\DRIVERS\RAMDRIVE.SYS 1024 512 128 /E

creates a 1Mbyte RAM disk with 512 byte sectors and 128 directory entries in extended memory.

TIP

Where RAM space is at a premium, use a small sector size (e.g. 128 bytes). This works because DOS does not allow files to share the same sector – a 513 byte file would occupy two sectors with 511 bytes wasted! If, however, memory is not limited, it is better to use a relatively large sector size in order to reduce access time.

TIP

Remember that the data stored in a RAM drive will be lost when the power is removed from the system. It is vital to backup your data before switching off!

TIP

A RAM drive can provide a quick method of copying disks on a system which has only one disk drive. You simply use **VDISK** or **RAMDRIVE** to establish a RAM drive with identical features to your existing (single) drive and then use **DISKCOPY**. The parameters for standard drives are:

Drive type	RAMDRIVE or VDISK parameters
5.25" 360Kbytes	360 512 112 /E or /A, as required
5.25" 1.2Mbytes	1200 512 224 /E or /A, as required
3.5" 720Kbytes	720 512 112 /E or /A, as required
3.5" 1.44Mbytes	1440 512 224 /E or /A, as required
3.5" 2.88Mbytes	2880 512 240 /E or /A, as required

Using DRIVER.SYS

DRIVER.SYS can be used to configure a system for use with a non-standard or an external disk drive.

Examples:

DEVICE = C:\DOS\DRIVER.SYS /D:2 /F:0 /S:9 /T:40

designates a third floppy disk drive in a system which already has two disk drives (the parameter following the **/D** switch is the 'physical drive number') having a capacity of 360K, 9 sectors per track and 40 tracks.

DEVICE = C:\DOS\DRIVER.SYS /D:2 /F:0 /S:9 /T:40
DEVICE = C:\DOS\DRIVER.SYS /D:2 /F:0 /S:9 /T:40

specifies *two* further disk drives (D: and E:), each 360Kbytes, 9 sectors per track, with 40 tracks. Each time the driver is loaded, the physical disk drive is assigned an additional valid drive letter automatically (D: the first time, E: the second time, and so on).

DEVICE = C:\DOS\DRIVER.SYS /F:1 /T:80 /S:15 /H:2 /C

specifies a conventional 1.2Mbyte 5¼" floppy disk drive (incorporating a disk change line).

DEVICE = C:\DOS\DRIVER.SYS /F:2 /T:80 /S:9 /H:2 /C

specifies a conventional 720Kbyte 3½" floppy disk drive (incorporating a disk change line).

DEVICE = C:\DOS\DRIVER.SYS /F:7 /T:80 /S:18 /H:2 /C

specifies a conventional 1.44Mbyte 3½" floppy disk drive (incorporating a disk change line).

Using EMM386

The EMM386 memory manager requires an 80386 (or later) CPU and provides a means of accessing the unused parts of the upper memory area. The memory manager also allows you to use your system's extended memory to simulate expanded memory. Note that EMM386 is provided as EMM386.SYS with MS-DOS 4.0 and DR-DOS 6.0 but as EMM386.EXE with MS-DOS5.0 (and later).

Examples:

DEVICE = C:\DOS\EMM386.SYS

installs the memory manager and takes 256Kbytes (the default) of extended memory to provide expanded memory (MS-DOS 4.0).

DEVICE = C:\DOS\EMM386.SYS 1024

installs the memory manager and takes 1Mbyte of extended memory to provide expanded memory (MS-DOS 4.0).

DEVICE = C:\DOS\EMM386.EXE 1024 RAM

provides access to the upper memory area and also uses 1024Kbytes of your computer's extended memory as expanded memory (MS-DOS 5.0 and later).

DEVICE = C:\DOS\EMM386.EXE NOEMS
provides access to all available portions of the upper memory area but without functioning as an expanded memory emulator (MS-DOS 5.0 and later).

DEVICE = C:\DRDOS\EMM386.SYS /F=NONE /B=AUTO /E=E800-FFFF
autoscans upper memory from C000 to FFFF (the default) but specifically excludes the area from E800 to FFFF. No LIM page frame is set up and the DOS kernel is loaded into upper memory or, if there is not enough upper memory, it is loaded into high memory (DR-DOS 6.0).

DEVICE = C:\DRDOS\EMM386.SYS /FRAME=C400 /KB=2048 /BDOS=FFFF
autoscans upper memory from C000 to FFFF (the default) and sets up a LIM window with 2Mbytes available. BDOS is located to segment address FFFF in high memory (DR-DOS 6.0).

TIP

The optimum sequence in which device drivers should appear within your CONFIG.SYS file is as follows:

1. HIMEM.SYS
2. An expanded memory manager (if your system is fitted with expanded memory.
3. Any device drivers that use extended memory.
4. EMM386.EXE (do not use EMM386 if you are using an expanded memory manager).
5. Any device drivers that use expanded memory.
6. Any device drivers that use the upper memory area.

Using DISPLAY.SYS

DISPLAY.SYS enables you to switch code pages without restarting DOS and PRINTER.SYS enables you to download a font table to supported printers so that they can print non-English language and graphic characters.

The DISPLAY.SYS utility caters for different display types and for specified code pages. You do not have to include DISPLAY.SYS if you do not use code-page switching. Valid display types are:

Display type	Meaning
MONO	Monochrome adapter
CGA	Colour-graphics adapter
EGA	Enhanced colour-graphics adapter or PS/2 or VGA
LCD	Convertible LCD

Valid code pages are:

Code page	Country
437	United States
850	Multilingual
860	Portugal
863	Canadian-French
865	Norway

The number specified within the DISPLAY.SYS command is the maximum number of additional code pages that the adapter can use

Example:

DEVICE = C:\DOS\DISPLAY.SYS CON: = (EGA,850,2)
specifies an EGA (or VGA) display using the multilingual code page 850 with two code pages.

DEVICE = C:\SYS\DISPLAY.SYS CON = (EGA,437,1)

specifies an EGA (or VGA) display using 437 as the starting code page together with one additional code page.
DEVICE = C:\SYS\DISPLAY.SYS CON = (EGA,850,863,2)
selects an EGA (or VGA) display and a code page of 863 (French-Canadian) together with the multilingual code page, 850.

TIP

If your existing code page is not 437 (United States or United Kingdom) always use 850 as the new code page and 2 as the number of additional code pages.

TIP

If you use ANSI.SYS and DISPLAY.SYS together in your CONFIG.SYS file, the ANSI.SYS command must be used before the DISPLAY.SYS directive. ANSI.SYS will not take effect when the order is reversed.

Using PRINTER.SYS

You can use PRINTER.SYS to print the required code page characters on supported printers (or on printers that provide emulation for the supported types). Note that MS-DOS 3.3 supports code pages on only two printers:
IBM ProPrinter Model 4201
IBM Quietwriter III Model 5202
MS-DOS 4.0 and MS-DOS 5.0 provide additional support for the following printers:
IBM ProPrinter Model 4202
IBM ProPrinter Model 4207
IBM ProPrinter Model 4208
Valid code pages are:

Code page	**Country**
437	United States
850	Multilingual
860	Portugal
863	Canadian-French
865	Norway

Example:
DEVICE = C:\DOS\PRINTER.SYS LPT1=(4201,850,2)
specifies the IBM ProPrinter Model 4201 connected to the parallel printer port and using the multilingual code page as the built-in character set. You can specify two code pages for the printer and then switch between them.

Using AUTOEXEC.BAT

The AUTOEXEC.BAT file allows you to automatically execute a series of programs and DOS utilities to add further functionality to your system when the system is initialised. AUTOEXEC.BAT normally contains a sequence of DOS commands but in addition it can also contain the name of an application or shell that will be launched automatically when the system is booted. This is a useful facility if you always use the same shell or application whenever you power-up your system or if you wish to protect the end-user from the need to remember rudimentary DOS commands (such as **MD**, **CD**, **XCOPY** etc.).

AUTOEXEC.BAT is typically used to:

1. Set up the system prompt (see page 185).
2. Define the path for directory searches (using **SET PATH**, see page 185).
3. Execute certain DOS utilities (e.g. **SHARE**).
4. Load a mouse driver (e.g. MOUSE.COM).
5. Change directories (e.g. from the root directory to a 'working' directory).
6. Launch an application or shell program (e.g. PCSHELL, Windows etc.).

The example CONFIG.SYS and AUTOEXEC.BAT files which follow should give you plenty of food for thought!

TIP

Microsoft's Windows and some DOS programs (e.g. AutoCAD) have their own built-in mouse drivers and can thus communicate directly with the mouse. However, if you regularly use a mouse with DOS applications, you will probably wish to include reference to your mouse driver within the AUTOEXEC.BAT file.

TIP

Don't be afraid to experiment with your CONFIG.SYS and AUTOEXEC.BAT files but do make sure that you keep back up copies of your original files (CONFIG.BAK, CONFIG.OLD etc.). Each time, use the MEM command with the /**PROGRAM**, /**DEBUG**, or /**CLASSIFY** switches to see the effect of your drivers and memory managers.

Example CONFIG.SYS and AUTOEXEC.BAT files

2Mbyte notebook for Windows 3.1 and MS-DOS 5.0

File	Content	Notes
CONFIG.SYS	DEVICE=C:\WINDOWS\HIMEM.SYS	Load the Windows high memory device driver
	DOS=HIGH	Load DOS into high memory
	FILES=40	Allow for up to 40 files
	BUFFERS=10	Provide 10 file buffers
	STACKS=9,256	Create 9 stacks each of 256 bytes
AUTOEXEC.BAT	PROMPT PG	Prompt with current directory path
	SET PATH=C:\DOS;C:\WINDOWS	Search DOS and Windows directories for executable files
	SET TEMP=C:\TEMP	Directory for Windows swap files
	C:\DOS\SHARE.EXE	Permits file sharing and locking
	C:\WINDOWS\SMARTRDV.EXE	Establish a disk cache
	CD WINDOWS	Change to the Windows directory . . .
	WIN	and run Windows!

COMMENT: Windows performance will be disappointing with limited memory, however, the disk cache will improve disk access time.

4Mbyte business machine for Windows 3.1 and MS-DOS 5.0

File	Content	Notes
CONFIG.SYS	DEVICE=C:\WINDOWS\HIMEM.SYS	Load the Windows high memory device driver
	DOS=HIGH	Load DOS in high memory
	FILES=64	Allow for up to 64 files
	BUFFERS=16	Provide 16 file buffers
	STACKS=9,256	Set up 9 stacks each of 256 bytes
	SHELL=C:\DOS\COMMAND.COM C:\DOS /E:1024 /P	Specify the command interpreter and a 1Kbyte environment
AUTOEXEC.BAT	PROMPT PG	Prompt with current directory path
	SET PATH=C:\DOS;C:\WINDOWS	Search DOS and Windows directories for executable files
	SET TEMP=C:\TEMP	Directory for Windows swap files
	LOADHIGH=C:\DOS\SHARE.EXE	Permits file sharing and locking
	C:\WINDOWS\SMARTRDV.EXE	Establishes a disk cache
	SET COMSPEC=C:\DOS\COMMAND.COM	Specify the location of the command interpreter
	CD WINDOWS	Change to the Windows directory . . .
	WIN	and run Windows!

COMMENT: With more memory space available it is possible to allocate more buffers and provide for more files.

4Mbyte business machine for Windows 3.1 and DOS applications running under MS-DOS 5.0

File	Content	Notes
CONFIG.SYS	DEVICE=C:\WINDOWS\HIMEM.SYS	Load the Windows high memory device driver
	DEVICE=C:\WINDOWS\EMM386.EXE RAM NOEMS	Load the memory manager
	DOS=HIGH,UMB	Load DOS into a UMB
	DEVICEHIGH=C:\WINDOWS\MOUSE.SYS /Y	Load the mouse driver into high memory
	SHELL=C:\DOS\COMMAND.COM C:\DOS /E:1024 /P	Specify the command interpreter and a 1Kbyte environment
	FILES=64	Allow for up to 64 files
	BUFFERS=16	Provide 16 file buffers
	STACKS=9,256	Set up 9 stacks each of 256 bytes
AUTOEXEC.BAT	PROMPT PG	Prompt with current directory path
	SET PATH=C:\DOS;C:\WINDOWS	Search DOS and Windows directories for executable files
	SET TEMP=C:\TEMP	Directory for Windows swap files
	LOADHIGH=C:\DOS\SHARE.EXE	Permits file sharing and locking
	C:\WINDOWS\SMARTRDV.EXE	Establishes a disk cache
	LOADHIGH C:\DOS\KEYB UK,,C:\DOS\KEYBOARD.SYS	Specify a UK keyboard layout
	LOADHIGH C:\DOS\DOSKEY	Remember last used commands
	SET COMSPEC=C:\DOS\COMMAND.COM	Specify the location of the command interpreter

COMMENT: A more elaborate configuration is required for this system which is used for both DOS and Windows applications.

4Mbyte machine for network use, MS-DOS 5.0

File	Content	Notes
CONFIG.SYS	DEVICE=C:\WINDOWS\HIMEM.SYS	Load the Windows high memory device driver
	DEVICE=C:\WINDOWS\EMM386.EXE RAM NOEMS	Load the memory manager
	DOS=HIGH,UMB	Load DOS in high memory
	DEVICEHIGH=C:\WINDOWS\MOUSE.SYS /Y	Load the mouse driver into high memory
	SHELL=C:\DOS\COMMAND.COM C:\DOS /E:1024 /P	Specify the command interpreter and a 1Kbyte environment
	FILES=80	Allow for up to 80 files
	BUFFERS=16	Provide 16 file buffers
	STACKS=9,256	Set up 9 stacks each of 256 bytes
AUTOEXEC.BAT	PROMPT PG	Prompt with directory path
	SET PATH=C:\DOS;C:\WINDOWS	Search DOS and Windows directories for executable files
	SET TEMP=C:\TEMP	Directory for Windows swap files
	LOADHIGH=C:\DOS\SHARE.EXE	Permits file sharing and locking
	C:\WINDOWS\SMARTRDV.EXE	Establishes a disk cache
	LOADHIGH C:\DOS\KEYB UK,,C:\DOS\KEYBOARD.SYS	Specify a UK keyboard layout
	LOADHIGH C:\DOS\DOSKEY	Remember last used commands
	LOADHIGH C:\NETWARE\IPX.COM	Load Netware drivers into high memory (if available)
	LOADHIGH C:\NETWARE\NETX.COM	
	SET COMSPEC=C:\DOS\COMMAND.COM	Specify the location of the command interpreter

COMMENT: Notice the Netware drivers, IPX.COM and NETX.COM. Both are loaded into high memory.

4Mbyte home computer for games, MS-DOS 5.0

File	Content	Notes
CONFIG.SYS	DEVICE=C:\DOS\HIMEM.SYS	Load the Windows high memory device driver
	DEVICE=C:\WINDOWS\EMM386.EXE 1024 RAM	Load the memory manager
	DOS=HIGH,UMB	Loads DOS in high memory
	DEVICEHIGH=C:\WINDOWS\MOUSE.SYS /Y	Load the mouse driver into high memory
	FILES=20	Allow for only 20 files
	BUFFERS=10	Provide 10 file buffers
	STACKS=2,256	Set up 2 stacks each of 256 bytes
AUTOEXEC.BAT	PROMPT PG	Prompt with directory path
	SET PATH=C:\DOS;C:\GAMES	Search DOS and Games directories for executable files

COMMENT: Many modern games require an appreciable amount of base memory (as much as 600Kbytes in some cases). This configuration maximises the amount of base RAM available for use by a games program.

2Mbyte laptop for DOS, DR-DOS 6.0

File	Content	Notes
CONFIG.SYS	DEVICE=C:\DRDOS\EMM386.SYS	Load the memory manager
	HIDEVICE=C:\DRDOS\ANSI.SYS	Load the ANSI screen driver
	FILES=48	Allow for 48 files
	BUFFERS=25	Provide 25 file buffers
	FASTOPEN=512	Reduces file access time
	HISTORY=ON,256,OFF	Remember last used commands
	COUNTRY=001,,C:\DRDOS\COUNTRY.SYS	Specify a US keyboard
AUTOEXEC.BAT	PROMPT PG	Prompt with directory path
	SET PATH=C:\DOS;C:\UTILITY;C:\APPS	Search DOS, Utility and Apps directories for Executable files

COMMENT: The limited RAM available on this machine does not affect its performance when running basic DOS applications. Some of the DOS programs and utilities used on this system make use of the ANSI.SYS screen driver.

4Mb '486 based notebook for MS-DOS 6.2 and Windows 3.1

File	Content	Notes
CONFIG.SYS	DEVICE=C:\DOS\HIMEM.SYS	Load the Windows high memory device driver
	DEVICE=C:\DOS\EMM386.EXE RAM	Load the memory manager
	BUFFERS=40	Provide 40 file buffers
	FILES=30	Allow for up to 30 files
	LASTDRIVE=E	Allow for external Zip drive D:
	DEVICEHIGH /L:1,12048 =C:\DOS\SETVER.EXE	Allow older applications to function correctly
	DOS=HIGH,UMB	Use high memory for DOS
	COUNTRY=044,,C:\DOS\COUNTRY.SYS	Specify the UK keyboard layout
	DEVICEHIGH /L:2,15792 =C:\DOS\DISPLAY.SYS CON=(EGA,,1)	Set up display driver in high memory
	STACKS=9,256	Set up 9 stacks each of 256 bytes
	DEVICEHIGH=C:\DOS\DBLSPACE.SYS /MOVE	Set up Doublespace utility
AUTOEXEC.BAT	LH /L:0;1,45456 /S C:\DOS\SMARTDRV.EXE /X	Load the disk cache into high memory
	@ECHO OFF	Disable screen messages
	PROMPT pg	Set up conventional prompt
	PATH=C:\WINDOWS;C:\DOS;C:\UTILITY;C:\ODAPI	
	SET TEMP=C:\DOS	
	MODE CON CODEPAGE PREPARE=((437) C:\DOS\EGA.CPI)	Set up code page
	MODE CON CODEPAGE SELECT=437	
	LH /L:1,16656 KEYB UK,,C:\DOS\KEYBOARD.SYS	Set up keyboard driver
	LH /L:2,6384 DOSKEY	And DOS 6.2 DOSKEY utility
	C:\MOUSE\MOUSE /MI	Load Microsoft Mouse driver
	C:\TOOLS_31\GUEST.EXE	Install Zip drive driver
	CLS	Clear the screen
	ECHO ==================================	Display message
	ECHO Property of John Smith	
	ECHO Tel: 01223–768123	
	ECHO ==================================	

COMMENT: This system is used not only for mainstream Windows applications but also with some mouse drive DOS applications. The hard disk uses disk compression and a Zip drive is used for backup purposes.

TIP

Within CONFIG.SYS, the command that loads DOS into high memory (DOS=HIGH,UMB) must follow the command that loads the high memory device driver, HIMEM.SYS.

TIP

You can easily include a message within the AUTOEXEC-.BAT file to name the owner of the system:

```
@ECHO OFF
ECHO ********************************
ECHO * This system belongs to: *
ECHO *         A. N. Other       *
ECHO *   Tel: 081–123–45678   *
ECHO ********************************
```

Using DEBUG

One of the most powerful (but often neglected) tools available within the MS-DOS environment is the debugger, DEBUG.COM. This program provides a variety of facilities including single-stepping a program to permit examination of the CPU registers and the contents of memory after execution of each instruction.

The debug command line can accept several arguments. Its syntax is as follows:

DEBUG [filespec] [parm1] [parm2]

where [filespec] is the specification of the file to be loaded into memory, [parm1] and [parm2] are optional parameters for the specified file.

As an example, the following MS-DOS command will load debug along with the file MYPROG.COM (taken from the disk in drive B:) ready for debugging:

DEBUG B:\MYPROG.COM

When debug has been loaded, the familiar MS-DOS prompt is replaced by a hyphen (-). This indicates that DEBUG is awaiting a command from the user. Commands comprise single letters (in either upper or lower case). Delimiters are optional between commands and parameters. They must, however, be used to seperate adjacent hexadecimal values.

<CTRL-BREAK> can be used to abort a DEBUG command whilst <CTRL-NUM.LOCK> can be used to pause the display (any other keystroke restarts the output). Commands may be edited using the keys available for normal MS-DOS command editing.

TIP

All debug commands accept parameters (except the Q command). You can separate parameters with commas or spaces, but these separators are required only between two hexadecimal values. Therefore the following commands are equivalent:

D CS:100 110
DCS:100 110
D,CS:100,110

TIP

Hard copy of Debug sessions can sometimes be very useful. If you need this facility, just type <CTRL-P> before the DEBUG command and then all your screen output will be echoed to your printer. Press <CTRL-P> a second time in order to cancel the printer echo.

Debug commands

Command	Meaning	Function
A [addr]	Assemble	Assemble mnemonics into memory from the specified address. If no address is specified, the code will be assembled into memory from address CS:0100. The <ENTER> key is used to terminate assembly and return to the debug prompt. Examples: **A 200** starts assembly from address CS:0200. **A 4E0:100** starts assembly from address 04E0:0100 (equivalent to a physical address of 04F00).
C range addr	Compare	Compare memory in the specified range with memory starting at the specified address.
D [addr]	Dump	Dump (display) memory from the given starting address. If no start address is specified, the dump will commence at DS:0100. Examples: **D 400** dumps memory from address DS:0400. **D CS:0** dumps memory from address CS:0000.
D [range]		Dump (display) memory within the specified range. Example: **D DS:200 20F** displays 16 bytes of memory from DS:0200 to DS:0210 inclusive.
E addr [list]	Enter	Enter (edit) bytes into memory starting at the given address. If no list of data bytes is specified, byte values are displayed and may be sequentially overwritten. <SPACE> may be used to advance, and <-> may be used to reverse the memory pointer. Example: **E 200,3C,FF,1A,FE** places byte values of 3C, FF, 1A and FE into four consecutive memory locations commencing at DS:0200.
F range list	Fill	Fills memory in the given range with data in the list. The list is repeated until all memory locations have been filled. Examples: **F 100,10F,FF**

		fills 16 bytes of memory with FF commencing at address DS:0100. **F 0, FFFF,AA,FF** fills 65536 bytes of memory with alternate bytes of AA and FF.
G [=addr]	Go	Executes the code starting at the given address. If no address is specified, execution commences at address CS:IP. Example: **G =100** executes the code starting at address CS:0100.
G [=addr] [addr] [addr]		Executes the code starting at the given address with the specified breakpoints. Example: **G =100 104 10B** executes the code starting at address CS:0100 and with breakpoints at addresses CS:0104 and CS:010B.
H value value	Hexadecimal	Calculates the sum and difference of two hexadecimal values.
I port	Port input	Inputs a byte value from the specified I/O port address and displays the value. Example: **I 302** inputs the byte value from I/O port address 302 and displays the value returned.
L [addr]	Load	Loads the file previously specified by the Name (N) command. The file specification is held at address CS:0080. If no load address is specified, the file is loaded from address CS:0100.
M range addr	Move	Moves (replicates) memory in the given range so that it is replicated starting at the specified address.
N filespec	Name	Names a file to be used for a subsequent Load (L) or Write (W) command. Example: **N B:\MYPROG.COM** names the file MYPROG.COM stored in the root directory of drive B for a subsequent load or write command.
O port byte	Port output	Output a given byte value to the specified I/O port address. Example: **O 303 FE** outputs a byte value of FE from I/O port address 303.
P [=addr] [instr]	Proceed	Executes a subroutine, interrupt, loop or string operation and resumes control at the next instruction. Execution starts at the specified address and continues for the specified number of instructions. If no address is specified, execution commences at the address given by CS:IP.
Q	Quit	Exits debug and return control to the current MS-DOS shell.
R [regname]	Register	Displays the contents of the specified register and allows the contents to be

		modified. If a name is not specified, the contents of all of the CPU registers (including flags) are displayed together with the next instruction to be executed (in hexadecimal and in mnemonic format).
S range list		Search memory within the specified range for the listed data bytes. Example: **S 0100 0800 20,1B** searches memory between address DS:0100 and DS:0800 for consecutive data values of 20 and 1B.
T [=addr] [instr]	Trace	Traces the execution of a program from the specified address and executing the given number of instructions. If no address is specified, the execution starts at address CS:IP. If a number of instructions is not specified then only a single instruction is executed. A register dump (together with a disassembly of the next instruction to be executed) is displayed at each step. Examples: **T** traces the execution of the single instruction referenced by CS:IP. **T =200,4** traces the execution of four instructions commencing at address CS:0200.
U [addr]	Unassemble	Unassemble (disassemble) code into mnemonic instructions starting at the specified address. If no address is specified, disassembly starts from the address given by CS:IP. Examples: **U** disassembles code starting at address CS:IP. **U 200** disassembles code starting at address CS:0200.
U [range]		Unassemble (disassemble) code into mnemonic instructions within the specified range of addresses. Example: **U 200 400** disassembles the code starting at address CS:0200 and ending at address CS:0400.
W [addr]	Write	Writes data to disk from the specified address. The file specification is taken from a previous Name (N) command. If the address is not specified, the address defaults to that specified by CS:IP. The file specification is located at CS:0080.

Notes:

(a) Parameters enclosed in square brackets ([and]) are optional.

(b) The equal sign (=) must precede the start address used by the following commands; Go (G), Proceed (P) and Trace (T).

(c) Parameters have the following meanings:

Parameter	Meaning
addr	Address (which may be quoted as an offset or as the contents of a segment register or segment address followed by an offset). The following are examples of acceptable addresses: **CS:0100** **04C0:0100** **0200**
byte	A byte of data (i.e. a value in the range 0 to FF). The following are examples of acceptable data bytes: **0** **1F** **FE**
filespec	A file specification (which may include a drive letter and sub-directory etc.). The following are examples of acceptable file specifications: **MYPROG.COM** **B:MYPROG.COM** **B:P\PROGS\MYPROG.COM**
instr	The number of instructions to be executed within a Trace (T) or Proceed (P) command.
list	A list of data bytes, ASCII characters (which must be enclosed in single quotes), or strings (which must be enclosed in double quotes). The following examples are all acceptable data lists: **3C,2F,C2,00,10** **'A',':','/'** **"Insert disk and press ENTER"**
port	A port address. The following are acceptable examples of port addresses: E (the DMA controller) 30C (within the prototype range) 378 (the parallel printer)
range	A range of addresses which may be expressed as an address and offset (e.g. CS:100,100) or as an address followed by a size (e.g. DS:100 L 20).
regname	A register name (see (d)). The following are acceptable examples of register names: **AX** **DS** **IP**
value	A hexadecimal value in the range 0 to FFFF.

(d) The following register and flag names are used within debug:

AX, BX, CX, DX	16-bit general purpose registers
CS, DS, ES, SS	Code, data, extra and stack segment registers
SP, BP, IP	Stack, base and instruction pointers
SI, DI	Source and destination index registers
F	Flag register.

(e) The following abbreviations are used to denote the state of the flags in conjunction with the Register (R) and Trace (T) commands:

Flag	Abbreviation	Meaning/status
Overflow	OV	Overflow
	NV	No overflow
Carry	CY	Carry
	NC	No carry
Zero	ZR	Zero
	NZ	Non-zero
Direction	DN	Down
	UP	Up
Interrupt	EI	Interrupts enabled
	DI	Interrupts disabled
Parity	PE	Parity even
	PO	Parity odd
Sign	NG	Negative
	PL	Positive
Auxiliary	AC	
Carry	NC	

(f) All numerical values within Debug are in hexadecimal.

A Debug walkthrough

The following 'walkthrough' has been provided in order to give you an insight into the range of facilities offered by Debug. We shall assume that a short program TEST.EXE has been written to test a printer connected to the parallel port. The program is designed to generate a single line of upper and lower case characters but, since an error is present, the compiled program prints only a single character. The source code for the program (TEST.ASM) is shown in Figure 14.1:

The first stage in the debugging process is to invoke Debug from MS-DOS using the command:

DEBUG TEST.EXE

The command assumes that TEST.EXE is present in the current directory and that DEBUG.EXE is acceptable either directly or via previous use of the SET PATH command.

```
COMMENT |
*******************************************************************
File:           TEST
History:        Started 8/8/92
Purpose:        Displays ASCII characters as a line on the printer, LPT1
Format:         No calling conventions
*******************************************************************|

                TITLE   test                ;
                DOSSEG                      ; Conventional segment allocation
                .MODEL  SMALL               ;
                .STACK  100h                ; 256 byte stack

; *** Data ***

                .DATA
message         DB      "Printer Test Program",13,10
lmessage        EQU     $ - message

; *** Code ***

                .CODE
start:          mov     ax,@DATA            ;
                mov     ds,ax               ; segment location of data
                mov     bx,1                ; handle for standard output
                mov     cx,lmessage         ; length of message
                mov     dx,OFFSET message           ; address of messaage
                mov     ah,40h              ; DOS write function
                int     21h                 ; call DOS
                mov     dl,41h              ; First character to print is A
                mov     cl,3Eh              ; Number of characters to print
                mov     ah,05h              ; Set up the function code
                int     21h                 ; and print the character
prch:           inc     dl                  ; Get the next character
                loop    prch                ; and go round again
                mov     al,0                ; Set up the return error-level
                mov     ah,4Ch              ; DOS exit function
                int     21h                 ; call DOS
                END     start
```

Figure 14.1 Source code for the program TEST.ASM

```
d0
1CF5:0000  00 00 00 00 00 00 00 00-00 00 00 00 00 00 00 00   ................
1CF5:0010  B8 F8 1C 8E D8 BB 01 00-B9 16 00 BA 04 00 B4 40   ...............@
1CF5:0020  CD 21 B2 41 B1 3E B4 05-CD 21 FE C2 E2 FC B0 00   .!.A.>...!......
1CF5:0030  B4 4C CD 21 50 72 69 6E-74 65 72 20 54 65 73 74   .L.!Printer Test
1CF5:0040  20 50 72 6F 67 72 61 6D-0D 0A 00 00 00 7E FF DB    Program.....~..
1CF5:0050  FF FF C3 E7 FF FF 7E 00-00 00 00 00 00 6C FE FE   ......~......l..
1CF5:0060  FE FE 7C 38 10 00 00 00-00 00 10 38 7C FE 7C      ..|8........8|.|
1CF5:0070  38 10 00 00 00 00 00 00-18 3C 3C E7 E7 E7 18 18   8........<<.....
-
```

Figure 14.2 Using DEBUG's Dump (D) command to display TEST.COM in memory

After the Debug hyphen prompt appears, we can check that our code has loaded, we use the Dump (D) command. Entering the command D0 produces the display shown in Figure 14.2:

The extreme left hand column gives the address (in segment register: offset format). The next 16 columns comprise hexadecimal data showing the bytes stored at the 16 address locations starting at the address shown in the left hand column. The 16 bytes in the block (addresses ICF5:0000 to ICF5.000F) all have values of 00. The value of the byte at ICF5:0010 is B8, whilst that at ICF5:0011 is F8, and so on. The last byte in the block (address ICF5:007F) has the value 18.

An ASCII representation of the data is shown in the right hand column of the screen dump. Byte values that do not correspond to printable ASCII characters are shown simply as a full-stop. Hence B8 and F8 (which are both non-printable characters) are shown by full-stops whilst 21H appears as !, and 41H as A.

```
1CF5:0010 B8F81C        MOV     AX,1CF8
1CF5:0013 8ED8          MOV     DS,AX
1CF5:0015 BB0100        MOV     BX,0001
1CF5:0018 B91600        MOV     CX,0016
1CF5:001B BA0400        MOV     DX,0004
1CF5:001E B440          MOV     AH,40
1CF5:0020 CD21          INT     21
1CF5:0022 B241          MOV     DL,41
1CF5:0024 B13E          MOV     CL,3E
1CF5:0026 B405          MOV     AH,05
1CF5:0028 CD21          INT     21
1CF5:002A FEC2          INC     DL
1CF5:002C E2FC          LOOP    002A
1CF5:002E B000          MOV     AL,00
1CF5:0030 B44C          MOV     AH,4C
1CF5:0032 CD21          INT     21
-
```

Figure 14.3 Using DEBUG's Unassemble (U) command to disassemble TEST.COM

The hexadecimal/ASCII dump shown earlier is not particularly useful and a more meaningful representation can be achieved by using the Unassemble (U) command. Since the program commences 16 bytes from the start of the block (i.e. at ICF5:0010) we shall unassemble the code from the address by specifying an offset of 10. We shall end the code disassembly at address offset 32 (this corresponds to the return to DOS). Hence the command we require is U10,32 and this results in the display of Figure 14.3 which shows the 16 instructions starting from address ICF5:0010:

The first instruction occupies 3 bytes of memory (addresses ICF5:0010, 1CF5:0011 and 1CF5:0012). The instruction comprises a move of 16-bits of immediate data (ICF8) into the AX register. The last program instruction is at address ICF5:0032 and is a software interrupt relating to address 21 in the interrupt vector table.

At this point it is worth mentioning that the Unassemble command can sometimes produce some rather odd displays. This is simply because the command is unable to distinguish valid program code from data; Unassemble will quite happily attempt to disassemble something which is not actually a program!

Having disassembled the program code resident in memory we can check it against the original source code file. Normally, however, this will not be necessary unless the object code file has become changed or corrupted in some way.

The next stage is that of tracing program execution. The Debug Trace (T) command could be employed for this function, however, it is better to make use of the Proceed (P) command to avoid tracing execution of the DOS interrupt routines in order to keep the amount of traced code manageable.

The Proceed command expects its first parameter to be the address of the first instruction to be executed. This must then be followed by a second parameter which gives the number of instructions to be traced. In this case, and since our program terminates normally, we can supply any sufficiently large number of instructions as the second parameter to the Proceed command. Hence the required command is P=100,100 and the resulting trace dump is shown in Figure 14.4:

The state of the CPU registers is displayed as each instruction is executed together with the next instruction in disassembled format. Taking the results of executing the first instruction (MOV AX,1CF8) as an example, we see that 1C has appeared in the upper byte of AX

```
AX=1CF8  BX=0000  CX=004A  DX=0000  SP=0100  BP=0000  SI=0000  DI=0000
DS=1CF5  ES=1CF5  SS=1CFA  CS=1CF5  IP=0013   NV UP EI PL NZ NA PO NC
1CF5:0013 8ED8          MOV     DS,AX

AX=1CF8  BX=0000  CX=004A  DX=0000  SP=0100  BP=0000  SI=0000  DI=0000
DS=1CF8  ES=1CF5  SS=1CFA  CS=1CF5  IP=0015   NV UP EI PL NZ NA PO NC
1CF5:0015 BB0100        MOV     BX,0001

AX=1CF8  BX=0001  CX=004A  DX=0000  SP=0100  BP=0000  SI=0000  DI=0000
DS=1CF8  ES=1CF5  SS=1CFA  CS=1CF5  IP=0018   NV UP EI PL NZ NA PO NC
1CF5:0018 B91600        MOV     CX,0016

AX=1CF8  BX=0001  CX=0016  DX=0000  SP=0100  BP=0000  SI=0000  DI=0000
DS=1CF8  ES=1CF5  SS=1CFA  CS=1CF5  IP=001B   NV UP EI PL NZ NA PO NC
1CF5:001B BA0400        MOV     DX,0004

AX=1CF8  BX=0001  CX=0016  DX=0004  SP=0100  BP=0000  SI=0000  DI=0000
DS=1CF8  ES=1CF5  SS=1CFA  CS=1CF5  IP=001E   NV UP EI PL NZ NA PO NC
1CF5:001E B440          MOV     AH,40

AX=40F8  BX=0001  CX=0016  DX=0004  SP=0100  BP=0000  SI=0000  DI=0000
DS=1CF8  ES=1CF5  SS=1CFA  CS=1CF5  IP=0020   NV UP EI PL NZ NA PO NC
1CF5:0020 CD21          INT     21
Printer Test Program

AX=0016  BX=0001  CX=0016  DX=0004  SP=0100  BP=0000  SI=0000  DI=0000
DS=1CF8  ES=1CF5  SS=1CFA  CS=1CF5  IP=0022   NV UP EI PL NZ NA PO NC
1CF5:0022 B241          MOV     DL,41

AX=0016  BX=0001  CX=0016  DX=0041  SP=0100  BP=0000  SI=0000  DI=0000
DS=1CF8  ES=1CF5  SS=1CFA  CS=1CF5  IP=0024   NV UP EI PL NZ NA PO NC
1CF5:0024 B13E          MOV     CL,3E

AX=0016  BX=0001  CX=003E  DX=0041  SP=0100  BP=0000  SI=0000  DI=0000
DS=1CF8  ES=1CF5  SS=1CFA  CS=1CF5  IP=0026   NV UP EI PL NZ NA PO NC
1CF5:0026 B405          MOV     AH,05

AX=0516  BX=0001  CX=003E  DX=0041  SP=0100  BP=0000  SI=0000  DI=0000
DS=1CF8  ES=1CF5  SS=1CFA  CS=1CF5  IP=0028   NV UP EI PL NZ NA PO NC
1CF5:0028 CD21          INT     21
A
AX=0541  BX=0001  CX=003E  DX=0041  SP=0100  BP=0000  SI=0000  DI=0000
DS=1CF8  ES=1CF5  SS=1CFA  CS=1CF5  IP=002A   NV UP EI PL NZ NA PO NC
1CF5:002A FEC2          INC     DL

AX=0541  BX=0001  CX=003E  DX=0042  SP=0100  BP=0000  SI=0000  DI=0000
DS=1CF8  ES=1CF5  SS=1CFA  CS=1CF5  IP=002C   NV UP EI PL NZ NA PE NC
1CF5:002C E2FC          LOOP    002A

AX=0541  BX=0001  CX=0000  DX=007F  SP=0100  BP=0000  SI=0000  DI=0000
DS=1CF8  ES=1CF5  SS=1CFA  CS=1CF5  IP=002E   NV UP EI PL NZ NA PO NC
1CF5:002E B000          MOV     AL,00

AX=0500  BX=0001  CX=0000  DX=007F  SP=0100  BP=0000  SI=0000  DI=0000
DS=1CF8  ES=1CF5  SS=1CFA  CS=1CF5  IP=0030   NV UP EI PL NZ NA PO NC
1CF5:0030 B44C          MOV     AH,4C

AX=4C00  BX=0001  CX=0000  DX=007F  SP=0100  BP=0000  SI=0000  DI=0000
DS=1CF8  ES=1CF5  SS=1CFA  CS=1CF5  IP=0032   NV UP EI PL NZ NA PO NC
1CF5:0032 CD21          INT     21

Program terminated normally
-
```

Figure 14.4 DEBUG program trace of TEST.COM

(AH), F8 has appeared in the lower byte of AX (AL) and the instruction pointer (IP) has moved on to offset address 0013. The next instruction to be executed (located at the address which IP is pointing to) is MOV DS,AX. The state of the CPU flags is also shown within the register dump. In this particular case, none of the flags has been changed as a result of executing the instruction.

In order to obtain a hard copy of the program trace, a <CTRL-P> command can be issued immediately before issuing the Proceed (P) command. From that point onwards, screen output was echoed to the printer. Since the program directs its own output to the printer, this also appears amidst the traced output. The screen output, 'Printer Test Program' appears after execution of the seventh instruction (INT 21).

A single character, A, is printed after the eleventh instruction. Thereafter, the program executes the loop formed by the instructions at offset addresses 002A and 002C. However, no printing takes place within this loop even though the DL register is incremented through the required range of ASCII codes (41 to 7F). Clearly the loop is not returning to the INT 21 instruction which actually makes the required calls into DOS.

```
p=10,100

AX=1CF8  BX=0000  CX=004A  DX=0000  SP=0100  BP=0000  SI=0000  DI=0000
DS=1CE5  ES=1CE5  SS=1CFA  CS=1CF5  IP=0013   NV UP EI PL NZ NA PO NC
1CF5:0013 8ED8          MOV     DS,AX

AX=1CF8  BX=0000  CX=004A  DX=0000  SP=0100  BP=0000  SI=0000  DI=0000
DS=1CF8  ES=1CE5  SS=1CFA  CS=1CF5  IP=0015   NV UP EI PL NZ NA PO NC
1CF5:0015 BB0100        MOV     BX,0001

AX=1CF8  BX=0001  CX=004A  DX=0000  SP=0100  BP=0000  SI=0000  DI=0000
DS=1CF8  ES=1CE5  SS=1CFA  CS=1CF5  IP=0018   NV UP EI PL NZ NA PO NC
1CF5:0018 B91600        MOV     CX,0016

AX=1CF8  BX=0001  CX=0016  DX=0000  SP=0100  BP=0000  SI=0000  DI=0000
DS=1CF8  ES=1CE5  SS=1CFA  CS=1CF5  IP=001B   NV UP EI PL NZ NA PO NC
1CF5:001B BA0400        MOV     DX,0004

AX=1CF8  BX=0001  CX=0016  DX=0004  SP=0100  BP=0000  SI=0000  DI=0000
DS=1CF8  ES=1CE5  SS=1CFA  CS=1CF5  IP=001E   NV UP EI PL NZ NA PO NC
1CF5:001E B440          MOV     AH,40

AX=40F8  BX=0001  CX=0016  DX=0004  SP=0100  BP=0000  SI=0000  DI=0000
DS=1CF8  ES=1CE5  SS=1CFA  CS=1CF5  IP=0020   NV UP EI PL NZ NA PO NC
1CF5:0020 CD21          INT     21
Printer Test Program

AX=0016  BX=0001  CX=0016  DX=0004  SP=0100  BP=0000  SI=0000  DI=0000
DS=1CF8  ES=1CE5  SS=1CFA  CS=1CF5  IP=0022   NV UP EI PL NZ NA PO NC
1CF5:0022 B241          MOV     DL,41

AX=0016  BX=0001  CX=0016  DX=0041  SP=0100  BP=0000  SI=0000  DI=0000
DS=1CF8  ES=1CE5  SS=1CFA  CS=1CF5  IP=0024   NV UP EI PL NZ NA PO NC
1CF5:0024 B13E          MOV     CL,3E

AX=0016  BX=0001  CX=003E  DX=0041  SP=0100  BP=0000  SI=0000  DI=0000
DS=1CF8  ES=1CE5  SS=1CFA  CS=1CF5  IP=0026   NV UP EI PL NZ NA PO NC
1CF5:0026 B405          MOV     AH,05

AX=0516  BX=0001  CX=003E  DX=0041  SP=0100  BP=0000  SI=0000  DI=0000
DS=1CF8  ES=1CE5  SS=1CFA  CS=1CF5  IP=0028   NV UP EI PL NZ NA PO NC
1CF5:0028 CD21          INT     21
A
AX=0541  BX=0001  CX=003E  DX=0041  SP=0100  BP=0000  SI=0000  DI=0000
DS=1CF8  ES=1CE5  SS=1CFA  CS=1CF5  IP=002A   NV UP EI PL NZ NA PO NC
1CF5:002A FEC2          INC     DL

AX=0541  BX=0001  CX=003E  DX=0042  SP=0100  BP=0000  SI=0000  DI=0000
DS=1CF8  ES=1CE5  SS=1CFA  CS=1CF5  IP=002C   NV UP EI PL NZ NA PE NC
1CF5:002C E2FA          LOOP    0028
BCDEFGHIJKLMNOPQRSTUVWXYZ[\]^_`abcdefghijklmnopqrstuvwxyz{¦}~
AX=057E  BX=0001  CX=0000  DX=007F  SP=0100  BP=0000  SI=0000  DI=0000
DS=1CF8  ES=1CE5  SS=1CFA  CS=1CF5  IP=002E   NV UP EI PL NZ NA PO NC
1CF5:002E B000          MOV     AL,00

AX=0500  BX=0001  CX=0000  DX=007F  SP=0100  BP=0000  SI=0000  DI=0000
DS=1CF8  ES=1CE5  SS=1CFA  CS=1CF5  IP=0030   NV UP EI PL NZ NA PO NC
1CF5:0030 B44C          MOV     AH,4C

AX=4C00  BX=0001  CX=0000  DX=007F  SP=0100  BP=0000  SI=0000  DI=0000
DS=1CF8  ES=1CE5  SS=1CFA  CS=1CF5  IP=0032   NV UP EI PL NZ NA PO NC
1CF5:0032 CD21          INT     21

Program terminated normally
-
```

Figure 14.5 Program trace of the corrected TEST.COM code

Fortunately, we can easily overcome this problem from within the debugger without returning to the macro assembler. We simply need to modify the LOOP instruction at offset address 002C. To do this we can make use of the Assemble (A) command to over-write the existing instruction. The required command is:

A 2C

The CS:IP prompt is then displayed (in this case it shows 1CF5:002C) after which we simply enter:

LOOP 28

The CS:IP prompt is incremented however, since we need to make no further changes to the code, we can simply escape from the Debug line assembler by simply pressing <RETURN>.

Having modified our code, we can again trace the program using the Proceed (P) command exactly as before. The traced output produced by the modified program is shown in Figure 14.5. Note that we have now succeeded in producing a line of printed output showing the full range of characters.

```
COMMENT |
***********************************************************************
File:              TEST
History:           Started 8/8/92
Purpose:           Displays ASCII characters as a line on the printer, LPT1
Format:            No calling conventions
***********************************************************************|

                   TITLE   test                ;
                   DOSSEG                      ; Conventional segment allocation
                   .MODEL  SMALL               ;
                   .STACK  100h                ; 256 byte stack

; *** Data ***

                   .DATA
message            DB      "Printer Test Program",13,10
lmessage           EQU     $ - message

; *** Code ***

                   .CODE
start:             mov     ax,@DATA            ;
                   mov     ds,ax               ; segment location of data
                   mov     bx,1                ; handle for standard output
                   mov     cx,lmessage         ; length of message
                   mov     dx,OFFSET message        ; address of messaage
                   mov     ah,40h              ; DOS write function
                   int     21h                 ; call DOS
                   mov     dl,41h              ; First character to print is A
                   mov     cl,3Eh              ; Number of characters to print
                   mov     ah,05h              ; Set up the function code
prch:              int     21h                 ; and print the character
                   inc     dl                  ; Get the next character
                   loop    prch                ; and go round again
                   mov     al,0                ; Set up the return error-level
                   mov     ah,4Ch              ; DOS exit function
                   int     21h                 ; call DOS
                   END     start
```

Figure 14.6 Corrected source code for TEST.ASM

Since no further errors have been found, we can exit from Debug, load the macro assembler, make the necessary changes to our source code, assemble and link to produce a modified EXE program file. The corrected source code is shown in Figure 14.6.

Using Debug's line assembler

Debug has an inbuilt line assembler which can be used to generate simple programs. The assembler is accessible from within Debug (as described in the previous section) but can also be accessed by means of a 'script file' which can be generated by any word processor or text editor capable of producing an ASCII text file (or even by means of the DOS COPY command).

During execution, Debug will take its input (redirected from the keyboard) from the script file. The script file will contain a sequence of Debug commands (which can include assembly language statements).

The two examples which follow show how Debug's assembler can be used to generate programs to respectively perform a 'warm' and 'cold' reboot:

Warm reboot

The following script file can be used with Debug to generate a program (WARM.COM). This program directs the program counter to the start of ROM BIOS but avoids the power-on memory check routine.

Assuming that the script file is to be produced by means of the DOS COPY command, the following keyboard entries will be required:

```
COPY CON WARM.DBG
A
XOR, AX,AX
MOV ES,AX
MOV DI,0472
MOV AX,1234
STOSW
JMP FFF:0000
(leave one blank line here)
NWARM.COM
RCX
10
W
Q
^Z
```

It is important to note that a newline (enter) should be used to terminate each line and the input should be terminated (after the newline which follows 'Q') by means of <CTRL-Z> (shown as ^Z). The <CTRL-Z> should also be followed by a newline.

The keystrokes will generate a file (WARM.DBG) which can be used as input to Debug by means of the following command:

DEBUG < WARM.DBG

Debug will assemble the statements contained in the script file in order to generate an executable file, WARM.COM. This program can be executed directly from the DOS prompt by typing WARM followed by enter (N.B. this will reboot your system!).

Cold reboot

If a cold boot is required, the assembly code should be modified by changing the MOV AX,1234 to MOV AX,0. The following keyboard entries are required:

```
COPY CON COLD.DBG
A
XOR AX,AX
MOV ES,AX
MOV DI,0472
MOV AX,0
STOSW
JMP FFF:0000
(leave one blank line here)
NCOLD.COM
RCX
10
W
Q
^Z
```

Again, note that the input should be terminated (after the newline which follows 'Q') by means of <CTRL-Z> (shown as ^Z) followed by enter.

The keystrokes will generate a file (COLD.DBG) which can be used as input to Debug by means of the following command:

DEBUG < COLD.DBG

Debug will assemble the statements contained in the script file in order to generate an executable file, COLD.COM. This program can be executed directly from the DOS prompt by typing COLD followed by enter. This should again reboot your system but this time the initial memory check routines will be performed.

15
Windows troubleshooting

This chapter explains how you can get the best out of Windows. The content relates to the most noteworthy features of the three major versions of Windows used with the vast majority of today's home and small-business computer systems.

Windows 3.0 and Windows 3.1

Following its introduction in 1990, Windows 3.0 rapidly became established as the most popular operating environment for the PC. Windows 3.1 was released in April 1992. This put right many of the problems associated with Windows 3.0. Not only was 3.1 more stable than its predecessor but it performed better and provided many new and upgraded features (notably network and multimedia capabilities). Windows 3.1 quickly became the *de facto* operating system for the PC and the majority of its users were able to operate in blissful ignorance of the underlying DOS operating system.

Windows 3.1 operates in two distinct modes; '386 enhanced mode' (for a PC with an 80386 or later CPU and a minimum of 2Mbyte RAM) or 'standard mode' (for a PC with an 80286 or later CPU and a minimum of 1Mbyte RAM). Windows 3.0 also supported 'real mode' (for a PC with an 8088 or 8086 CPU and a minimum of 640Kbyte RAM).

Initialisation files

Windows 3.1 uses two initialisation files to configure the Windows environment:

- WIN.INI which configures the Windows environment and caters for your own individual preferences
- SYSTEM.INI which configures Windows for your own particular hardware.

Other Windows programs create their own initialisation files. For example, the Windows Program Manager has an initialisation file called PROGMAN.INI.

WIN.INI

WIN.INI is divided into sections which group together settings which have related functions, as follows:

Section	Function
[windows]	Controls the appearance of the Windows environment.
[extensions]	Controls file associations (extensions to applications).
[mci extensions]	Controls file associations in conjunction with the high-level Media Control Interface.
[embedding]	Lists the associations between objects and servers used by OLE.

[programs]	Lists the additional paths used to search for program files when you open a document file that has an OLE association.
[desktop]	Controls the appearance of the desktop and the position of windows and icons.
[intl]	Controls the format of dates, times and currency.
[Windows Help]	Controls the appearance of the Help window and the help text.
[sounds]	Lists the sound files associated with the Windows events (a sound driver capable of playing .WAV files is required).
[colour]	Contains the colour definitions for the Windows user interface.
[fonts]	Lists the typefaces available and the location of the font defining them (if no path is specified, fonts are assumed to be located in the \WINDOWS\SYSTEM directory).
[Font Substitutes]	Provides compatibility with Windows 3.0 and allows you to re-map typefaces used by older Windows applications to TrueType fonts.
[TrueType]	Describes the settings that control TrueType fonts.
[ports]	Lists all the ports and files that can be used by the (parallel port) printer devices and defines default parameters for (serial port) communications.
[PrinterPorts]	Lists the printers that are available to Windows and their current port assignment and time-out values.
[devices]	As for PrinterPorts but with no time-out values.
[network]	Contains network settings.

SYSTEM.INI

SYSTEM.INI is also divided into sections which group together settings which have related functions, as follows:

Section	**Function**
[boot]	Contains a list of device drivers and Windows modules that configure Windows each time it is started.
[boot description]	Used to specify the devices that can be changed when the Windows Setup program is run.
[drivers]	Lists aliases assigned to Windows drivers.
[keyboard]	Provides information about the keyboard.
[mci]	Lists the device drivers used by the Media Control Interface to play media files.
[standard]	Determines how Windows runs in Standard Mode.
[386Enh]	Determines how Windows runs in 386 Enhanced Mode.
[NonWindowsApp]	Determines how DOS applications run and how they appear when run in a Window.

> **TIP**
>
> You can edit WIN.INI and SYSTEM.INI using the Windows System Editor utility, SYSEDIT.EXE. You will find this program in the \WINDOWS\STSTEM directory. When run, it opens the following files simultaneously for editing:
>
> - CONFIG.SYS
> - AUTOEXEC.BAT
> - WIN.INI
> - SYSTEM.INI
>
> Each file is displayed in its own window and they may be tiled or cascaded during an editing session.

> **TIP**
>
> Incorrect settings within SYSTEM.INI may cause your system to lock-up or immediately return to DOS. It is important to modify only one or two settings at a time and also to have a backup of your original SYSTEM.INI file available!

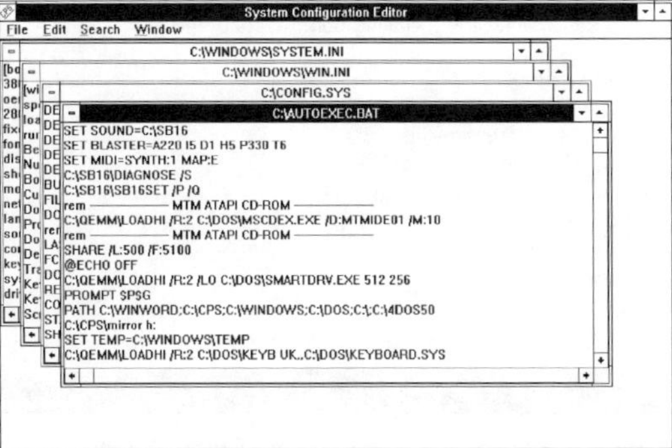

Figure 15.1 The Windows 3.1 System Configuration Editor

Windows 95

Microsoft made another significant advance in the development of Windows with the release of Windows 95. Microsoft had a number of objectives in mind when Windows 95 was developed, including that of making the Windows more intuitive and accessible to new users and making the interface more customisable and ultimately more productive.

Windows 95 contains the basic code present in DOS and also does not require CONFIG.SYS or AUTOEXEC.BAT to be present. These two files do, however, need to be present if you wish to configure a system for running DOS applications.

The Registry

Windows 95 makes it easier to install and configure new hardware by means of its 'Plug and Play' capability. This important feature helps to avoid the problems of conflict that may arise as a result of duplicate IRQ settings, I/O addresses and DMA channels. In order to keep track of settings, Windows 95 keeps a database of system information known as the 'Registry'.

The Registry is a vital part of Windows and it should be treated with respect. To examine (and, if necessary, edit) the Registry you can make use of the Windows Registry Editor (RegEdit.EXE). You will find this utility in the \WINDOWS directory.

TIP

Incorrect entries in the Registry can cause unpredictable results (or Windows 95 may simply refuse to run). You should therefore not make changes to the Registry unless you are completely confident that you know what you are doing! Never make changes to the Registry without first making a back up copy (see below).

TIP

If your Windows Registry becomes corrupted (and you have not kept a back up copy) you can restore the corrupted files from DOS by entering the following commands at the DOS prompt:

```
c:
cd \windows
attrib -r -h -s system.da0
attrib -r -h -s system.dat
ren system.dat system.old
ren system.da0 system.dat
attrib -r -h -s user.da0
attrib -r -h -s user.dat
ren user.dat user.old
ren user.da0 user.dat
```

TIP

You can also create a back up copy of the Registry on a floppy disk. This will protect you against the unlikely (but nonetheless possible) event of losing or corrupting both the Registry and its back up. You can do this by inserting a formatted floppy disk into drive A: and then entering the following commands in a DOS window:

```
c:
cd \windows
attrib -r -h -s system.dat
attrib -r -h -s user.dat
copy system.dat a:\system.dat
copy user.dat a:\user.dat
```

(Note that if you have a *very* large Registry file you may have to compress the file (using a ZIP utility) *before* saving it to floppy disk.)

> **TIP**
>
> The Windows 95 Registry Editor does not provide you with the registry data in the form of a single editable file. If you find this an inconvenient way of displaying/editing the Registry files, you can use the Export Registry File option to create a text file containing the Registry contents (the file created will have a .REG file extension). You can also import all (or part) of a modified Registry data file. However, if you do this you must take great care to edit the file as an ASCII file and introduce no extra codes or unwanted formatting.

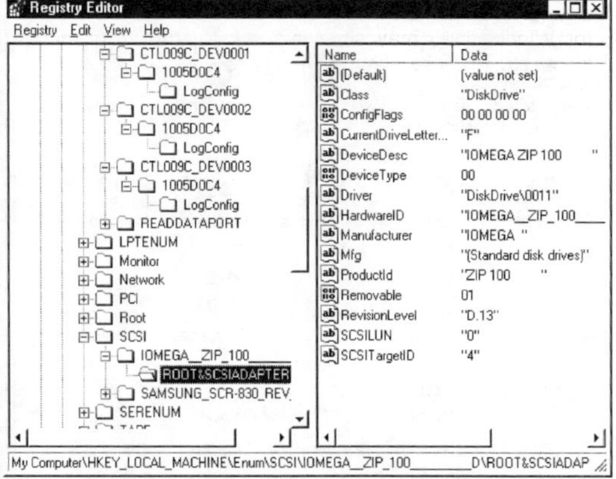

Figure 15.2 The Windows 95 Registry Editor showing the entry for an IOMEGA ZIP drive configured as an SCSI device

Filenames

Filenames in Windows 95 are not limited to the 'eight characters plus three character extension' used in DOS and Windows 3.1. In fact, filenames in Windows 95 can be up to 255 characters in length. If an application does not recognise long filenames, Windows 95 will truncate the name that the application uses so that it is compatible with standard DOS filenames.

> **TIP**
>
> Because of the different ways in which filenames are handled, you must never use file utility software designed for DOS and earlier versions of Windows in a system running Windows 95. Failure to observe this precaution can result in lost and unrecoverable files!

Installing Windows 95

Windows 95 requires at least 40–55Mbyte of free hard disk space plus additional hard disk space in which to create a swap file (this should typically be 2 to 3 times the size of the RAM fitted to the machine). Before installing Windows 95 you should:

- turn off any screen saver that might be active
- unload any background utilities
- check that your hard disk is free from any virus infection
- de-fragment the hard disk
- backup important system files (including AUTOEXEC.BAT and CONFIG.SYS).

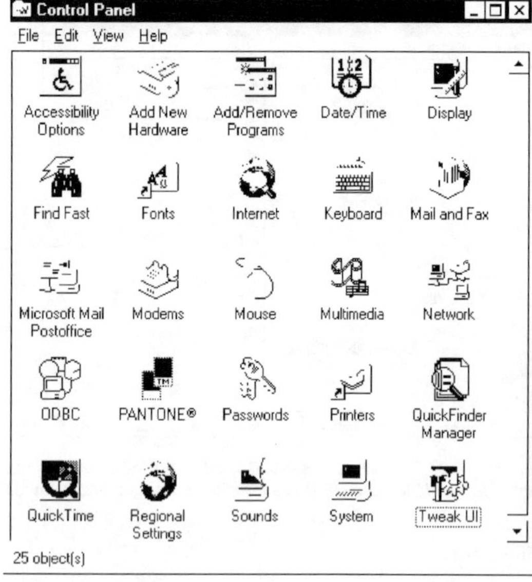

Figure 15.3 The Windows 95 Control Panel

Boot hot-keys

Windows 95 allows you to determine its start-up configuration during the boot sequence. This useful feature provides you with several options including booting into the previous version of DOS (if installed on your system), booting into a 'safe' mode, or ignoring the whole or part of the DOS configuration files (CONFIG.SYS and AUTOEXEC.BAT) when booting into Windows. The following hot-keys are available:

Key	Action
<F4>	Boots the computer using the previous version of DOS (if present).
<F5>	Boots Windows 95 in 'safe' mode.
<Shift-F5>	Boots Windows 95 without processing the DOS configuration files, CONFIG.SYS and AUTOEXEC.BAT.

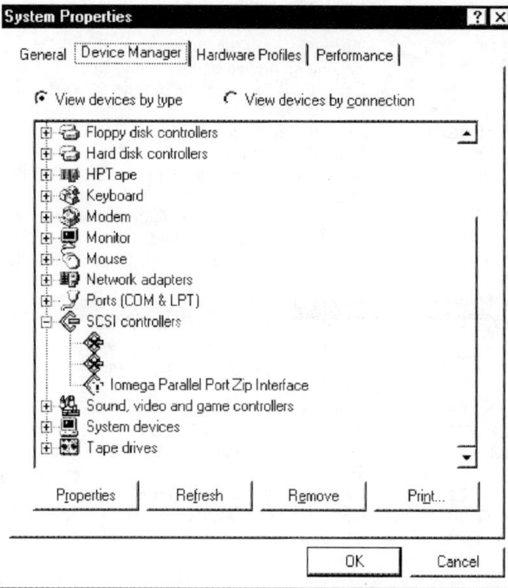

Figure 15.4 The Device Manager tab selected from the System icon within the Windows 95 Control Panel

<F6>	Boots Windows 95 in 'safe' mode with network support.
<F8>	Runs the Windows 95 start-up menu.
<Shift-F8>	Executes CONFIG.SYS and AUTOEXEC.BAT one line at a time (giving you the option of skipping each line).

Windows 95 Explorer

The Windows 95 Explorer allows you to gain an overview of the file and directory structure of your computer. Explorer displays icons arranged hierarchically in its left window pane. The right window pane provides details of the folders and files including name, size, type and the date that the file was last modified. These two views are independent of one another – you can expand or contract the tree structure in the left pane whilst, at the same time, displaying file and folder information in the right pane.

Keyboard shortcuts

The following keyboard shortcuts are available in Windows 95 Explorer:

Key	Action
<F1>	Help.
<F2>	Rename the highlighted file or folder.
<F3>	Bring up the Find dialog.
<F4>	Toggle the drop-down list from the Toolbar.

<F5>	Refresh the window display.
<F6>	Move the current focus.
<F10>	Put the focus in the menu bar on the File menu.
<ALT-*>	Expand all branches in the folder tree.
<*>	Expand all branches below the focused node, folder or disk.
<BACKSPACE>	Move up one level in the folder hierarchy.
<TAB>	Move the current focus.
<Arrow keys>	Move up and down the folder tree or list of files and folders.
<Right arrow>	Expand the highlighted folder. If already expanded go to the parent folder.
<Left arrow>	Collapse the highlighted folder. If not expanded go to the parent folder.
<CTRL-Arrows>	Scroll within current pane (leave focus unchanged).
<PGUP>	Scroll up within current pane (leave focus unchanged).
<PGDN>	Scroll down within current pane (leave focus unchanged).
<ENTER>	Runs the file or opens the folder in the right pane.
<SHIFT-F10>	Same as a right mouse click.
<ALT-SPACE>	Opens the system menu (allows you to move, size or close the folder).
<ALT-ENTER>	Displays the folder's properties.
<CTRL-G>	Opens the Go To dialog box.
<ALT-F4>	Closes the window.

Upgrading Windows

Microsoft have provided a continuous upgrade path right from the earliest version of Windows (designed for AT computers with 80286 processors) through to the latest Windows 98. Undoubtedly the question of whether you should, or should not, attempt to upgrade a system from one version of Windows to the next (e.g. from Windows 3.11 to Windows 95) depends on three main factors. The first of these is whether the hardware platform can satisfactorily support the new version (notably whether sufficient RAM and hard disk space is available). The second item to consider is whether, or not, you intend to run applications that are designed to take advantage of the later version of Windows. The third factor is whether or not you need the features offered by an updated Windows interface. This might be important if, for example, you need to achieve a very high level of integration between Web pages and your desktop!

Windows 3.1 to Windows 95

In general, it is worth considering upgrading from Windows 3.1 to Windows 95 if:

- you have at least 12Mbyte and preferably more than 16Mbyte RAM fitted
- you suffer from occasional crashes caused by General Protection Faults (GPF's) – the dreaded 'blue screen of death'!
- you need to run newer 32 bit Windows applications
- you have at least 120Mbyte of hard disk space free (remember also that your 32 bit Windows applications will make heavy demands on your precious hard disk space – you don't just need 60Mbytes for Windows)
- you have a '486 DX or later processor.

It is not even worth considering upgrading to Windows 95 if:

- you are entirely satisfied with the performance of your system and don't need to upgrade your Windows applications
- you only have 4Mbyte of RAM (or less) and don't intend to upgrade it
- you have a '486 SX (or earlier processor)
- your hard disk space is limited and less than 60Mbytes is available (remember that you will need hard disk space for any new applications).

TIP

If you have any doubts as to whether your hardware will support Windows 95, Microsoft has produced a System Check Utility that will confirm whether or not your Windows 3.1 based system is good enough to operate satisfactorily under Windows 95. You can download this utility from:
http://microsoft.com/windows95/infor/w95syschk.htm.

TIP

Microsoft Plus! for Windows 95 adds more functions to the basic Windows 95 package. Microsoft Plus! is a suite of programs and utilities that include Internet Explorer, Dial-Up Networking Server, improved DriveSpace compression and personalised desktop themes.

Windows 95 to Windows 98

Whilst Windows 95 represents a significant upgrade from Windows 3.1, the same cannot be said of the relationship between Windows 98 and Windows 95.

In general, it is worth considering upgrading from Windows 95 to Windows 98 if:

- you wish to have virtually seamless integration between the Web and your computer's 'desktop'
- you have at least 16Mbyte and preferably 32Mbyte, or more, RAM fitted
- you have at least 180Mbyte of hard disk space free (your 32-bit Windows applications will make heavy demands on your precious hard disk space)
- you have a Pentium or equivalent processor.

It is not even worth considering a machine to Windows 95 if:

- the Windows 95 interface already does everything you want
- if you have less than 16Mbyte of RAM
- you have no wish to use the Internet
- if your hard disk space is limited and less than 200Mbyte is available (remember that you will need plenty of space for your new 32-bit applications).

TIP

Microsoft is currently planning a single release version of Windows 98 that will *directly* upgrade both Windows 3.1 and Windows 95 to Windows 98. If you plan to make the jump from Windows 3.1 to Windows 98 it is *essential* that you should ensure that your hardware platform is good enough to support Windows 98!

TIP

When running a DOS session in a window, you can toggle between the window and full-screen DOS by pressing <ALT-ENTER>.

TIP

Windows 95 contains a hard disk compression utility called DriveSpace. To run DriveSpace click on Start, select Programs and Accessories, then System Tools and finally click on DriveSpace. After choosing which drive to compress from the Drive menu, choose Compress and then Start. If you have not backed up your files, click on Back Up Files and then follow the instructions on screen before selecting Compress Now.

TIP

Unused fonts can consume large amounts of hard disk space (often between 60 and 100Kbytes for each installed font). To remove unused fonts double-click on Fonts from within the Control Panel. Select the font that you wish to remove, then click on Delete from the File menu. If you want to remove more than one installed font in a single operation you need only hold down <CTRL> as you make each selection.

Improving the performance of Windows

Fortunately, there are several ways of improving Windows 95 without having to face a full upgrade to Windows 98. We shall begin by looking at two methods of extending the functionality of Windows 95 using two of Microsoft's excellent (and currently free) programs.

Microsoft's PowerToys

Microsoft's PowerToys were developed by the Windows Shell Development Team. They are a set of utilities that add more functionality to the Windows 95 interface. Don't be fooled into thinking that they are a mere 'afterthought' on Microsoft's part – they actually represent a suite of utilities that members of the Windows 95 development team developed to meet their own needs. As such, they are not an officially supported part of Windows 95 – you use them entirely 'at your own risk'.

The PowerToys currently supplied by Microsoft include:

PowerToy	Function
Desktop Menu	Open items on your desktop from a convenient menu on the taskbar (Windows NT and Windows 95).
CAB View	Allows you to treat .CAB files like folders, look inside, then drag files in and out with ease (Windows 95).
CD AutoPlay Extender	Provides an auto-play facility on any non-audio CD and provides speedy access to individual programs (Windows 95).
Contents Menu	Allows you to locate your files without having to open their folders (Windows 95).
Explore From Here	Opens the Windows 95 Explorer from any location (Windows NT and Windows 95).
FlexiCD	Provides convenient audio CD control directly from the Windows 95 taskbar (Windows 95).
QuickRes	Allows you to change the screen's resolution from the Windows 95 taskbar without having to reboot (Windows 95).
Round Clock	A round analogue clock (Windows 95).
Find X 1.2	Allows you to customise your Find menu with drag-and-drop facilities (Windows NT and Windows 95).
Send To X 1.4	Provides a facility to send a file to any Folder (Windows NT and Windows 95).
Shortcut Target Menu 1.2	Allows you to get the properties for a shortcut's target simply by right-clicking the shortcut (Windows NT and Windows 95).
Tweak UI 1.1	This is arguably the most useful of all of the PowerToys as it allows you to optimise several aspects of the Windows user interface, including menu speed, window animation, and Internet Explorer (Windows NT and Windows 95).
XMouse 1.2	Makes the Windows focus follow your mouse without the need for clicking (Windows 95).
Command Prompt Here 1.1	Allows you to start a command prompt in the folder of your choice by clicking the mouse button (Windows NT and Windows 95).
Telephony Location Selector	Provides laptop computer users with a facility that can change their dialling location with ease (Windows 95).

Installing the PowerToys

PowerToys can be downloaded from:

http:/microsoft.com/windows95/info/powertoys.htm and
http:/www.eu.microsoft.com/windows95/info/powertoys.htm.

The following steps are required to install PowerToys:

1. Create a folder on the C: drive to hold the PowerToy utilities. To do this you need to right-click on the desktop and choose New:Folder from the pop-up menu, then name the folder 'Power'.
2. Download the PowerToys from the Internet site (above) by clicking on the link on the PowerToy page to download the file

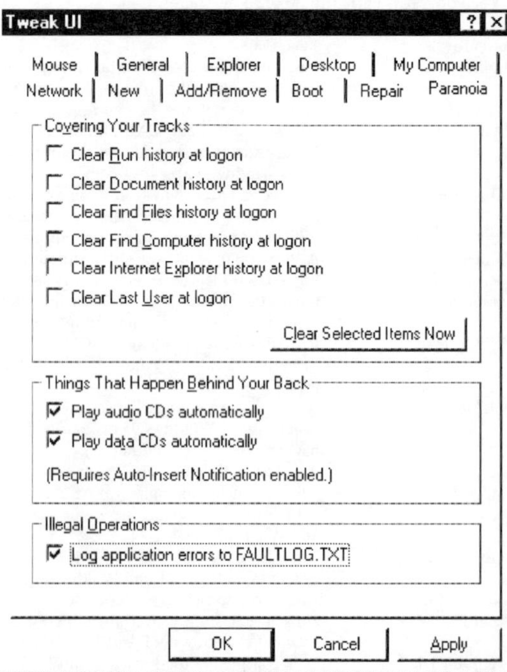

Figure 15.5 The Paranoia tab selected from the Tweak UI icon within the Windows 95 Control Panel (note that Tweak UI is available as part of the Windows 95 PowerToys set and must be installed before its icon will appear in the Control Panel window – see figure 15.3)

'PowerToy.EXE'. (If you don't need all of the PowerToy utilities you may select them individually.) Save PowerToy.EXE in the Power folder that you created in Step 1.

3. De-compress the file 'PowerToy.exe'. To do this you need to open the Power folder and simply double-click the file 'PowerToy.EXE'. This will create a number of new files in the Power folder.
4. Install each of the PowerToys. Do this by finding the set-up information files (the icons for .INF files look like notepads with a small yellow gear on each). Right-click each one in turn then choose Install. Ignore the dialogue box that asks you whether you wish to restart your system for each change to take effect – you can restart at the end when all of the PowerToys have been installed.

Kernel Toys

Not to be outdone, the Windows 95 kernel team have produced their own set of utilities to rival those produced by the Windows shell team. Like the Power Toys, the Kernel Toys are also not officially supported by Microsoft. Once again, you use them 'at your own risk'.

The Kernel Toys currently supplied by Microsoft include:

Kernel Toy	**Function**
Memory Tracker	Provides information on the use of conventional memory.
MS-DOS Mode Wizard	This tool provides you with a way of customising your system for DOS applications.
Time Zone Editor	Allows you to easily modify the Windows Time Zone setting.
Keyboard Re-map	Control Panel Keyboard extension.
Process Watcher	Lets you monitor CPU usage by program.
Windows Key Control	Allows you to control the behaviour of the 'Windows Key' on a Windows 95 keyboard.

Installing the Kernel Toys
KernelToys can be downloaded from:

http:/microsoft.com/windows95/info/kerneltoys.htm and
http:/www.eu.microsoft.com/windows95/info/kerneltoys.htm.

The following steps are required to install KernelToys:

1. Create a folder on the C: drive to hold the KernelToy utilities. To do this you need to right-click on the desktop and choose New:Folder from the pop-up menu, then name the folder 'kernltoys'.
2. Download the KernelToys from the Internet site (above) by clicking on the link on the KernelToy page to download the file 'KernlToy.EXE'. (If you don't need all of the KernelToy utilities you may select them individually.) Save KernlToy.EXE in the kernltoys folder that you created in Step 1.
3. De-compress the file 'KernlToy.exe'. To do this you need to open the Kernel folder and simply double-click the file 'KernlToy.EXE'. This will create a number of new files in the kernltoys folder.
4. Install each of the KernelToys. Do this by finding the set-up information files (the icons for .INF files look like notepads with a small yellow gear on each). Right-click each one in turn then choose Install. Ignore the dialogue box that asks you whether you wish to restart your system for each change to take effect – you can restart at the end when all of the KernelToys have been installed.

Internet Explorer 4

Windows 95 can be made to look and feel more like Windows 98 by making use of the interface provided by Microsoft's Internet Explorer 4. This powerful Web browser treats the desktop as a Web page, making the screen save show Web content, replacing the background of windows with HTML, and changing the usual Windows 95 double-click mouse action to the single-click action normally associated with Web browsers. Internet Explorer 4 can thus be considered to be something of an intermediate step between Windows 95 and Windows 98. Furthermore, since Internet Explorer 4 is currently available from Microsoft free of charge, Windows 95 users can get to grips with the Windows 98 interface without actually having to make the jump. Internet Explorer 4 (and Windows 98, for that matter) can be highly recommended if you wish to have a very high level of integration between your desktop and the Web. If this is not the case (or if you have no Internet connection) then much of the rationale for changing to Windows 98 becomes lost!

Internet Explorer 4 can be downloaded from:

http:/microsoft.com/ie/ie40/ and http:/www.eu.microsoft.com/ie/ie40/.

OSR2

Microsoft Windows 95 OEM Service Release 2 (OSR2) is an update to the Microsoft Windows 95 operating system intended to add support for new and emerging hardware, and to include various updates to Windows 95 which were formerly available separately. Because most of the functionality in OSR2 is applicable only to new hardware devices, the OSR2 release version of Windows is usually only shipped with new systems. For users of early versions of Windows 95, some of the OSR2 components are available for downloading from Microsoft's Web sites: http:/microsoft.com/windows95/info/updates.htm and http:/www.eu.microsoft.com/windows95/info/updates.htm.

Some of the notable features of OSR2 are:

FAT32	Enhancements to the Windows 95 FAT file system designed to efficiently support large hard disks, up to 2Tbytes in size. Includes updates to FDISK, Format, Scandisk and Defrag disk utilities to support FAT32 partitions.
DriveSpace	Windows 95 DriveSpace compression utility now supports compressed volumes up to 2Gbytes in size. (Note that DriveSpace compression is not supported on FAT32 volumes.)
Power	Advanced Power Management (APM) 1.2 BIOS, wake-on-ring for modems, multi-battery PCs, drive spin down and powering down of inactive PCMCIA modems.
Storage	Support for IDE Bus Mastering, 120Mbyte Floptical disk drives, removable IDE media, Zip drives and CD-ROM Changers.
PCMCIA	Adds support for new PC Card 32 (Cardbus) bridges, PCMCIA cards that operate at 3.3V rather than 5V, multifunction PCMCIA network/modem cards and PCMCIA Global Positioning Satellite (GPS) devices.
CD-ROMs	File system enhancements that support for ISO 9660 disks up to 4Gbytes in size, and CD-I format CD-ROMs.
PCI	Support for PCI devices for use in PCI docking stations. Support for new PCI interrupt routers.
Internet	Internet Explorer 3 with support for ActiveX, HTML style sheets, frames and Java. Internet connection Wizard for connection to world-wide Internet Service Providers.
e-mail	Send and receive e-mail quickly with SMTP and POP3 mail client.
Games	Direct-X high-performance 2-D and 3-D graphics, sound, input and communications for games. High quality playback of video, including QuickTime and MPEG-1 formats.
MMX	Support for third parties to build software that exploits the Intel Pentium Multimedia Extensions (MMX) for fast audio and video support on the latest generation of Intel Pentium processors.
Networking	Various networking enhancements including 32-bit Data Link Control and Infrared LAN connectivity.
Desktop	Desktop Management Interface (DMI) 1.1 – allows

	a desktop management application to monitor devices on the PC.
Display	Support for dynamically changing screen resolution and colour depth. Adapter refresh rate can also be set with most newer display driver chipsets.
Imaging	View image data using Wang Imaging from a variety of different file formats, including JPG, XIF, TIFF, BMP and FAX. Scan and annotate images with built-in TWAIN scanner support.
Scandisk	Scandisk will automatically run at the next reboot in order to check for damaged files in the event that the PC does not shut down normally.

Performance enhancement

Few Windows users can remain unaware of the Control Panel for very long. Unfortunately, the Control Panel's default settings invariably represent something of a compromise. Indeed, new systems are often supplied with settings that are less than optimum. That said, a judicious choice of Control Panel settings can usually help you to achieve a significant improvement in performance.

Optimising the File System

Start by double-clicking on the System icon from within the Windows 95 Control Panel. Next select the Performance tab and click on the File System button. There are two settings in the Hard Disk dialog box. The setting labelled 'Typical role of this machine' determines how much memory space is reserved to handle path and filename caching. The default 'Desktop computer' selection allocates space for a mere 32 paths and 677 filenames, whereas the 'Network server' setting increases these settings to 64 paths and 2,729 filenames. Even if your computer is used only for standard desktop applications, it is worth changing the 'Typical role . . .' to 'Network server'. It is important to note that, if you are using the original release of Windows 95 (not the updated OSR2 version) you will also have to correct a 'bug' in the Windows 95 Registry. If this is the case, use the Windows 95 Registry Editor (Regedit.exe from the Windows directory) to change the value of

HKEY_LOCAL_MACHINE\SOFTWARE\Microsoft\Windows \CurrentVersion\FS Templates\Server\NameCache to A9 0A 00 00, and \PathCache to 40 00 00 00.

Read-ahead optimisation

The File System's Hard Disk settings will also let you adjust the amount of memory used to buffer data. Adjustment is carried out by means of the Read-Ahead Optimisation slider. This determines how much additional data Windows 95 should fetch every time you retrieve data from your hard disk (read-ahead buffering improves performance by reducing the number of times your machine has to access the relatively slow hard disk to retrieve data). With today's applications it is usually best to set the slider to its maximum (right-most) position. This will provide Windows with the maximum 64Kbyte of read-ahead buffering.

Supplemental cache optimisation

The File System Properties dialogue box also lets you adjust the size of the memory that acts as a read-ahead cache for data from a

CD-ROM. To adjust the cache size, simply select the CD-ROM tab and then move the Supplemental Cache Size slider. If you use your CD-ROM drive frequently, you should move the Supplemental Cache Size slider to 'Large', and specify that you have a Quad Speed or Higher CD. This will set aside more than 1Mbyte for the read-ahead cache and it will ensure that the CD-ROM drive will run as fast as possible.

Speeding up virtual memory

Within the System Properties dialogue, the Virtual Memory button will allow you to set aside a dedicated amount of hard disk memory for use as a swap file. Windows 95 is usually set-up to automatically manage the size of the swap file. However, you can control the size of the swap file by manually entering maximum and minimum sizes for the swap file. If you have plenty of hard disk space available and you regularly run memory-intensive applications like Microsoft Office 97 or Adobe Photoshop, judicious adjustments to the size of the swap file can help to speed things up.

Furthermore, if you have more than one physical drive, you should ensure that the swap file is set-up on your fastest hard drive. However, it is first worthwhile defragmenting the drive (using Defrag.exe from the Windows directory) on the drive where the swap file will be located. To minimise swap file access times, set the minimum and maximum size of the swap file to the same value, approximately 2.5 to 3 times the size of your main memory. For example, if you have 16Mbytes of RAM, you should set it to 48Mbytes. Having made the necessary changes you should restart Windows to allow the new settings to take effect.

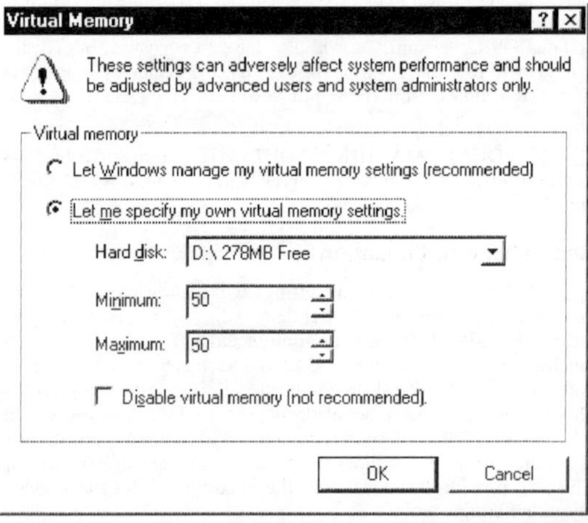

Figure 15.6 Adjusting the Virtual Memory settings after selecting the Performance tab from the System icon within the Windows 95 Control Panel

TIP

WINCheckIT, or an equivalent program, will allow you to measure the performance of your system before and after carrying out any adjustments. Each time you run WIN-CheckIT it will gather data on your system and allow you to compare the new data with that obtained from previous tests. WINCheckIT also contains a database of data obtained from a number of 'reference' systems. By comparing results (either in WINCheckIT's tabular or graphical forms) you will be able to gauge the effectiveness of your 'tune-up' efforts!

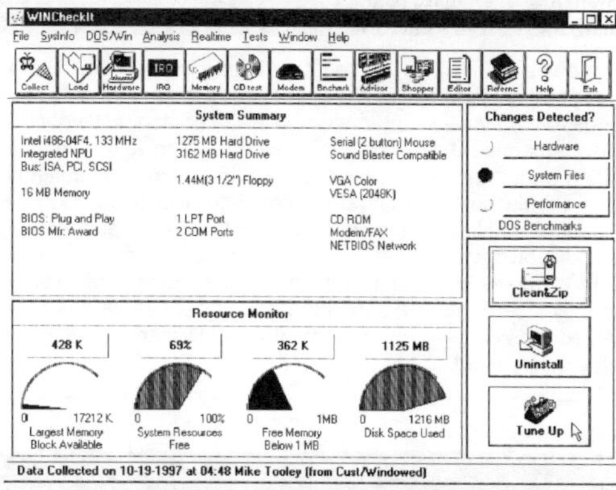

Figure 15.7 Using WINCheckIt to obtain information on a system

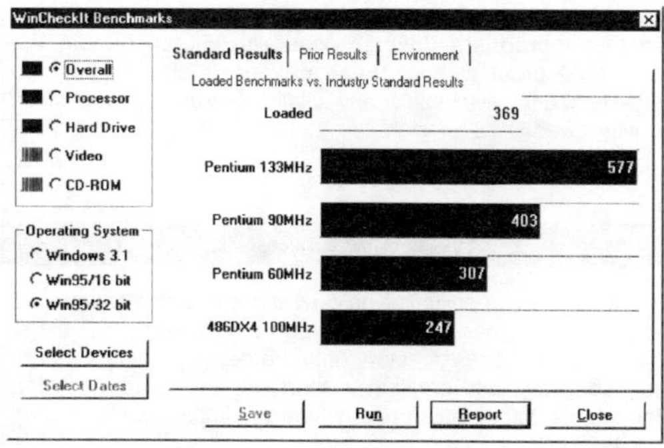

Figure 15.8 WINCheckIt's benchmarking facility can be used to compare a system's performance before and after making configuration adjustments as well as comparing it with a number of reference systems

TIP

Windows 95 works best when used with more recent Plug and Play drivers. These drivers support new features, tend to be more stable and consume fewer resources than older drivers. In order to maintain compatibility with older Windows 3.1 applications and 'legacy' hardware, Windows 95 will make use of an older Windows 3.1 driver if a Plug and Play driver is not available. If you find that you have to continue to use Windows 3.1 drivers it may be worth contacting the supplier to see if an updated Windows 95 driver is available.

TIP

Windows 95 will allow you to disable certain hardware acceleration features of the graphics adapter card in situations that may cause intermittent crashes or incorrectly generated screens. Disabling acceleration will, however, reduce video performance. To check your video acceleration settings you should select the System icon from within the Control Panel, then click on the Performance tab and Graphics button. If you suspect that your graphics performance is poor with Windows 95 it might be worth considering upgrading your graphics card (making sure that the replacement card is optimised for Windows 95 and has at least 1Mbyte (and preferably more) RAM.

TIP

If you find that your CD-ROM drive is not recognised when you boot into a pure DOS session or exit to DOS from Windows 95, you should ensure that the DOS configuration files (CONFIG.SYS and AUTOEXEC.BAT) contain references to the appropriate drivers. Windows 95 can handle the CD-ROM drive without these drivers. It also makes the CD-ROM drive available to any applications that operate within a windowed DOS session.

TIP

To launch a screen saver quickly and easily in Windows 95 whenever you need it, simply drag the required .SCR file(s) from your Windows directory onto the desktop using the right mouse button and creating a short cut. Thereafter, you can launch the screen saver at any time by simply double clicking on its icon.

TIP

Occasionally you may find that a program requires one of several of the Visual Basic Runtime Modules in order to run. This is because the run-time modules (.DLL files) are often not distributed with the program files – the supplier simply assumes that you already have the required .DLL file installed on your system! Unfortunately, this situation is further complicated by the fact that each version of Visual Basic has its own VBRUN file, which will work with any program written in that version of Visual Basic (but not with programs written in other versions).

There are currently five different sets of VBRUN modules which are available from various online sites for download (they can also be obtained from several of the more popular magazine cover CD-ROMs). The currently available versions are listed below:

Visual Basic version	**Application size**	**VBRUN .DLL filename**
1.0	16-bit	VBRUN100.DLL
2.0	16-bit	VBRUN200.DLL
3.0	16-bit	VBRUN300.DLL
4.0	16-bit	VB40016.DLL
4.0	32 bit	VB40032.DLL

Note that if you download these files they may be supplied either in the form of self-extracting .EXE files or .ZIP files. The latter require unzipping using an appropriate un-ZIP utility. Whatever method is used to obtain these files it is important that their final resting place on your system is within the C:\WINDOWS\SYSTEM directory since this is where Visual Basic programs expect to find them (along with your other Dynamic Link Library files).

16
Tools and test equipment

This chapter describes the tools and test equipment necessary to locate basic hardware faults. Fault location to board or 'replaceable unit' level requires nothing more than a screwdriver, a multimeter and a diagnostic disk. Component level fault-finding, on the other hand, is much more demanding and requires an appreciable investment in specialised tools and test equipment. Despite this, you can achieve a great deal with only a modest initial outlay; more complex tools and test equipment can be acquired as you develop confidence.

Tools

To help you prioritise your spending at the outset, I have included 'minimum' and 'extended' lists for both tools and test equipment. The 'minimum' list of tools represents the minimum complement of items necessary for basic service work (e.g. fault-finding to board level on conventional circuit boards). The 'extended' list, on the other hand, includes many items that may only be used infrequently as well as those that are required for repairs to boards using surface mounted components.

Minimum list of tools

- One small pair of side cutters.
- One small pair of pliers.
- One pair combination pliers and cutters.
- Set of flat-bladed screwdrivers.
- Set of cross-point screwdrivers.
- Set of trimming/adjusting tools.
- Set of hexagon keys.
- One miniature soldering iron (15–25W) with set of bits.
- One desoldering tool.
- Set of i.c. extracting tools.
- One anti-static mat (with grounding leads).

Extended list of tools

As 'minimum' list plus the following additional items:

- One pair of wire strippers.
- One medium mains tester screwdriver.
- Set of jeweller's screwdrivers.
- One trimming knife.
- One pair of good quality tweezers.
- One bench magnifying glass.
- One Anglepoise (or similar) adjustable bench lamp.
- One combination wire-wrapping/unwrapping tool.
- Set of open ended metric spanners (M2.5 to M6).
- One portable soldering iron (12V or rechargeable type).
- One temperature controlled soldering iron.
- One i.c. desoldering tools (with set of bits).
- One PCB cleaner.
- One desolder wick.

TIP

Good quality tools can be expected to last a lifetime provided they are properly used and cared for. It is therefore wise to purchase the best quality that you can afford – there is little sense in buying inferior items that will need replacing every few years.

Test equipment

As you might expect, test equipment tends to vary not only in specification but also in price. At one extreme are such everyday items as basic analogue multimeters costing less than £20. At the other extreme can be found sophisticated signature and logic analysers costing around £5,000.

Fortunately, only a few basic items of test equipment are required to successfully diagnose the vast majority of hardware faults. The three most commonly used items in my workshop are a digital multimeter, a logic probe and a breakout box – an invaluable trio of instruments that cost me less than £80!

TIP

Choosing the right test instrument for the job can be all-important. Familiarity is the key to getting the best from your test gear and, at least in the initial stages, it is wise to learn how to use one instrument at a time.

Items on the 'minimum' list become essential if you are to adequately cope with *every* hardware fault that you are likely to encounter. There is, however, no reason why you should not make a start with only a good multi-range meter and a logic probe. Other items of test equipment (including those on the 'extended' list) can be acquired over a period of time. In any event, it is best not to be in too much of a hurry to extend the range of facilities available – you will soon get to know which instrument you derive most benefit from and this will help point the way to future purchases.

Minimum list of test equipment

- Multi-range meter (good quality analogue or digital type).
- Logic probe.
- Breakout box (RS-232).
- Null-modem (or null-modem cable).
- Test prods.
- Selection of IC test clips.
- Selection of leads and connectors.

Extended list of test equipment

As 'minimum' list plus the following additional items:

- Oscilloscope (preferably dual beam 50MHz type).
- Oscilloscope probes ('×1' and '×10').
- Logic pulser.
- Current tracing probe.
- Logic test clip.
- Line monitor (RS-232).
- Patch box (RS-232).

- Gender changer (RS-232).
- Null-modem (RS-232).

Multi-range meters

A good quality multi-range meter is undoubtedly an excellent investment if you intend to regularly tackle hardware faults. The instrument can be used for checking voltage (a.c. and d.c.), current (a.c. or d.c.) and resistance ('ohms'). As many as eight or nine measuring functions may be provided with a maximum of six or eight ranges on each. Besides the normal voltage, current and resistance functions, some meters also include facilities for checking transistors and measuring capacitance. Meters may also be either analogue or digital types but will usually operate from internal batteries so that they are independent of the mains supply.

Analogue instruments employ conventional moving coil meters and the display takes the form of a pointer moving across a calibrated scale. This arrangement is not so convenient to use as that provided by digital instruments. It does, however, offer some advantages, not the least of which is that it is very difficult to make adjustments using a digital readout to monitor varying circuit conditions, and in this application the analogue meter is therefore superior. Its scale can be easily interpreted; a movement in one direction represents an increase and in the other a decrease. The principal disadvantage of many analogue meters is the rather cramped and sometimes confusing scale calibration. To determine the exact reading requires first an estimation of the pointer's position and then the application of some mental arithmetic based on the range switch setting.

Digital meters, on the other hand, are usually extremely easy to read and have displays that are clear, unambiguous and capable of providing a very high resolution. It is thus possible to distinguish readings that are very close. This is just not possible with an analogue instrument. Another very significant difference between analogue and digital instruments is the input resistance that they present to the circuit under investigation when taking voltage measurements.

TIP

The resistance of a reasonable quality non-electronic analogue meter can be as low as 50kΩ on the 2.5V range. With a digital instrument the input resistance is typically 10MΩ on the 2V (1.999V max) range. The digital instrument is thus to be preferred when accurate readings are to be taken. While this may be of little concern when checking the voltages of supply rails and in TTL circuits generally, it does become extremely important when measurements are to be made on circuits which use CMOS devices.

Low-cost digital multimeters have been made possible by the advent of mass-produced LSI devices and liquid crystal displays. A three-digit display is the norm, consisting of three full digits which can display 0 to 9 and a fourth (most significant) digit which can only display 1. Thus, the maximum display indication, ignoring the range switching and decimal point, is 1999; anything greater over-ranges the display. Nearly all digital meters contain automatic zero and polarity indicating facilities and some also have auto-ranging. This feature, which is usually only found in the more sophisticated instruments, automatically changes the range setting so that maximum resolution is obtained without over-ranging. There is thus no need for manual operation of the range switch once the indicating mode has been selected. This is an extremely useful facility since it frees the user from the need to make repeated adjustments to the range switch while measurements are being made.

For portable applications an LCD instrument is, by virtue of its small size, low weight and minimal power consumption, much to be preferred. Most LCD meters will provide around 200 hours of continuous operation from one set of batteries but a comparable LED instrument may only operate for some 20–30 hours. As with analogue multimeters, it is wise to select an instrument that has a clear display and sensible range switching.

TIP

Many digital multimeters use a multiplicity of push-buttons and this can be particularly confusing when a combination of several push-buttons have to be used to select a particular range. In general, instruments that employ a conventional rotary switch, augmented if necessary by one or two push-buttons or slide switches, are much easier to use.

TIP

The most common use of a multimeter is checking supply rail voltages. The nominal 5V rail should normally be within the range 4.75–5.25V and the 12V rail between 11.4–12.6V. Voltages outside this range don't always indicate a fault – in some cases they can indicate that the power supply is inadequately rated!

Oscilloscopes

An oscilloscope will allow you to display time-related voltage waveforms such as those which appear on a clock or bus line. Such an item represents a considerable capital investment, however, it can become invaluable in a number of applications such as disk drive head alignment, checking for 'glitches' and supply borne noise, faulty bus lines and certain timing problems.

The oscilloscope display is generally provided by a cathode ray tube (CRT) which has a typical screen area of around 80 × 100mm. The CRT is fitted with a graticule, which may be either integral with the tube face or a separate translucent sheet. The graticule is usually ruled with a 1cm grid to which further bold lines may be added to mark the major axes on the central viewing area. Accurate voltage and time measurements may be made with reference to the graticule, applying a scale factor derived from the appropriate range switch. A word of caution is appropriate at this stage, however.

TIP

Before taking accurate measurements from the CRT screen it is essential to ensure that the relevant front panel controls are set to the 'calibrate' (CAL) position. If you fail to do this, any readings which you take are liable to be inaccurate! (Many oscilloscopes have an in-built calibrate facility – consult your operations manual for details.)

For personal computer servicing, it is essential to have an oscilloscope with a vertical bandwidth of at least 30MHz and a reliable trigger (preferably incorporating a 'delayed trigger' facility). The timebase ranges should similarly extend to at least 0.1μs/cm, or less. Ideally the oscilloscope should have a dual trace capability although this is not absolutely essential. A vertical amplifier sensitivity of 10mV/cm is quite adequate and an input impedance of 1MΩ shunted by about 30pF is the norm.

TIP

The use of a correctly designed and matched oscilloscope probe is essential in order to avoid the effects of capacitive loading. Many probes provide switched '×1' and '×10' facilities and they should normally be used in the latter position when examining digital signals.

Logic probes

Surprisingly, the most regularly used item of test gear in my own workshop is also the least expensive. It is, as you may have guessed, nothing more than a simple hand-held logic probe. The supply to the probe (usually +5V and 'ground') is connected via a short length of cable terminated in a pair of crocodile clips. These may be attached to the positive supply and 0V rails at suitably accessible points on the circuit under investigation. Most probes will accept supplies in the range 4.75–18V and are usually protected against inadvertent polarity reversal.

TIP

Some manufacturers supply their logic probes with a range of interchangeable probe tips. These can be an asset when the probe is to be attached to a wide variety of components.

As with other items of test equipment, there is some variation in the facilities offered by logic probes but invariably three LEDs are provided to indicate the logical state of the probe tip, which may be either 'HIGH' (logic 1), 'LOW' (logic 0) or PULSE (alternating between the two states). The relative brightness of the 'HIGH' and 'LOW' indicators gives an approximate indication of the duty cycle of the pulse train. The indications provided by a typical low-cost logic probe are shown in Table 16.1.

More sophisticated logic probes provide pulse-stretching facilities so that pulses of very short duration can be recognised. Other types incorporate a 'memory' mode that can catch a narrow pulse and display it continuously until the mode is cancelled or the probe is disconnected from its supply. Note that when using such a probe it is usually necessary to ensure that the probe tip is connected to the circuit at the point under investigation before switching to the 'memory' mode. If this precaution is not observed, the action of connecting the floating probe tip is likely to produce an erroneous trigger pulse.

Logic probes are usually available in two varieties (or may be switched into one of two modes): either TTL or CMOS. In the TTL mode 'HIGH' and 'LOW' signal levels are defined as greater than 2.25V and less than 0.8V, respectively, whereas in the CMOS mode these levels are represented by 70% and 30% of the probe supply voltage. While it is possible to use a high input impedance TTL logic probe

Table 16.1 Logic probe indications

LED indicator			State	Waveform
Low	Pulse	High		
OFF	OFF	ON	Steady logic 1	
ON	OFF	OFF	Steady logic 0	
OFF	OFF	OFF	Open circuit or undefined level	
OFF	BLINK	OFF	Pulse train of near 50% duty cycle at >1 MHz	
ON	BLINK	ON	Pulse train of near 50% duty cycle at <1 MHz	
OFF	BLINK	ON	Pulse train of high mark:space ratio	
ON	BLINK	OFF	Pulse train of low mark:space ratio	

for fault tracing in CMOS circuits, the use of a CMOS probe in TTL circuits is not generally to be recommended.

Typical logic probe indications CPU and bus lines are shown in Table 16.2 but it is important to note that older logic probes may fail to respond at the fast clock rates of many of the more recent processors. In such cases an oscilloscope will be required in order to test for activity on the various CPU lines. Lower speed bus lines will, however, produce indications on most types of logic probe.

TIP

A 'stuck' or 'floating' bus line is easy to detect using a logic probe. However, before checking the bus lines for activity it is worth checking the bus clock, interrupt and reset lines (see Table 16.2).

Logic pulsers

Like logic probes, pulsers are simple hand-held instruments that derive their power supply from the circuit under investigation. A narrow pulse of short duration is generated whenever a push-button is depressed. Alternatively, a continuous train of pulses is generated if the button is held down. When the button is released, the probe assumes a high impedance state. The output of the probe can typically source or sink currents of up to several hundred milliamps (equivalent to 50 or more conventional TTL loads). The pulse width is made fairly narrow, being typically 1μs and 10μs in the TTL and CMOS modes, respectively.

The primary function of the logic pulser is to achieve a momentary change of state at a node in a circuit. More sophisticated pulsers use comparator techniques to sense the state of the node before applying a pulse of the correct (opposite) polarity. If the test point is high the

Table 16.2 Typical logic probe indications for PC bus lines

Signal	Abbreviation	State
Address lines	A0-Ann	Pulsing
Address latch enable	ALE#	Pulsing
Address enable	AEN#	Pulsing
Chip select	CS#	High/pulsed low
Clock	CLK	Pulsing (square wave)
Common	GND	Low (0V)
Data lines	D0-Dnn	Pulsing
Interrupt request lines	IR(Q)n	Pulsing
Interrupt acknowledge	INTA#	Pulsing
Lock	LOCK	Pulsing
Memory read	RD#	Pulsing
Min/max. mode	MN/MX	Low
Non-maskable interrupt	NMI	Low
Queue status	QSn	Pulsing
Ready	READY	Pulsing
Request/grant	RQ/GTn	High/pulsing
Reset (active high)	RESET#	High
Reset (active low)	RESET	Low
Status	Sn	Pulsing
Supply	Vcc	+5V
Test	TEST	High
Write	WR#	Pulsing

Note: # indicates active low (asserted low)

pulse goes low, and vice versa. After the pulse has been emitted another comparison is made and, if a change of node state has occurred, the next pulse generated will be of opposite polarity. This useful facility permits continuous triggering of the circuit under investigation regardless of its actual logic state.

When using a logic pulser it should be remembered that, since an appreciable current may be sourced or sunk by the device, the return current flowing in the supply common lead will also be considerable. Thus, to prevent erroneous triggering, it is essential to derive the pulser's supply from a low impedance point on the supply rails and not merely clip the leads to the nearest available integrated circuit. While this latter technique may prove satisfactory for use with logic probes, it is definitely not recommended where logic pulsers are concerned. A suitable connecting point is directly across the terminals of an electrolytic supply decoupling capacitor of 100μF minimum.

IC test clips

The clearance between the pins of a conventional dual-in-line integrated circuit is of the order of 1.3mm, or less. In view of this, the use of conventional test prods is likely to be a hazardous process since there is a considerable risk of inadvertent short circuits when making a connection to a device. Spring-loaded dual-in-line test clips facilitate the attachment of a variety of test instruments using conventional hook-type test prods. Test clips come in a variety of sizes and it is wise to have several available including 16-pin, 28-pin and 40-pin types.

Logic monitors

Various forms of logic state monitor are available, ranging from simple clip-on indicators to sophisticated multi-channel bench instruments.

In all cases, however, LEDs are used to display the logical state of each of the pins of the IC under investigation. It is then possible to monitor, simultaneously, the logical state of all of the inputs and outputs of a digital IC.

Simple logic monitors generally contain 16 LEDs and can be used in conjunction with 8-pin, 14-pin and 16-pin devices. These are invariably circuit powered, automatically deriving their supplies from the highest and lowest voltages appearing at the 16 points of connection. Since only one LED is available for each pin, a single logic threshold is recognised. This is usually the same as that for a logic probe 'HIGH' (i.e. greater than 2.25V or 70% of the supply voltage for TTL and CMOS monitors, respectively). Pulse trains appear as LEDs with less than full intensity, the relative brightness giving an approximate indication of the duty cycle. More complex logic monitors may provide remote display facilities, a choice of logic thresholds (appropriate to either TTL or CMOS) and up to 40 display channels.

Current tracers

When fault tracing, it is sometimes advantageous to be able to measure the current at strategic points in a circuit. Such a measurement becomes necessary when, for example, we are concerned with the supply current drawn by an integrated circuit. Where devices are mounted in sockets, conventional multi-range meters may be used. The procedure involves first removing the integrated circuit from its socket, bending the relevant pin through 90 degrees, then re-inserting the device and connecting the milliammeter between the bent-out pin and the appropriate point in the circuit. This method is, of course, inappropriate when a chip is soldered into the PCB. There is, however, no need to cut the PCB tracks if a current tracer is available. Such an instrument can measure, to a reasonable approximation, the current flowing in standard size PCB tracks without the need to break the circuit.

Two forms of current tracer are available; one operates by sensing the magnetic field in the vicinity of the track and the other measures the voltage drop across a short length of track. For accurate measurements, the PCB is assumed to be standard 35μm (306g/m^2) track and calibration is usually supplied for 1–2mm width track. Current tracers will typically respond to currents of 10mA or less and it is thus possible to check the operating current of a single TTL gate with a reasonable degree of accuracy. More sophisticated current tracers of the magnetic sensing variety may be used to 'follow' the path of direct current in the PCB. Such devices can thus be extremely useful in detecting such PCB faults as dry joints, hair-line cracks, solder splashes, shorted tracks and open-circuit plated through holes.

TIP

A reasonably sensitive multimeter can be used to provide a rough indication of the relative magnitude of current present in a PCB track. Simply connect the probe tips to the ends of each track in turn and select a low voltage range (e.g. 200mV full-scale). A high voltage drop will indicate the presence of a larger than normal current.

Logic comparators

It is often necessary to determine whether or not a logic gate is functioning correctly and, while a simple method of checking an integrated circuit using a logic probe has already been described, this may not cover every case and a more rigorous substitution test may be preferred. Such a test would verify all of the gates contained within a single IC at the same time without the need to transfer a logic probe from pin to pin.

Substitution testing is a relatively easy matter when devices are mounted in sockets but it may not even be considered when a device has to be desoldered (particularly when a double-sided PCB is involved!). We have therefore to leave the IC in circuit. However, since we have immediate access to all of its pins it is possible to duplicate its operation externally, using a known good device and then compare the results obtained. A device that performs this function is a logic comparator and such an instrument can permit rapid in-circuit dynamic testing of a wide variety of logic devices.

The output of the gate on test is compared with that derived from a reference gate using an exclusive-OR gate when both gates are fed with the same inputs. If the gate on test is producing the same logic function as that of the reference gate, the output of the exclusive-OR gate will be at logic 0. If, on the other hand, there is a difference between the outputs of the gate on test and the reference gate, the output provided by the exclusive-OR gate will be at logic 1.

The logic comparator is normally connected to the suspect device by means of an IC test clip and multi-way ribbon cable. To be useful, the logic comparator must be accompanied by a wide range of known reference devices. So if you are lucky enough to own such an instrument it is worth building up a reasonable stock of logic gates, over and above those one would normally keep in stock for replacement purposes.

Diagnostic adapters

Finally, several manufacturers make use of specialised adapter cards to diagnose faults on systems which refuse to boot normally (i.e. when the system won't even run the diagnostic code within the BIOS ROM). As the display will not normally be operational in such an eventuality, these adapter cards provide their output on an external display or on a printer.

Diagnostic adapter cards provide a very effective means of fault-finding a system that fails the standard bootstrap diagnostics or that manifestly fails to execute any of the BIOS code. Unfortunately, such items are not widely available and furthermore their usefulness is generally restricted to a particular machine type or family.

Data communications test equipment

Several specialised test instruments and accessories are required for testing asynchronous serial data communications systems. The following items are available from a number of manufacturers and suppliers.

Patch boxes

These low-cost devices facilitate the cross connection of RS-232 (or equivalent) signal lines. The equipment is usually fitted with two D-type connectors (or ribbon cables fitted with a plug and socket) and all lines are brought out to a patching area into which links may be plugged. In use, these devices are connected in series with the RS-232 serial data path and various patching combinations are tested until a functional interface is established. If desired, a dedicated cable may then be manufactured in order to replace the patch box.

Gender changers

Gender changers normally comprise an extended RS-232 connector which has a male connector at one end and a female connector at the other. Gender changers permit mixing of male and female connector types (note that the convention is male at the DTE and female at the DCE).

Null modems

Like gender changers, these devices are connected in series with an RS-232C serial data path. Their function is simply that of changing the signal lines so that a DTE is effectively configured as a DCE. Null modems can easily be set up using a patch box or purchased as a dedicated null-modem cable.

Line monitors

Line monitors display the logical state (in terms of MARK or SPACE) present on the most commonly used data and handshaking signal lines. Light emitting diodes (LED) provide the user with a rapid indication of which signals are present and active within the system.

Breakout boxes

Breakout boxes provide access to the signal lines and invariably combine the features of patch boxes and line monitors. In addition, switches or jumpers are usually provided for linking lines on either side of the box. Connection is almost invariably via two 25-way ribbon cables terminated with connectors.

Interface testers

Interface tests are somewhat more complex than simple breakout boxes and generally incorporate facilities for forcing lines into MARK or SPACE states, detecting glitches, measuring baud rates and also displaying the format of data words. Such instruments are, not surprisingly, rather expensive but could be invaluable for anyone who is regularly carrying out fault finding on asynchronous serial equipment.

17
Reference section

Glossary of terms

Accelerator

A board which replaces the CPU with circuitry to increase the speed of processing.

Access time

The time taken to retrieve data from a memory/storage device, i.e. the elapsed time between the receipt of a read signal at the device and the placement of valid data on the bus. Typical access times for semiconductor memory devices are in the region 100–200ns whilst average access times for magnetic disks typically range from 10–50ms.

Accumulator

A register within the central processing unit (CPU) in which the result of an operation is placed.

Acknowledge (ACK)

A signal used in serial data communications which indicates that data has been received without error.

Active high

A term used to describe a signal which is asserted in the high (logic 1) state.

Active low

A term used to describe a signal which is asserted in the low (logic 0) state.

Address

A reference to the location of data in memory or within I/O space. The CPU places addresses (in binary coded form) on the address bus.

Address bus

The set of lines used to convey address information. The IBM-PC bus has 20 address lines (A0 to A19) and these are capable of addressing more than a million address locations. One byte of data may be stored at each address.

Address decoder

A hardware device (often a single integrated circuit) which provides chip select or chip enable signals from address patterns which appear on an address bus.

Address selection

The process of selecting a specific address (or range of addresses). In order to prevent conflicts, expansion cards must usually be configured (by means of DIP switches or links) to unique addresses within the I/O address map.

Amplifier

A circuit or device which increases the power of an electrical signal.

Analogue

The representation of information in the form of a continuously variable quantity (e.g. voltage).

AND

Logical function which is asserted (true) when all inputs are simultaneously asserted.

ANSI character set

The American National Standard Institute's character set which is based on an 8-bit binary code and which provides 256 individual characters (see also ASCII).

Archive

A device or medium used for storage of data which need not be instantly accessible (e.g. a tape cartridge).

ASCII

A code which is almost universally employed for exchanging data between microcomputers. Standard ASCII is based on a 7-bit binary code and caters for alphanumeric characters (both upper and lower case), punctuation and special control characters. Extended ASCII employs an eighth bit to provide an additional 128 characters (often used to represent graphic symbols).

Assembly language

A low-level programming language which is based on mnemonic instructions. Assembly language is often unique to a particular microprocessor or microprocessor family.

Asserted

A term used to describe a signal when it is in its logically true state (i.e. logic 1 in the case of an active high signal or logic 0 in the case of an active low signal).

Asynchronous transmission

A data transmission method in which the time between transmitted characters is arbitrary. Transmission is controlled by start and stop bits (no additional synchronising or timing information is required).

ATAPI

The ATAPI (or Advanced Technology Attachment Packet Interface) standard provides a simple means of connecting a CD-ROM drive to an EIDE adapter. Without such an interface, a CD-ROM drive will require either a dedicated interface card or an interface provided on a sound card.

AUTOEXEC.BAT

A file which contains a set of DOS commands and/or program names which is executed automatically whenever the system is initialised and provides a means of configuring a system.

Backup

A file or disk copy made in order to avoid the accidental loss, damage or erasure of programs and/or data.

Basic input output system (BIOS)

The BIOS is the part of the operating system which handles communications between the microcomputer and peripheral devices (such as keyboard, serial port etc.). The BIOS is supplied as firmware and is contained in a read-only memory (ROM).

Batch file

A file containing a series of DOS commands which are executed when the file name is entered after the DOS prompt. Batch files are given a BAT file extension. A special type of batch file (AUTOEXEC.BAT) is executed (when present) whenever a system is initialised. See also AUTOEXEC.BAT.

Baud rate

The speed at which serial data is transferred between devices.

Binary file

A file which contains binary data (i.e. a direct memory image). This type of file is used for machine readable code, program overlays and graphics screens.

Bit

A contraction of 'binary digit'; a single digit in a binary number.

Boot

The name given to the process of loading and initialising an operating system (part of the operating system is held on disk and must be loaded from disk into RAM on power-up).

Boot record

A single-sector record present on a disk which conveys information about the disk and instructs the computer to load the requisite operating system files into RAM (thus booting the machine).

Buffer

In a hardware context, a buffer is a device which provides a degree of electrical isolation at an interface. The input to a buffer usually exhibits a much higher impedance than its output (see also 'Driver'). In a software context, a buffer is a reserved area of memory which provides temporary data storage and thus may be used to compensate for a difference in the rate of data flow or time of occurrence of events.

Bus

An electrical highway for signals which have some common function. Most microprocessor systems have three distinct buses; an address bus, data bus and control bus. A local bus can be used for high-speed data transfer between certain devices (e.g. CPU, graphics processors and video memory).

Byte

A group of eight bits which are operated on as a unit.

Cache

A high-speed random-access memory which is used to store copies of the data from the most recent main memory or hard disk accesses. Subsequent accesses fetch data from this area rather than from the slower main memory or hard disk.

Central processing unit (CPU)

The part of a computer that decodes instructions and controls the other hardware elements of the system. The CPU comprises a control unit, arithmetic/logic unit and internal storage. In microcomputers, a microprocessor acts as the CPU (see also Microprocessor).

Channel

A path along which signals or data can be sent.

Character set

The complete range of characters (letters, numbers and punctuation) which are provided within a system. See also ANSI and ASCII.

Checksum

Additional binary digits appended to a block of data. The value of the appended digits is derived from the sum of the data present within the block. This technique provides a means of error checking (validation).

Chip

The term commonly used to describe an integrated circuit.

CISC

The term CISC refers to a 'Complex Instruction Set Computer' – the standard Intel family of CPUs all conform to this model rather than the alternative 'Reduced Instruction Set Computer' (RISC). There is much debate about the advantages and disadvantages of these two design methodologies but, in fact, neither of these two contrasting approaches has actually demonstrated clear superiority over the other (see also CISC).

Clock

A source of timing signals used for synchronising data transfers within a microprocessor or microcomputer system.

Cluster

A unit of space allocated on the surface of a disk. The number of sectors which make up a cluster varies according to the DOS version and disk type (see also Sector).

Command

An instruction (entered from the keyboard or contained within a batch file) which will be recognised and executed by a system (see also Batch file).

Common

A return path for a signal (often ground).

CONFIG.SYS

A file which contains DOS configuration commands which are used to configure the system at start-up. The CONFIG.SYS file specifies device drivers which are loaded during initialisation and which extend the functionality of a system by allowing it to communicate with additional items of hardware (see also Device driver).

Controller

A sub-system within a microcomputer which controls the flow of data between the system and an I/O or storage device (e.g. a CRT controller, hard disk controller etc.). A controller will generally be based on one, or more, programmable VLSI devices.

Coprocessor

A second processor which shares the same instruction stream as the main processor. The coprocessor handles specific tasks (e.g. mathematics) which would otherwise be performed less efficiently (or not at all) by the main processor.

Cylinder

The group of tracks which can be read from a hard disk at any instant of time (i.e. without steeping the head in or out). In the case of a floppy disk (where there are only two surfaces), each cylinder comprises two tracks. In the case of a typical IDE hard disk, there may be two platters (i.e. four surfaces) and thus four tracks will be present within each cylinder.

Daisy chain

A method of connection in which signals move in a chained fashion from one device to another. This form of connection is commonly used with disk drives.

Data

A general term used to describe numbers, letters and symbols present with a computer system. All such information is ultimately represented by patterns of binary digits.

Data bus

A highway (in the form of multiple electrical conductors) which conveys data between the different elements within a microprocessor system.

Data file

A file which contains data (rather than a program) and which are used by applications such as spreadsheet and database applications. Note that data may or may not be stored in directly readable ASCII form.

Device

A hardware component such as a memory card, sound card, modem or graphics adapter.

Device driver

A term used to describe memory resident software (specified in the CONFIG.SYS system file) which provides a means of interfacing specialised hardware (e.g. expanded memory adapters) (see CONFIG-.SYS).

Direct memory access

A method of fast data transfer in which data moves between a peripheral device (e.g. a hard disk) and main memory without direct control of the CPU.

Directory

A catalogue of disk files (containing such information as filename, size, attributes, and date/time of creation). The directory is stored on the disk and updated whenever a file is amended, created or deleted. A directory entry usually comprises 32 bytes for each file.

DIP switch

A miniature PCB-mounted switch that allows configuration options (such as IRQ or DMA settings) to be selected.

Disk operating system (DOS)

A group of programs which provide a low-level interface with the system hardware (particularly disk I/O). Routines contained within system resident portions of the operating system may be used by the programmer. Other programs provided as part of the system include those used for formatting disks, copying files etc.

Double word

A data value which comprises a group of 32-bits (or two words) (see also Word).

DRAM

DRAM (or Dynamic Random Access Memory) refers to the semi-conductor read/write memory of a PC. DRAM requires periodic 'refreshing' and therefore tends not to offer the highest speeds required of specialised memories (such as cache memory). DRAM is, however, relatively inexpensive.

Driver

In a software context, a driver is a software routine which provides a means of interfacing a specialised hardware device (see also Device driver). In a hardware context, a driver is an electrical circuit which provides an electrical interface between an output port and an output transducer. A driver invariably provides power gain (i.e. current gain and/or voltage gain) (see also Amplifier).

EIDE

EIDE (or Enhanced Integrated Drive Electronics) is the most widely-used interface for connecting hard disk drives to a PC. Most mother-boards now incorporate an on-board EIDE controller rather than having to make use of an adapter card. This allows one or two hard disk drives to be connected directly to the motherboard.

Expanded memory (EMS memory)

Memory which is additional to the conventional 'base' memory available within the system. This memory is 'paged' into the base memory space whenever it is accessed. The EMS specification uses four contiguous 16Kbyte pages of physical memory (64Kbyte total) to access up to 32Mbyte of expanded memory space (see also Expanded memory manager).

Expanded memory manager

An expanded memory manager (such as EMM386.EXE included with MS-DOS 5.0 and later) provides a means of establishing and controlling the use of expanded memory (i.e. memory above the DOS 1Mbyte limit). Unlike DOS and Windows 3.1, Windows 95 incorporates its own memory management and thus EMM386 (or its equivalent) is not required (see also Expanded memory).

Extended memory (XMS memory)

Memory beyond the 1Mbyte range ordinarily recognised by MS-DOS. The XMS memory specification resulted from collaboration between Lotus, Intel and Microsoft (sometimes known as LIM specification).

File

Information (which may comprise ASCII encoded text, binary coded data and executable programs) stored on a floppy or hard disk. Files may be redirected from one logical device to another using appropriate DOS commands.

File allocation table (FAT)

The file allocation table (or FAT) provides a means of keeping track of the physical location of files stored on a floppy disk or hard disk. Part of the function of DOS is to keep the FAT up to date whenever a file operation is carried out. DOS does not necessarily store files in physically contiguous clusters on a disk and it is the FAT that maintains the addresses of clusters occupied by a particular file. These clusters may, in fact, be scattered all over the surface of the disk (in which case we describe the file as having been 'fragmented').

File attributes

Information which indicates the status of a file (e.g. hidden, read-only, system etc.).

Filter

In a software context, a filter is a software routine which removes or modifies certain data items (or data items within a defined range). In a hardware context, a filter is an electrical circuit which modifies the frequency distribution of a signal. Filters are often categorised as low-pass, high-pass, band-pass or band-stop depending upon the shape of their frequency response characteristic.

Firmware

A program (software) stored in read-only memory (ROM). Firmware provides non-volatile storage of programs.

Fixed disk

A disk which cannot be removed from its housing. Note that, whilst the terms 'hard' and 'fixed' are often used interchangeably, some forms of hard disk are exchangeable.

Font

A set of characters (letters, numbers and punctuation) with a particular style and size.

Format

The process in which a magnetic disk is initialised so that it can accept data. The process involves writing a magnetic pattern of tracks and sectors to a blank (uninitialised) disk. A disk containing data can be reformatted, in which case all data stored on the disk will be lost. An MS-DOS utility program (FORMAT.COM) is supplied in order to carry out the formatting of floppy disks (a similar utility is usually provided for formatting the hard disk).

Graphics adapter

An option card which provides a specific graphics capability (e.g. CGA, EGA, HGA, VGA). Graphics signal generation is not normally part of the functionality provided within a system motherboard.

Handshake

An interlocked sequence of signals between peripheral devices in which a device waits for an acknowledgement of the receipt of data before sending new data.

Hard disk

A non-flexible disk used for the magnetic storage of data and programs (see also Fixed disk).

Hardware

The physical components (e.g. system board, keyboard etc.) which make up a microcomputer system.

High state

The more positive of the two voltage levels used to represent binary logic states. A high state (logic 1) is generally represented by a voltage in the range 2.0–5.0V.

High memory

The first 64Kbyte of extended memory. This area is used by some DOS applications and also by Windows (see Extended memory).

IDE

IDE (or Integrated Drive Electronics) is the forerunner of the EIDE interface used in most modern PCs (see EIDE).

Input/output (I/O)

Devices and lines used to transfer information to and from external (peripheral) devices.

Integrated circuit

An electronic circuit fabricated on a single wafer (chip) and packaged as a single component.

Interface

A shared boundary between two or more systems, or between two or more elements within a system. In order to facilitate interconnection of systems, various interface standards are adopted (e.g. RS-232 in the case of asynchronous data communications).

Interleave

A system of numbering the sectors on a disk in a non-consecutive fashion in order to optimise data access times.

Interrupt

A signal generated by a peripheral device when it wishes to gain the attention of the CPU. The Intel 80x86 family of microprocessors support both software and hardware interrupts. The former provide a means of invoking BIOS and DOS services whilst the latter are generally managed by an interrupt controller chip (e.g. 8259).

ISA

ISA (or Industry Standard Architecture) is the long-surviving standard for connecting multiple interface adapters to the PC bus. Due to speed limitations, the ISA bus is no longer used for hardware that requires fast data throughput and local bus schemes (such as VL-bus or PCI-bus) are much preferred.

Joystick

A device used for positioning a cursor, pointer or output device using switches or potentiometers which respond to displacement of the stick in the x and y directions.

Jumper

Jumpers, like DIP switches, provide a means of selecting configuration options on adapter cards (see DIP switch).

Keyboard buffer

A small area in memory which provides temporary storage for keystrokes (see Buffer).

Kilobyte (K)

1,024 bytes (note that $2^{10} = 1{,}024$).

Logical device

A device which is normally associated with microcomputer I/O, such as the console (which comprises keyboard and display) and printer.

Low state

The more negative of the two voltage levels used to represent the binary logic states. A low state (logic 0) is generally represented by a voltage in the range 0V–0.8V.

Megabyte (M)

1,048,576 bytes (note that $2^{20} = 1{,}048{,}576$). The basic addressing range of the 8086 (which has 20 address bus lines) is 1Mbyte.

Memory

That part of a microcomputer system into which information can be placed and later retrieved. Storage and memory are interchangeable terms. Memory can take various forms including semiconductor (RAM and ROM), magnetic (floppy and hard disks) and optical disks. Note that memory may also be categorised as read-only (in which case data cannot subsequently be written to the memory) or read/write (in which case data can both be read from and written to the memory).

Memory resident program

See TSR.

Microprocessor

A central processing unit fabricated on a single chip.

MIDI

The MIDI (or Musical Instrument Digital Interface) is the current industry standard for connecting musical instruments to a PC.

Modem

A contraction of modulator-demodulator; a communications interface device that enables a serial port to be interfaced to a conventional voice-frequency telephone line.

Modified frequency modulation (MFM)

A method of data encoding employed with hard disk storage. This method of data storage is 'self-clocking'.

Motherboard

The motherboard (or system board) is the mother printed circuit board which provides the basic functionality of the microcomputer system including CPU, RAM and ROM. The system board is fitted with connectors which permit the installation of one, or more, option cards (e.g. graphics adapters, disk controllers etc.).

Multimedia

A combination of various media technologies including sound, video, graphics and animation.

Multitasking

A process in which several programs are running simultaneously.

NAND

Inverse of the logical AND function.

Negative acknowledge (NAK)

A signal used in serial data communications which indicates that erroneous data has been received.

Network

A system which allows two or more computers to be linked via a physical communications medium (e.g. coaxial cable) in order to exchange information and share resources.

Nibble

A group of four bits which make up one half of a byte. A hexadecimal character can be represented by such a group.

Noise

Any unwanted signal component which may appear superimposed on a wanted signal.

NOR

Inverse of the logical OR function.

Operating system

A control program which provides a low-level interface with the system hardware. The operating system thus frees the programmer from the need to produce hardware specific I/O routines (e.g. those associated with disk filing) (see also Disk operating system).

Option card

A printed circuit board (adapter card) which complies with the physical and electrical specification for a particular system and which provides the system with additional functionality (e.g. asynchronous communications facilities).

OR

Logical function which is asserted (true) when any one or more of its inputs are asserted.

Page

A contiguous area of memory of defined size (often 256 bytes but can be larger, see Expanded memory).

Paragraph

Sixteen consecutive bytes of data. The segment address can be incremented to point to consecutive paragraphs of data.

Parallel interface (parallel port)

A communications interface in which data is transferred a byte at a time between a computer and a peripheral device, such as a printer.

PCI

The PCI (or Peripheral Component Interconnect) standard provides a means of connecting 32-bit or 64-bit expansion cards to a motherboard. PCI expansion slots are available in most modern PCs.

PCMCIA

The PCMCIA (or simply PC Card) standard provides a means of connecting a sub-miniature expansion card (such as a memory card or modem) to a laptop or book computer.

Peripheral

An external hardware device whose activity is under the control of the microcomputer system.

Port

A general term used to describe an interface circuit which facilitates transfer of data to and from external devices (peripherals).

Program

A sequence of executable microcomputer instructions which have a defined function. Such instructions are stored in program files having EXE or COM extensions.

Propagation delay

The time taken for a signal to travel from one point to another. In the case of logic elements, propagation delay is the time interval between the appearance of a logic state transition at the input of a gate and its subsequent appearance at the output.

Protocol

A set of rules and formats necessary for the effective exchange of data between intelligent devices.

Random access

An access method in which each word can be retrieved in the same amount of time (i.e. the storage locations can be accessed in any desired order). This method should be compared with sequential access in which access times are dependent upon the position of the data within the memory.

Random access memory (RAM)

A term which usually refers to semiconductor read/write memory (in which access time is independent of actual storage address). Note that semiconductor read-only memory (ROM) devices also provide random access.

Read

The process of transferring data to a processor from memory or I/O.

Read-only memory (ROM)

A memory device which is permanently programmed. Erasable-programmable read only memory (EPROM) devices are popular for storage of programs and data in stand-alone applications and can be erased under ultraviolet light to permit reprogramming.

Register

A storage area within a CPU, controller or other programmable device, in which data (or addresses) are placed during processing. Registers will commonly hold 8, 16 or 32-bit values.

RISC

The term RISC refers to a 'Reduced Instruction Set Computer' – a computer based on a processor that accepts only a limited number of basic instructions but which decodes and executes them faster than the alternative technology (CISC) (see also CISC).

Run length limited (RLL)

A method of data encoding employed with hard disk storage. This method is more efficient than conventional MFM encoding.

Root directory

The principal directory of a disk (either hard or floppy) which is created when the disk is first formatted. The root directory may contain the details of further sub-directories which may themselves contain yet more sub-directories, and so on.

SCSI

The SCSI (or Small Computer Systems Interface) provides a means of interfacing up to eight peripheral devices (such as hard disks, CD-ROM drives and scanners) to a microcomputer system. With its roots in larger minicomputer systems, SCSI tends to be more complex and expensive in comparison with EIDE.

Sector

The name given to a section of the circular track placed (during formatting) on a magentic disk. Tracks are commonly divided into 10 sectors (see also Format).

Segment

64Kbytes of contiguous data within memory. The starting address of such a block of memory may be contained within one of the four segment registers (DS, CS, SS or ES).

Serial interface (serial port)

A communications interface in which data is transferred a bit at a time between a computer and a peripheral device, such as a modem. In serial data transfer, a byte of data (i.e. eight bits) is transmitted by sending a stream of bits, one after another. Furthermore, when such data is transmitted asynchronously (i.e. without a clock), additional bits must be added for synchronisation together with further bits for error (parity) checking (if enabled).

Server

A computer which provides network accessible services (e.g. hard disk storage, printing etc.).

Shell

The name given to an item of software which provides the principal user interface to a system. The DOS program COMMAND.COM provides a simple DOS shell, however, later versions of MS-DOS and DR-DOS provide much improved graphical shells (DOSSHELL and VIEWMAX, respectively).

Signal

The information conveyed by an electrical quantity.

Signal level

The relative magnitude of a signal when considered in relation to an arbitrary reference (usually expressed in volts, V).

SIMM

SIMMs (or Single In-line Memory Modules) are used to house the DRAM chips used in all modern PCs. The modular packaging and standard pin connections makes memory expansion very straightforward.

Software

A series of computer instructions (i.e. a program).

Sub-directory

A directory which contains details of a group of files and which is itself contained within another directory (or within the root directory).

System board

See motherboard.

Swap file

A swap file is a file that resides on a hard disk and is used to provide 'virtual memory'. Swap files may be either 'permanent' or 'temporary' (see also Virtual memory).

System file

A file that contains information required by DOS. Such a file is not normally shown in a directory listing.

Terminal emulation

The ability of a microcomputer to emulate a hardware terminal.

TSR

A terminate-and-stay-resident program (i.e. a program which, once loaded, remains resident in memory and which is available for execution from within another application).

UART

UART (or Universal Asynchronous Transmitter/Receiver) is the name given to the chip that controls the PC's serial interface. Most modern PCs are fitted with 16550 or 16650 UARTs.

Upper memory

The 384Kbyte region of memory which extends beyond the 640Kbyte of conventional memory. This region of memory is not normally available to applications and is reserved for system functions such as the video display memory. Some applications (such as Windows running in enhanced mode) can access unused portions of the upper memory area).

Validation

A process in which input data is checked in order to identify incorrect items. Validation can take several forms including range, character and format checks.

Verification

A process in which stored data is checked (by subsequent reading) to see whether it is correct.

Virtual memory

A technique of memory management which uses disk swap files to emulate random-access memory. The extent of RAM can be increased by this technique by an amount which is equivalent to the total size of the swap files on the hard disk.

Visual display unit (VDU)

An output device (usually based on a cathode ray tube) on which text and/or graphics can be displayed. A VDU is normally fitted with an integral keyboard in which case it is sometimes referred to as a console.

Volume label

A disk name (comprising up to 11 characters). Note that hard disks may be partitioned into several volumes, each associated with its own logical drive specifier (i.e. C:, D:, E:, etc).

VRAM

VRAM (or Video Random Access Memory) is a high-speed type of DRAM fitted to a graphics controller card. This type of memory is preferred for the fast throughput of data which is essential when manipulating high-resolution screen images (see also DRAM).

Word

A data value which comprises a group of 16-bits and which constitutes the fundamental size of data which an 8086 processor can accept and manipulate as a unit.

Write

The process of transferring data from a CPU to memory or to an I/O device.

Hex, binary, decimal, and ASCII/IBM extended character set

Hex.	Binary	Decimal	ASCII/IBM (see note on p. 272)
00	00000000	0	
01	00000001	1	^A
02	00000010	2	^B
03	00000011	3	^C
04	00000100	4	^D
05	00000101	5	^E
06	00000110	6	^F
07	00000111	7	^G
08	00001000	8	^H
09	00001001	9	^I
0A	00001010	10	^J
0B	00001011	11	^K
0C	00001100	12	^L
0D	00001101	13	^M
0E	00001110	14	^N
0F	00001111	15	^O
10	00010000	16	^P
11	00010001	17	^Q
12	00010010	18	^R
13	00010011	19	^S
14	00010100	20	^T

15	00010101	21	^U
16	00010110	22	^V
17	00010111	23	^W
18	00011000	24	^X
19	00011001	25	^Y
1A	00011010	26	^Z
1B	00011011	27	^[
1C	00011100	28	^\
1D	00011101	29	^]
1E	00011110	30	^^
1F	00011111	31	^
20	00100000	32	
21	00100001	33	!
22	00100010	34	“
23	00100011	35	#
24	00100100	36	$
25	00100101	37	%
26	00100110	38	&
27	00100111	39	‘
28	00101000	40	(
29	00101001	41	)
2A	00101010	42	*
2B	00101011	43	+
2C	00101100	44	,
2D	00101101	45	-
2E	00101110	46	.
2F	00101111	47	/
30	00110000	48	0
31	00110001	49	1
32	00110010	50	2
33	00110011	51	3
34	00110100	52	4
35	00110101	53	5
36	00110110	54	6
37	00110111	55	7
38	00111000	56	8
39	00111001	57	9
3A	00111010	58	:
3B	00111011	59	;
3C	00111100	60	<
3D	00111101	61	=
3E	00111110	62	>
3F	00111111	63	?
40	01000000	64	@
41	01000001	65	A
42	01000010	66	B
43	01000011	67	C
44	01000100	68	D
45	01000101	69	E
46	01000110	70	F
47	01000111	71	G
48	01001000	72	H
49	01001001	73	I
4A	01001010	74	J
4B	01001011	75	K
4C	01001100	76	L
4D	01001101	77	M
4E	01001110	78	N
4F	01001111	79	O
50	01010000	80	P

51	01010001	81	Q
52	01010010	82	R
53	01010011	83	S
54	01010100	84	T
55	01010101	85	U
56	01010110	86	V
57	01010111	87	W
58	01011000	88	X
59	01011001	89	Y
5A	01011010	90	Z
5B	01011011	91	[
5C	01011100	92	\
5D	01011101	93	]
5E	01011110	94	^
5F	01011111	95	_
60	01100000	96	`
61	01100001	97	a
62	01100010	98	b
63	01100011	99	c
64	01100100	100	d
65	01100101	101	e
66	01100110	102	f
67	01100111	103	g
68	01101000	104	h
69	01101001	105	i
6A	01101010	106	j
6B	01101011	107	k
6C	01101100	108	l
6D	01101101	109	m
6E	01101110	110	n
6F	01101111	111	o
70	01110000	112	p
71	01110001	113	q
72	01110010	114	r
73	01110011	115	s
74	01110100	116	t
75	01110101	117	u
76	01110110	118	v
77	01110111	119	w
78	01111000	120	x
79	01111001	121	y
7A	01111010	122	z
7B	01111011	123	{
7C	01111100	124	|
7D	01111101	125	}
7E	01111110	126	~
7F	01111111	127	
80	10000000	128	Ç
81	10000001	129	ü
82	10000010	130	é
83	10000011	131	â
84	10000100	132	ä
85	10000101	133	à
86	10000110	134	å
87	10000111	135	ç
88	10001000	136	ê
89	10001001	137	ë
8A	10001010	138	è
8B	10001011	139	ï
8C	10001100	140	î

8D	10001101	141	ì
8E	10001110	142	Ä
8F	10001111	143	Å
90	10010000	144	É
91	10010001	145	æ
92	10010010	146	Æ
93	10010011	147	ô
94	10010100	148	ö
95	10010101	149	ò
96	10010110	150	û
97	10010111	151	ù
98	10011000	152	ÿ
99	10011001	153	Ö
9A	10011010	154	Ü
9B	10011011	155	¢
9C	10011100	156	£
9D	10011101	157	¥
9E	10011110	158	₧
9F	10011111	159	ƒ
A0	10100000	160	á
A1	10100001	161	í
A2	10100010	162	ó
A3	10100011	163	ú
A4	10100100	164	ñ
A5	10100101	165	Ñ
A6	10100110	166	ª
A7	10100111	167	º
A8	10101000	168	¿
A9	10101001	169	⌐
AA	10101010	170	¬
AB	10101011	171	½
AC	10101100	172	¼
AD	10101101	173	¡
AE	10101110	174	«
AF	10101111	175	»
B0	10110000	176	░
B1	10110001	177	▒
B2	10110010	178	▓
B3	10110011	179	│
B4	10110100	180	┤
B5	10110101	181	╡
B6	10110110	182	╢
B7	10110111	183	╖
B8	10111000	184	╕
B9	10111001	185	╣
BA	10111010	186	║
BB	10111011	187	╗
BC	10111100	188	╝
BD	10111101	189	╜
BE	10111110	190	╛
BF	10111111	191	┐
C0	11000000	192	└
C1	11000001	193	┴
C2	11000010	194	┬
C3	11000011	195	├
C4	11000100	196	─
C5	11000101	197	┼
C6	11000110	198	╞
C7	11000111	199	╟
C8	11001000	200	╚

C9	11001001	201	╔
CA	11001010	202	╩
CB	11001011	203	╦
CC	11001100	204	╠
CD	11001101	205	═
CE	11001110	206	╬
CF	11001111	207	╧
D0	11010000	208	╨
D1	11010001	209	╤
D2	11010010	210	╥
D3	11010011	211	╙
D4	11010100	212	╘
D5	11010101	213	╒
D6	11010110	214	╓
D7	11010111	215	╫
D8	11011000	216	╪
D9	11011001	217	┘
DA	11011010	218	┌
DB	11011011	219	█
DC	11011100	220	▄
DD	11011101	221	▌
DE	11011110	222	▐
DF	11011111	223	▀
E0	11100000	224	α
E1	11100001	225	ß
E2	11100010	226	Γ
E3	11100011	227	π
E4	11100100	228	Σ
E5	11100101	229	σ
E6	11100110	230	µ
E7	11100111	231	τ
E8	11101000	232	Φ
E9	11101001	233	Θ
EA	11101010	234	Ω
EB	11101011	235	δ
EC	11101100	236	∞
ED	11101101	237	φ
EE	11101110	238	ε
EF	11101111	239	∩
F0	11110000	240	≡
F1	11110001	241	±
F2	11110010	242	≥
F3	11110011	243	≤
F4	11110100	244	⌠
F5	11110101	245	⌡
F6	11110110	246	÷
F7	11110111	247	≈
F8	11111000	248	°
F9	11111001	249	∙
FA	11111010	250	·
FB	11111011	251	√
FC	11111100	252	ⁿ
FD	11111101	253	²
FE	11111110	254	■
FF	11111111	255	

Note: IBM and compatible equipment does not use standard ASCII characters below 32 decimal. These non-displayable ASCII characters are referred to as control characters. When output to the IBM display, these characters appear as additional graphics characters (not shown in the table).

IBM POST and diagnostic error codes

Indeterminate (01x)

01x	indeterminate problem

Power supply (02x)

02x	power supply fault

System board (1xx)

101	interrupt failure
102	BIOS ROM checksum error (PC, XT); timer (AT, MCA)
103	BASIC ROM checksum error (PC, XT); timer interrupt (AT, MCA)
104	interrupt controller (PC, XT); protected mode (AT, MCA)
105	timer (PC, XT); keyboard controller (MCA)
106	system board
107	system board adapter card or maths coprocessor, NMI test (MCA)
108	system board; timer bus (MCA)
109	DMA test; memory
110	system board memory (ISA); system board parity check (MCA)
111	adapter memory (ISA); memory adapter parity check (MCA)
112	adapter; watchdog time-out (MCA)
113	adapter; DMA arbitration time-out (MCA)
114	external ROM checksum (MCA)
115	80386 protect mode
121	unexpected hardware interrupt
131	cassette wrap test (PC)
132	DMA extended registers
133	DMA verify logic
134	DMA arbitration logic
151	real-time clock (or CMOS RAM)
152	system board (ISA); real time clock or CMOS (MCA)
160	system board ID not recognised (MCA)
161	system options (dead battery) (CMOS chip lost power)
162	system options (run Setup) (CMOS does not match system)
163	time and date (run Setup) (clock not updating)
164	memory size (run Setup) (CMOS does not match system)
165	adapter ID mismatch (MCA)
166	adapter time-out; card busy (MCA)
167	system clock not updating (MCA)
199	incorrect user device list

Memory (2xx)

201	memory error (number preceding 201 indicates specific location)
202	memory address line 0-15
203	memory address line 16-23; line 16-31 (MCA)

204	relocated memory (PS/2)
205	error in first 128Kbytes (PS/2 ISA); CMOS (PS/2 MCA)
207	ROM failure
211	system board memory; system board 64Kbytes (MCA)
215	memory address error; 64Kbytes on daughter/ SIP 2 (70)
216	system board memory; 64Kbytes on daughter/ SIP 1 (70)
221	ROM to RAM copy (MCA)
225	wrong speed memory on system board (MCA)

Keyboard (3xx)

301	keyboard did not respond correctly, or stuck key detected (the hexadecimal number preceding 301 is the scan code for the faulty key) keyboard interface (MCA)
302	user-indicated error from keyboard test (PC, XT)
302	keyboard locked (AT, models 25, 30)
303	keyboard/system board interface
304	keyboard or system unit error; keyboard clock (MCA)
305	keyboard fuse on system board (50, 60, 80); +5V error (70)
341	keyboard
342	keyboard cable
343	enhancement card or cable
365	keyboard (replace keyboard)
366	interface cable (replace cable)
367	enhancement card or cable (replace)

Monochrome display (4xx)

401	memory, horizontal sync frequency or vertical sync test
408	user-indicated display attributes
416	user-indicated character set
424	user-indicated 80 × 25 mode
432	monochrome card parallel port test

Color/graphics display (5xx)

501	memory, horizontal sync frequency or vertical sync test
508	user-indicated display attributes
516	user-indicated character set
524	user-indicated 80 × 25 mode
532	user-indicated 40 × 25 mode
540	user-indicated 320 × 200 graphics mode
548	user-indicated 640 × 200 graphics mode
556	light pen test
564	user-indicated screen paging test

Diskette drives and/or adapter (6xx)

601	diskette/adapter test failure; drive or controller (MCA)
602	diskette test (PC, XT); diskette boot record (MCA)

603	diskette size error
606	diskette verify function
607	write protected diskette
608	bad command; diskette status returned
610	diskette initialisation (PC, XT)
611	timeout; diskette status returned
612	bad NEC; diskette status returned
613	bad DMA; diskette status returned
614	DMA boundary error
621	bad seek; diskette status returned
622	bad CRC; diskette status returned
623	record not found; diskette status returned
624	bad address mark; diskette status returned
625	bad NEC seek; diskette status returned
626	diskette data compare error
627	diskette change line error
628	diskette removed
630	drive A: index stuck high
631	drive A: index stuck low
632	drive A: track 0 stuck off
633	drive A: track 0 stuck on
640	drive B: index stuck high
641	drive B: index stuck low
642	drive B: track 0 stuck off
643	drive B: track 0 stock on
650	drive speed
651	format failure
652	verify failure
653	read failure
654	write failure
655	controller
656	drive
657	write protect stuck protected
658	change line stuck changed
659	write protect stuck unprotected
660	change line stuck unchanged

Math coprocessor (7xx)

702	exception errors test
703	rounding test
704	arithmetic test 1
705	arithmetic test 2
706	arithmetic test 3
707	combination test
708	integer store test
709	equivalent expressions
710	exceptions
711	save state
712	protected mode test
713	voltage/temperature sensitivity test

Parallel printer adapter (9xx)

901	data register latch
902	control register latch
903	register address decode
904	address decode
910	status line wrap connector
911	status line bit 8 wrap
912	status line bit 7 wrap

913	status line bit 6 wrap
914	status line bit 5 wrap
915	status line bit 4 wrap
916	interrupt wrap
917	unexpected interrupt
92x	feature register

Alternate printer adapter (10xx)

10xx	adapter test failure
1002	jumpers (IBM models 25, 30)

Communications device asynchronous communications adapter System board, asynchronous port (MCA), 16550 internal modem (PS/2) (11xx)

1101	adapter test failure
1102	card-selected feedback
1103	port 102 register test
1106	serial option
1107	communications cable or system board (MCA)
1108	IRQ 3
1109	IRQ 4
1110	modem status register not clear 16550 chip register
1111	ring-indicate 16550 control line internal wrap test
1112	trailing edge ring-indicate 16550 control line external wrap test
1113	receive and delta receive line signal detect 16550 transmit
1114	receive line signal detect 16550 receive
1115	delta receive line signal detect 16550 transmit and receive data unequal
1116	line control register: all bits cannot be set 16550 interrupt function
1117	line control register: all bits cannot be reset 16550 baud rate test
1118	transmit holding and/or shift register stuck on 16550 interrupt-driven receive external data wrap test
1119	data ready stuck on 16550 FIFO
1120	interrupt enable register: all bits cannot be set
1121	interrupt enable register: all bits cannot be reset
1122	interrupt pending stuck on
1123	interrupt ID register stuck on
1124	modem control register: all bits cannot be set
1125	modem control register: all bits cannot be reset
1126	modem status register: all bits cannot be set
1127	modem status register: all bits cannot be reset
1128	interrupt ID
1129	cannot force overrun error
1130	no modem status interrupt
1131	invalid interrupt pending
1132	no data ready

1133	no data available interrupt
1134	no transmit holding interrupt
1135	no interrupts
1136	no received line status interrupt
1137	no receive data available
1138	transmit holding register
1139	no modem status interrupt
1140	transmit holding register to empty
1141	no interrupts
1142	no IRQ4 interrupt
1143	no IRQ3 interrupt
1144	no data transferred
1145	maximum baud rate
1146	minimum baud rate
1148	timeout error
1149	invalid data returned
1150	modem status register error
1151	no DSR and delta DSR
1152	no DSR
1153	no delta DSR
1154	modem status register
1155	no CTS and delta CTS
1156	no CTS
1157	no delta CTS

Alternate communications device, asynchronous communications adapter (ISA), dual asynchronous communications (DAC) adapter (MCA), 16550 internal modem (12xx)

12xx	same as 1100-1157ISA systems, except for PS/2 codes listed below
1202	jumpers (models 25, 30)
1202 or 06	serial device (e.g. dual asynchronous adapter)
1208 or 09	serial device (e.g. dual asynchronous adapter)
1212	dual async adapter or system board
1218 or 19	dual async adapter or system board
1227	dual async adapter or system board
1233 or 34	dual async adapter or system board

Game control adapter (13xx)

1301	adapter failure
1302	joystick test

Color/graphics printer (14xx)

1401	printer test failure
1402	not ready; out of paper
1403	no paper; interrupt failure
1404	matrix printer test failure; system board time-out
1405	parallel adapter
1406	presence test

Synchronous data link control (SDLC) communications adapter (15xx)

1501	adapter test failure
1510	8255 port B
1511	8255 port A
1512	8255 port C

1513	8253 timer #1 did not reach terminal count
1514	8253 timer #1 output stuck on
1515	8253 timer #0 did not reach terminal count
1516	8253 timer #0 output stuck on
1517	8253 timer #2 did not reach terminal count
1518	8253 timer #2 output stuck on
1519	8273 port B error
1520	8273 port A error
1521	8273 command/read time-out
1522	interrupt level 4 (timer and modem change)
1523	ring indicator stuck on
1524	received clock stuck on
1525	transmit clock stuck on
1526	test indicate stuck on
1527	ring indicate not on
1528	receive clock not on
1529	transmit clock not on
1530	test indicate not on
1531	data set ready not on
1532	carrier detect not on
1533	clear-to-send not on
1534	data set ready stuck on
1535	carrier detect stuck on
1536	clear-to-send stuck on
1537	level 3 (transmit/receive) interrupt
1538	receive interrupt results error
1539	wrap data miscompare error
1540	DMA channel 1 transmit error
1541	DMA channel 1 receive error
1542	8273 error-checking or status-reporting error
1547	level 4 stray interrupt
1548	level 3 stray interrupt
1549	interrupt presentation sequence time-out

Display station emulation adapter (DSEA) (16xx)

(N.B. try removing non-IBM adapters and then repeat the POST checks)

1604 or 08	DSEA or system twin-axial network problem
1624 or 34	DSEA
1644 or 52	DSEA
1654 or 58	DSEA
1662	interrupt level switches set wrong or defective DSEA
1664	DSEA
1668	see 1662
1669 or 74	if early version of IBM diagnostics diskette, replace with version 3.0 (or later) and repeat diagnostic checks
1674	station address which is set wrong or defective DSEA
1684 or 88	feature not installed, device address switches set wrong, or DSEA

Fixed (hard) disk/adapter (17xx)

1701	drive not ready (PC, XT) fixed disk/adapter test (AT, PS/2)
1702	time-out (PC, XT); fixed disk/adapter (AT, PS/2)
1703	drive (PC, XT, PS/2)

1704	controller (PC, XT), adapter, or drive error (AT, PS/2)
1705	no record found
1706	write fault
1707	track 0 error
1708	head select error
1709	bad ECC (AT)
1710	read buffer overrun
1711	bad address mark
1712	bad address mark (PC, AT); error of undetermined cause (AT)
1713	data compare error
1714	drive not ready
1730	adapter
1731	adapter
1732	adapter
1750	drive verify
1751	drive read
1752	drive write
1753	random read test
1754	drive seek test
1755	controller
1756	controller ECC test
1757	controller head select
1780	hard disk drive C fatal; time-out
1781	hard disk drive D fatal; time-out
1782	hard disk controller (no IPL from hardfile)
1790	drive C non-fatal error (can attempt to run IPL from drive)
1791	drive D non-fatal error (can attempt to run IPL from drive)

Expansion unit (PC, XT only) (18xx)

1801	expansion unit POST error
1810	enable/disable
1811	extender card wrap test failure while disabled
1812	high-order address lines failure while disabled
1813	wait state failure while disabled
1814	enable/disable could not be set on
1815	wait state failure while enabled
1816	extender card wrap test failure while enabled
1817	high-order address lines failure while enabled
1818	disable not functioning
1819	wait request switch not set correctly
1820	receiver card wrap test or an adapter card in expansion unit
1821	receiver high-order address lines

Bisynchronous communications (BSC) adapter (20xx)

2001	adapter test failure
2010	8255 port A
2011	8255 port B
2012	8255 port C
2013	8253 timer #1 did not reach terminal count
2014	8253 timer #1 output stuck on
2015	8253 timer #2 did not reach terminal count
2016	8253 timer #2 output stuck on
2017	8251 data-set-ready failure to come on

2018	8251 clear-to-send not sensed
2019	8251 data-set-ready stuck on
2020	8251 clear-to-send stuck on
2021	8251 hardware reset
2022	8251 software reset command
2023	8251 software error-reset command
2024	8251 transmit-ready did not come on
2025	8251 receive-ready did not come on
2026	8251 could not force overrun error status
2027	interrupt-transmit; no timer interrupt
2028	interrupt-transmit; replace card or planar
2029	interrupt-transmit; replace card only
2030	interrupt-transmit; replace card or planar
2031	interrupt-transmit; replace card only
2033	ring-indicate stuck on
2034	receive-clock stuck on
2035	transmit clock stuck on
2036	test indicate stuck on
2037	ring indicate not on
2038	receive clock not on
2039	transmit clock not on
2040	test indicate not on
2041	data-set-ready stuck on
2042	carrier detect not on
2043	clear-to-send not on
2044	data-set-ready stuck on
2045	carrier detect stuck on
2046	clear-to-send stuck on
2047	unexpected transmit
2048	unexpected receive interrupt
2049	transmit data did not equal receive data
2050	8251 detected overrun error
2051	lost data set ready during data wrap
2052	receive time-out during data wrap

Alternative bisynchronous communications adapter (21xx)

21xx	as for 2000 to 2052

Cluster adapter (22xx)

22xx	adapter test failure

Plasma monitor adapter (23xx)

23xx	adapter test failure

Enhanced graphics adapter systems board video (MCA) (24xx)

2401	adapter test failure
2402	monitor if colors change, otherwise system board
2408	user-indicated display attributes
2409	monitor
2410	system board
2416	user-indicated character set
2424	user-indicated 80 × 25 mode
2432	user-indicated 40 × 25 mode
2440	user-indicated 320 × 200 graphics mode
2448	user-indicated 640 × 200 graphics mode

2456	light pen test
2464	user-indicated screen paging test

Alternate enhanced graphics adapter (25xx)

25xx	adapter test failure

PC/370-M adapter (26xx)

2601 to 75	memory card
2677 to 80	processor card
2681	memory card
2682	processor card
2694	processor card
2695	memory card
2697	processor card

PC/3277 (27xx)

27xx	emulator test failure

3278/79 emulator, 3270 connection adapter (28xx)

28xx	adapter test failure

Color/graphics printer (29xx)

29xx	printer test failure

LAN (local area network) adapter (30xx)

3001	adapter ROM failure
3002	RAM
3003	digital loopback
3005	4V or 12V
3006	interrupt conflict
3007	analog
3008	reset command
3015	refer to PC Network Service Manual
3020	replace adapter with jumper W8 enabled
3040	LF translator cable
3041	refer to PC Network Service Manual

Primary PC network adapter (30xx)

3001	adapter test failure
3002	ROM
3003	ID
3004	RAM
3005	HIC
3006	12V d.c.
3007	digital loopback
3008	host-detected HIC failure
3009	sync fail and no-go bit
3010	HIC test OK and no-go bit
3011	go bit and no CMD 41
3012	card not present
3013	digital fall-through
3015	analog
3041	hot carrier on other card
3042	hot carrier on this card

Alternate LAN adapter (31xx)

31xx	as for 3000 to 3041
3115 or 40	LF translator cable

PC display adapter (32xx)

32xx	adapter test failure

Compact printer (PC, XT only) (33xx)

33xx	printer test failure

Enhanced display station emulator adapter (35xx)

3504	adapter connected to twin-axial cable during off-line test
3508	work station address in use by another work station, or diagnostic diskette from another PC was used
3509	diagnostic program failure; retry on new diskette
3540	work station address invalid, not configured at controller; twin-axial cable failure or not connected; or diagnostic diskette from another PC was used
3588	feature not installed or device I/O address switches set wrong
3599	diagnostic program failure; retry on new diskette

IEEE 488 adapter (36xx)

3601	adapter test failure (base address and read registers incorrect, following initialisation
3602	write to SPMR
3603	write to ADR or IEEE-488 adapter addressing problems
3610	adapter cannot be programmed to listen
3611	adapter cannot be programmed to talk
3612	adapter cannot take control with IFC
3613	adapter cannot go to standby
3614	adapter cannot take control asynchronously
3615	adapter cannot take control asynchronously
3616	adapter cannot pass control
3617	adapter cannot be addressed to listen
3618	adapter cannot be unaddressed to listen
3619	adapter cannot be addressed to talk
3620	adapter cannot be unaddressed to talk
3621	adapter cannot be addressed to listen with extended addressing
3622	adapter cannot be unaddressed to listen with extended addressing
3623	adapter cannot be addressed to talk with extended addressed
3624	adapter cannot be unaddressed to talk with extended addressing
3625	adapter cannot write to self
3626	adapter cannot generate handshake error
3627	adapter cannot detect DCL message
3628	adapter cannot detect SDC message
3629	adapter cannot detect END with EOI

3630	adapter cannot detect EOT with EOI
3631	adapter cannot detect END with 0-bit EOS
3632	adapter cannot detect END with 7-bit EOS
3633	adapter cannot detect GET
3634	mode 3 addressing not functioning
3635	adapter cannot recognise undefined command
3636	adapter cannot detect REM, REMC, LOK, or LOKC
3637	adapter cannot clear REM or LOK
3638	adapter cannot detect SRQ
3639	adapter cannot conduct serial poll
3640	adapter cannot conduct parallel poll
3650	adapter cannot DMA to 7210
3651	data error on DMA to 7210
3652	adapter cannot DMA from 7210
3653	data error on DMA from 7210
3658	uninvoked interrupt received
3659	adapter cannot interrupt on ADSC
3660	adapter cannot interrupt on ADSC
3661	adapter cannot interrupt on CO
3662	adapter cannot interrupt on DO
3663	adapter cannot interrupt on DI
3664	adapter cannot interrupt on ERR
3665	adapter cannot interrupt on DEC
3666	adapter cannot interrupt on END
3667	adapter cannot interrupt on DET
3668	adapter cannot interrupt on APT
3669	adapter cannot interrupt on CPT
3670	adapter cannot interrupt on REMC
3671	adapter cannot interrupt on LOKC
3672	adapter cannot interrupt on SRQI
3673	adapter cannot interrupt on terminal count on DMA to 7210
3674	adapter cannot interrupt on terminal count on DMA from 7210
3675	spurious DMA terminal count interrupt
3697	illegal DMA configuration setting detected
3698	illegal interrupt level configuration setting detected

Data acquisition adapter (38xx)

3801	adapter test failure
3810	timer read test
3811	timer interrupt test
3812	delay, BI 13 test
3813	rate, BI 13 test
3814	BO 14, ISIRQ test
3815	BO 0, count-in test
3816	BI STB, count-out test
3817	BO 0, BO CTS test
3818	BO 1, BI 0 test
3819	BO 2, BI 1 test
3820	BO 3, BI 2 test
3821	BO 4, BI 3 test
3822	BO 5, BI 4 test
3823	BO 6, BI 5 test
3824	BO 7, BI 6 test
3825	BO 8, BI 7 test
3826	BO 9, BI 8 test

3827	BO 10, BI 9 test
3828	BO 11, BI 10 test
3829	BO 12, BI 11 test
3830	BO 13, BI 12 test
3831	BO 15, AI CE test
3832	BO STB, BO GATE test
3833	BI CTS, BI HOLD test
3834	AI CO, BI 15 test
3835	counter interrupt test
3836	counter read test
3837	AO 0 ranges test
3838	AO 1 ranges test
3839	AI 0 values test
3840	AI 1 values test
3841	AI 2 values test
3842	AI 3 values test
3843	analog input interrupt test
3844	AI 23 address or value test

Professional graphics controller adapter (39xx)

3901	adapter test failure
3902	ROM1 self-test
3903	ROM2 self-test
3904	RAM self-test
3905	cold start cycle power
3906	data error in communications RAM
3907	address error in communications RAM
3908	bad data detected while read/write to 6845-like register
3909	bad data detected in lower hex-E0 bytes while reading or writing 6845 equivalent registers
3910	PGC display bank output latches
3911	basic clock
3912	command control error
3913	vertical sync scanner
3914	horizontal sync scanner
3915	intech
3916	LUT address error
3917	LUT red RAM chip error
3918	LUT green RAM chip error
3919	LUT blue RAM chip error
3920	LUT data latch error
3921	horizontal display
3922	vertical display
3923	light pen
3924	unexpected error
3925	emulator addressing error
3926	emulator data latch
3927	base for error codes 3928-3930 (emulator RAM)
3928	emulator RAM
3929	emulator RAM
3930	emulator RAM
3931	emulator H/V display problem
3932	emulator cursor position
3933	emulator attribute display problem
3934	emulator cursor display
3935	fundamental emulation RAM problem
3936	emulation character set problem

3937	emulation graphics display
3938	emulation character display problem
3939	emulation bank select
3940	display RAM U2
3941	display RAM U4
3942	display RAM U6
3943	display RAM U8
3944	display RAM U10
3945	display RAM U1
3946	display RAM U3
3947	display RAM U5
3948	display RAM U7
3949	display RAM U9
3950	display RAM U12
3951	display RAM U14
3952	display RAM U16
3953	display RAM U18
3954	display RAM U20
3955	display RAM U11
3956	display RAM U13
3957	display RAM U15
3958	display RAM U17
3959	display RAM U19
3960	display RAM U22
3961	display RAM U24
3962	display RAM U26
3963	display RAM U28
3964	display RAM U30
3965	display RAM U21
3966	display RAM U23
3967	display RAM U25
3968	display RAM U27
3969	display RAM U29
3970	display RAM U32
3971	display RAM U34
3972	display RAM U36
3973	display RAM U38
3974	display RAM U40
3975	display RAM U31
3976	display RAM U33
3977	display RAM U35
3978	display RAM U37
3979	display RAM U39
3980	PGC RAM timing
3981	PGC read/write latch
3982	SR bus output latches
3983	addressing error (vertical column of memory; U2 at top)
3984	addressing error (vertical column of memory; U4 at top)
3985	addressing error (vertical column of memory; U6 at top)
3986	addressing error (vertical column of memory; U8 at top)
3988	addressing error (vertical column of memory; U10 at top)
3989	horizontal bank latch errors
3990	horizontal bank latch errors
3991	horizontal bank latch errors
3992	RAG/CAG PGC

3993	multiple write modes, nibble mask errors
3994	row nibble (display RAM)
3995	PGC addressing

5278 display attachment unit and 5279 display (44xx)

44xx	display attachment test failure

IEEE-488 interface adapter (45xx)

45xx	adapter test failure

ARTIC multiport/2 interface adapter (46xx)

4611	adapter
4612 or 13	memory module
4630	adapter
4640 or 41	memory module
4650	interface cable

Internal modem (48xx)

48xx	modem test failure

Alternate internal modem (49xx)

49xx	modem test failure

Financial communication system (56xx)

56xx	system test failure

Chip set (Phoenix BIOS only) (70xx)

7000	CMOS failure
7001	shadow RAM failure (ROM not shadowed to RAM)
7002	CMOS configuration data error

Voice communications adapter (71xx)

7101	adapter test failure
7102	instruction or external data memory
7103	PC to VCA interrupt
7104	internal data memory
7105	DMA
7106	internal registers
7117	interactive shared memory
7108	VCA to PC interrupt
7109	DC wrap
7111	external analog wrap and tone output
7114	telephone attachment test

3.5-inch diskette drive (73xx)

7301	diskette drive/adapter test failure
7306	diskette change line error
7307	write-protected diskette
7308	bad command; drive error
7310	disk initialisation error; track zero bad
7311	time-out; drive error
7312	bad disk controller chip
7313	bad DMA controller; drive error
7314	DMA boundary error

7315	bad index timing; drive error
7316	speed error
7321	bad seek; drive error
7322	bad CRC; drive error
7323	record not found; drive error
7324	bad address mark; drive error
7325	bad drive controller chip; seek error

8514/A display adapter/A (74xx)

74xx	adapter test failure
7426	monitor
744x to 747x	8514 memory module

Pageprinter (76xx)

7601	adapter test failure
7602	adapter card
7603	printer
7604	printer cable

PS/2 speech adapter (84xx)

84xx	adapter test failure

2Mbyte extended memory adapter (85xx)

85xx	adapter test failure
850x or 851x	80286 Expanded Memory Adapter/A (model 50)
852x	80286 Expanded Memory Adapter/A, memory module (model 50)

PS/2 pointing device (mouse) (86xx)

8601	pointing device; mouse time-out (MCA)
8602	pointing device; mouse interface (MCA)
8603	system board; mouse interrupt (MCA)
8604	pointing device or system board

MIDI adapter (89xx)

89xx	adapter test failure

Multiprotocol communications adapter (100xx)

10002 or 06	any serial device, but most likely multiprotocol adapter
10007	multiprotocol adapter or communications cable
10008 or 09	any serial device, but most likely multiprotocol adapter
10012	multiprotocol adapter or system board
10018 or 19	multiprotocol adapter or system board
10042 or 56	multiprotocol adapter or system board

Modem and communications adapter/A (101xx)

101xx	system board
10102	card-selected feedback
10103	port 102 register test
10106	serial option
10108	IRQ 3
10109	IRQ 4
10110	16450 chip register

10111	16450 control line internal wrap test
10113	transmit
10114	receive
10115	transmit and receive data not equal
10116	interrupt function
10117	baud rate test
10118	interrupt driven receive external data wrap test
10125	reset result code
10126	general result code
10127	S register write/read
10128	echo on/off
10129	enable/disable result codes
10130	enable number/word result codes
10133	connect results for 300 baud not received
10134	connect results for 1,200 baud not received
10135	local analog loopback 300-baud test
10136	local analog loopback 1,200-baud test
10137	no response to escape/reset sequence
10138	S register 13 incorrect parity or number of data bits
10139	S register 15 incorrect bit rate

ESDI fixed disk or adapter (104xx)

10450	write/read test
10451	read verify test
10452	seek test
10453	wrong device type indicated
10454	controller failed sector buffer test
10455	controller
10456	controller diagnostic command
10461	format error
10462	controller head select
10463	write/read sector error
10464	drive primary map unreadable
10465	controller ECC 8-bit
10466	controller ECC 9-bit
10467	soft seek error
10468	hard seek error
10469	soft seek error count exceeded
10470	controller attachment diagnostic error
10471	controller wrap mode interface
10472	controller wrap mode drive select
10473	error during ESDI read verify test
10480	drive C, ESDI adapter or system board
10481	drive D seek failure, ESDI adapter or system board
10482	ESDI fixed disk adapter
10483	ESDI fixed disk adapter; controller reset; drive select 0
10484	controller head select 3 selected bad
10485	controller head select 2 selected bad
10486	controller head select 1 selected bad
10487	controller head select 0 selected bad
10488	controlled rg-cmd complete 2
10489	controlled wg-cmd complete 1
10490	drive C format; read failure; controller
10491	drive D format; read failure
10499	controller

5.25-inch external diskette drive or adapter (107xx)

107xx	drive or adapter test failure

SCSI adapter (112xx)

112xx	adapter test failure

Processor card for model 70, type 3 (129xx)

12901	processor portion of processor board
12902	cache portion of processor board

Plasma display and adapter (149xx)

14901 or 02	system board or plasma display
14922	system board or display adapter
14932	display adapter

6157 Streaming tape drive or tape attachment adapter (165xx)

165xx	adapter test failure
16520	streaming tape drive
16540	tape attachment adapter

Primary token-ring network PC adapter (166xx)

166xx	adapter test failure

Alternative token-ring network PC adapter (167xx)

167xx	adapter test failure

Adapter memory module (194xx)

194xx	adapter test failure

SCSI fixed disk and controller (210xx)

210xx	disk or controller test failure

SCSI CD-ROM system (215xx)

215xx	CD-ROM system test failure

Audible BIOS error codes

IBM BIOS

Indication	Meaning
One short beep	Normal POST – no error
Two short beeps	POST error – see screen for error code
No beeps	Power missing, loose card or short circuit
Continuous beep	Power missing, loose card or short circuit
Repeating short beep	Power missing, loose card or short circuit
One long and one short beep	System board error
One long and two short beeps	Video (mono/CGA display adapter)
One long and three short beeps	Video (EGA display adapter)
Three long beeps	Keyboard error
One beep, blank/incorrect display	Video display circuitry

AMI BIOS

Indication	Meaning
One short beep	DRAM refresh failure
Two short beeps	Parity circuit failure
Three short beeps	Base memory (64Kbyte) RAM failure
Four short beeps	System timer failure
Five short beeps	CPU failure
Six short beeps	Keyboard controller error
Seven short beeps	Virtual mode exception error
Eight short beeps	Display memory failure
Nine short beeps	ROM BIOS checksum failure
One long and three short beeps	Base/extended memory failure
One long and eight short beeps	Display/retrace test failure

Award BIOS

Indication	Meaning
One short beep	No error during POST
Two short beeps	Any non-fatal error
One long and two short beeps	Video error
One long and three short beeps	Keyboard controller error

Phoenix BIOS

Indication	Meaning
One, one and three beeps	CMOS read/write failure
One, one and four beeps	ROM BIOS checksum failure
One, two and one beep	Programmable interval timer failure
One, two and two beeps	DMA initialisation failure
One, two and three beeps	DMA page register read/write failure
One, three and one beep	RAM refresh verification error

One, three and three beeps	First 64Kbyte RAM chip/data line failure
One, three and four beeps	First 64Kbyte odd/even logic failure
One, four and one beep	Address line failure first 64Kbyte RAM
One, four and two beeps	Parity failure first 64Kbyte RAM
One, four and three beeps	Fail-safe timer feature (EISA only)
One, four and four beeps	Software NMI port failure (EISA only)
Two, one and up to four beeps	First 64Kbyte RAM chip/data line failure (bits 0 to 3, respectively)
Two, two and up to four beeps	First 64Kbyte RAM chip/data line failure (bits 4 to 7, respectively)
Two, three and up to four beeps	First 64Kbyte RAM chip/data line failure (bits 8 to 11, respectively)
Two, four and up to four beeps	First 64Kbyte RAM chip/data line failure (bits 12 to 15, respectively)
Three, one and one beep	Slave DMA register failure
Three, one and two beeps	Master DMA register failure
Three, one and three beeps	Master interrupt mask register failure
Three, one and four beeps	Slave interrupt register failure
Three, two and four beeps	Keyboard controller test failure
Three, three and four beeps	Screen initialisation failure
Three, four and one beep	Screen retrace test failure
Four, two and one beep	Timer tick failure
Four, two and two beeps	Shutdown test failure
Four, two and three beeps	Gate A20 failure
Four, two and four beeps	Unexpected interrupt in protected mode
Four, three and one beep	RAM text address failure
Four, three and three beeps	Interval timer channel 2 failure
Four, three and four beeps	Time of day clock failure
Four, four and three beeps	Maths coprocessor failure

Addresses of suppliers

Memory upgrades, chips and SIMMs

Advanced Business Computers (Europe) Ltd
36A, Kilburn High Road
London
NW6 5UA
Tel: (0171) 372 1917
Fax: (0171) 625 7649

AW Computer Memory Bargains
PO Box 6911
Dundee
DD2 1YL
Tel: (01382) 643739
Fax: (01382) 646243

Dealex Ltd
64, Chapel View
South Croydon
Surrey
CR2 7LF
Tel: (0181) 6684199
Fax: (0181) 6687429

Kingston Technology
Kingston Court
Brooklands Close
Sunbury-on-Thames
Middlesex
TW16 7EP
Tel: (01932) 738888
Fax: (01932) 738811

Memory Bank
The Powermark Centre
The Waterfront
Elstree Road
Elstree
Herts
WD6 3RP
Tel: (0181) 9567000
Fax: (0181) 9567100

Memory Direct Ltd.
42–44 Birchett Road
Aldershot
Hants
GU11 1LT
Tel: (01252) 316060

Oftek Ltd
Brymar House
Walford Drive
Solihull
West Midlands
B92 9DW
Tel: (0121) 7223993
Fax: (0121) 7439845

Portables and Upgrades Ltd
Dram House
Latham Close
Bredbury Industrial Park
Stockport
SK6 2SD
Tel: (0161) 4066486
Fax: (0161) 4949125

Powermark plc
Premier House
112 Station Road
Edgware
Middlesex
HA8 7AQ
Tel: (0181) 9513355
Fax: (0181) 9056233

Richnight Ltd
197, Brighton Road
Purley
Surrey
CR8 4HF
Tel: (0181) 6684199
Fax: (0181) 6687249

Motherboards, system upgrades

A+P Computers Ltd
35 Walnut Tree Close
Guildford
Surrey
GU1 4UN
Tel: (01483) 304118
Fax: (01483) 304124

A.C.C. Tronics Ltd
Unit 6
Chancel Way
Moor Lane Industrial Estate
Witton
Birmingham
B6 7AU
Tel: (0121) 3444911

Atom Computer Services Ltd
1–7 Mount Street
Stapleford
Nottingham
NG9 8AW
Tel: (01602) 491891
Fax: (01602) 491640

Choice Peripherals
Units 1 and 2
Highgrounds Way
Rhodesia
Worksop
Notts
S80 3AF
Tel: (0114) 2382000
Fax: (01909) 530261

Computer Mates (UK) Ltd
Pinewood Studios
Iver Heath
Bucks
SL0 0NH
Tel: (01753) 553535
Fax: (01753) 553530

DS Computers
Unit 206, Belgravia Workshops
157 Marlborough Road
London
N19 4NF
Tel: (0171) 2815096
Fax: (0171) 2817364

Fox Computer Systems
Unit C
Great Eastern Industrial Estate
Station Road
Maldon Essex
CM9 4LQ
Tel: (0990) 744500
Fax: (0990) 502207

Hobbykit Ltd
Unit 19
Capitol Industrial Park
Capitol Way
London
NW9 0EQ
Tel: (0181) 2057485
Fax: (0181) 2050603

Novatech
Blueprint 1400
Dundas Spur
Portsmouth
PO3 5RW
Tel: (0800) 666500
Fax: (01705) 322500

PGP Computers
Unit 14A
Sunrise Business Park
Blandford Forum
Dorset
DT11 8ST
Tel: (01258) 451347
Fax: (01258) 456046

Roldec Systems
Roldec House
504 Dudley Road
Wolverhampton
WV2 3AA
Tel: (01902) 456464
Fax: (01902) 452592

Simply Computers
Tel: (0181) 4982100
Fax: (0181) 5234002

SMC Computers plc
253–257 Farnham Road
Slough
Berks
SL2 1HA
Tel: (01753) 550333
Fax: (01753) 524443

Stak Trading
Stak House
Butlers Leap
Rugby
CV21 3RQ
Tel: (01788) 577497
Fax: (01788) 544584

Technomatic
Tel: (0990) 146111
Fax: (0990) 134988

Watford Electronics Ltd
Jessa House
Finway
off Dallow Road
Luton
LU1 1TR
Tel: (01582) 745555
Fax: (01582) 488588

Software

Elite Software Products Ltd
102–104 High Street
Coleshill
Warks
B46 3BL
Tel: (01675) 464488
Fax: (01675) 464685
(Agents for Addstor Inc. and distributors of SuperStor hard disk data compression software)

WCD Ltd
Rowlandson House
289–293 Ballards Lane
Finchley
London
N12 8NP
Tel: (0181) 3439899
Fax: (0181) 3438428
(Distributors of Landmark Research International's diagnostic software products including PC probe, AlignIt, Kickstart, ROM POST, Service Diagnostics etc.)

Systems, cards and accessories

Chipboards plc
Almac House
Church Lane
Bisley
Surrey
GU24 9DR
Tel: (01483) 797959
Fax: (01483) 797702

Codec Systems Ltd
173–181 St James's Road
Croydon
CR0 2BZ
Tel: (0181) 6648500

Computer Trading
Manor Development Centre
Units B10–B14
40 Alison Crescent
Sheffied
S2 1AS
Tel: (0114) 2531600
Fax: (0114) 2653606

Dabs Press
22 Warwick Street
Prestwich
Manchester
M25 7HN
Tel: (0161) 7738632
Fax: (01772) 623000

Evesham Micros Ltd
Unit 9
St Richards Road
Evesham
Worcs
WR11 6TD
Tel: (01386) 765500
Fax: (01386) 765354

Olympian Computer Systems
Imperial House
64 Willoughby Lane
London
N17 0SP
Tel: (0181) 8804222
Fax: (0181) 8804223

RSC Corporate
75–77 Queens Road
Watford
Herts
WD1 2QN
Tel: (01923) 243301
Fax: (01923) 237946

Scan International
Genesis House
Stopes Road
Little Lever
Bolton
Lancs
BL3 1NP
Tel: (0161) 7244910
Fax: (0161) 7259059

Silica Systems
1–4, The Mews
Hatherley Road
Sidcup
Kent
DA14 4DX
Tel: (0181) 3091111
Fax: (0181) 3080608

SJP
181 Melton Road
Leicester
LE4 6QT
Tel: (01533) 697270

SMC Computers
26 Farnham Road
Slough
Berks
SL1 3TA
Tel: (01753) 550333
Fax: (01753) 524443

Unimart Computers Ltd
Unit 15
Maple Industrial Estate
Maple Way
Feltham
Middlesex
TW13 7AW
Tel: (0181) 8932959
Fax: (0181) 8932961

Useful Web sites

Company	URL
AMD	http://www.amd.com
Caldera	http://www.caldera.co.uk
Carrera	http://www.carrera.co.uk
Computer Information Centre	http://www.compinfo.co.uk
Dan Technology	http://www.dan.co.uk
Dell	http://www.dell.com/uk
Dr Solomon's Software	http://www.drsolomon.com
Epson	http://www.epson.co.uk
Gateway	http://www.gw2k.co.uk
Hewlett Packard	http://www.hp.com
IBM	http://www.ibm.com
Kingston Technology	http://www.kingston.com
Matrox	http://www.matrox.com
Maxtor	http://www.maxtor.com
McAfee	http://www.mcafee.com
Mesh	http://www.meshplc.co.uk
Microsoft	http://www.microsoft.com
NEC	http://www.nec.com
Seagate	http://www.seagate.com
Symantec	http://www.symantec.com
Taxan	http://www.taxan.co.uk
US Robotics	http://www.usr.co.uk
Western Digital	http://www.wdc.com

N.B. Many companies maintain UK Web sites as well as sites in the USA. Where UK sites are known to exist these have been quoted.

18
Diagnostic software

This chapter provides you with the QuickBASIC source code for a number of complete diagnostic programs. These simple utilities will help you check and modify the configuration of your system as well as carry out routine tests and adjustments of such items as disk drives, printers and monitors.

Microsoft's QuickBASIC (or QBASIC) is still widely available (it was previously supplied as part of the MS-DOS utilities and it is eminently suitable for the complete beginner to programming.

TIP

When keying in the diagnostic programs into your computer, QuickBASIC will usually tell you if you make a mistake. The most common mistakes are:

- confusing letter O with figure 0 (they look alike and they are adjacent on the keyboard)
- confusing letter I with figure 1 (they look alike)
- confusing : with ;
- missing out one or more lines of text
- duplicating one or more lines of text
- missing off trailing $, #, :, ; and % signs (these are more important than you might think)
- missing spaces (although QuickBASIC is usually reasonably forgiving as far as this is concerned
- mis-spelling keywords like FILEATTR (two T's), ALIAS (one L) etc.

TIP

If you have the full version of QuickBASIC (rather than the cut-down version supplied as part of the MS-DOS package), you can compile the programs and make them into 'stand-alone' .EXE files. You will then be able to use them without first having to load QBASIC.

If you don't have access to Microsoft QuickBASIC, or if you would prefer not to type in the programs, these and other programs can be downloaded from the author's Web pages at:

http://members.aol.com/miketooley

All five programs may be freely adapted, copied and modified. You are encouraged to use them as the basis of your own personalised diagnostic programs. Finally, if you have any suggestions, modifications and/or improvements please let me know so that I can incorporate them in future releases.

Disk check

This program will allow you to quickly check the performance of the floppy and hard drives fitted to your system. The program will also provide you with some useful information about the organisation of your disk drives including the number of sectors per cluster, the number of bytes per sector, the number of sectors per disk and the total capacity of the disk.

The program will also allow you to carry out a disk write/read test. You should have a formatted disk with at least 32Kbytes free in each of the floppy drives that you wish to test. Similarly, you must have at least 32Kbytes free on each hard disk that is to be tested. Note that the test file created (TEST.DAT) is erased from the disk at the end of the test. The write/read test is repeated a total of 10 times and any errors reported (DOS would normally report these errors anyway).

```
' ****************************************************************
' ** Name:        DISK.BAS          Version: 0.17        **
' ** Function:    Checks drives A: to D:                 **
' ** Language:    Microsoft QuickBASIC                   **
' ** Notes:       Program creates a file, TEST.DAT       **
' **              on the specified drive which must      **
' **              have at least 32Kbytes free            **
' ****************************************************************
'
' Initialise
'
TYPE RegType
AX AS INTEGER
BX AS INTEGER
CX AS INTEGER
DX AS INTEGER
BP AS INTEGER
SI AS INTEGER
DI AS INTEGER
DS AS INTEGER
FLAGS AS INTEGER
END TYPE
'
ON ERROR GOTO warning
' Initialise in text mode
SCREEN 0
COLOR 15, 1
ul$ = STRING$(40, CHR$(205))
DIM InputRegs AS RegType, OutputRegs AS RegType
' Display main menu
DO
main:
```

```
CLS
PRINT ul$
PRINT " DISK CHECK "
PRINT ul$; ""
PRINT " Select option..."
PRINT " [T] = write/read test"
PRINT " [V] = get DOS version"
PRINT " [D] = disk information"
PRINT " [Q] = quit"
DO
  r$ = UCASE$(INKEY$)
LOOP UNTIL r$ <> "" AND INSTR("TVDQ", r$)
IF r$ = "Q" THEN CLS : SCREEN 0: END
'
PRINT ul$
IF r$ = "T" THEN GOSUB test
IF r$ = "V" THEN GOSUB version
IF r$ = "D" THEN GOSUB info
LOOP
'
test:
GOSUB which
' Use root directory
file$ = drive$ + ":\TEST.DAT"
' Reset error flag
flag% = 0
' Repeat the write/read test ten times
FOR no% = 1 TO 10
  GOSUB tidy
  LOCATE 10, 2
  PRINT "Writing data to "; file$
  LOCATE 11, 2
  PRINT "["; no%; "]"
  OPEN file$ FOR OUTPUT AS #1
  FOR ch% = 0 TO 4096
    PRINT #1, ch%
  NEXT ch%
  CLOSE #1
  GOSUB tidy
  LOCATE 10, 2
  PRINT "Reading data from "; file$
  LOCATE 11, 2
  PRINT "["; no%; "]"
  OPEN file$ FOR INPUT AS #1
```

```
  FOR dat% = 0 TO 4096
    INPUT #1, ch%
    IF ch% <> dat% THEN flag% = 1
  NEXT dat%
  CLOSE #1
NEXT no%
GOSUB tidy
IF flag% = 1 THEN
  LOCATE 10, 2
  PRINT "An error has occurred - check the disk!"
  ELSE
  LOCATE 10, 2
  PRINT "Test completed without error."
  LOCATE 11, 2
  PRINT "Erasing "; file$
  KILL file$
END IF
GOSUB waitkey
RETURN
'
version:
' Get DOS version
InputRegs.AX = &H3000
CALL INTERRUPT(&H21, InputRegs, OutputRegs)
majorver% = OutputRegs.AX AND 255
minorver% = OutputRegs.AX / 256
LOCATE 10, 2
PRINT "DOS version..."; majorver%; "."; minorver%
GOSUB waitkey
RETURN
'
info:
GOSUB which
IF drive$ = "A" THEN InputRegs.DX = &H1
IF drive$ = "B" THEN InputRegs.DX = &H2
IF drive$ = "C" THEN InputRegs.DX = &H3
IF drive$ = "D" THEN InputRegs.DX = &H4
InputRegs.AX = &H1C00
CALL INTERRUPT(&H21, InputRegs, OutputRegs)
sectors = OutputRegs.AX AND 255
bytes = OutputRegs.CX
clusters = OutputRegs.DX
IF clusters <= 0 THEN clusters = clusters + 65536
' Determine disk capacity
```

```
capacity = INT(sectors * bytes * clusters / 1000)
' Erase any existing screen data
GOSUB tidy
' Display the disk information
LOCATE 10, 2: PRINT "Information for drive: "; drive$
LOCATE 11, 2: PRINT "Sectors per cluster:  "; sectors
LOCATE 12, 2: PRINT "Bytes per sector:     "; bytes
LOCATE 13, 2: PRINT "Clusters per disk:    "; clusters
LOCATE 14, 2: PRINT "Disk capacity:        "; capacity
GOSUB waitkey
RETURN
'
which:
' Specify drive to be used
LOCATE 10, 2
PRINT "Which drive [A],[B],[C] or [D]?"
DO
  r$ = UCASE$(INKEY$)
LOOP UNTIL r$ <> "" AND INSTR("ABCD", r$)
drive$ = r$
LOCATE 10, 2
PRINT STRING$(39, " ")
RETURN
'
tidy:
' Erase any existing screen data
FOR cline% = 10 TO 14
  LOCATE cline%, 2
  PRINT STRING$(39, " ")
NEXT cline%
RETURN
'
waitkey:
PRINT ul$
PRINT " Press any key to continue..."
GOSUB keywait
RETURN
'
keywait:
DO
  r$ = INKEY$
LOOP UNTIL r$ <> ""
RETURN
'
```

```
warning:
PRINT ul$
PRINT " An error has occurred!"
GOSUB waitkey
RESUME main
```

Display check

This program will allow you to carry out various checks and adjustments on a variety of PC displays including basic text mode displays (80 × 25 monochrome), CGA, EGA and VGA colour types.

The program has two menu screens and it initialises in 'Text' mode. You can then either display a chequerboard (80 × 25 grid) by pressing <T> or move to the 'setup display' sub-menu by pressing <S>. Here you have a choice of a 'Text Mode', 'CGA' (320 × 200, 4 colours), 'EGA' (640 × 200, 16 colours), and 'VGA' (640 × 350, 16 colours).

One the required display mode has been selected, you should exit to the main menu and continue with one or more of the checks. Assuming that you have selected a graphics mode (CGA, EGA, or VGA) you can select from:

(i) Alignment test – this test displays a series of concentric circles and it is used for adjusting height, width, vertical linearity, and horizontal linearity.

(ii) Grid test – this test displays a grid (horizontal and vertical lines) and it is also used to check monitor convergence.

(iii) Dot test – this test displays a matrix of single-pixel dots. It can be used to check dynamic focus (all dots should be the same size).

(iv) Colour bars – this test displays 16 colours bars (four in CGA mode) and can be used for performing colour adjustments.

(v) Text display – this test displays a chequer board of text characters (ASCII 32 and 219, respectively). You should check that the 80 × 25 display fills the display with an adequate margin all round.

```
' ******************************************************************
' ** Name:       DISPLAY.BAS                                     **
' ** Function:   Checks Text/CGA/EGA/VGA displays                **
' ** Language:   Microsoft QuickBASIC                            **
' ** Notes:      Requires appropriate display                    **
' **             adapter card                                    **
' ******************************************************************
'
' Initialise
'
ON ERROR GOTO warning
' Initialise in text mode
SCREEN 0
COLOR 15, 1
```

```
xc = 0
mode$ = "Text"
ul$ = STRING$(40, CHR$(205))
' Display main menu
DO
main:
CLS
PRINT ul$
PRINT " DISPLAY CHECK     Current mode = "; mode$
PRINT ul$; ""
PRINT " Select option..."
IF xc <> 0 THEN
  PRINT " [A] = alignment test"
  PRINT " [G] = grid test"
  PRINT " [D] = dot test"
  PRINT " [C] = colour bars"
END IF
PRINT " [T] = text display"
PRINT " [S] = setup display mode"
PRINT " [Q] = quit"
DO
  r$ = UCASE$(INKEY$)
LOOP UNTIL r$ <> "" AND INSTR("AGDTCSQ", r$)
IF r$ = "Q" THEN CLS : SCREEN 0: END
'
PRINT ul$
IF xc <> 0 THEN
  IF r$ = "A" THEN GOSUB alignment
  IF r$ = "G" THEN GOSUB grid
  IF r$ = "D" THEN GOSUB dot
  IF r$ = "C" THEN GOSUB colours
END IF
IF r$ = "T" THEN GOSUB text
IF r$ = "S" THEN GOTO setup
LOOP
'
alignment:
CLS
FOR x = xc / 4 TO xc STEP xc / 4
  CIRCLE (xc, yc), x
NEXT x
LINE (0, yc)-(2 * xc, yc)
LINE (xc, 0)-(xc, 2 * yc)
GOSUB keywait
```

```
RETURN
'
grid:
CLS
FOR y = 0 TO 2 * yc STEP yc / 10
  LINE (0, y)-(2 * xc, y)
NEXT y
FOR x = 0 TO 2 * xc STEP xc / 15
  LINE (x, 0)-(x, 2 * yc)
NEXT x
GOSUB keywait
RETURN
'
dot:
CLS
FOR y = 0 TO 2 * yc STEP yc / 10
  FOR x = 0 TO 2 * xc STEP xc / 15
    PSET (x, y)
    NEXT x
  NEXT y
GOSUB keywait
RETURN
'
text:
CLS
IF mode$ <> "CGA" THEN xlim = 80 ELSE xlim = 40
FOR x = 1 TO xlim STEP 2
  FOR y = 1 TO 25 STEP 2
    LOCATE y, x
    PRINT CHR$(219);
  NEXT y
NEXT x
FOR x = 2 TO xlim STEP 2
  FOR y = 2 TO 25 STEP 2
    LOCATE y, x
    PRINT CHR$(219);
  NEXT y
NEXT x
GOSUB keywait
RETURN
'
colours:
IF mode$ <> "CGA" THEN
  COLOR 0, 0
```

```
  CLS
  x = 0
  xold = 0
  inc = xc / 8
  FOR colour = 0 TO 15
    x = x + inc
    LINE (xold, 0)-STEP(x, 2 * yc), colour, BF
    xold = x
  NEXT colour
ELSE
' CGA uses 4 colours...
  COLOR 0, 0, 1
  CLS
  x = 0
  xold = 0
  inc = xc / 2
  FOR colour = 0 TO 3
    x = x + inc
    LINE (xold, 0)-STEP(x, 2 * yc), colour, BF
    xold = x
  NEXT colour
END IF
GOSUB keywait
IF mode$ <> "CGA" THEN COLOR 15, 1 ELSE COLOR
1, 2, 1
RETURN
'
setup:
DO
' Display setup menu
CLS
PRINT ul$
PRINT " DISPLAY SETUP      Current mode = "; mode$
PRINT ul$; ""
PRINT " Select option..."
PRINT " [T] = Text Mode (80 col., 16 colours)"
PRINT " [C] = CGA (320 x 200, 4 colours)"
PRINT " [E] = EGA (640 x 200, 16 colours)"
PRINT " [V] = VGA (640 x 350, 16 colours)"
PRINT " [X] = exit to main menu"
DO
  r$ = UCASE$(INKEY$)
LOOP UNTIL r$ <> "" AND INSTR("TCEVX", r$)
IF r$ = "X" THEN GOTO main
```

```
PRINT ul$
IF r$ = "T" THEN
  SCREEN 2: SCREEN 0: COLOR 15, 1: xc = 0: yc = 0:
mode$ = "Text"
END IF
IF r$ = "C" THEN SCREEN 1: COLOR 1, 2, 1: xc = 160:
yc = 100: mode$ = "CGA"
IF r$ = "E" THEN SCREEN 8: COLOR 15, 1: xc = 320:
yc = 100: mode$ = "EGA"
IF r$ = "V" THEN SCREEN 9: COLOR 15, 1: xc = 320:
yc = 175: mode$ = "VGA"
LOOP
'
waitkey:
PRINT ul$
PRINT " Press any key to continue..."
GOSUB keywait
RETURN
'
keywait:
DO
  r$ = INKEY$
LOOP UNTIL r$ <> ""
RETURN
'
warning:
PRINT ul$
PRINT " An error has occurred!"
GOSUB waitkey
RESUME main
```

Printer check

This program will allow you to carry out a number of checks on an Epson-compatible printer connected to the PC's parallel port. You can print the standard (ASCII) and extended (non-ASCII) character sets (characters corresponding to codes from 32 to 127 and 128 to 255, respectively), print directly from the keyboard, send line feed and form feed characters, exercise the printer continuously and print a 'style sheet' for the printer.

You can also use the 'set up' option (press <S>) from the main menu in order to select the required print style and repeat any of the main menu tests, as required. The 'setup' option allows you to select condensed, double strike, emphasised, italic, normal, subscript, and superscript print modes (and allowable combinations of these basic styles).

```
' ******************************************************************
' ** Name:       PRINTER.BAS          Version: 0.15    **
' ** Function:   Checks Epson compatible printers    **
' ** Language:   Microsoft QuickBASIC                **
' ** Notes:      Use parallel printer port LPT1      **
' ******************************************************************
'
' Initialise
'
ON ERROR GOTO warning
SCREEN 0
COLOR 15, 1
ul$ = STRING$(31, CHR$(205))
'
' Check printer is on-line and ready
'
DEF SEG = &H40
status& = PEEK(9) * 256 + PEEK(8) + 1
IF INP(status&) <> 223 THEN
  CLS
  PRINT " Printer not ready!"
  DO
  LOOP UNTIL INP(status&) = 223
END IF
DEF SEG
' Reset printer to start
GOSUB cancel
' Set up print style flags
nf$ = "*": cf$ = "": bf$ = "": ef$ = ""
if$ = "": sbf$ = "": spf$ = ""
'
' Display main menu
'
DO
main:
CLS
PRINT ul$
PRINT " PRINTER CHECK"
PRINT ul$; ""
PRINT " Select option..."
PRINT " [A] = print standard ASCII character set"
PRINT " [E] = print extended character set"
PRINT " [K] = print from keyboard"
PRINT " [L] = send line feed"
```

```
PRINT " [F] = send form feed"
PRINT " [C] = continuous printing"
PRINT " [P] = print style check sheet"
PRINT " [S] = setup printer"
PRINT " [Q] = quit"
DO
  r$ = UCASE$(INKEY$)
LOOP UNTIL r$ <> "" AND INSTR("AEKLFCPSQ", r$)
IF r$ = "Q" THEN GOSUB cancel: CLS : END
'
PRINT ul$
IF r$ = "A" THEN GOSUB standard
IF r$ = "E" THEN GOSUB extended
IF r$ = "K" THEN GOSUB keyboard
IF r$ = "L" THEN GOSUB linefeed
IF r$ = "F" THEN GOSUB formfeed
IF r$ = "C" THEN GOSUB continuous
IF r$ = "P" THEN GOSUB style
IF r$ = "S" THEN GOTO setup
LOOP
'
standard:
PRINT " Standard ASCII character set..."
LPRINT
LPRINT "Standard ASCII character set..."
LPRINT
FOR char = 32 TO 79
  LPRINT CHR$(char);
NEXT char
LPRINT
FOR char = 80 TO 127
  LPRINT CHR$(char);
NEXT char
LPRINT
RETURN
'
extended:
PRINT " Extended character set..."
LPRINT
LPRINT "Extended character set (non-ASCII)..."
LPRINT
FOR char = 128 TO 191
  LPRINT CHR$(char);
NEXT char
```

```
LPRINT
FOR char = 192 TO 255
  LPRINT CHR$(char);
NEXT char
LPRINT
RETURN
'
keyboard:
PRINT " Printing from keyboard."
PRINT " Press [#] to quit..."
PRINT ul$
LPRINT
DO
  LOCATE , , 1          'turn cursor on for text entry
  r$ = INPUT$(1)
  IF r$ = "#" THEN
    LOCATE , , 0
    LPRINT
    GOSUB waitkey
    RETURN
  END IF
  PRINT r$;
  LPRINT r$;
LOOP
'
linefeed:
PRINT " Sending line feed..."
LPRINT CHR$(13);
RETURN
'
formfeed:
PRINT " Sending form feed..."
LPRINT CHR$(12);
RETURN
'
continuous:
PRINT " Continuous printing."
PRINT " Press [#] to quit..."
PRINT ul$
LPRINT
DO
  r$ = INKEY$
  LPRINT "H";
LOOP WHILE r$ <> "#"
```

```
LPRINT
RETURN
'
style:
PRINT " Printing style check sheet..."
GOSUB cancel
LPRINT CHR$(12);
FOR lin% = 1 TO 4
  LPRINT
NEXT
LPRINT STRING$(64, "_")
LPRINT
LPRINT "Style check sheet: "; TIME$; "    "; DATE$
LPRINT
LPRINT STRING$(64, "_")
LPRINT
test$ = ""
FOR char = 1 TO 40
  test$ = test$ + CHR$(char + 64)
NEXT char
' normal mode
GOSUB cancel
LPRINT "Normal:           "; test$
LPRINT
' condensed mode
LPRINT CHR$(15);
LPRINT "Condensed:        "; test$
LPRINT
GOSUB cancel
' double-strike mode
LPRINT CHR$(27); "G";
LPRINT "Double-strike:    "; test$
LPRINT
GOSUB cancel
' italic mode
LPRINT CHR$(27); "4";
LPRINT "Italic:           "; test$
LPRINT
GOSUB cancel
' emphasized mode
LPRINT CHR$(27); "E"
LPRINT "Emphasized:       "; test$
LPRINT
GOSUB cancel
```

```
' superscript mode
LPRINT CHR$(27); "S"; "0";
LPRINT "Superscript:        "; test$
LPRINT
GOSUB cancel
' subscript mode
LPRINT CHR$(27); "S"; "1";
LPRINT "Subscript:          "; test$
LPRINT
GOSUB cancel
LPRINT
LPRINT STRING$(64, "_")
LPRINT CHR$(12);
RETURN
'
setup:
DO
  '
  ' Display setup menu
  '
  CLS
  PRINT ul$
  PRINT " PRINTER SETUP"
  PRINT ul$; ""
  PRINT " Select option..."
  PRINT " [C] = condensed print   "; cf$
  PRINT " [B] = double strike     "; bf$
  PRINT " [E] = emphasized        "; ef$
  PRINT " [I] = italic print      "; if$
  PRINT " [N] = normal print      "; nf$
  PRINT " [S] = subscript         "; sbf$
  PRINT " [T] = superscript       "; spf$
  PRINT " [X] = exit to main menu"
  DO
    r$ = UCASE$(INKEY$)
  LOOP UNTIL r$ <> "" AND INSTR("CBENISTX", r$)
  IF r$ = "X" THEN GOTO main
  '
  PRINT ul$
  IF r$ = "C" THEN LPRINT CHR$(15); : cf$ = "*": nf$ = ""
  IF r$ = "B" THEN LPRINT CHR$(27); "G"; : bf$ = "*": nf$ = ""
  IF r$ = "E" THEN LPRINT CHR$(27); "E"; : ef$ = "*": nf$ = ""
  IF r$ = "I" THEN LPRINT CHR$(27); "4"; : if$ = "*": nf$ = ""
  IF r$ = "N" THEN
```

```
    GOSUB cancel
    nf$ = "*"
    cf$ = "": bf$ = "": ef$ = "": if$ = "": sbf$ = "": spf$ = ""
  END IF
  IF r$ = "S" THEN
    LPRINT CHR$(27); "S"; "0";
    sbf$ = "*": spf$ = "": nf$ = ""
  END IF
  IF r$ = "T" THEN
    LPRINT CHR$(27); "S"; "1";
    spf$ = "*": sbf$ = "": nf$ = ""
  END IF
LOOP
'
cancel:
LPRINT CHR$(18); : cf$ = "" ' cancel condensed mode
LPRINT CHR$(27); "F"; : ef$ = "" ' cancel emphasized
mode
LPRINT CHR$(27); "H"; : bf$ = "" ' cancel double strike
mode
LPRINT CHR$(27); "5"; : if$ = "" ' cancel italic mode
LPRINT CHR$(27); "T"; : sbf$ = "": spf$ = "": ' cancel
sub/super
RETURN
'
waitkey:
PRINT ul$
PRINT " Press any key to continue..."
DO
  r$ = INKEY$
LOOP UNTIL r$ <> ""
RETURN
'
warning:
PRINT ul$
PRINT " An error has occurred!"
GOSUB waitkey
RESUME main
```

Soak test

This program will allow you to soak test your system. It will continuously cycle through a series of routines which will exercise the items that you specify. You can interrupt program execution at the end of the current cycle by pressing <Q> at any point in the cycle (note that you will have to wait for the current cycle to complete before the program terminates and returns you to the DOS prompt).

The program will first request information on your system including the number of floppy and hard disk drives fitted, the type of display and whether you wish to test a printer connected to the parallel port (if you select this last option you must have a printer connected which is on-line and ready to go).

The program will also prompt you for your system clock speed. You should select from 4 to 12MHz (slow), 12 to 25MHz (medium) and 25 to 60MHz (fast). If you don't know the system clock speed, you should select the middle option (respond by pressing <B>).

You should have a formatted disk with at least 32Kbytes free in each of the floppy drives that you wish to test. Similarly, you must have at least 32Kbytes free on each hard disk that has been included in the system specification.

After responding to the various prompts and questions, your system configuration will be displayed and you will be asked to confirm your selection. If the selection is correct, the program will cycle through the various tests with each part exercised in turn until you decide to quit the program.

Finally, it is important to note that you don't have to put the whole system to test. You can exclude particular items from the soak test by simply omitting them from the initial system specification.

```
' *******************************************************************
' ** Name:        SOAK.BAS              Version: 0.17      **
' ** Function:    Performs system soak test                **
' ** Language:    Microsoft QuickBASIC                     **
' ** Notes:       Program creates files on each            **
' **              drive (32Kbytes of free space            **
' **              required on each drive)                  **
' *******************************************************************
'
' Initialise
'
ON ERROR GOTO warning
' Initialise in text mode
SCREEN 0
COLOR 15, 1
ul$ = STRING$(40, CHR$(205))
' Display main menu
r$ = ""
main:
DO
CLS
PRINT ul$
PRINT " SYSTEM SOAK TEST"
PRINT ul$; ""
PRINT " Please provide system information..."
'
```

```
PRINT " Number of floppy disk drives?"
PRINT " (0, 1, or 2)"
DO
   r$ = INKEY$
 LOOP UNTIL r$ <> "" AND INSTR("012", r$)
 fdrives = VAL(r$)
 '
 PRINT " Number of hard disk drives?"
 PRINT " (0, 1, or 2)"
 DO
   r$ = INKEY$
 LOOP UNTIL r$ <> "" AND INSTR("012", r$)
 hdrives = VAL(r$)
 '
 PRINT " Type of graphics adapter?"
 PRINT " (C=CGA, E=EGA, V=VGA)"
 DO
   r$ = UCASE$(INKEY$)
 LOOP UNTIL r$ <> "" AND INSTR("CEV", r$)
 display$ = r$
 '
 PRINT " Parallel printer check (Y/N)?"
 DO
   r$ = UCASE$(INKEY$)
 LOOP UNTIL r$ <> "" AND INSTR("YN", r$)
 testprint$ = r$
 '
 PRINT " System clock speed range?"
 PRINT " (A=4-12MHz, B=12-25MHz, C=25-66MHz)"
 DO
   r$ = UCASE$(INKEY$)
 LOOP UNTIL r$ <> "" AND INSTR("ABC", r$)
 speed$ = r$
 '
 ' Display users specification
 '
 CLS
 PRINT ul$
 PRINT " SELECTED SYSTEM SPECIFICATION"
 PRINT ul$; ""
 d$(1) = "": d$(2) = "": d$(3) = "": d$(4) = ""
 '
 PRINT " Number of floppy disk drives: "; fdrives
 IF fdrives > 0 THEN
```

```
    IF fdrives = 1 THEN d$(1) = "A"
    IF fdrives = 2 THEN d$(1) = "A": d$(2) = "B"
    PRINT " Floppy drive(s): "; d$(1); d$(2)
  END IF
  '
  PRINT " Number of hard disk drives: "; hdrives
  IF hdrives > 0 THEN
    IF hdrives = 1 THEN d$(3) = "C"
    IF hdrives = 2 THEN d$(3) = "C": d$(4) = "D"
    PRINT " Hard drive(s): "; d$(3); d$(4)
  END IF
  '
  PRINT " Display type: "; display$; "GA"
  '
  IF testprint$ = "Y" THEN
    PRINT " Parallel printer checking enabled"
  ELSE
    PRINT " Parallel printer checking disabled"
  END IF
  '
  IF speed$ = "A" THEN
    lim% = 10000
    PRINT " Clock speed range 4-12MHz (slow)"
  END IF
  IF speed$ = "B" THEN
    lim% = 20000
    PRINT " Clock speed range 12-25MHz (medium)"
  END IF
  IF speed$ = "C" THEN
    lim% = 30000
    PRINT " Clock speed range 25-66MHz (fast)"
  END IF
  '
  PRINT ul$
  PRINT " Is this configuration correct (Y/N)?"
  DO
    r$ = UCASE$(INKEY$)
  LOOP UNTIL r$ <> "" AND INSTR("YN", r$)
LOOP WHILE r$ = "N"
'
' Warn user to prepare for soak tests...
'
CLS
PRINT ul$
```

```
PRINT " ABOUT TO CARRY OUT SOAK TESTS"
PRINT ul$
IF print$ = "Y" THEN
  PRINT "WARNING: Check printer is on-line and
ready!"
END IF
FOR n% = 1 TO 2
  IF d$(n%) <> "" THEN
    PRINT " WARNING: Insert a formatted disk with "
    PRINT "                    at least 32K available in "; d$(n%)
  END IF
NEXT n%
FOR n% = 3 TO 4
  IF d$(n%) <> "" THEN
    PRINT " WARNING: You must have at least 32K "
    PRINT "                     free space on drive "; d$(n%)
  END IF
NEXT n%
GOSUB waitkey
'
cycle% = 1
  DO
  CLS
  PRINT ul$
  PRINT " SOAK TESTING SYSTEM"
  PRINT ul$
  PRINT " Soak test cycle: "; cycle%
  PRINT " Press <Q> during cycle to quit at"
  PRINT " end of current cycle."
  '
  ' First test; sound speaker
  '
  LOCATE 8, 2
  FOR n% = 1 TO 4
    BEEP
    GOSUB delay1
  NEXT n%
  '
  ' Second test; write to display using text mode
  '
  CLS
  FOR c% = 53 TO 48 STEP -1
    FOR location% = 0 TO (25 * 80)
     PRINT CHR$(c%);
```

```
  NEXT location%
NEXT c%
'
' Third test; write to display using graphics mode
'
' Set up graphics mode...
IF display$ = "C" THEN
  SCREEN 1: COLOR 1, 2, 1: xc = 160: yc = 100
END IF
IF display$ = "E" THEN
  SCREEN 8: COLOR 15, 1: xc = 320: yc = 100
END IF
IF display$ = "V" THEN
  SCREEN 9: COLOR 15, 1: xc = 320: yc = 175
END IF
' Display colour bars
CLS
IF display$ <> "C" THEN
  COLOR 0, 0
  CLS
  x = 0
  xold = 0
  inc = xc / 8
  FOR colour = 0 TO 15
   x = x + inc
   LINE (xold, 0)-STEP(x, 2 * yc), colour, BF
   xold = x
  NEXT colour
ELSE
  ' CGA uses only 4 colours...
  COLOR 0, 0, 1
  CLS
  x = 0
  xold = 0
  inc = xc / 2
  FOR colour = 0 TO 3
   x = x + inc
   LINE (xold, 0)-STEP(x, 2 * yc), colour, BF
   xold = x
  NEXT colour
END IF
' Hold display on screen for a while
GOSUB delay2
' Reset screen mode to text
```

```
SCREEN 2: SCREEN 0: COLOR 15, 1
'
' Fourth test; exercise each disk drive in turn
'
CLS
PRINT ul$
PRINT " Checking disk drives, please wait..."
PRINT ul$
FOR n% = 1 TO 4
  IF d$(n%) <> "" THEN
   ' Use root directory
   file$ = d$(n%) + ":\TEST.DAT"
   ' Reset error flag
   flag% = 0
   GOSUB tidy
   LOCATE 6, 2
   PRINT "Writing data to "; file$
   OPEN file$ FOR OUTPUT AS #1
   FOR ch% = 0 TO 4096
   PRINT #1, ch%
   NEXT ch%
   CLOSE #1
   GOSUB tidy
   LOCATE 6, 2
   PRINT "Reading data from "; file$
   OPEN file$ FOR INPUT AS #1
   FOR dat% = 0 TO 4096
   INPUT #1, ch%
   IF ch% <> dat% THEN flag% = 1
   NEXT dat%
   CLOSE #1
   GOSUB tidy
   IF flag% = 1 THEN
   LOCATE 6, 2
   PRINT "An error has occurred!"
   ELSE
   LOCATE 6, 2
   PRINT "Drive "; d$(n%); " tested without error."
   LOCATE 7, 2
   PRINT "Erasing "; file$
   KILL file$
   END IF
  END IF
  GOSUB delay2
```

```
  NEXT n%
  '
  ' Fifth test: write to parallel printer
  '
  IF testprint$ = "Y" THEN
    LPRINT
    FOR c% = 32 TO 95
     LPRINT CHR$(c%);
    NEXT c%
    LPRINT
    FOR c% = 96 TO 159
     LPRINT CHR$(c%);
    NEXT c%
    LPRINT
    FOR c% = 160 TO 223
     LPRINT CHR$(c%);
    NEXT c%
    LPRINT
    FOR c% = 224 TO 255
     LPRINT CHR$(c%);
    NEXT c%
    LPRINT " Soak test cycle ="; cycle%
  END IF
  '
  cycle% = cycle% + 1
  '
  ' Does user want to quit?
  '
  r$ = UCASE$(INKEY$)
  IF r$ = "Q" THEN COLOR 15, 0: CLS : END
LOOP
'
' Utility subroutines
'
tidy:
' Erase any existing screen data
FOR cline% = 6 TO 10
  LOCATE cline%, 2
  PRINT STRING$(39, " ")
NEXT cline%
RETURN
'
waitkey:
PRINT ul$
```

```
PRINT " Press any key to continue..."
GOSUB keywait
RETURN
'
keywait:
DO
  r$ = INKEY$
LOOP UNTIL r$ <> ""
RETURN
'
delay1:
t% = 0
FOR t% = 0 TO lim%: NEXT t%
RETURN
'
delay2:
u% = 0
FOR u% = 0 TO 20
  GOSUB delay1
NEXT u%
RETURN
'
warning:
PRINT ul$
PRINT " An error has occurred!"
GOSUB waitkey
RESUME main
```

System check

This utility will tell you a lot about your system. It will display the system type (PC, XT, AT or PS/2), the system identification byte, the current video mode and number of screen columns, the amount of conventional (base) RAM present, the number of floppy drives, serial ports and printers connected. The program will also let you know whether a PC games adapter, DMA controller, maths coprocessor and internal modem is present. The program also displays the ROM creation date.

The program will also provide you with an approximate indication of the clock speed of your system compared with a basic specification AT machine. Note that the value indicated is *not* the clock speed of your system. Instead, it is the clock rate that an AT specification computer would have to operate at in order to achieve an equivalent processing speed. Indications will range from about 22MHz for a fairly basic 80386SX machine to well over 200MHz for a 80486DX operating at 33MHz.

```
' ****************************************************************
' ** Name:        SYSTEM.BAS          Version: 0.1     **
' ** Function:    Checks and displays system info.     **
' ** Language:    Microsoft QuickBASIC                 **
' ** Notes:       Assumes conventional ROM BIOS        **
' **              organisation                         **
' ****************************************************************
'
' Initialise
'
ON ERROR GOTO warning
' Initialise in text mode
SCREEN 0
COLOR 15, 1
ul$ = STRING$(40, CHR$(205))
' Display main menu
DO
main:
CLS
PRINT ul$
PRINT " SYSTEM BOARD CHECK             "
PRINT ul$; ""
PRINT " Select option..."
PRINT " [I] = system information"
PRINT " [S] = speed check"
PRINT " [Q] = quit"
DO
  r$ = UCASE$(INKEY$)
LOOP UNTIL r$ <> "" AND INSTR("ISQ", r$)
IF r$ = "Q" THEN CLS : SCREEN 0: END
'
PRINT ul$
IF r$ = "S" THEN GOSUB speed
IF r$ = "I" THEN GOSUB information
LOOP
'
speed:
LOCATE 10, 2
PRINT "Checking clock speed..."
start! = TIMER
FOR i = 1 TO 10000
NEXT i
time! = TIMER
elapsed = time! - start!
```

```
LOCATE 10, 2
PRINT "Equiv. clock speed (AT): "; INT(60 / elapsed);
"MHz"
GOSUB waitkey
RETURN
'
information:
' Get system ID byte from ROM
DEF SEG = &HF000
ident% = PEEK(&HFFFE)
' Determine type standard (PC, XT, AT etc)
IF ident% = 255 THEN type$ = "PC"
IF ident% = 254 OR ident% = 251 THEN type$ = "XT"
IF ident% = 253 THEN type$ = "PC Junior"
IF ident% = 252 THEN type$ = "AT or PS/2"
IF ident% = 250 THEN type$ = "PS/2 Model 30"
IF ident% = 249 THEN type$ = "PC Convertible"
IF ident% = 248 THEN type$ = "PS/2 Model 80"
' Get ROM creation date
DEF SEG = &HFFFF
dat$ = ""
FOR location% = 12 TO 5 STEP -1
  dat$ = CHR$(PEEK(location%)) + dat$
NEXT location%
' Get installed equipment list from RAM
DEF SEG = &H0
equlo% = PEEK(&H410)
equhi% = PEEK(&H411)
' Get usable memory
memlo% = PEEK(&H413)
memhi% = PEEK(&H414)
' Get keyboard status
kbdlo% = PEEK(&H417)
kbdhi% = PEEK(&H418)
' Get disk status
disks% = PEEK(&H441)
' Get video mode
vmode% = PEEK(&H449)
' Get column width
colum% = PEEK(&H44A)
' Determine number of floppy drives present
ndriv% = 1 + ((equlo% AND 192) / 64)
' Determine number of serial ports present
nserp% = (equhi% AND 6) / 2
```

```
' Determine number of printers present
nprin% = ((equhi% AND 192) / 64)
' Determine whether a games adapter is present
IF (equhi% AND 16) THEN gam$ = "Yes" ELSE gam$ = "No"
' Determine whether a DMA controller is present
IF (equhi% AND 1) THEN dma$ = "No" ELSE dma$ = "Yes"
' Determine whether a maths coprocessor is present
IF (equlo% AND 2) THEN cop$ = "Yes" ELSE cop$ = "No"
' Determine whether a serial printer is present
IF (equhi% AND 32) THEN ser$ = "Yes" ELSE ser$ = "No"
' Display the information
LOCATE 9, 2: PRINT "System type:          "; type$
LOCATE 10, 2: PRINT "System ID:      "; HEX$(ident%)
LOCATE 11, 2: PRINT "Video mode:          "; vmode%
LOCATE 12, 2: PRINT "Screen columns:      "; colum%
LOCATE 13, 2: PRINT "Conventional RAM:    "; 256 *
memhi% + memlo%; "kbytes"
LOCATE 14, 2: PRINT "Floppy drives:       "; ndriv%
LOCATE 15, 2: PRINT "Serial ports:        "; nserp%
LOCATE 16, 2: PRINT "Printers:            "; nprin%
LOCATE 17, 2: PRINT "PC games adapter:    "; gam$
LOCATE 18, 2: PRINT "DMA controller:      "; dma$
LOCATE 19, 2: PRINT "Maths coprocessor:   "; cop$
LOCATE 20, 2: PRINT "Internal modem:      "; ser$
LOCATE 21, 2: PRINT "ROM creation date:   "; dat$
GOSUB waitkey
RETURN
'
waitkey:
PRINT ul$
PRINT " Press any key to continue..."
GOSUB keywait
RETURN
'
keywait:
DO
  r$ = INKEY$
LOOP UNTIL r$ <> ""
RETURN
'
warning:
PRINT ul$
PRINT " An error has occurred!"
GOSUB waitkey
RESUME main
```

Index

F8 = safe mode

Alt <enter> small dos window

Alt tab toggle thro' running apps